Volumes 1-3 are still available, so you have no excuse not to support us.
HE'S COPPING AN ATTITUDE AT THE MOMENT.
What are you doing, Izumi-san?
Sumikko is out for a walk.

TENSHI JA NAI!!

Translation —Akira Tsubasa
Adaptation -- Jamie S. Rich
Production Assistant – Mallory Reaves
Lettering – Jennifer Skarupa
Production Manager – James Dashiell
Editor – Jake Forbes

A Go! Comi manga

Published by Go! Media Entertainment, LLC

Tenshi Ja Nai!! Volume 4
© TAKAKO SHIGEMATSU 2005
Originally published in Japan in 2005 by Akita Publishing Co., Ltd., Tokyo.
English translation rights arranged with Akita Publishing Co., Ltd.
through TOHAN CORPORATION, Tokyo.

Visit us online at www.gocomi.com
e-mail: info@gocomi.com

ISBN 1-933617-03-9

First printed in July 2006

1 2 3 4 5 6 7 8 9

Manufactured in the United States of America

TENSHI JA NAI!!

I'm No Angel!

Volume 4

Story and Art by
Takako Shigematsu

go!comi

Concerning Honorifics

At Go! Comi, we do our best to ensure that our translations read seamlessly in English while respecting the original Japanese language and culture. To this end, the original honorifics (the suffixes found at the end of characters' names) remain intact. In Japan, where politeness and formality are more integrated into every aspect of the language, honorifics give a better understanding of character relationships. They can be used to indicate both respect and affection. Whether a person addresses someone by first name or last name also indicates how close their relationship is.

Here are some of the honorifics you might encounter in reading this book:

-san: This is the most common and neutral of honorifics. The polite way to address someone you're not on close terms with is to use "-san." It's kind of like Mr. or Ms., except you can use "-san" with first names as easily as family names.

-chan: Used for friendly familiarity, mostly applied towards young girls. "-chan" also carries a connotation of cuteness with it, so it is frequently used with nick-names towards both boys and girls (such as "Na-chan" for "Natsu").

-kun: Like "-chan," it's an informal suffix for friends and classmates, only "-kun" is usually associated with boys. It can also be used in a professional environment by someone addressing a subordinate.

-sama: Indicates a great deal of respect or admiration.

Sempai: In school, "sempai" is used to refer to an upperclassman or club leader. It can also be used in the workplace by a new employee to address a mentor or staff member with seniority.

Sensei: Teachers, doctors, writers or any master of a trade are referred to as "sensei." When addressing a manga creator, the polite thing to do is attach "-sensei" to the manga-ka's name (as in Shigematsu-sensei).

Onii: This is the more casual term for an older brother. Usually you'll see it with an honorific attached, such as "onii-chan."

Onee: The casual term for older sister, it's used like "onii" with honorifics.

[blank]: Not using an honorific when addressing someone indicates that the speaker has permission to speak intimately with the other person. This relationship is usually reserved for close friends and family.

TENSHI JA NAI!!

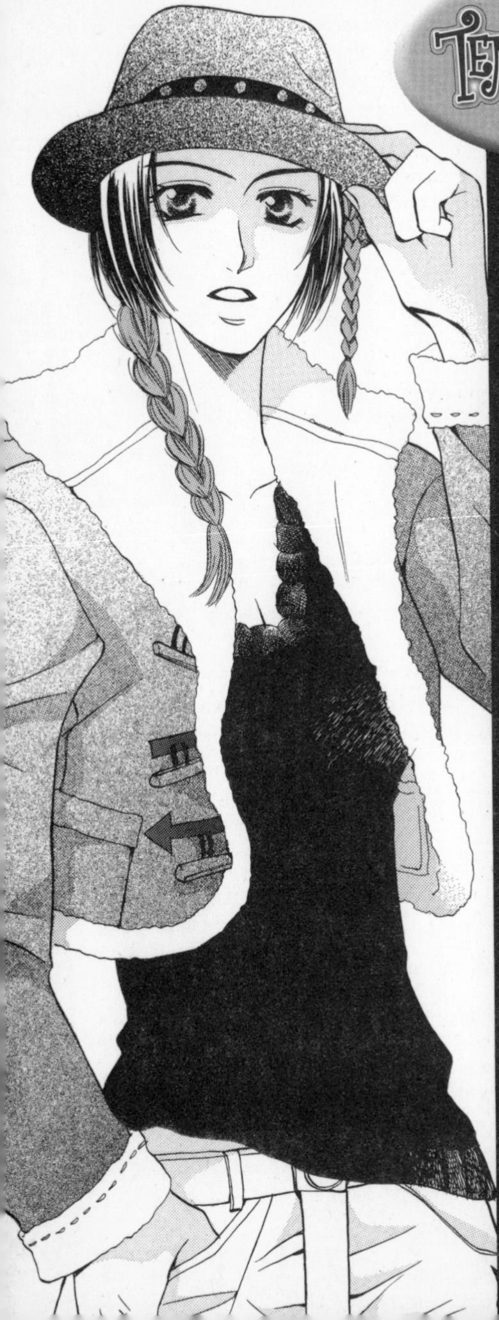

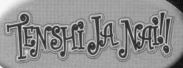

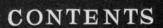

CONTENTS

VOL. 4

Hikaru Takabayashi

The reluctant star of the series. Hikaru wants nothing more than to be left alone, but ever since she transferred to the prestigious Seika Academy, she's been stuck in the spotlight. Being roommates with a cross-dressing pop idol is bad enough, but now Izumi is blackmailing her into helping with his modeling job. Will Hikaru ever catch a break?

Izumi is one of the hottest new female pop idols in Japan. The only problem is...she's a guy! Only two people knew his secret—Yasukuni, his bodyguard and childhood friend, and Akizuki his manager. When Hikaru finds out, Izumi blackmails her into helping him maintain his secret. Izumi needs the modeling money to pay off his father's medical bills.

Izumi Kido

Yasukuni Inukai

Yasukuni is fiercely loyal to Izumi. A bastard child disowned by his father, Izumi is the only family he has. Now that Hikaru has won his trust, he's taken to looking out for her, as well. Much of his past remains a mystery, such as why he's missing his right eye. He does double duty as the school janitor so he can always be close to Izumi.

SUMIKKO

Hikaru's best friend in the world. Yasukuni takes care of her while Hikaru's at school.

Momochi

Star reporter for the school paper, Momochi is always on the lookout for gossip!

Akizuki

President of the Akizuki Talent Agency and Izumi's manager.

Cast of Characters

Wall of Memories

A New School

When her mom and step-dad move to France, Hikaru transfers to her mother's alma mater, the prestigious Seika Academy, an all-girls finishing school.

Childhood memories

When she was seven years old, Hikaru modeled in a series of ads. Her jealous classmates picked on her relentlessly so now Hikaru's greatest wish is to be left alone.

BLACKMAIL!!!

To keep Hikaru quiet and in order to enlist her help, Izumi and Yasukuni blackmail Hikaru with naked photos.

She's a GUY!?

Hikaru discovers that her roommate, Izumi, is actually a guy!

Izumi's Confidant

Hikaru turns out to be a blessing in disguise for Izumi. Having a female conspirator by his side helps him maintain his cover in the trickiest circumstances.

When Fans Attack!

It's not easy being a celebrity on campus. Half the students worship Izumi, the other half resent her. And Hikaru's stuck in the middle!

A Shocking Past

After being betrayed and left for broke, Izumi's father attempted to commit suicide but ended up in a coma. Now Izumi has to work as a model to pay off his dad's medical bills.

TENSHI JA NAI!!
I'm No Angel!

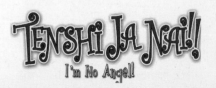

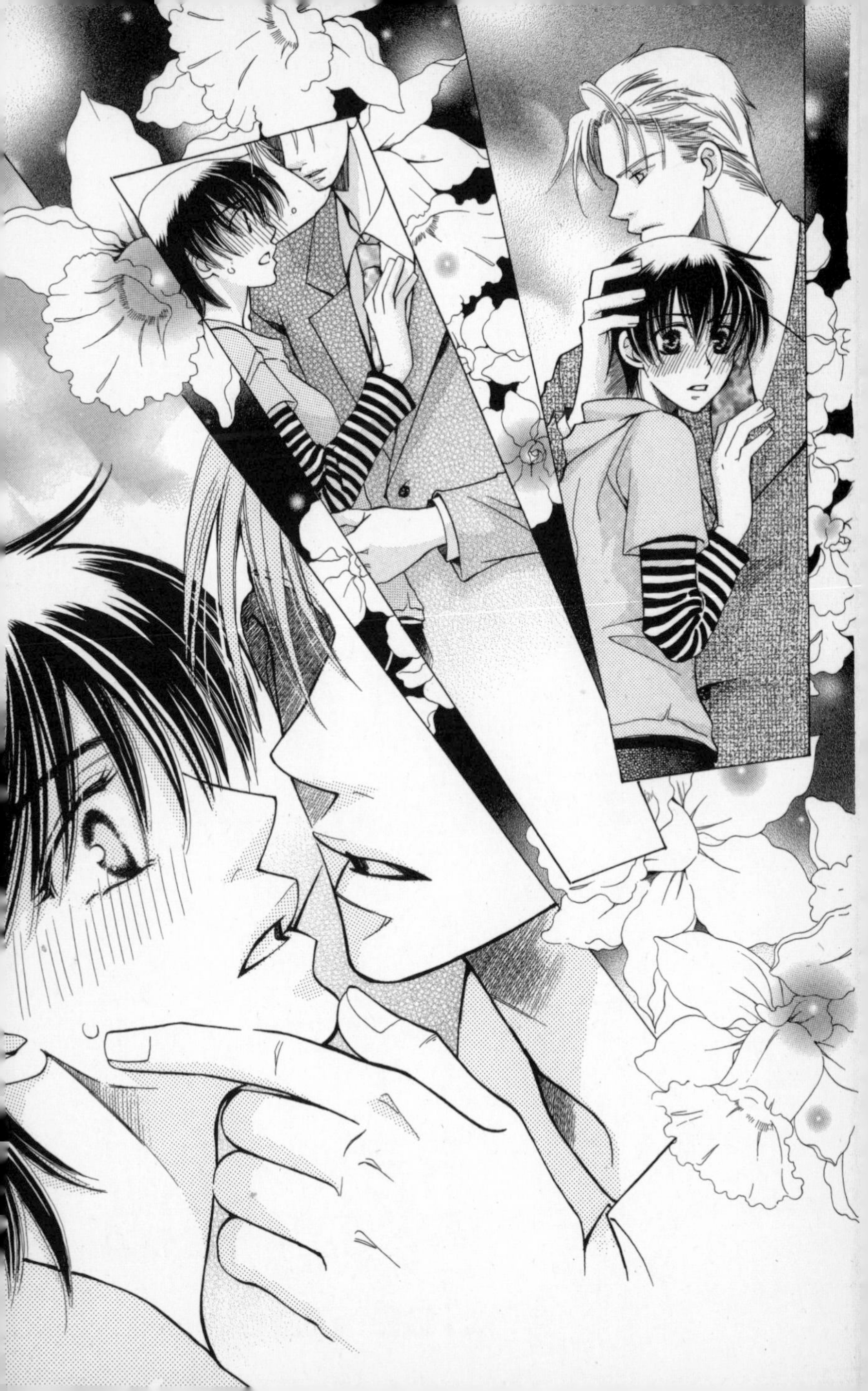

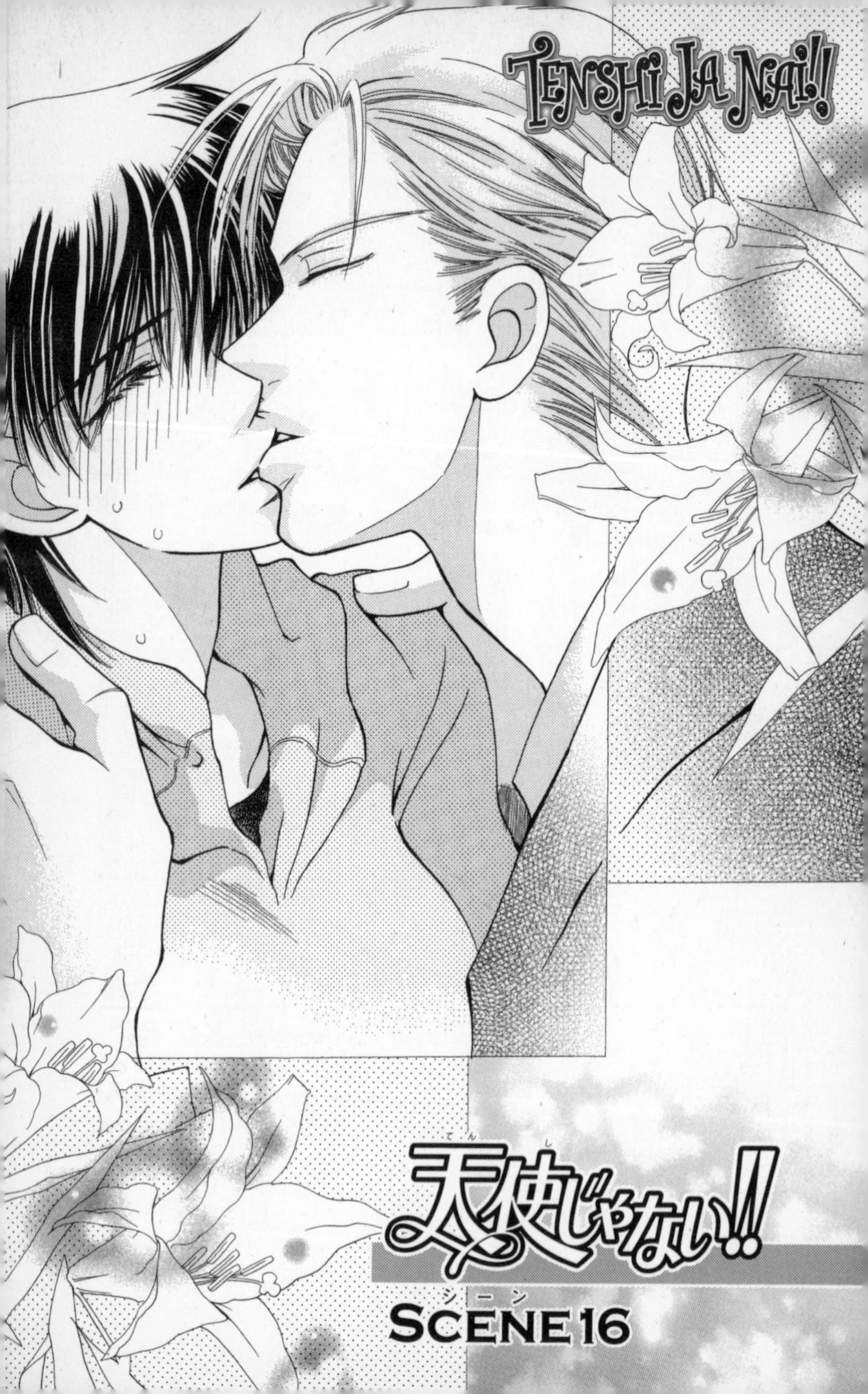
TENSHI JA NAI!!
天使じゃない!!
SCENE 16

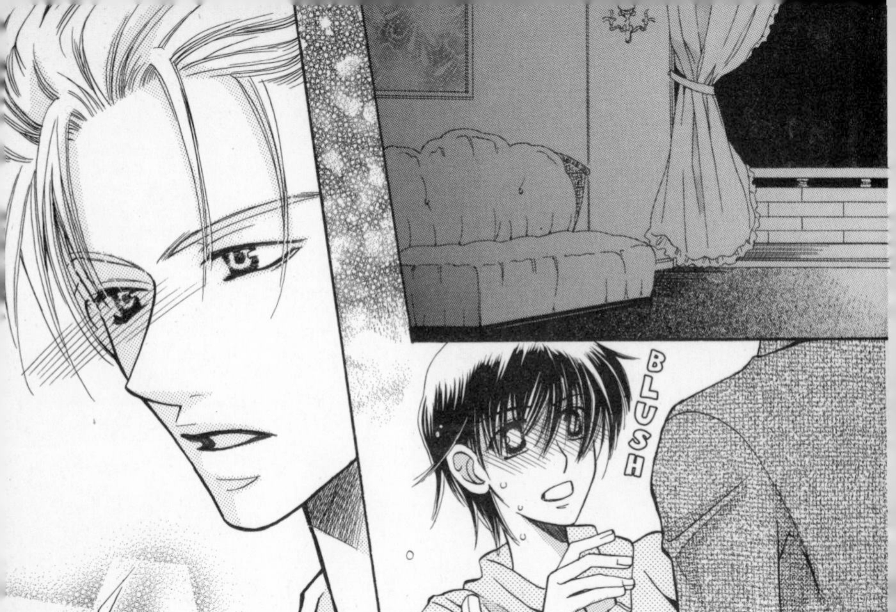
BLUSH
SE...
...SENSEI?
WHEN I SAW YOU AND THAT MAN GOING INTO THE HOTEL ROOM TO-GETHER...
...I CAME TO REALIZE...

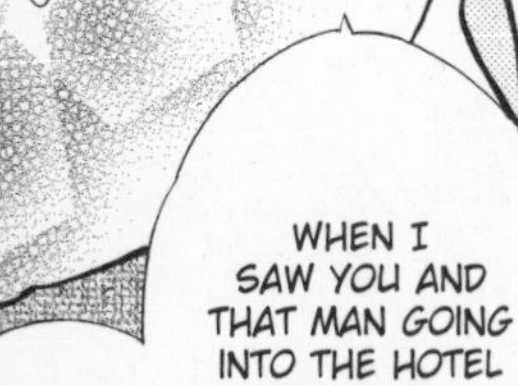
Greetings.

Hello to all of you who may be reading this series for the first time, and also to all of my regular readers! Thank you for picking up Tenshi Ja Nai!! volume 4. I hope that you enjoy reading it, and that you'll like it enough to come back...

--Takako Shigematsu
October 25, 2004

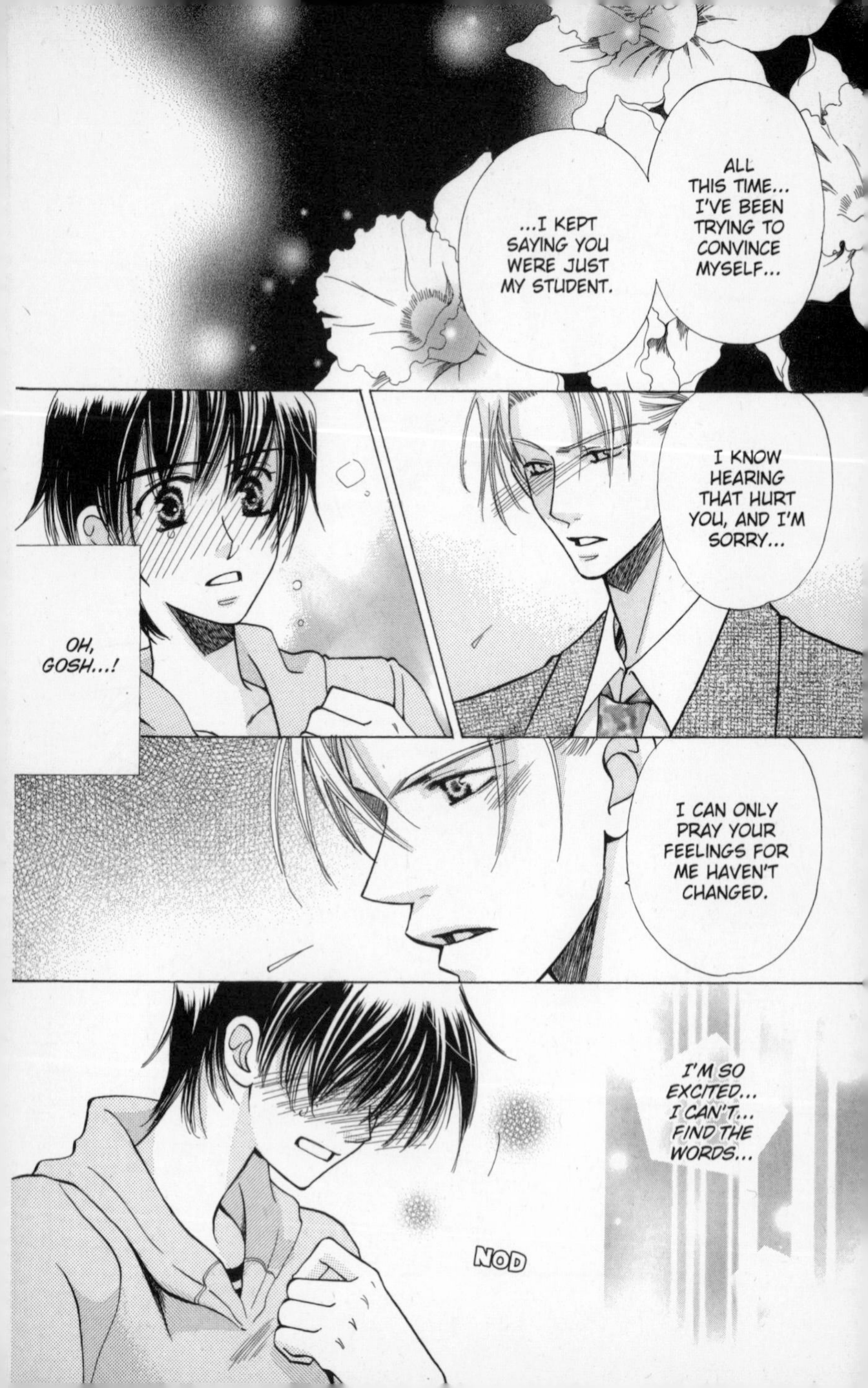
ALL THIS TIME... I'VE BEEN TRYING TO CONVINCE MYSELF...
...I KEPT SAYING YOU WERE JUST MY STUDENT.
I KNOW HEARING THAT HURT YOU, AND I'M SORRY...
OH, GOSH...!
I CAN ONLY PRAY YOUR FEELINGS FOR ME HAVEN'T CHANGED.
I'M SO EXCITED... I CAN'T... FIND THE WORDS...
NOD

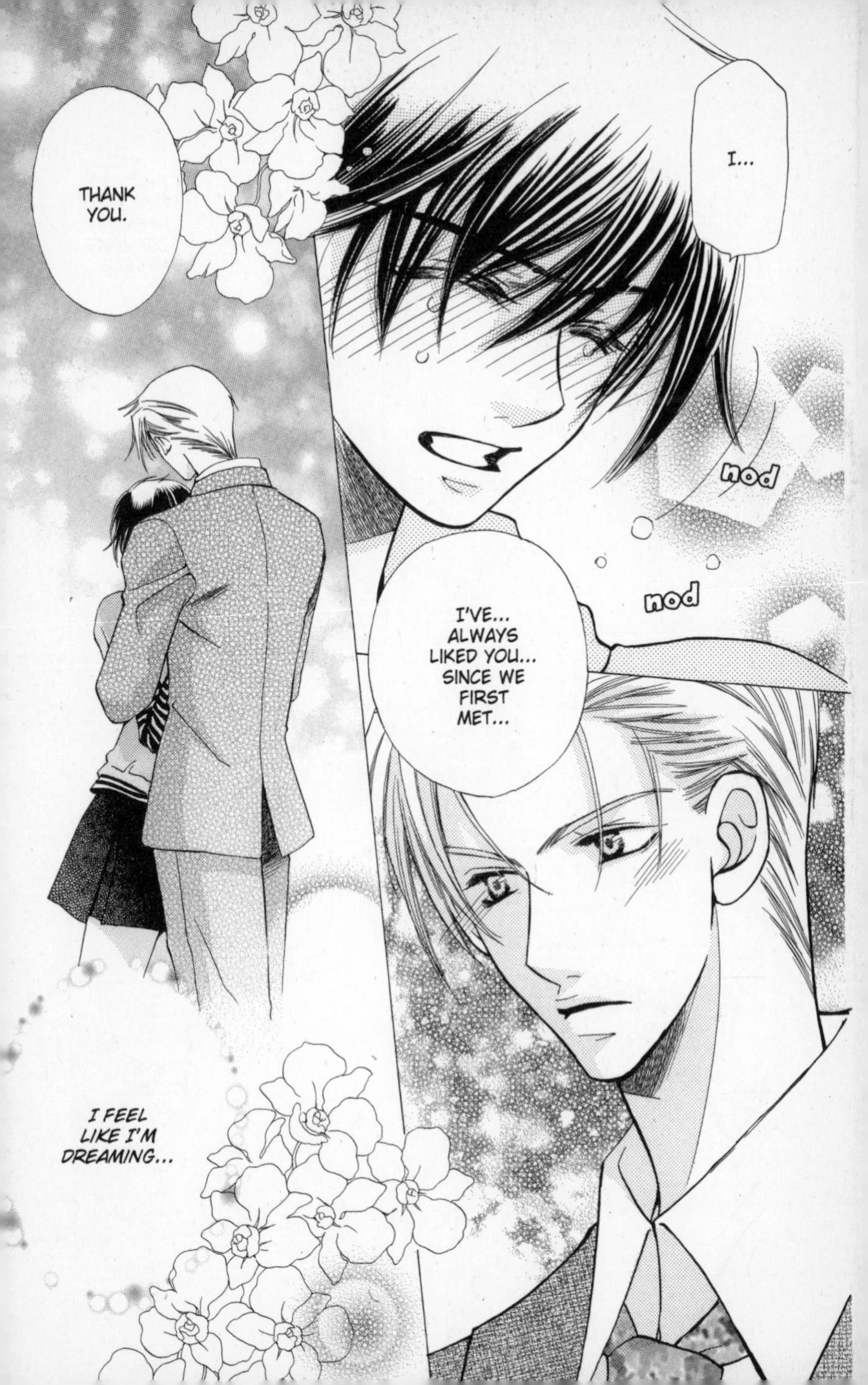
I...
nod
nod
I'VE... ALWAYS LIKED YOU... SINCE WE FIRST MET...
THANK YOU.
I FEEL LIKE I'M DREAMING...

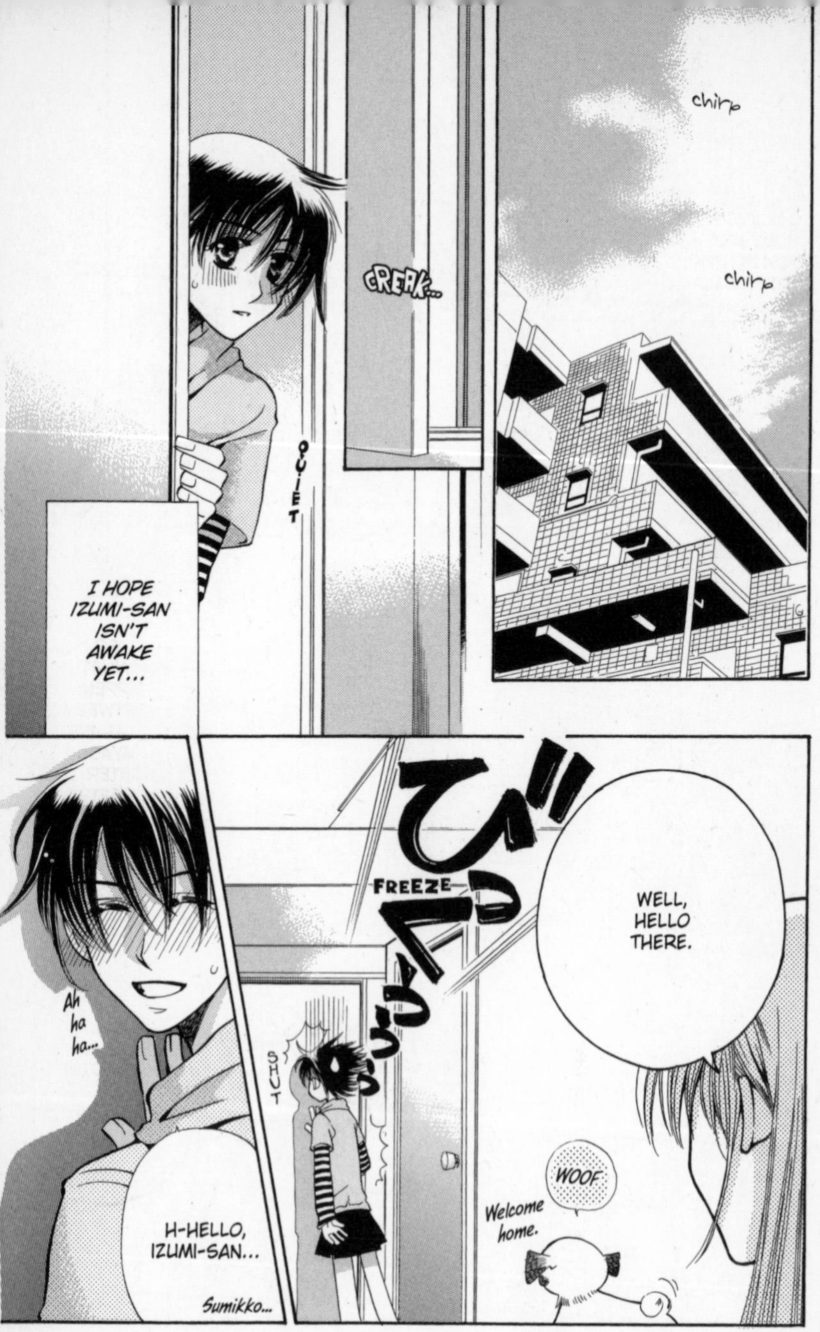
chirp
chirp
CREAK...
QUIET
I HOPE IZUMI-SAN ISN'T AWAKE YET...
WELL, HELLO THERE.
FREEZE
WOOF
Welcome home.
SHUT
Ah ha ha...
H-HELLO, IZUMI-SAN...
Sumikko...

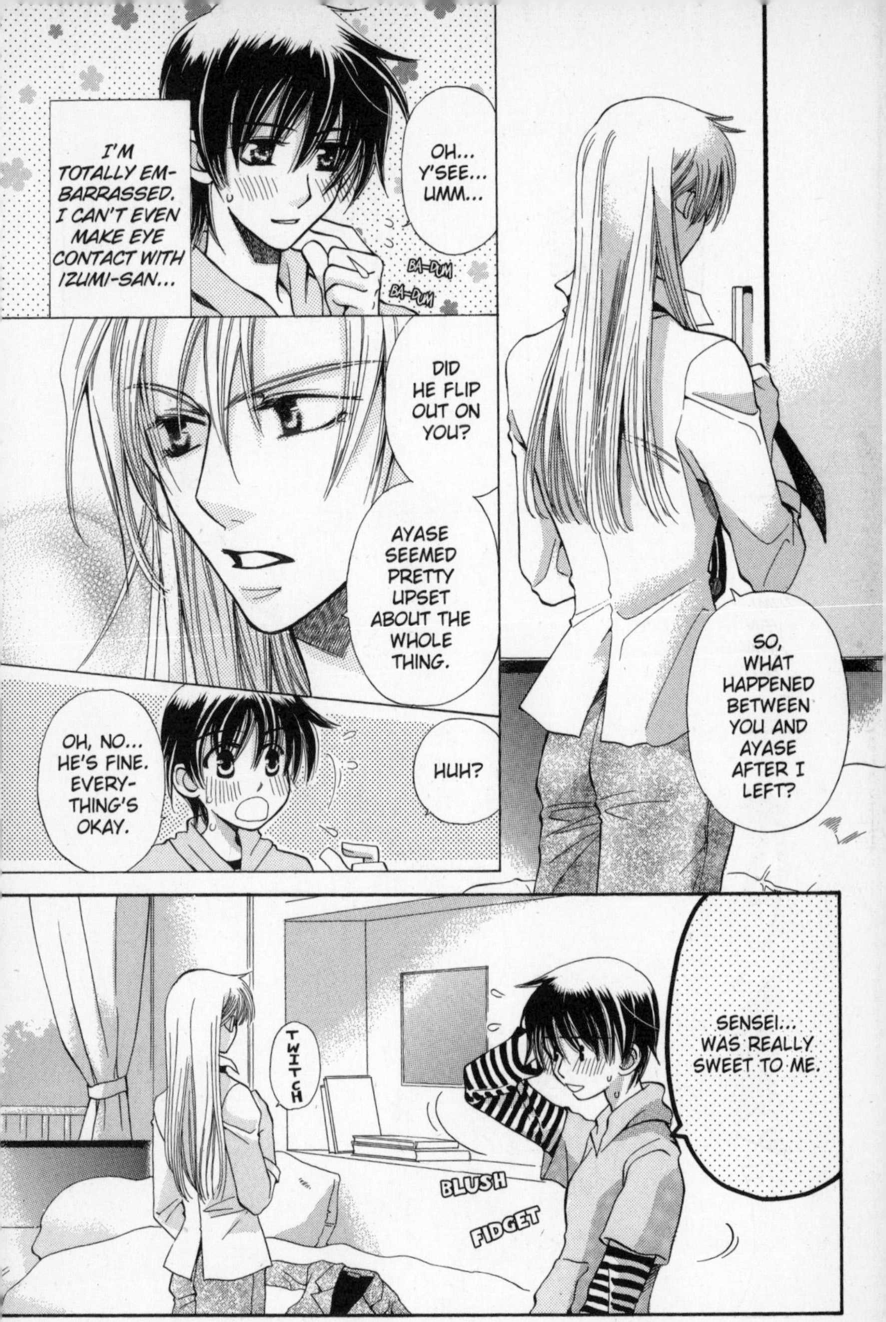
SO, WHAT HAPPENED BETWEEN YOU AND AYASE AFTER I LEFT?
OH... Y'SEE... UMM...
I'M TOTALLY EM-BARRASSED. I CAN'T EVEN MAKE EYE CONTACT WITH IZUMI-SAN...
BA-DUM
BA-DUM
DID HE FLIP OUT ON YOU?
AYASE SEEMED PRETTY UPSET ABOUT THE WHOLE THING.
HUH?
OH, NO... HE'S FINE. EVERY-THING'S OKAY.
SENSEI... WAS REALLY SWEET TO ME.
TWITCH
BLUSH
FIDGET

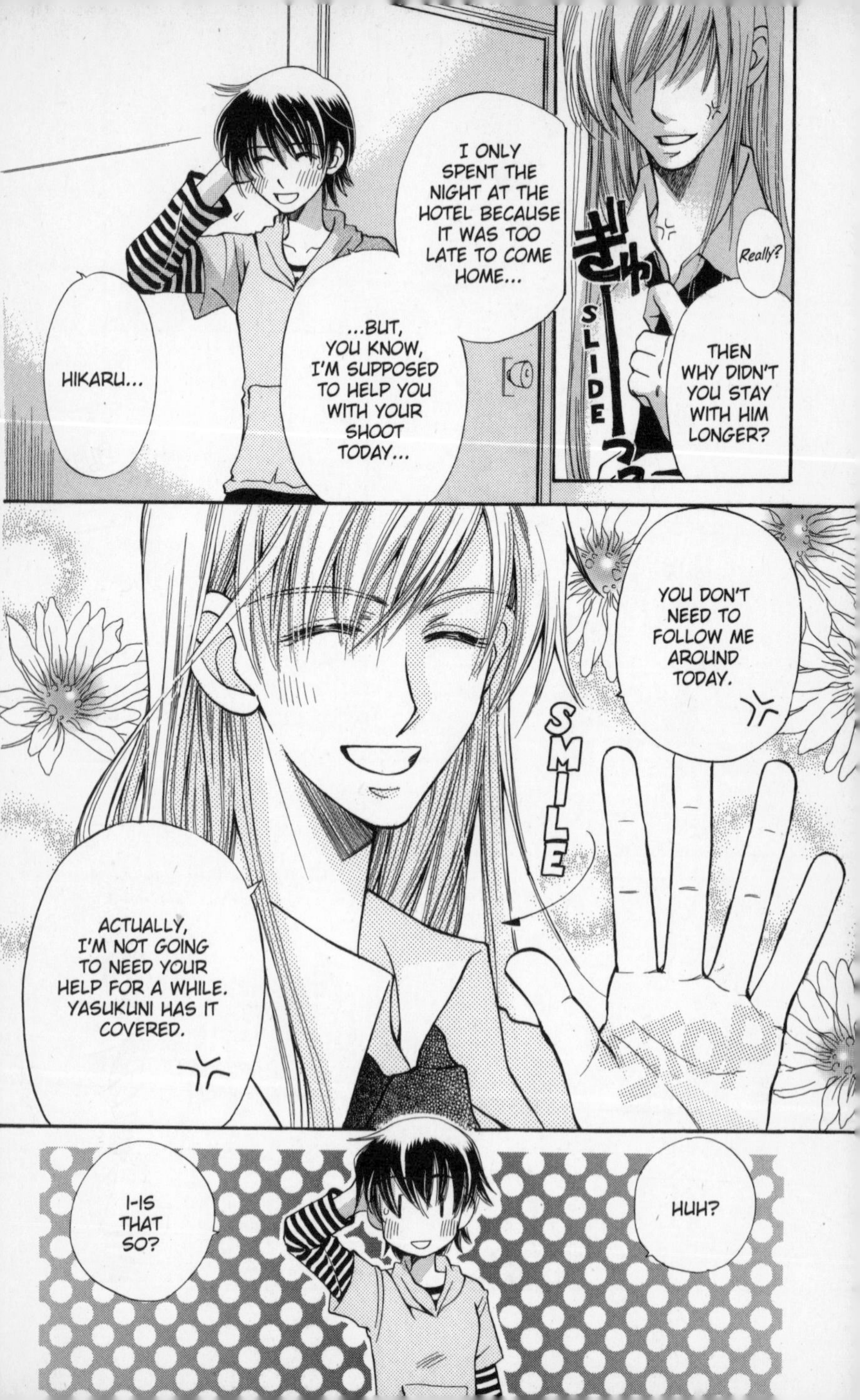
Really?
ぎゅ
SLIDE
THEN WHY DIDN'T YOU STAY WITH HIM LONGER?
I ONLY SPENT THE NIGHT AT THE HOTEL BECAUSE IT WAS TOO LATE TO COME HOME...
...BUT, YOU KNOW, I'M SUPPOSED TO HELP YOU WITH YOUR SHOOT TODAY...
HIKARU...
YOU DON'T NEED TO FOLLOW ME AROUND TODAY.
SMILE
STOP
ACTUALLY, I'M NOT GOING TO NEED YOUR HELP FOR A WHILE. YASUKUNI HAS IT COVERED.
HUH?
I-IS THAT SO?

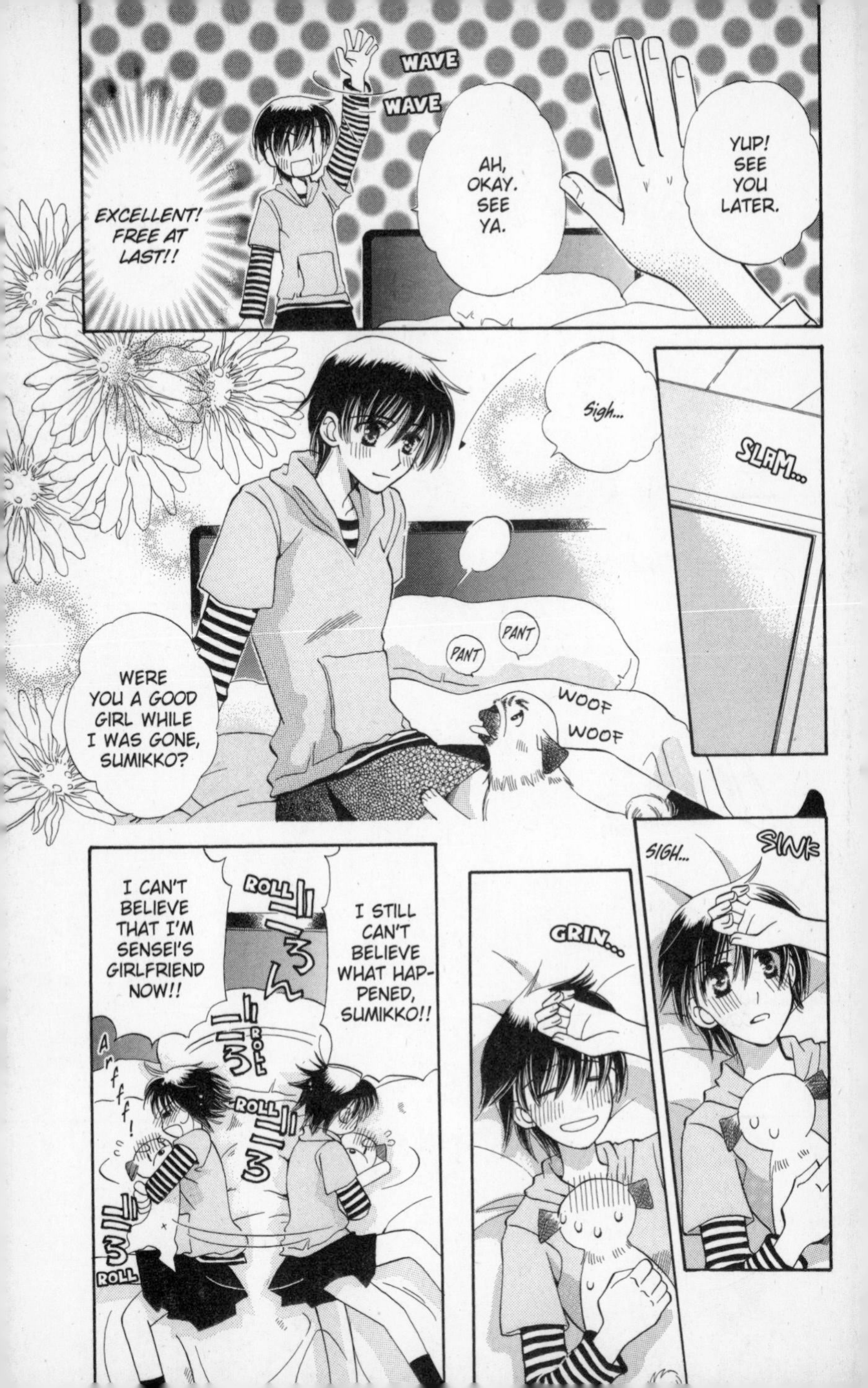
YUP! SEE YOU LATER.
AH, OKAY. SEE YA.
WAVE
WAVE
EXCELLENT! FREE AT LAST!!
SLAM...
Sigh...
PANT
PANT
WOOF
WOOF
WERE YOU A GOOD GIRL WHILE I WAS GONE, SUMIKKO?
SINK
SIGH...
GRIN...
I STILL CAN'T BELIEVE WHAT HAP-PENED, SUMIKKO!!
ROLL
I CAN'T BELIEVE THAT I'M SENSEI'S GIRLFRIEND NOW!!
ROLL
ROLL
Arfff!
ROLL

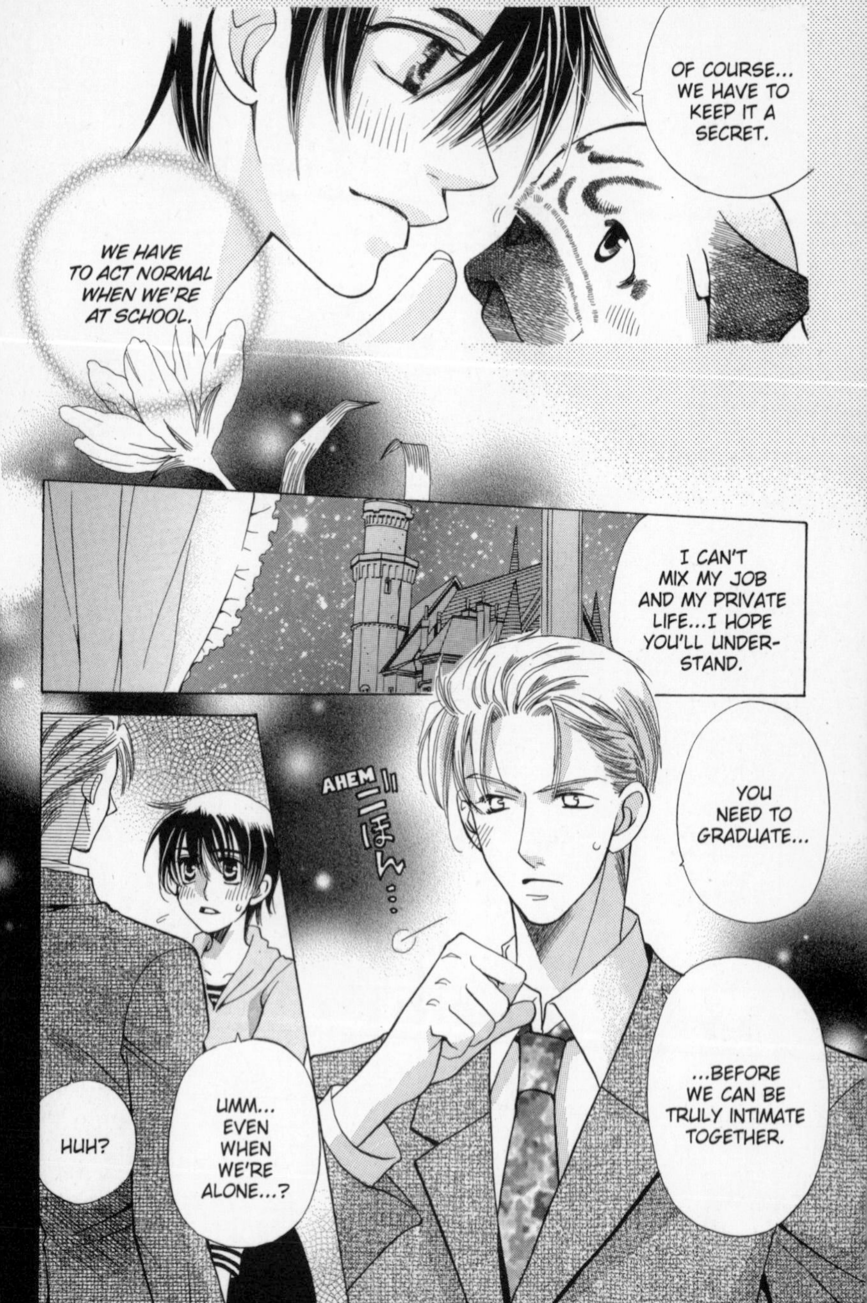
OF COURSE... WE HAVE TO KEEP IT A SECRET.
WE HAVE TO ACT NORMAL WHEN WE'RE AT SCHOOL.
I CAN'T MIX MY JOB AND MY PRIVATE LIFE...I HOPE YOU'LL UNDER-STAND.
YOU NEED TO GRADUATE...
...BEFORE WE CAN BE TRULY INTIMATE TOGETHER.
AHEM
こほん…
UMM... EVEN WHEN WE'RE ALONE...?
HUH?

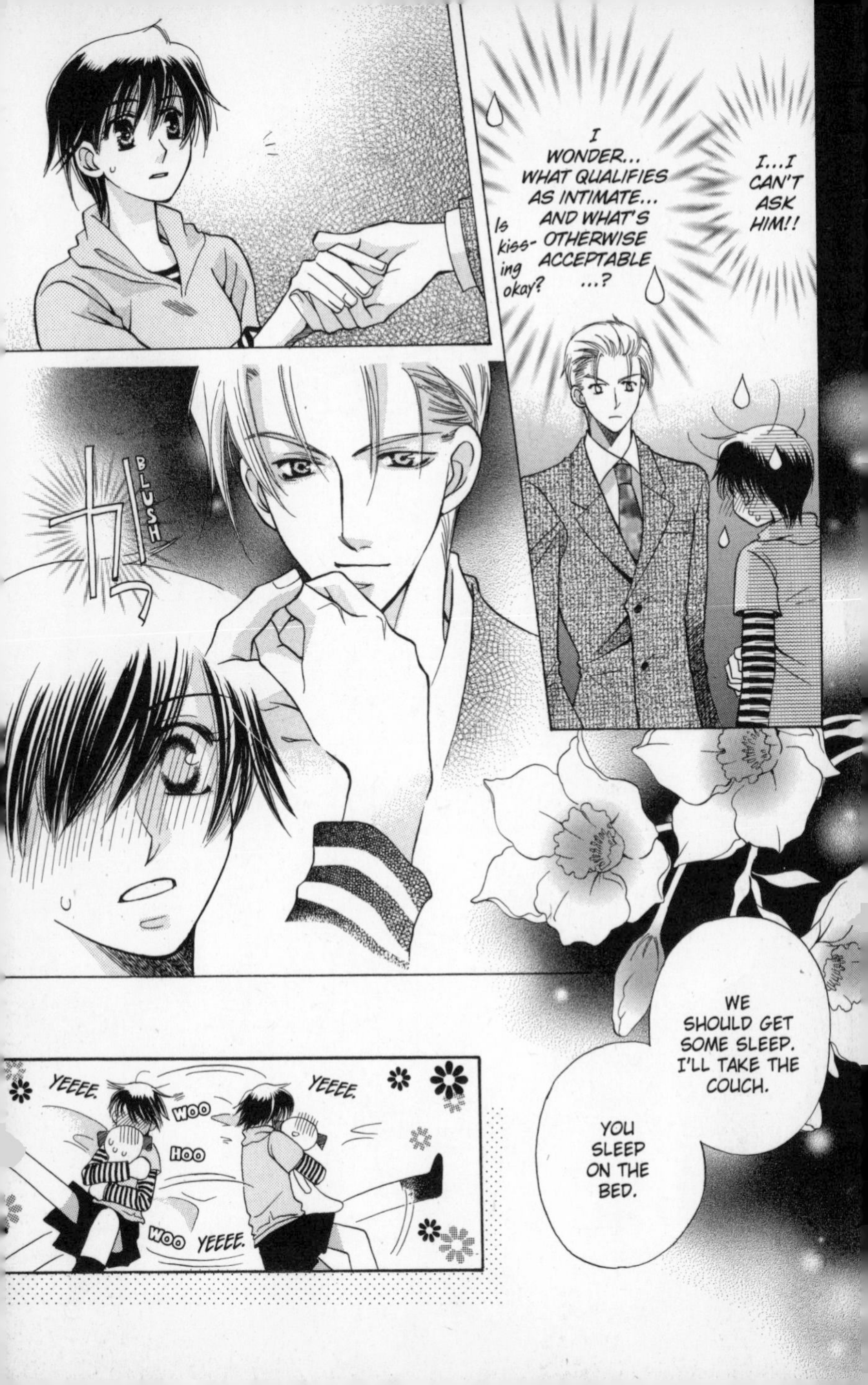

I... I CAN'T ASK HIM!!
I WONDER... WHAT QUALIFIES AS INTIMATE... AND WHAT'S OTHERWISE ACCEPTABLE ...?
Is kiss-ing okay?
BLUSH
WE SHOULD GET SOME SLEEP. I'LL TAKE THE COUCH.
YOU SLEEP ON THE BED.
YEEEE.
YEEEE.
WOO
HOO
WOO YEEEE.

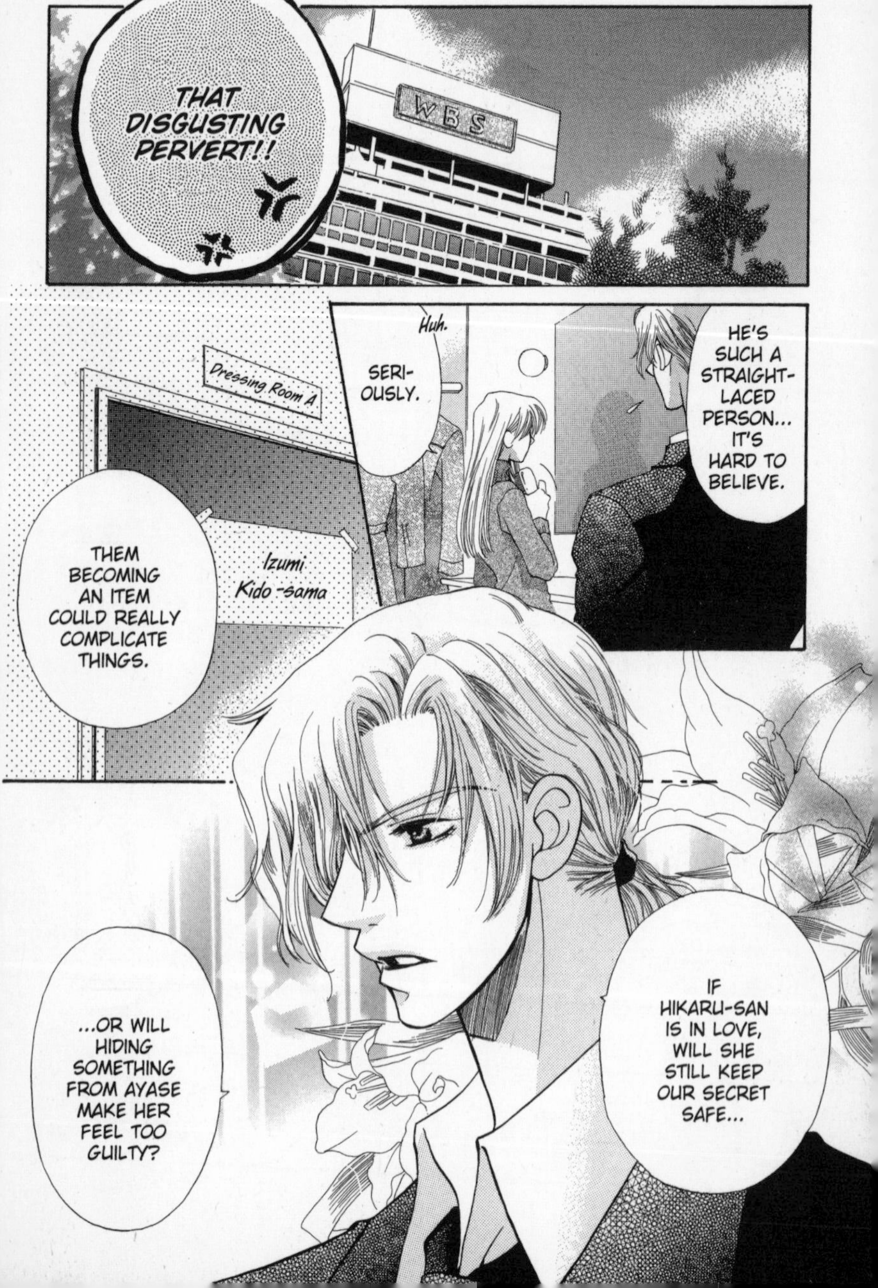
THAT DISGUSTING PERVERT!!
WBS
HE'S SUCH A STRAIGHT-LACED PERSON... IT'S HARD TO BELIEVE.
Huh.
SERI-OUSLY.
Dressing Room A
Izumi Kido-sama
THEM BECOMING AN ITEM COULD REALLY COMPLICATE THINGS.
IF HIKARU-SAN IS IN LOVE, WILL SHE STILL KEEP OUR SECRET SAFE...
...OR WILL HIDING SOMETHING FROM AYASE MAKE HER FEEL TOO GUILTY?

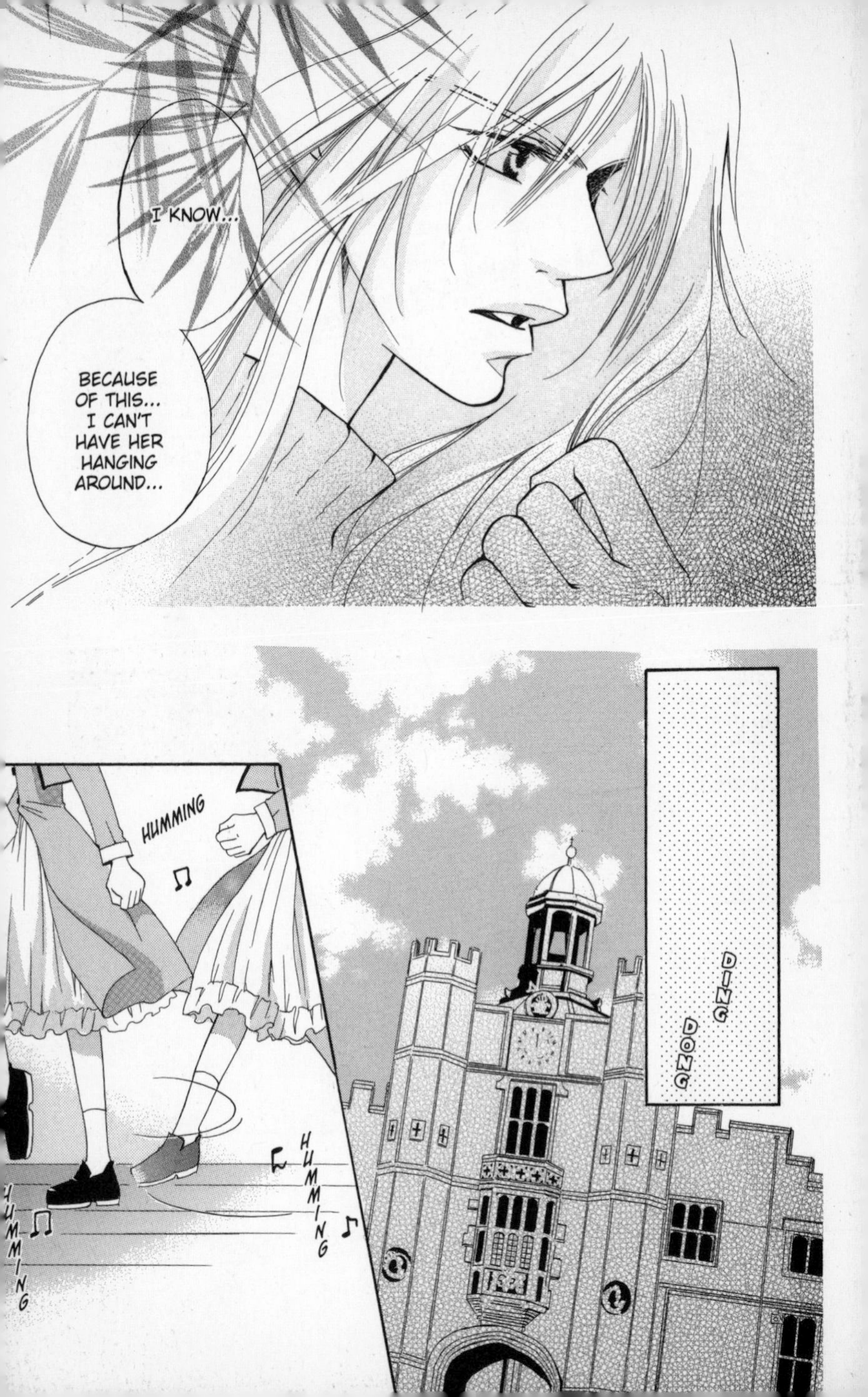
I KNOW...
BECAUSE OF THIS... I CAN'T HAVE HER HANGING AROUND...
DING DONG
HUMMING
HUMMING
HUMMING

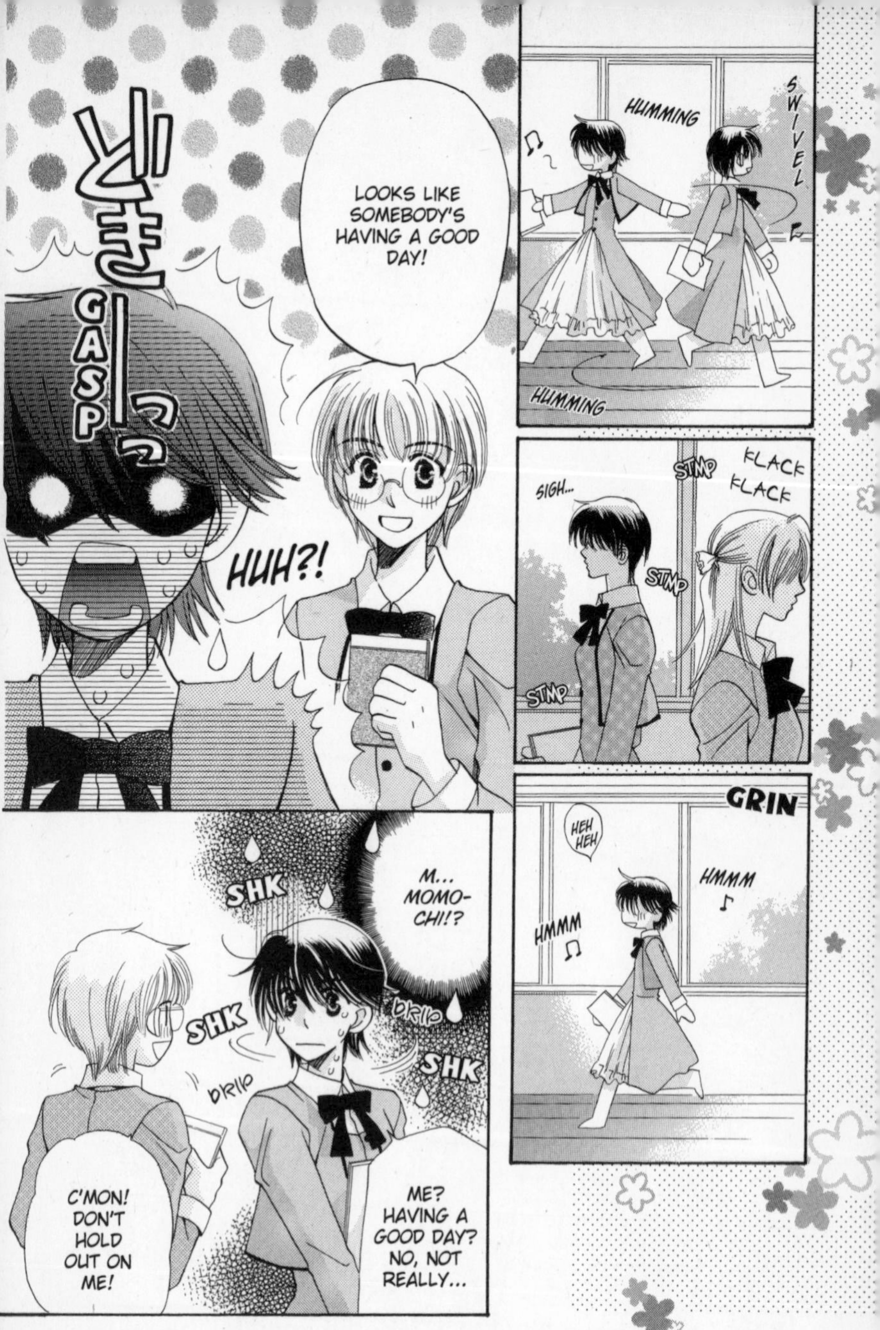
HUMMING
SWIVEL
HUMMING
SIGH...
STMP
KLACK KLACK
STMP
STMP
GRIN
HEH HEH
HMMM ♪
HMMM ♫
LOOKS LIKE SOMEBODY'S HAVING A GOOD DAY!
どきーっ
GASP
HUH?!
M... MOMO-CHI!?
SHK
DRIP
SHK
SHK
DRIP
ME? HAVING A GOOD DAY? NO, NOT REALLY...
C'MON! DON'T HOLD OUT ON ME!

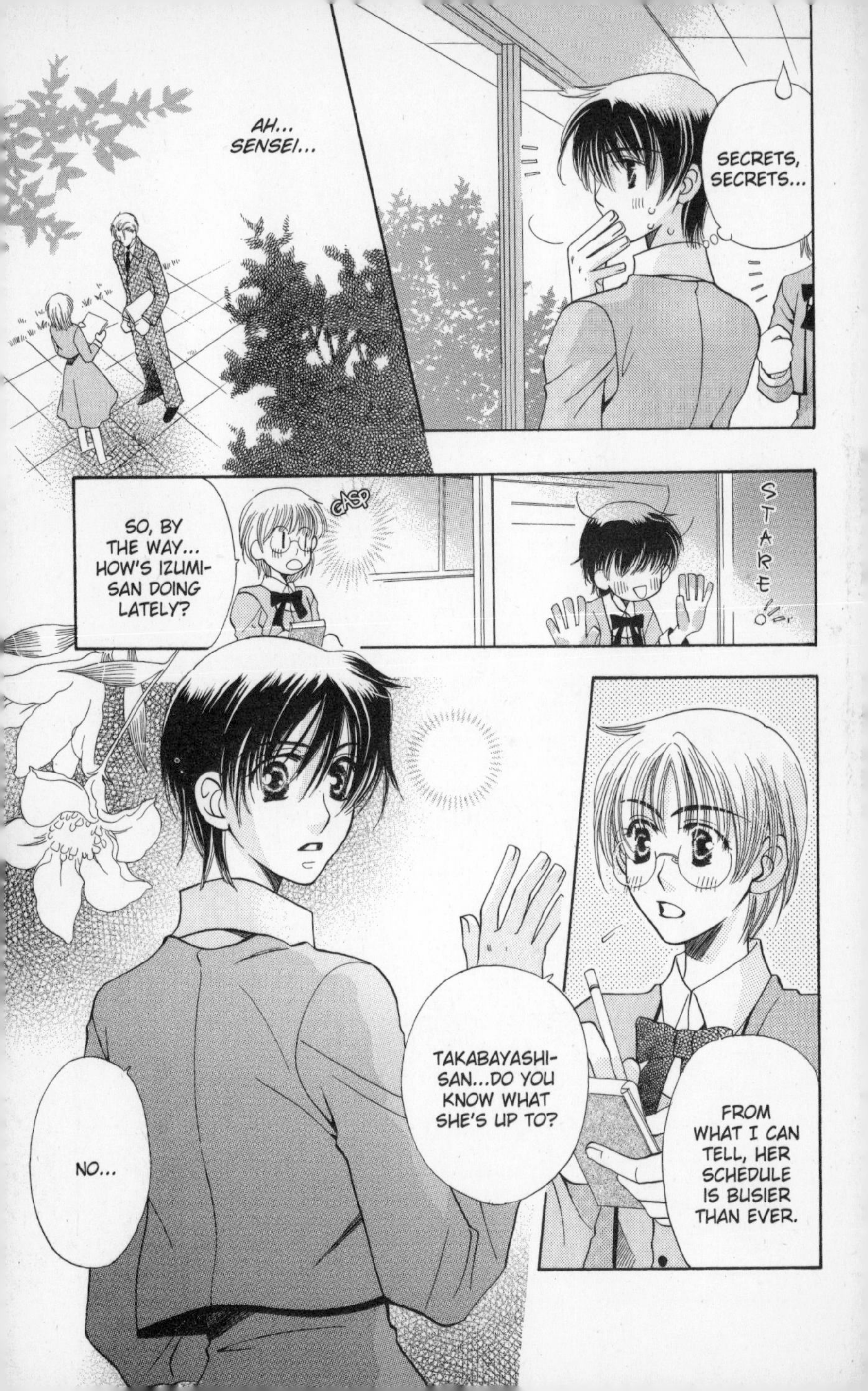
SECRETS, SECRETS...
AH... SENSEI...
STARE
GASP
SO, BY THE WAY... HOW'S IZUMI-SAN DOING LATELY?
TAKABAYASHI-SAN...DO YOU KNOW WHAT SHE'S UP TO?
FROM WHAT I CAN TELL, HER SCHEDULE IS BUSIER THAN EVER.
NO...

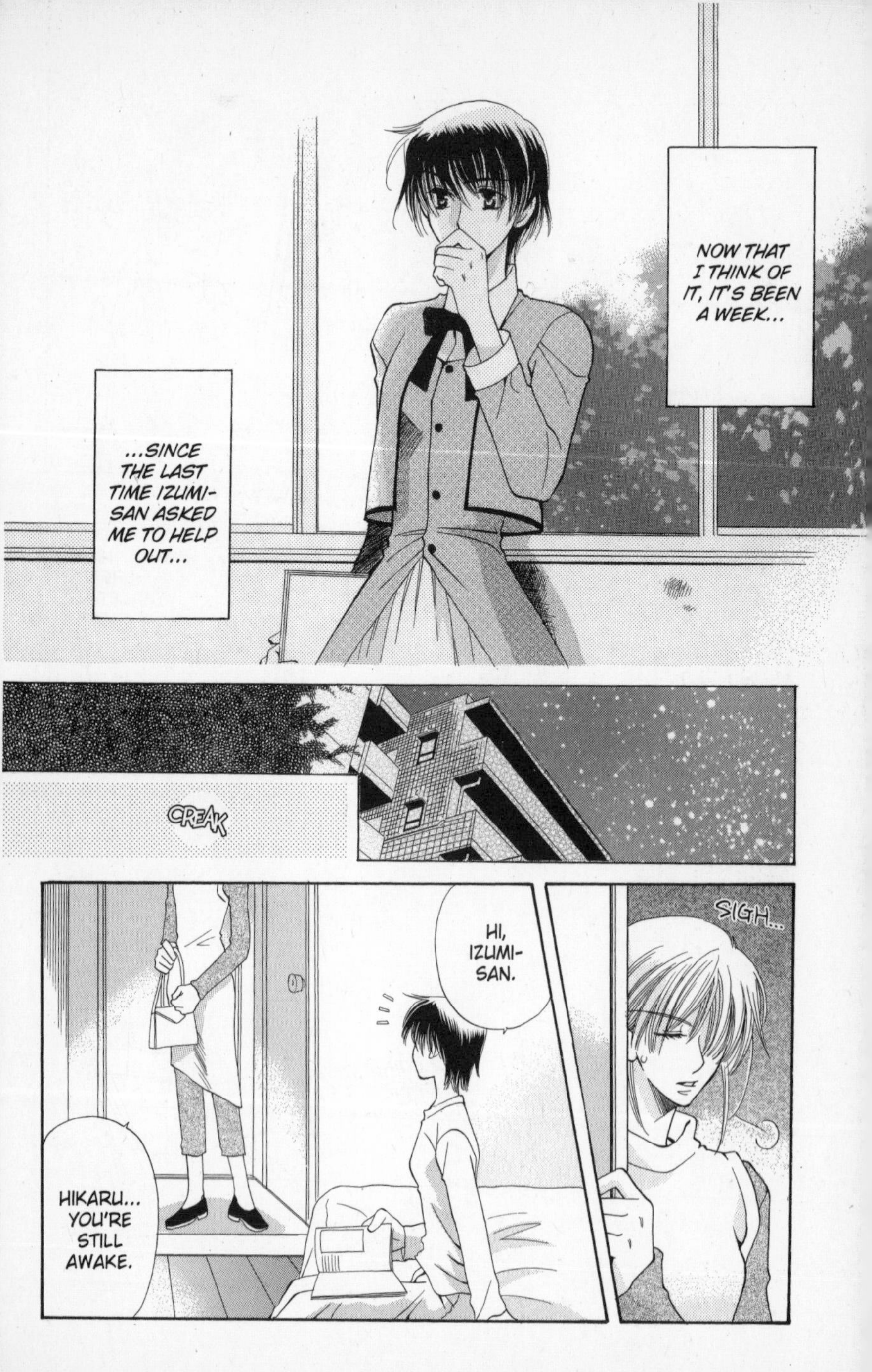
NOW THAT I THINK OF IT, IT'S BEEN A WEEK...
...SINCE THE LAST TIME IZUMI-SAN ASKED ME TO HELP OUT...
CREAK
SIGH...
HI, IZUMI-SAN.
HIKARU... YOU'RE STILL AWAKE.

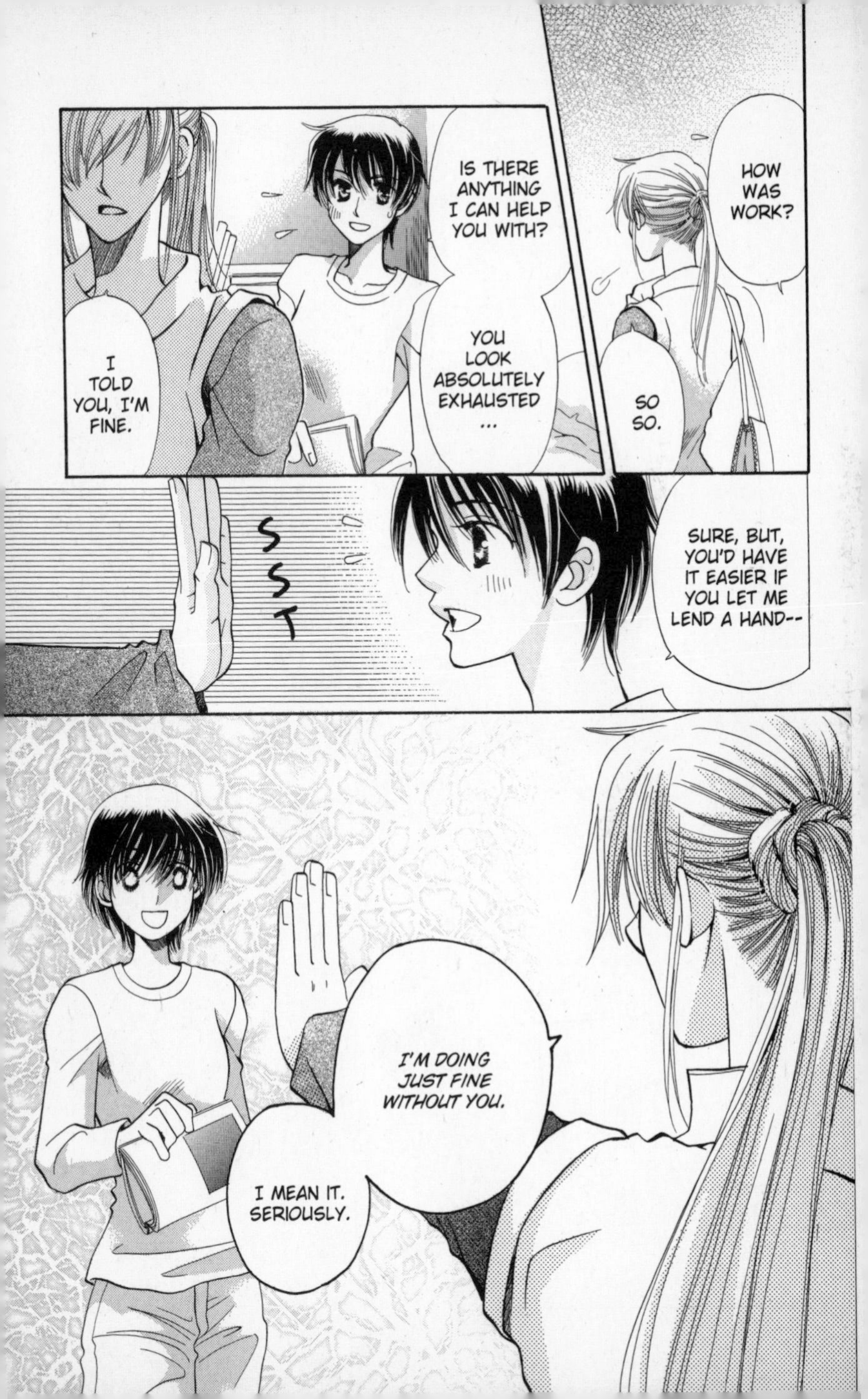
HOW WAS WORK?
SO SO.
IS THERE ANYTHING I CAN HELP YOU WITH?
YOU LOOK ABSOLUTELY EXHAUSTED ...
I TOLD YOU, I'M FINE.
SURE, BUT, YOU'D HAVE IT EASIER IF YOU LET ME LEND A HAND--
SST
I'M DOING JUST FINE WITHOUT YOU.
I MEAN IT. SERIOUSLY.

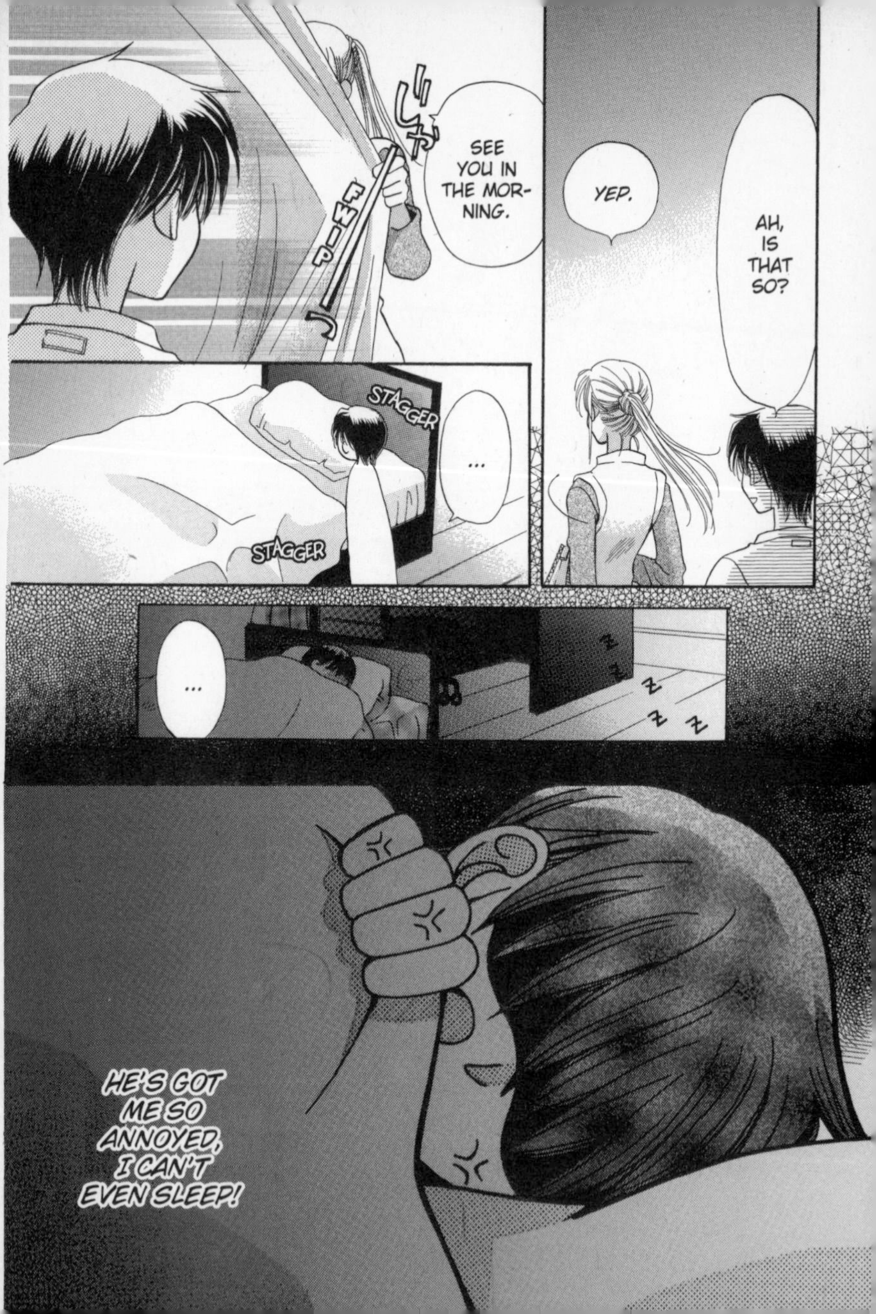
AH, IS THAT SO?
YEP.
SEE YOU IN THE MORNING.
FWIP
STAGGER
...
STAGGER
Z Z Z Z Z
...
HE'S GOT ME SO ANNOYED, I CAN'T EVEN SLEEP!

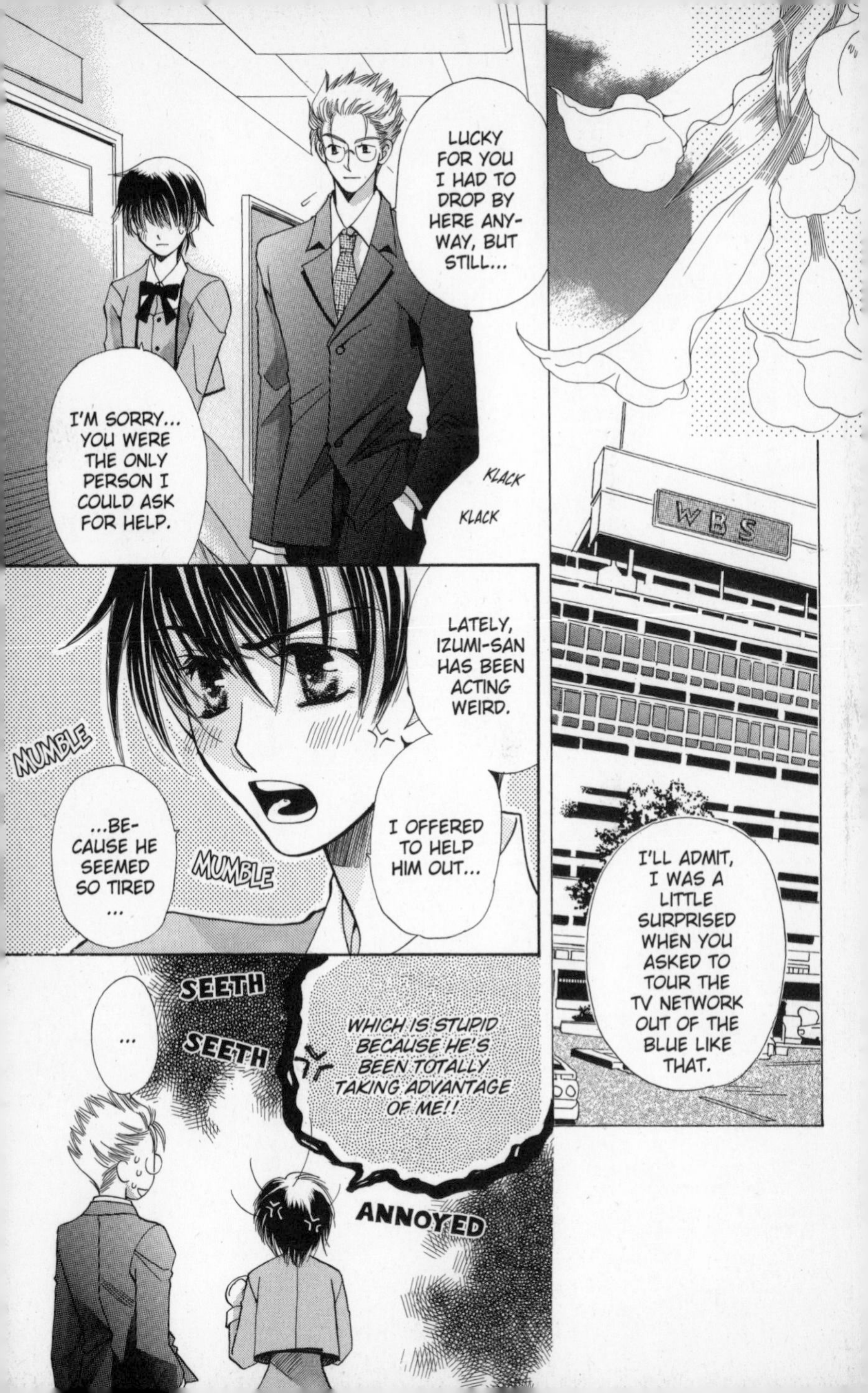

I'LL ADMIT, I WAS A LITTLE SURPRISED WHEN YOU ASKED TO TOUR THE TV NETWORK OUT OF THE BLUE LIKE THAT.
WBS
LUCKY FOR YOU I HAD TO DROP BY HERE ANYWAY, BUT STILL...
I'M SORRY... YOU WERE THE ONLY PERSON I COULD ASK FOR HELP.
KLACK
KLACK
LATELY, IZUMI-SAN HAS BEEN ACTING WEIRD.
I OFFERED TO HELP HIM OUT...
MUMBLE
...BE-CAUSE HE SEEMED SO TIRED ...
MUMBLE
WHICH IS STUPID BECAUSE HE'S BEEN TOTALLY TAKING ADVANTAGE OF ME!!
SEETH
SEETH
...
ANNOYED

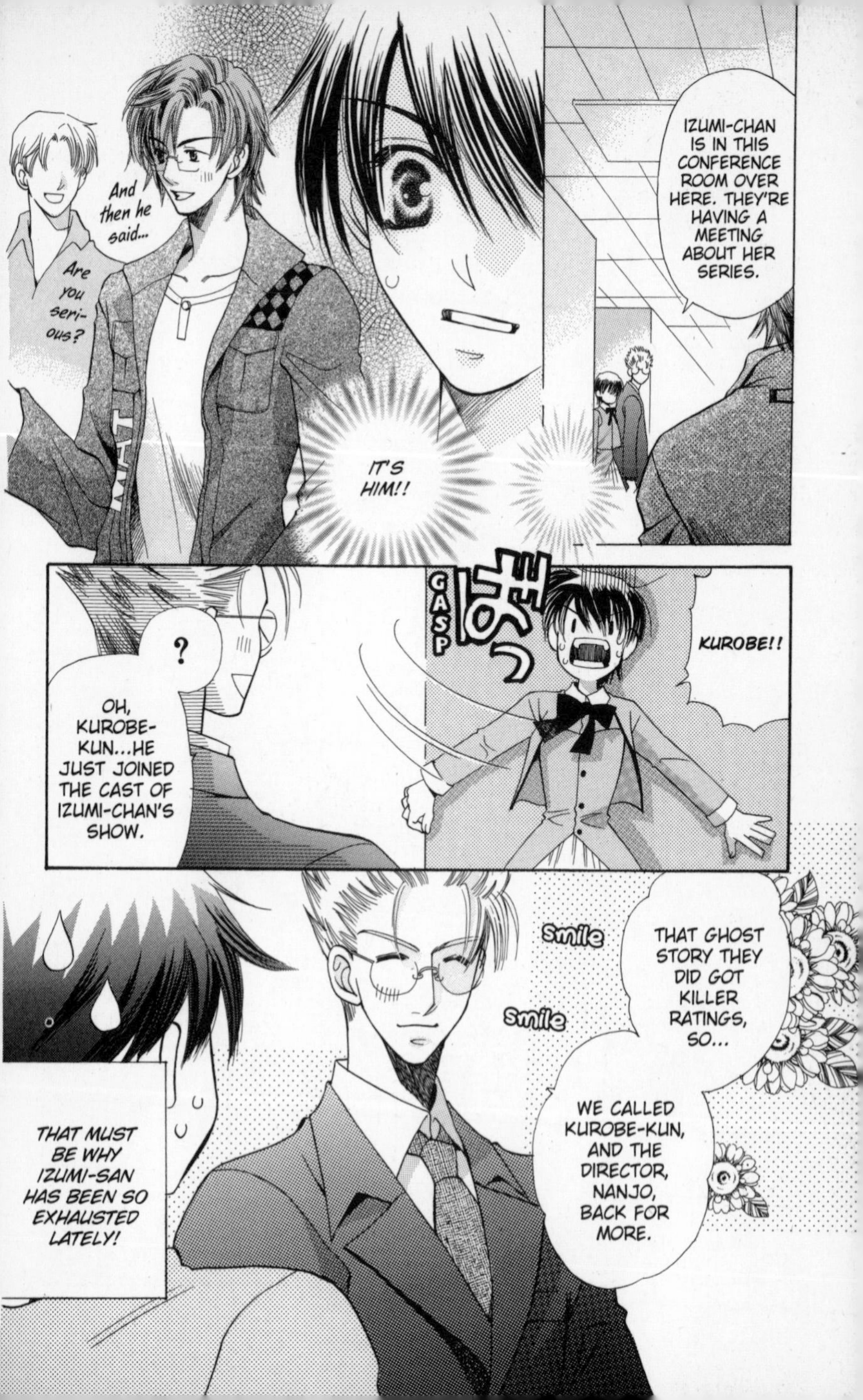
IZUMI-CHAN IS IN THIS CONFERENCE ROOM OVER HERE. THEY'RE HAVING A MEETING ABOUT HER SERIES.
And then he said...
Are you seri-ous?
IT'S HIM!!
KUROBE!!
ぱっ
GASP
?
OH, KUROBE-KUN...HE JUST JOINED THE CAST OF IZUMI-CHAN'S SHOW.
THAT GHOST STORY THEY DID GOT KILLER RATINGS, SO...
Smile
Smile
WE CALLED KUROBE-KUN, AND THE DIRECTOR, NANJO, BACK FOR MORE.
THAT MUST BE WHY IZUMI-SAN HAS BEEN SO EXHAUSTED LATELY!

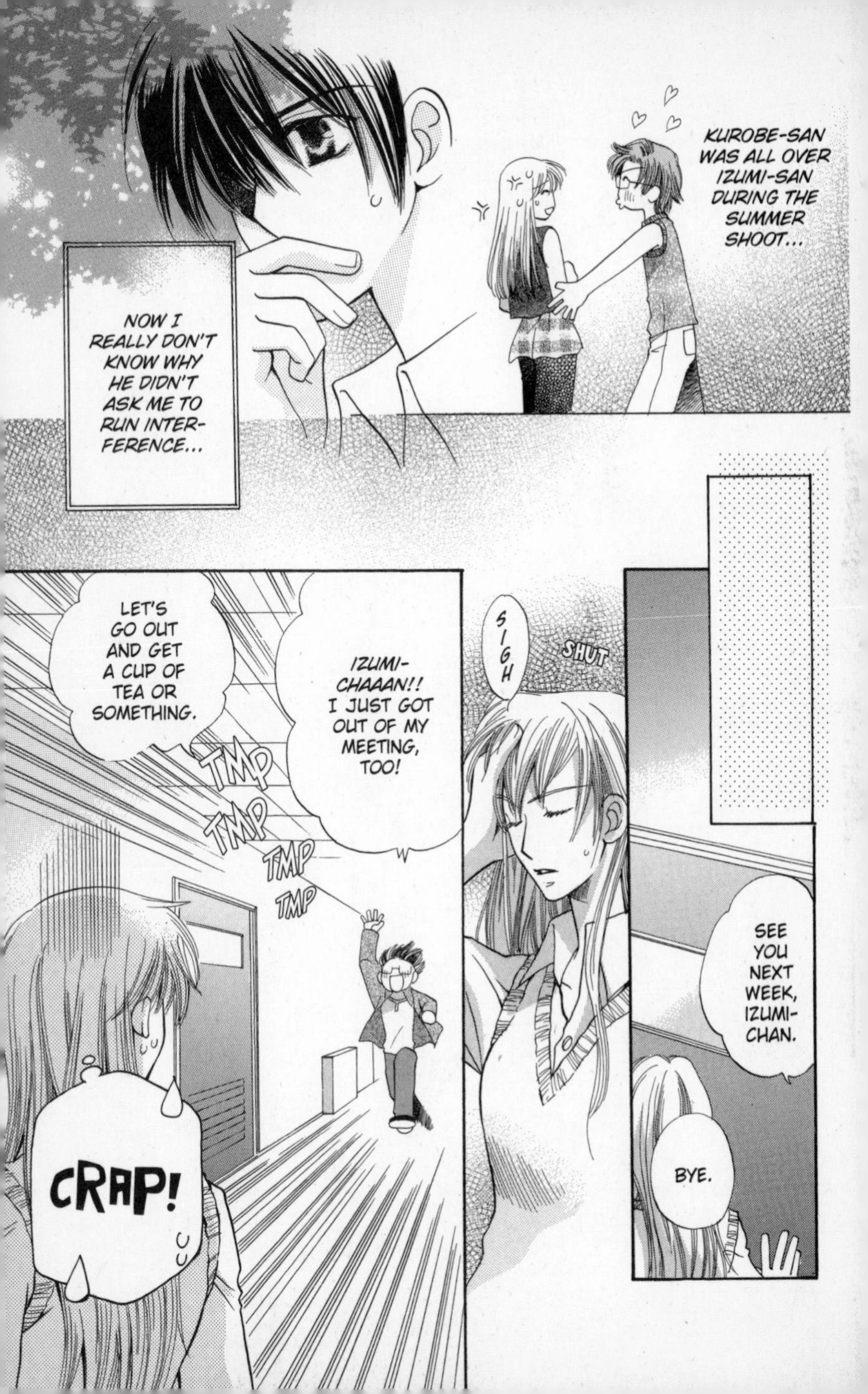
KUROBE-SAN WAS ALL OVER IZUMI-SAN DURING THE SUMMER SHOOT...
NOW I REALLY DON'T KNOW WHY HE DIDN'T ASK ME TO RUN INTER-FERENCE...
SEE YOU NEXT WEEK, IZUMI-CHAN.
BYE.
SHUT
SIGH
IZUMI-CHAAAN!! I JUST GOT OUT OF MY MEETING, TOO!
LET'S GO OUT AND GET A CUP OF TEA OR SOMETHING.
TMP
TMP
TMP
TMP
CRAP!

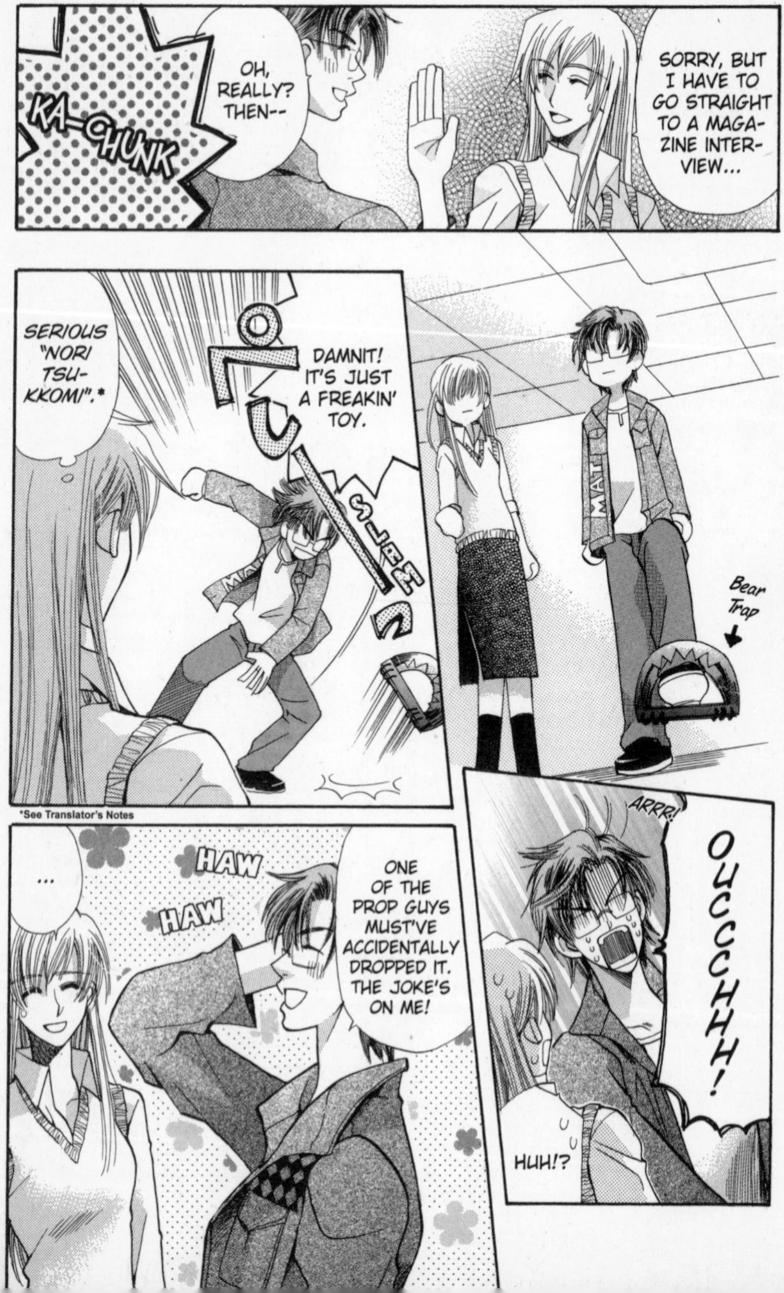
SORRY, BUT I HAVE TO GO STRAIGHT TO A MAGAZINE INTERVIEW...
OH, REALLY? THEN--
KA-CHUNK
Bear Trap
DAMNIT! IT'S JUST A FREAKIN' TOY.
SLAM
SERIOUS "NORI TSUKKOMI".*
ARRR!
OUCCHHH!
HUH!?
ONE OF THE PROP GUYS MUST'VE ACCIDENTALLY DROPPED IT. THE JOKE'S ON ME!
HAW
HAW
...

*See Translator's Notes

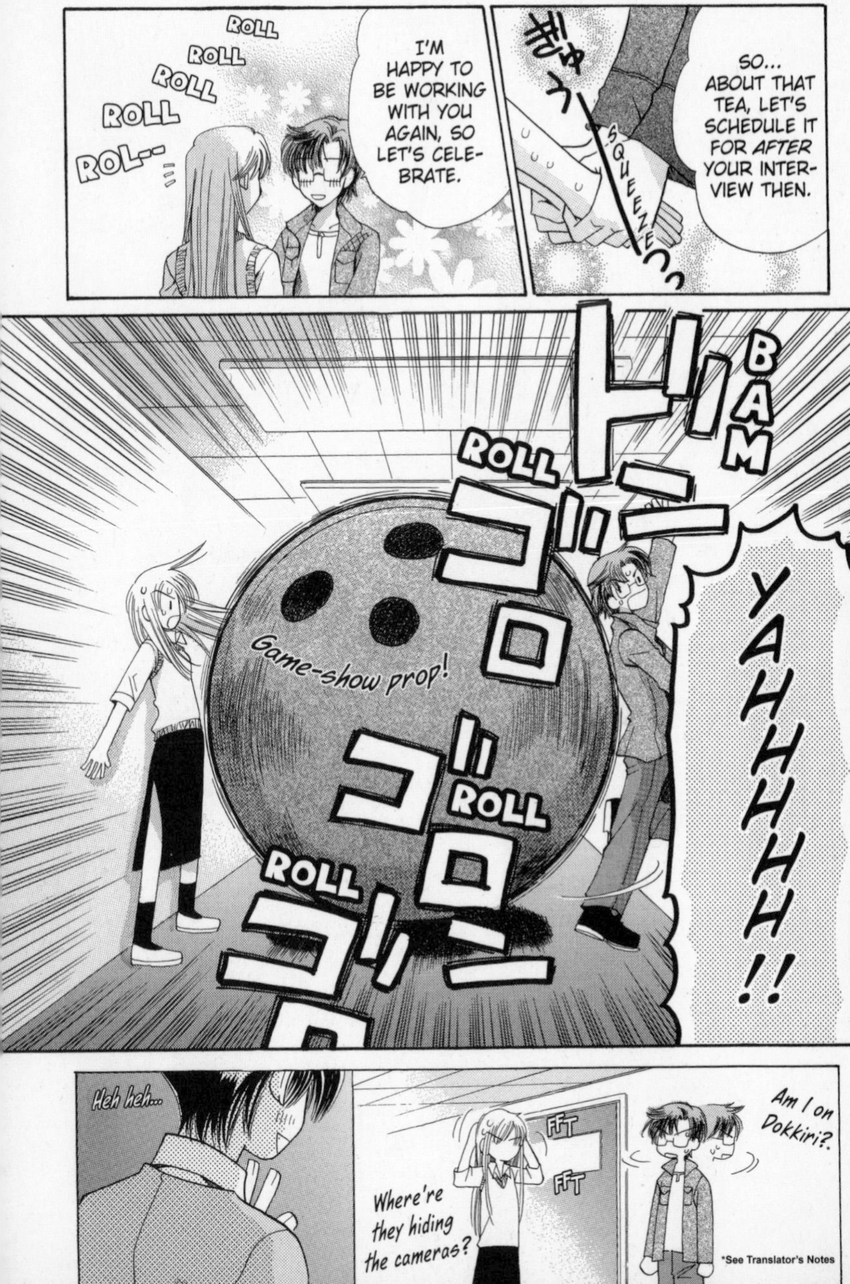
ぎゅっ
SQUEEZE
SO... ABOUT THAT TEA, LET'S SCHEDULE IT FOR *AFTER* YOUR INTER- VIEW THEN.
ROLL
ROLL
ROLL
ROLL
ROL--
I'M HAPPY TO BE WORKING WITH YOU AGAIN, SO LET'S CELE- BRATE.
ドーン
BAM
YAHHHHH!!
ゴロ
ROLL
Game-show prop!
ゴロ
ROLL
ゴロ
ROLL
Am I on Dokkiri?*
FFT
FFT
Where're they hiding the cameras?
Heh heh...

*See Translator's Notes

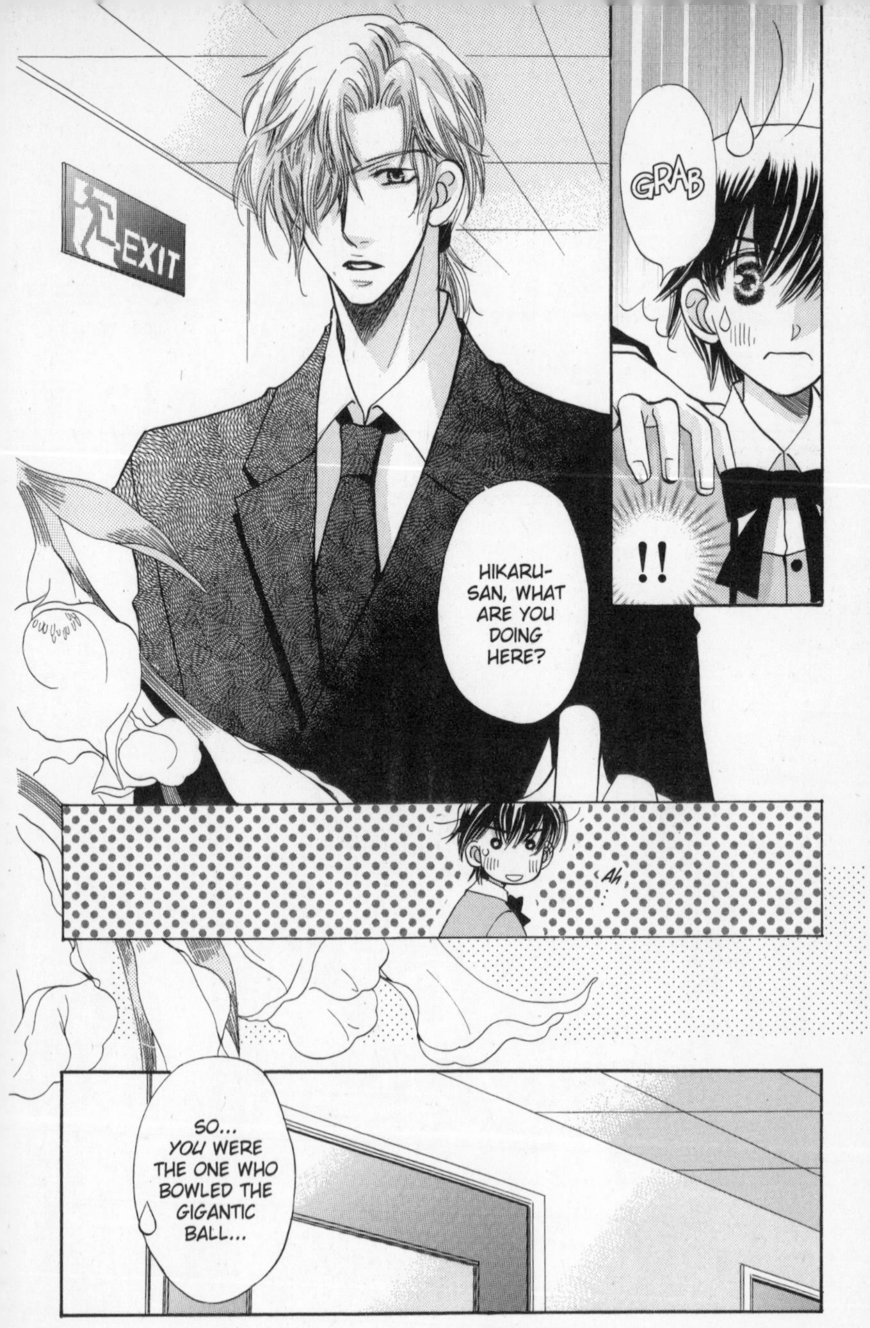
GRAB
!!
EXIT
HIKARU-SAN, WHAT ARE YOU DOING HERE?
Ah
SO... *YOU* WERE THE ONE WHO BOWLED THE GIGANTIC BALL...

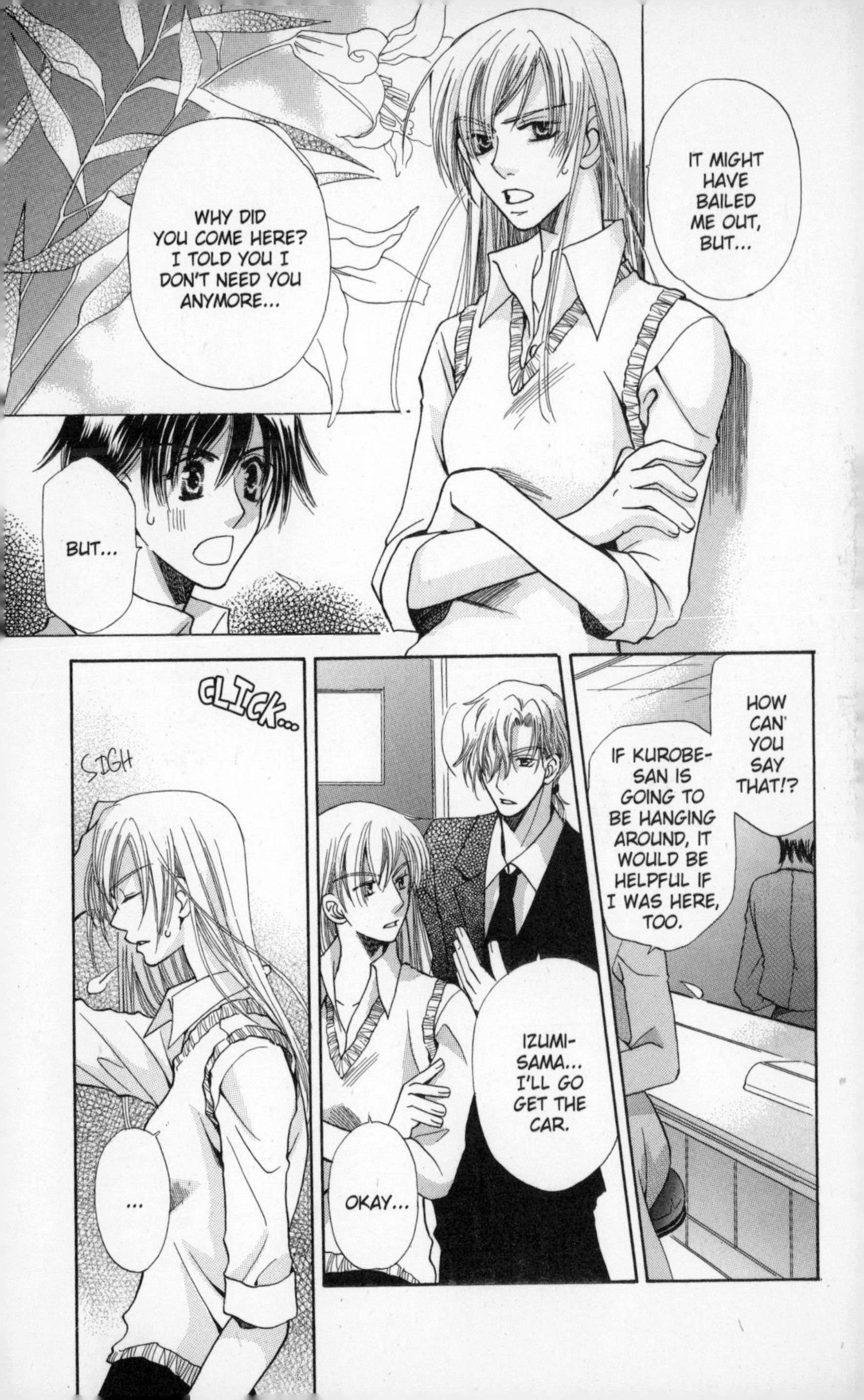
IT MIGHT HAVE BAILED ME OUT, BUT...
WHY DID YOU COME HERE? I TOLD YOU I DON'T NEED YOU ANYMORE...
BUT...
HOW CAN' YOU SAY THAT!?
IF KUROBE-SAN IS GOING TO BE HANGING AROUND, IT WOULD BE HELPFUL IF I WAS HERE, TOO.
IZUMI-SAMA... I'LL GO GET THE CAR.
OKAY...
CLICK...
SIGH
...

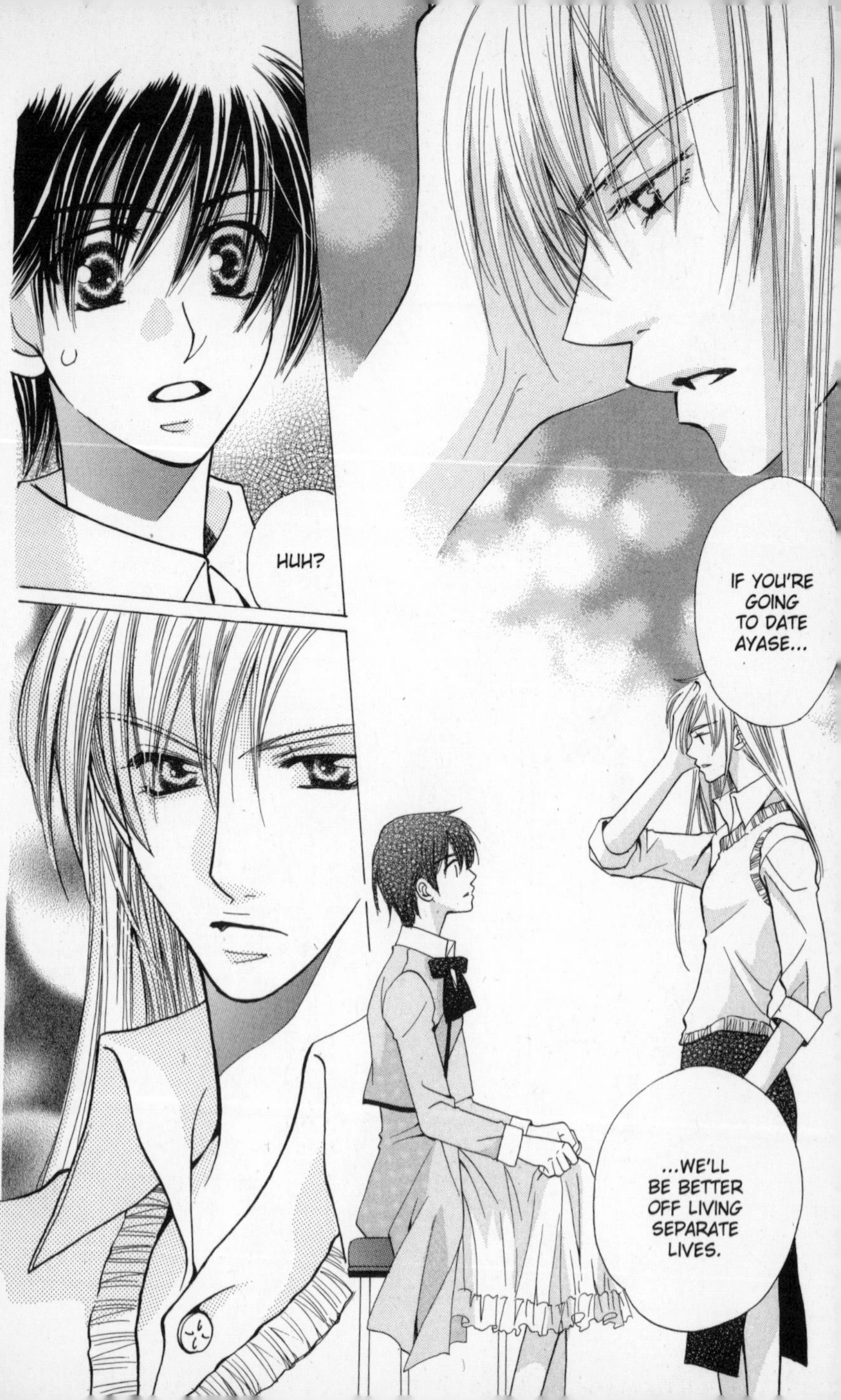
IF YOU'RE GOING TO DATE AYASE...
...WE'LL BE BETTER OFF LIVING SEPARATE LIVES.
HUH?

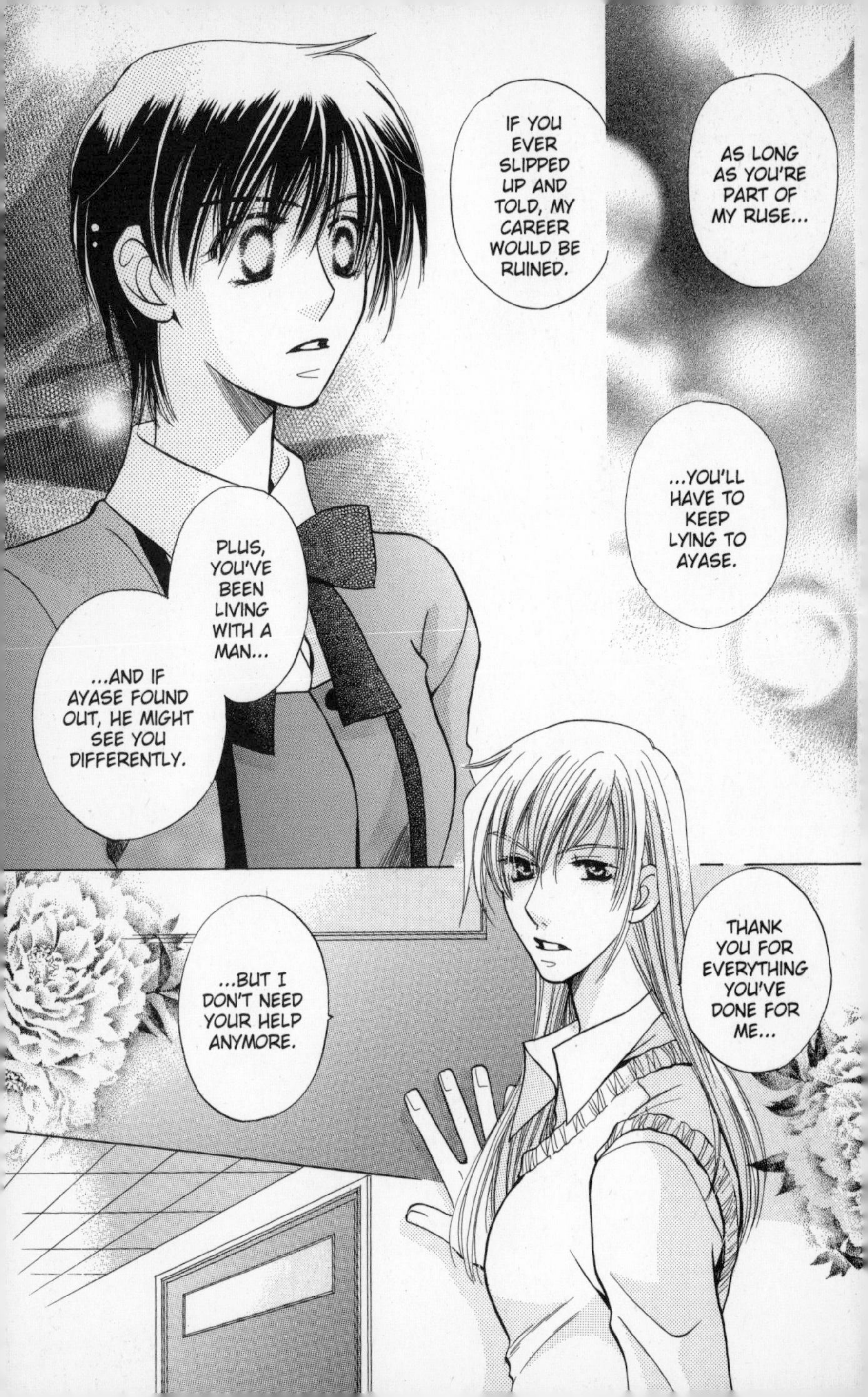
AS LONG AS YOU'RE PART OF MY RUSE...
...YOU'LL HAVE TO KEEP LYING TO AYASE.
IF YOU EVER SLIPPED UP AND TOLD, MY CAREER WOULD BE RUINED.
PLUS, YOU'VE BEEN LIVING WITH A MAN...
...AND IF AYASE FOUND OUT, HE MIGHT SEE YOU DIFFERENTLY.
THANK YOU FOR EVERYTHING YOU'VE DONE FOR ME...
...BUT I DON'T NEED YOUR HELP ANYMORE.

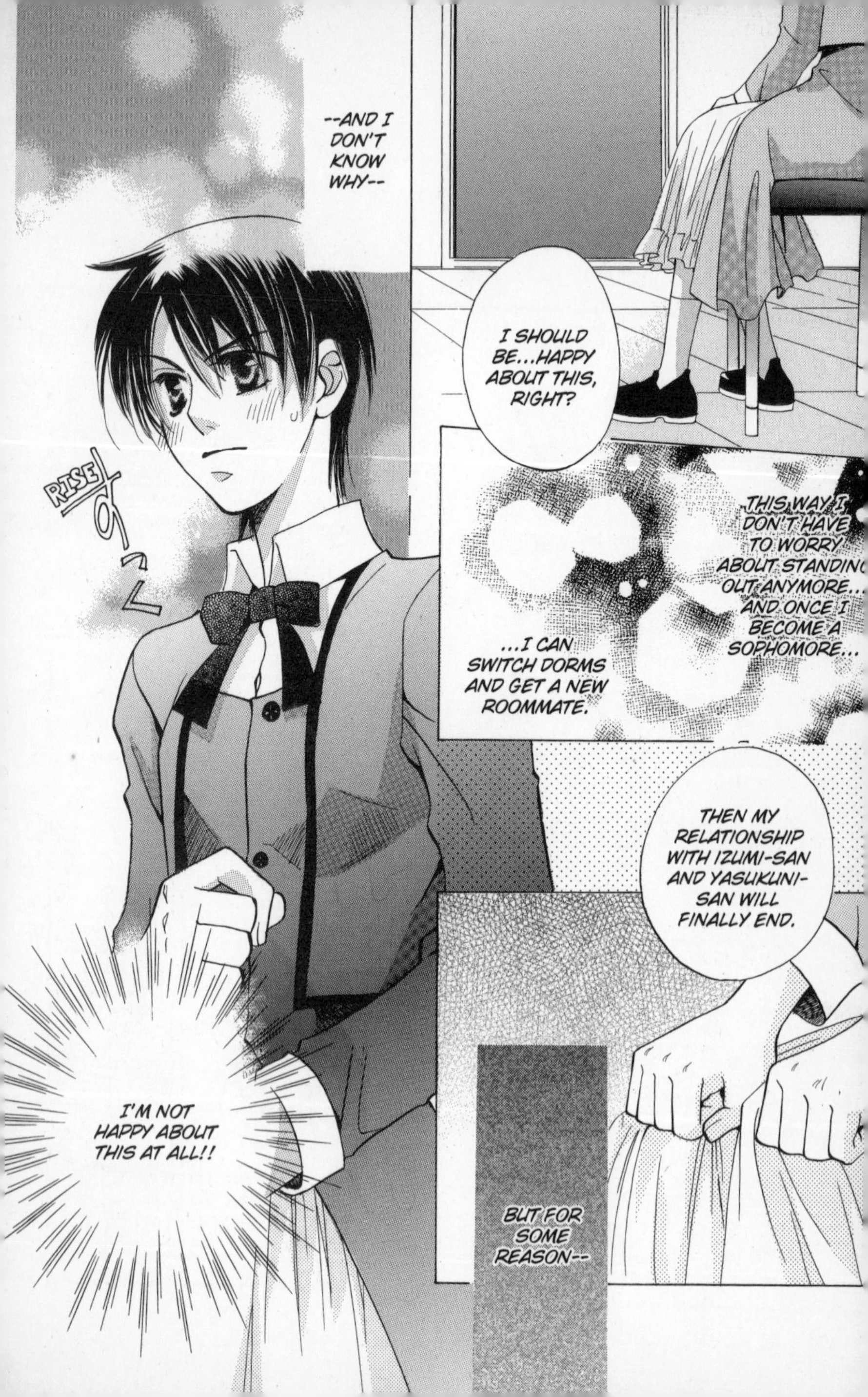
I SHOULD BE...HAPPY ABOUT THIS, RIGHT?
THIS WAY I DON'T HAVE TO WORRY ABOUT STANDING OUT ANYMORE... AND ONCE I BECOME A SOPHOMORE...
...I CAN SWITCH DORMS AND GET A NEW ROOMMATE.
THEN MY RELATIONSHIP WITH IZUMI-SAN AND YASUKUNI-SAN WILL FINALLY END.
BUT FOR SOME REASON--
--AND I DON'T KNOW WHY--
RISE
I'M NOT HAPPY ABOUT THIS AT ALL!!

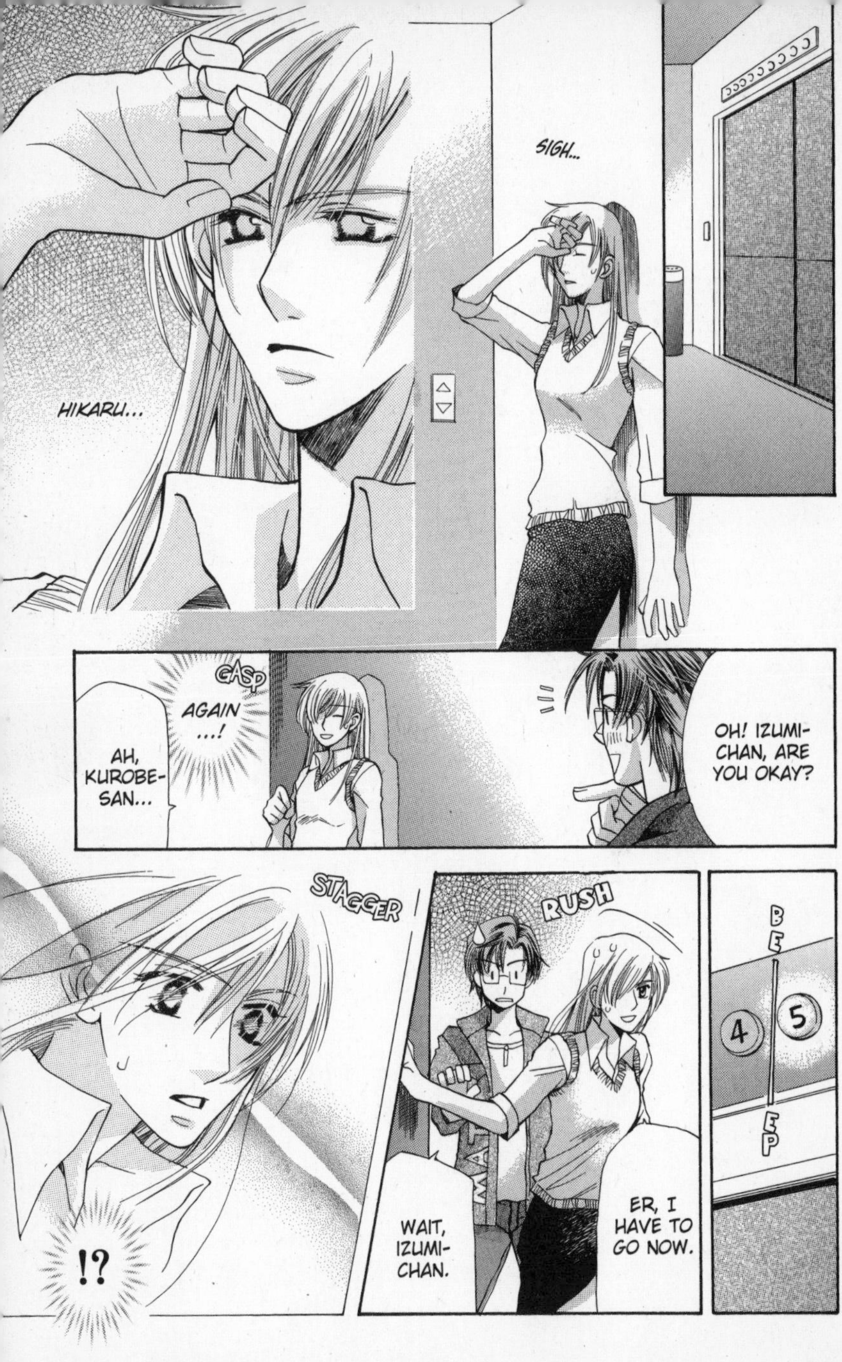

SIGH...
HIKARU...
OH! IZUMI-CHAN, ARE YOU OKAY?
GASP
AGAIN ...!
AH, KUROBE-SAN...
BE EP
RUSH
ER, I HAVE TO GO NOW.
WAIT, IZUMI-CHAN.
STAGGER
!?

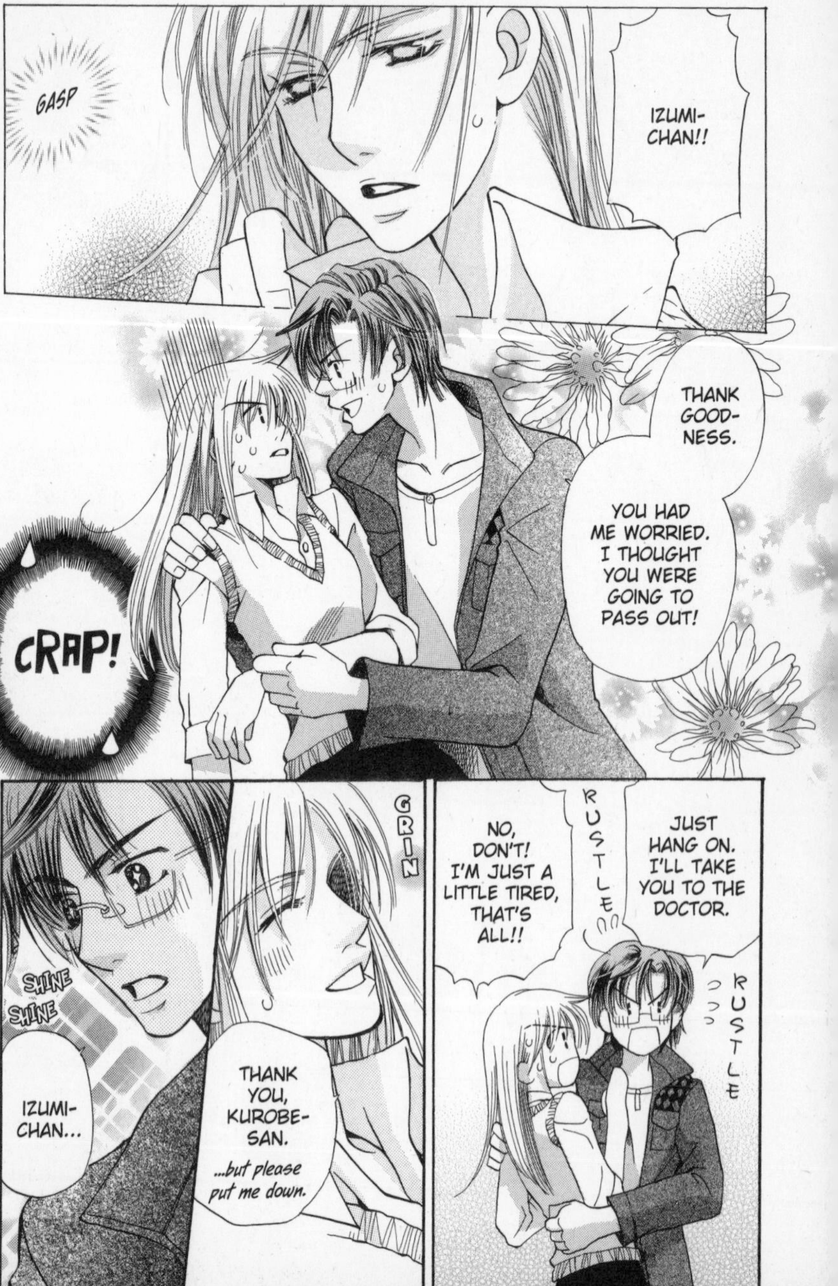
IZUMI-CHAN!!
GASP
THANK GOOD-NESS.
YOU HAD ME WORRIED. I THOUGHT YOU WERE GOING TO PASS OUT!
CRAP!
JUST HANG ON. I'LL TAKE YOU TO THE DOCTOR.
RUSTLE
NO, DON'T! I'M JUST A LITTLE TIRED, THAT'S ALL!!
RUSTLE
GRIN
THANK YOU, KUROBE-SAN.
...but please put me down.
SHINE
SHINE
IZUMI-CHAN...

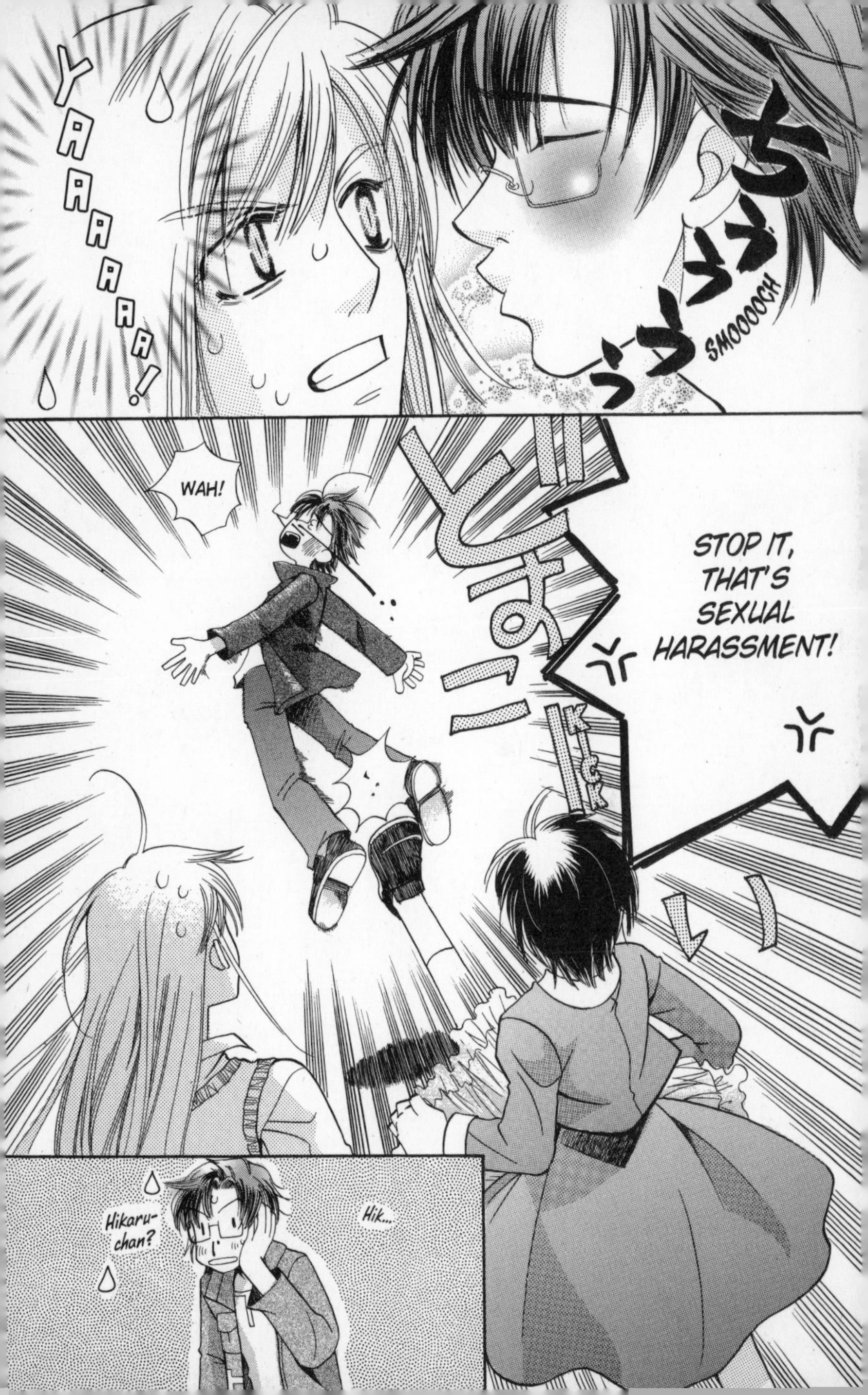
SMOOOOCH
YAAAAAAA!
STOP IT, THAT'S SEXUAL HARASSMENT!
KICK
WAH!
Hik...
Hikaru-chan?

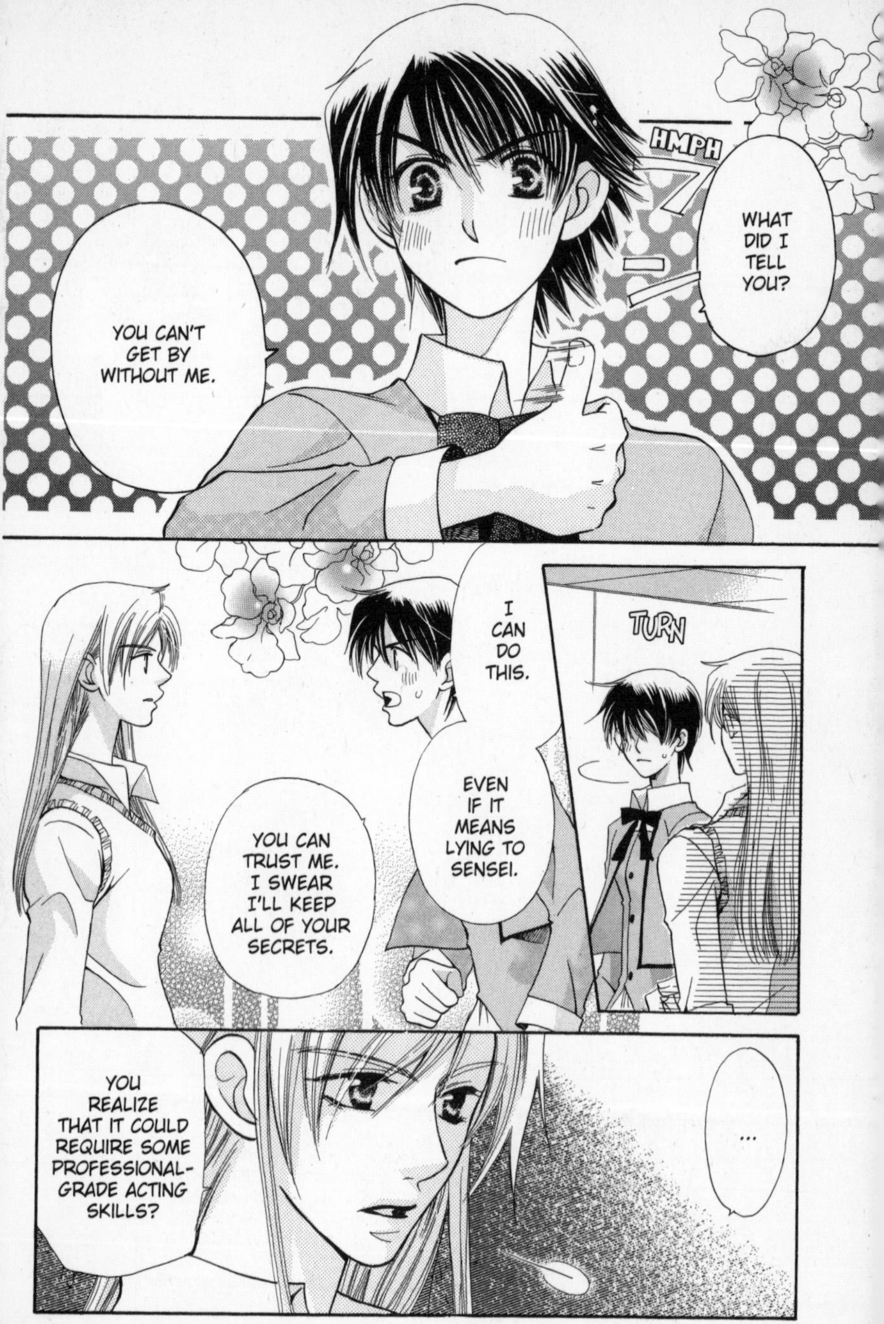
HMPH
WHAT DID I TELL YOU?
YOU CAN'T GET BY WITHOUT ME.
TURN
I CAN DO THIS.
EVEN IF IT MEANS LYING TO SENSEI.
YOU CAN TRUST ME. I SWEAR I'LL KEEP ALL OF YOUR SECRETS.
...
YOU REALIZE THAT IT COULD REQUIRE SOME PROFESSIONAL-GRADE ACTING SKILLS?

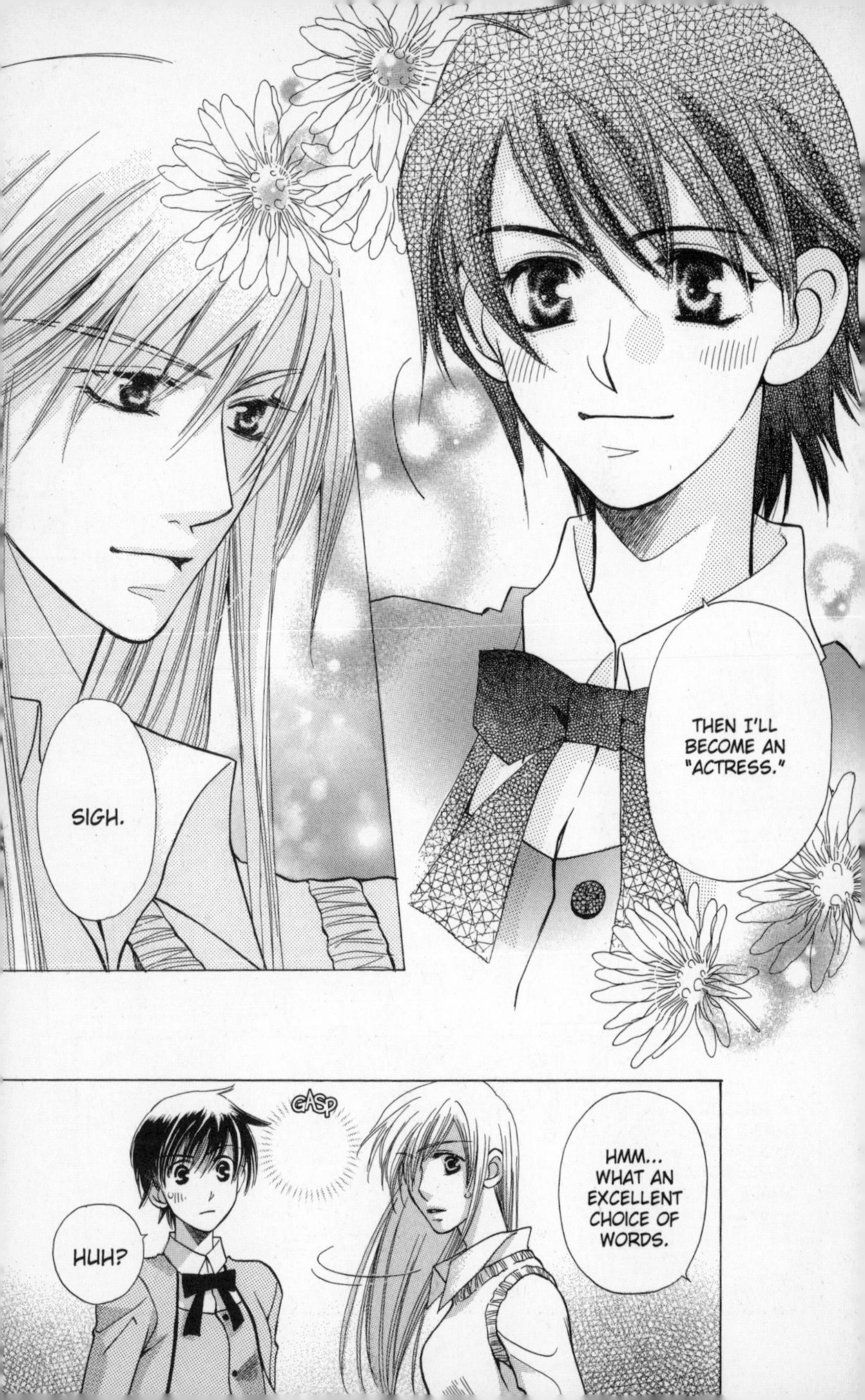
THEN I'LL BECOME AN "ACTRESS."
SIGH.
HMM... WHAT AN EXCELLENT CHOICE OF WORDS.
GASP
HUH?

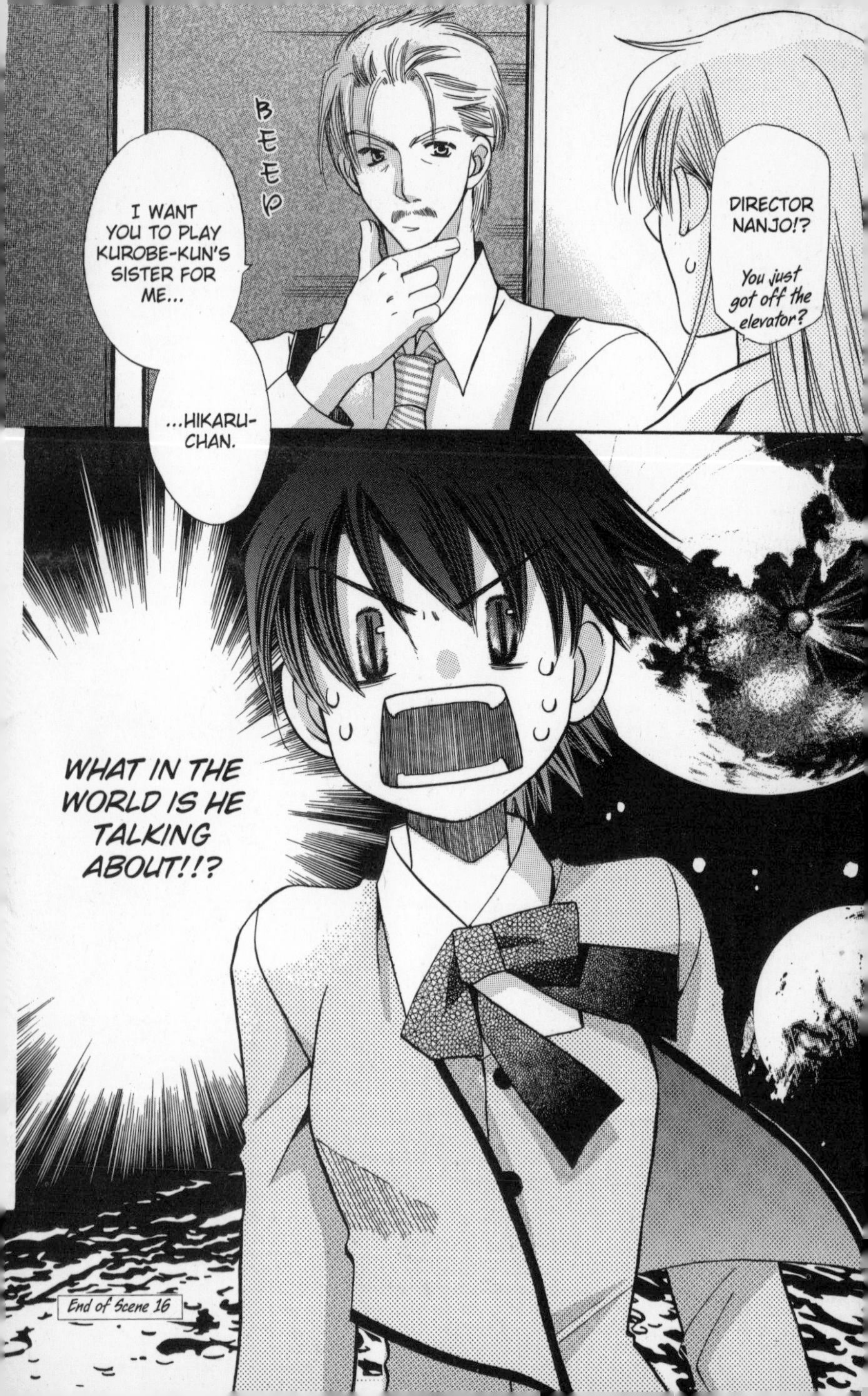
DIRECTOR NANJO!?
You just got off the elevator?
BEEP
I WANT YOU TO PLAY KUROBE-KUN'S SISTER FOR ME...
...HIKARU-CHAN.
WHAT IN THE WORLD IS HE TALKING ABOUT!!?
End of Scene 16

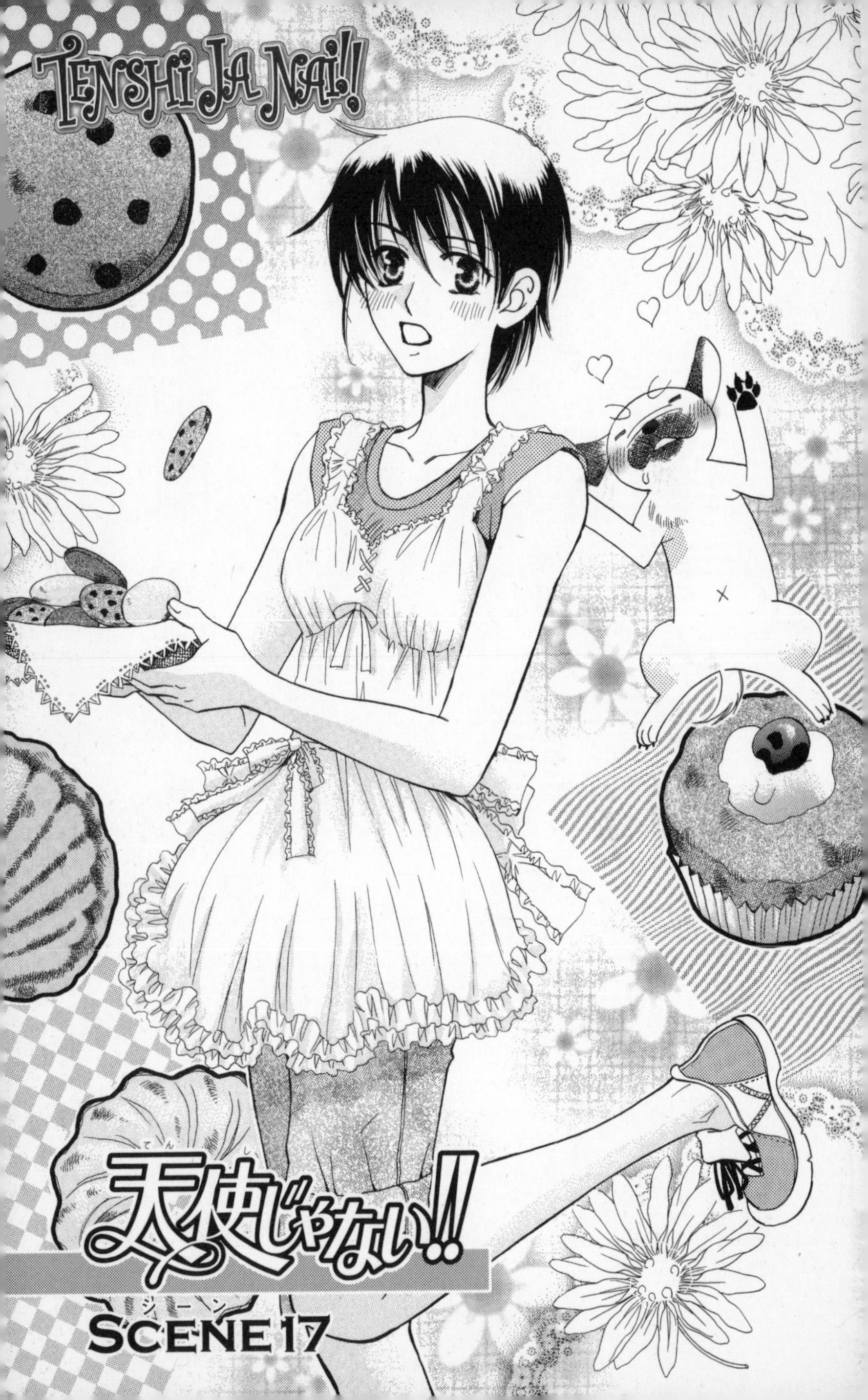
TENSHI JA NAI!!
天使じゃない!!
SCENE 17

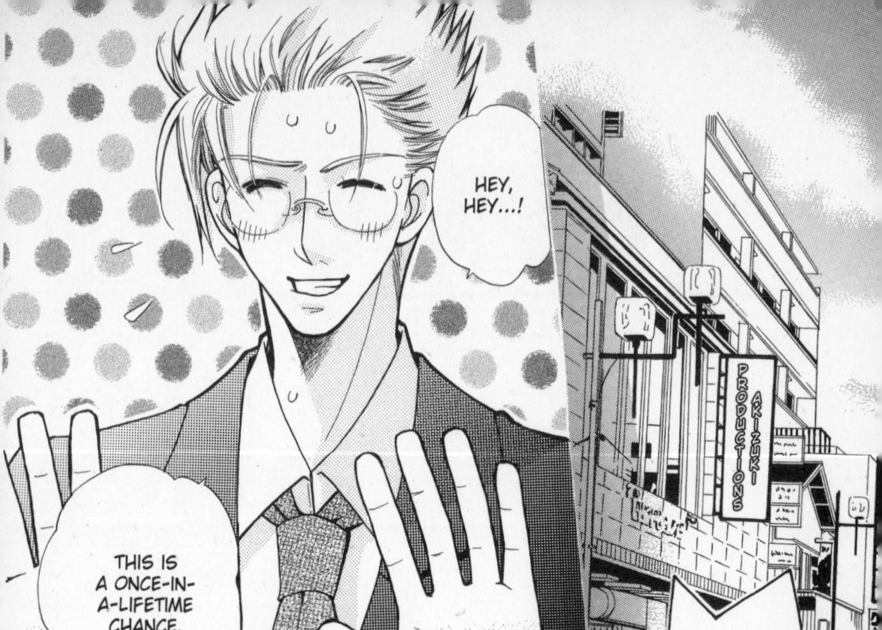
AKIZUKI PRODUCTIONS
THERE'S NO WAY I'M GOING TO DO THIS!
HEY, HEY...!
THIS IS A ONCE-IN-A-LIFETIME CHANCE, HIKARU-CHAN.
BESIDES, YOU'LL BE WITH IZUMI-CHAN ON A DAILY BASIS, SO ALL THE BETTER TO PROTECT "HER" SECRET...
BU... BUT ...

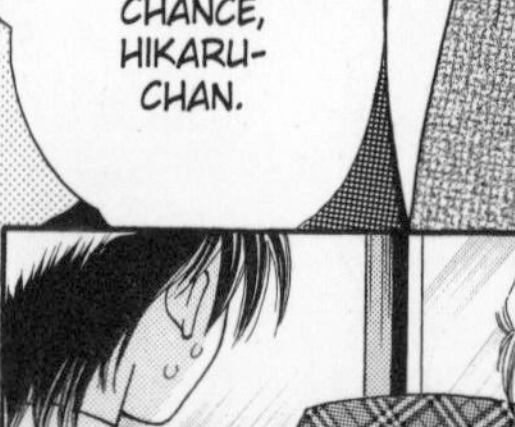
Aw come on, guys. I'm just a side character so a photo really isn't necessary...

Yuichi Akizuki (33 years old)
Born on September 9.
Blood type is O.

He shouldn't be trusted easily, because he's a cunning fellow. During the night, he's popular in the red-light districts. It's always hard to tell what he's up to. Izumi doesn't like him very much. He's a hedonist.

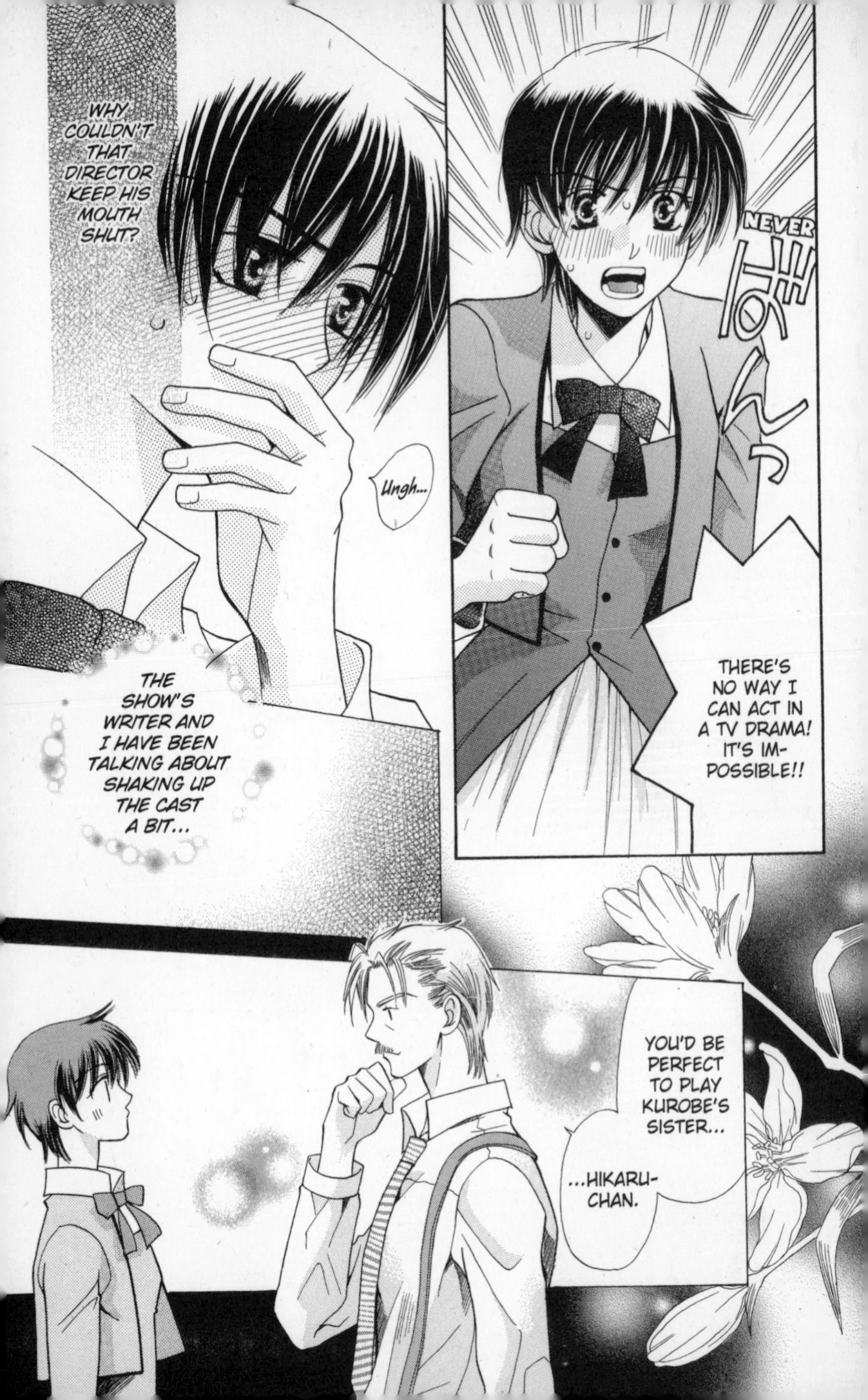
NEVER
THERE'S NO WAY I CAN ACT IN A TV DRAMA! IT'S IM-POSSIBLE!!
WHY COULDN'T THAT DIRECTOR KEEP HIS MOUTH SHUT?
Ungh...
THE SHOW'S WRITER AND I HAVE BEEN TALKING ABOUT SHAKING UP THE CAST A BIT...
YOU'D BE PERFECT TO PLAY KUROBE'S SISTER...
...HIKARU-CHAN.

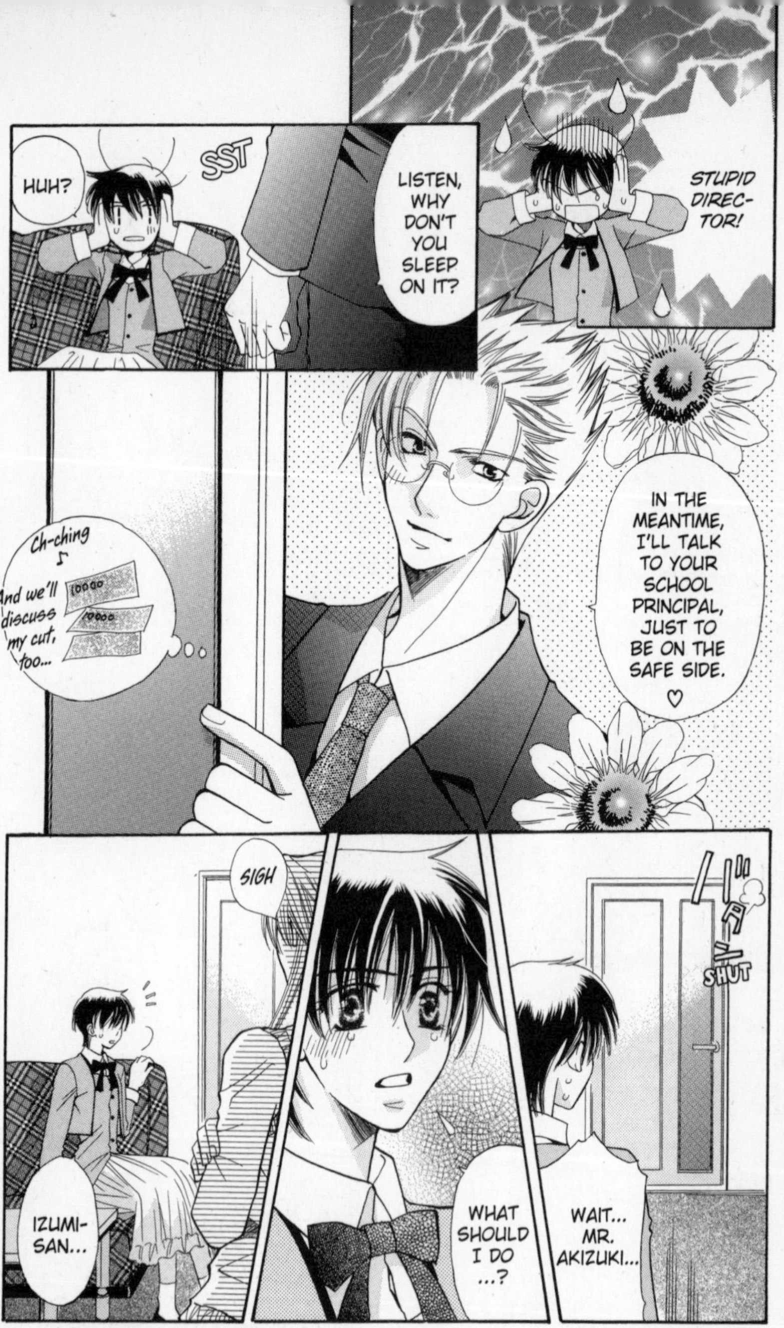
STUPID DIRECTOR!
LISTEN, WHY DON'T YOU SLEEP ON IT?
SST
HUH?
IN THE MEANTIME, I'LL TALK TO YOUR SCHOOL PRINCIPAL, JUST TO BE ON THE SAFE SIDE. ♡
Ch-ching ♪
And we'll discuss my cut, too...
SHUT
WAIT... MR. AKIZUKI...
SIGH
WHAT SHOULD I DO ...?
IZUMI-SAN...

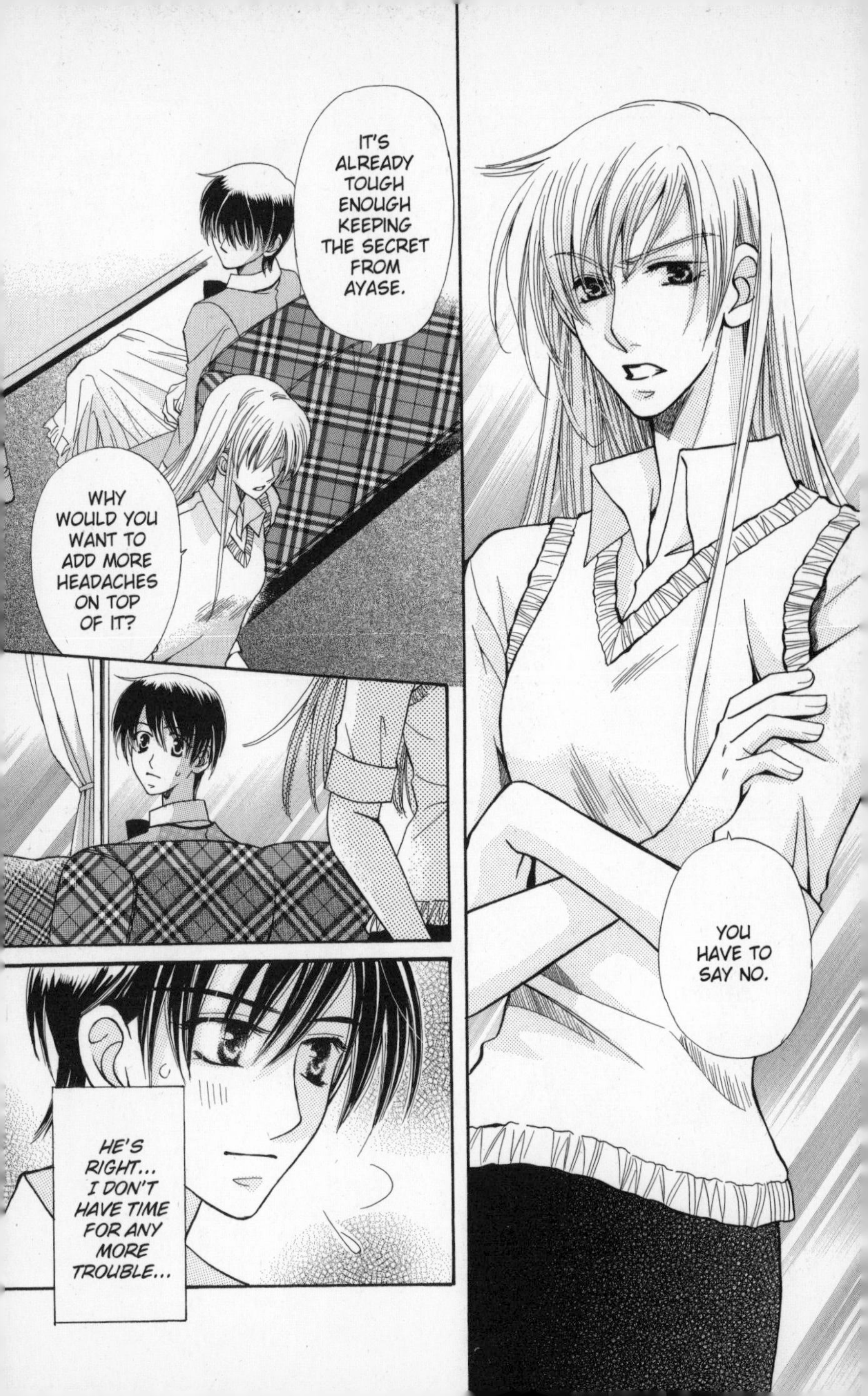
YOU HAVE TO SAY NO.
IT'S ALREADY TOUGH ENOUGH KEEPING THE SECRET FROM AYASE.
WHY WOULD YOU WANT TO ADD MORE HEADACHES ON TOP OF IT?
HE'S RIGHT... I DON'T HAVE TIME FOR ANY MORE TROUBLE...

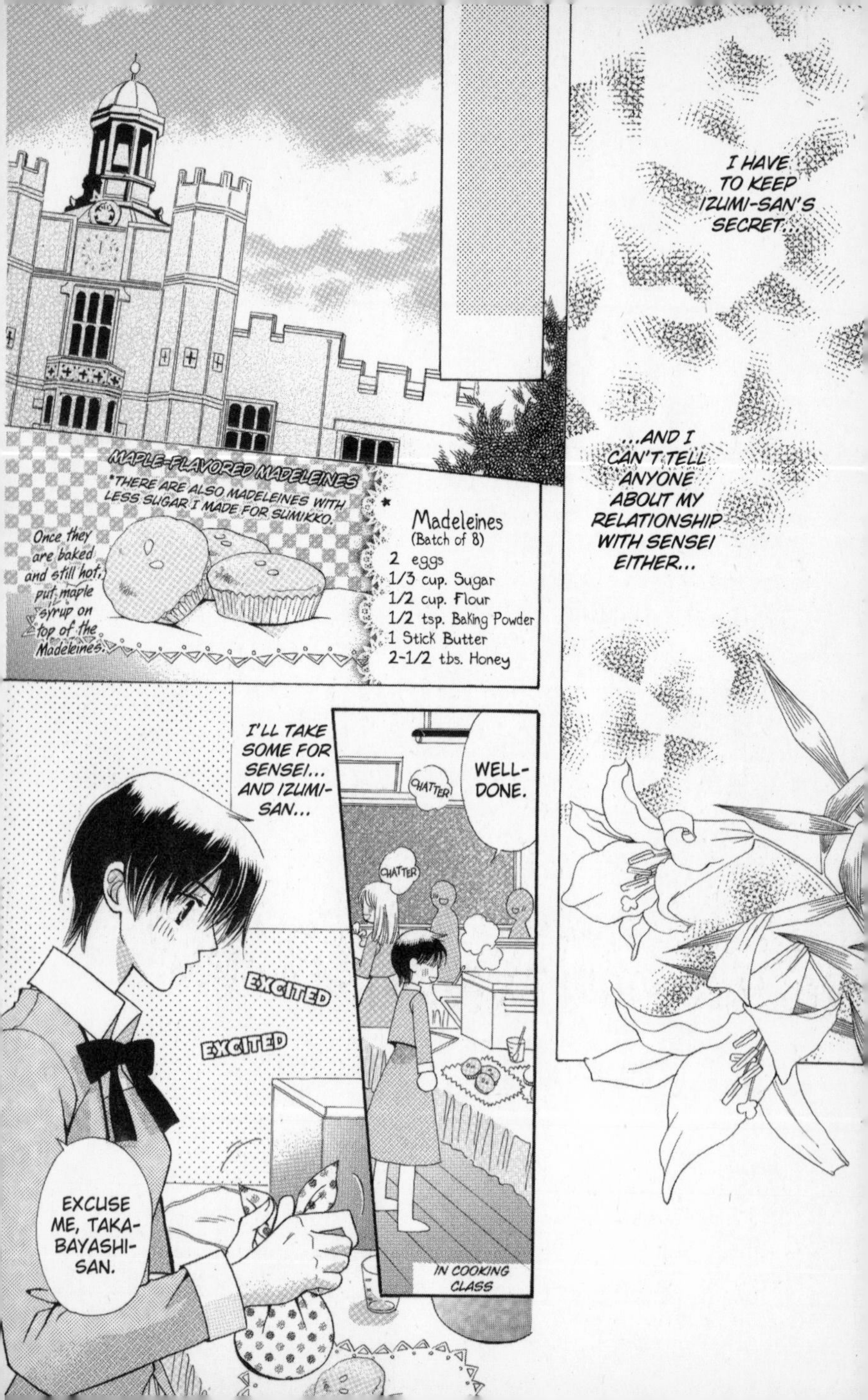
I HAVE TO KEEP IZUMI-SAN'S SECRET...
...AND I CAN'T TELL ANYONE ABOUT MY RELATIONSHIP WITH SENSEI EITHER...
MAPLE-FLAVORED MADELEINES
*THERE ARE ALSO MADELEINES WITH LESS SUGAR I MADE FOR SUMIKKO.
Once they are baked and still hot, put maple syrup on top of the Madeleines.
* Madeleines
(Batch of 8)
2 eggs
1/3 cup. Sugar
1/2 cup. Flour
1/2 tsp. Baking Powder
1 Stick Butter
2-1/2 tbs. Honey
WELL-DONE.
CHATTER
CHATTER
IN COOKING CLASS
I'LL TAKE SOME FOR SENSEI... AND IZUMI-SAN...
EXCITED
EXCITED
EXCUSE ME, TAKA-BAYASHI-SAN.

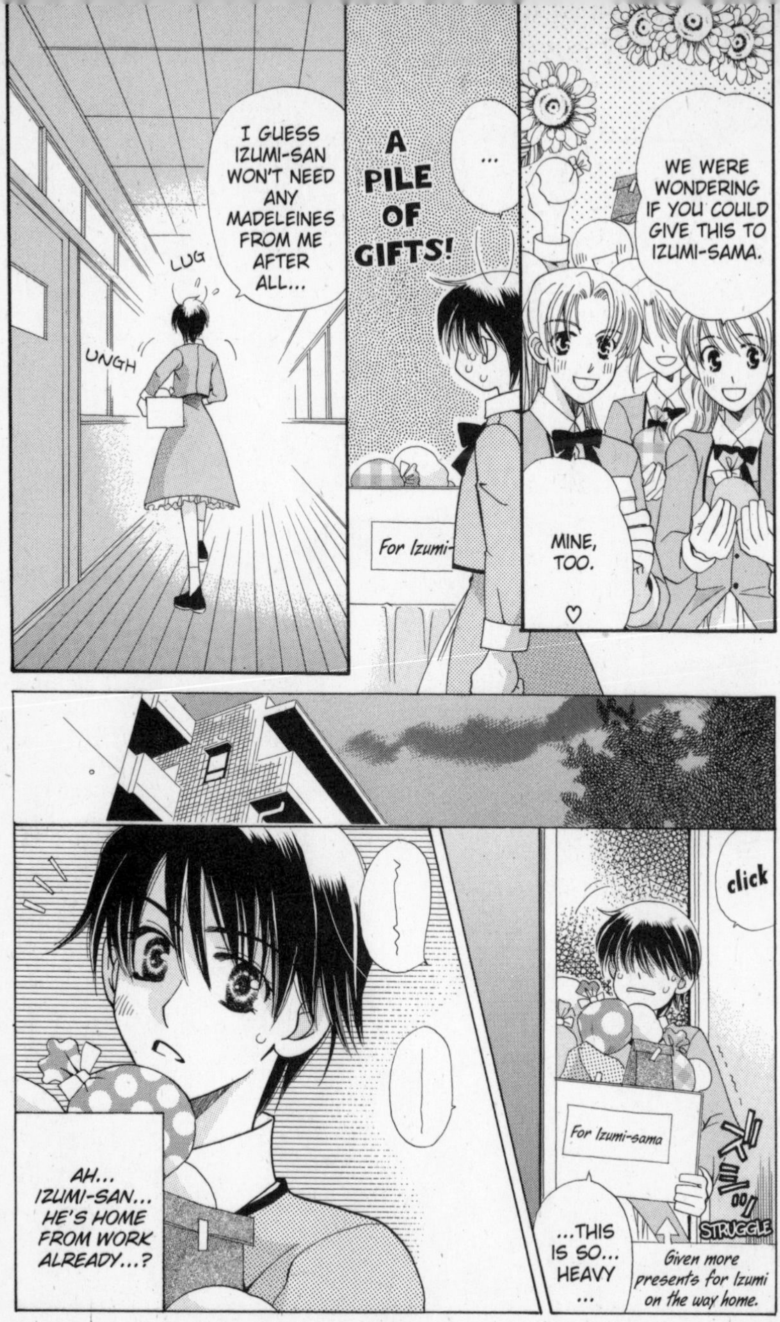
WE WERE WONDERING IF YOU COULD GIVE THIS TO IZUMI-SAMA.
MINE, TOO. ♡
...
A PILE OF GIFTS!
For Izumi-
I GUESS IZUMI-SAN WON'T NEED ANY MADELEINES FROM ME AFTER ALL...
LUG
UNGH
click
For Izumi-sama
STRUGGLE
...THIS IS SO... HEAVY ...
Given more presents for Izumi on the way home.
AH... IZUMI-SAN... HE'S HOME FROM WORK ALREADY...?

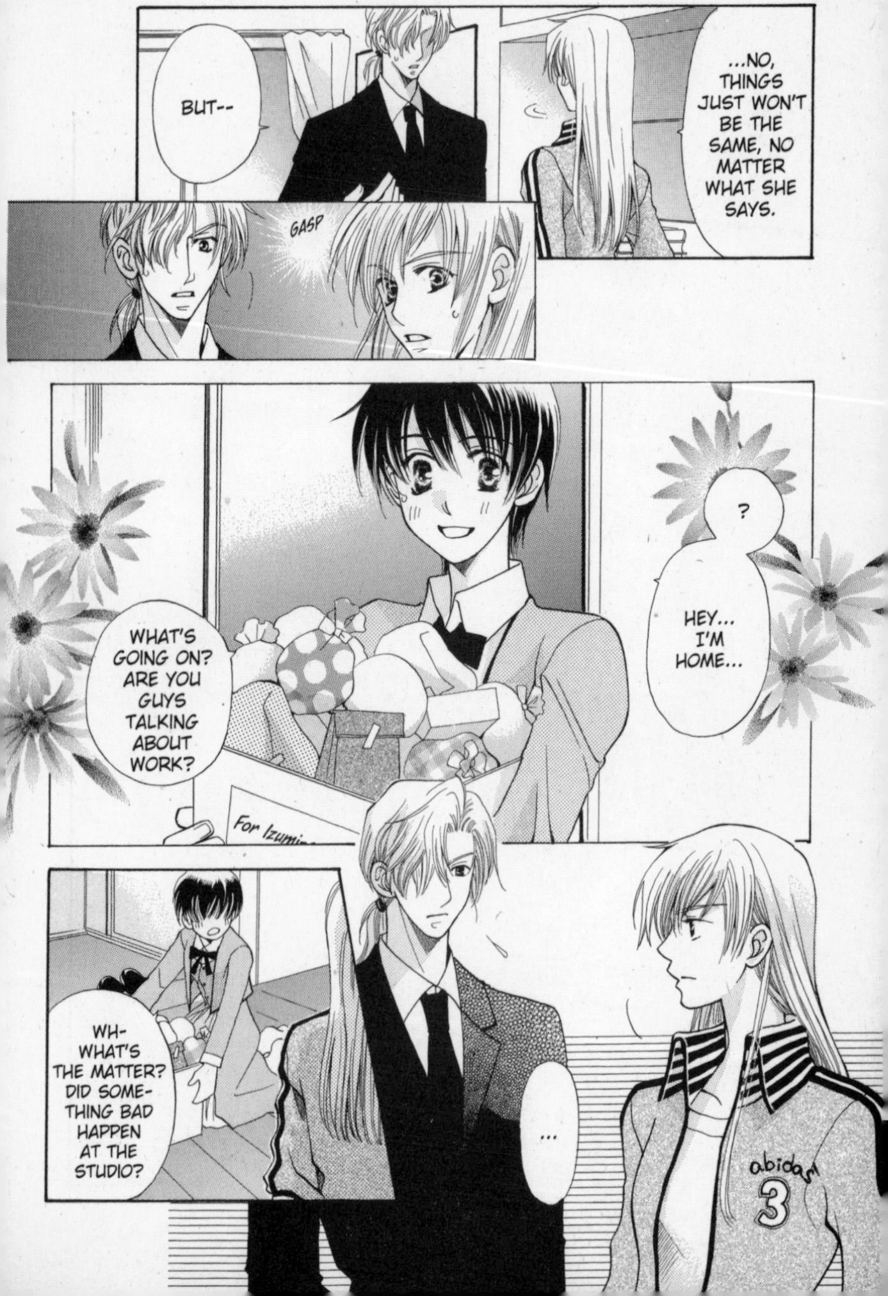
...NO, THINGS JUST WON'T BE THE SAME, NO MATTER WHAT SHE SAYS.
BUT--
GASP
?
HEY... I'M HOME...
WHAT'S GOING ON? ARE YOU GUYS TALKING ABOUT WORK?
...
abidas 3
WH-WHAT'S THE MATTER? DID SOME-THING BAD HAPPEN AT THE STUDIO?

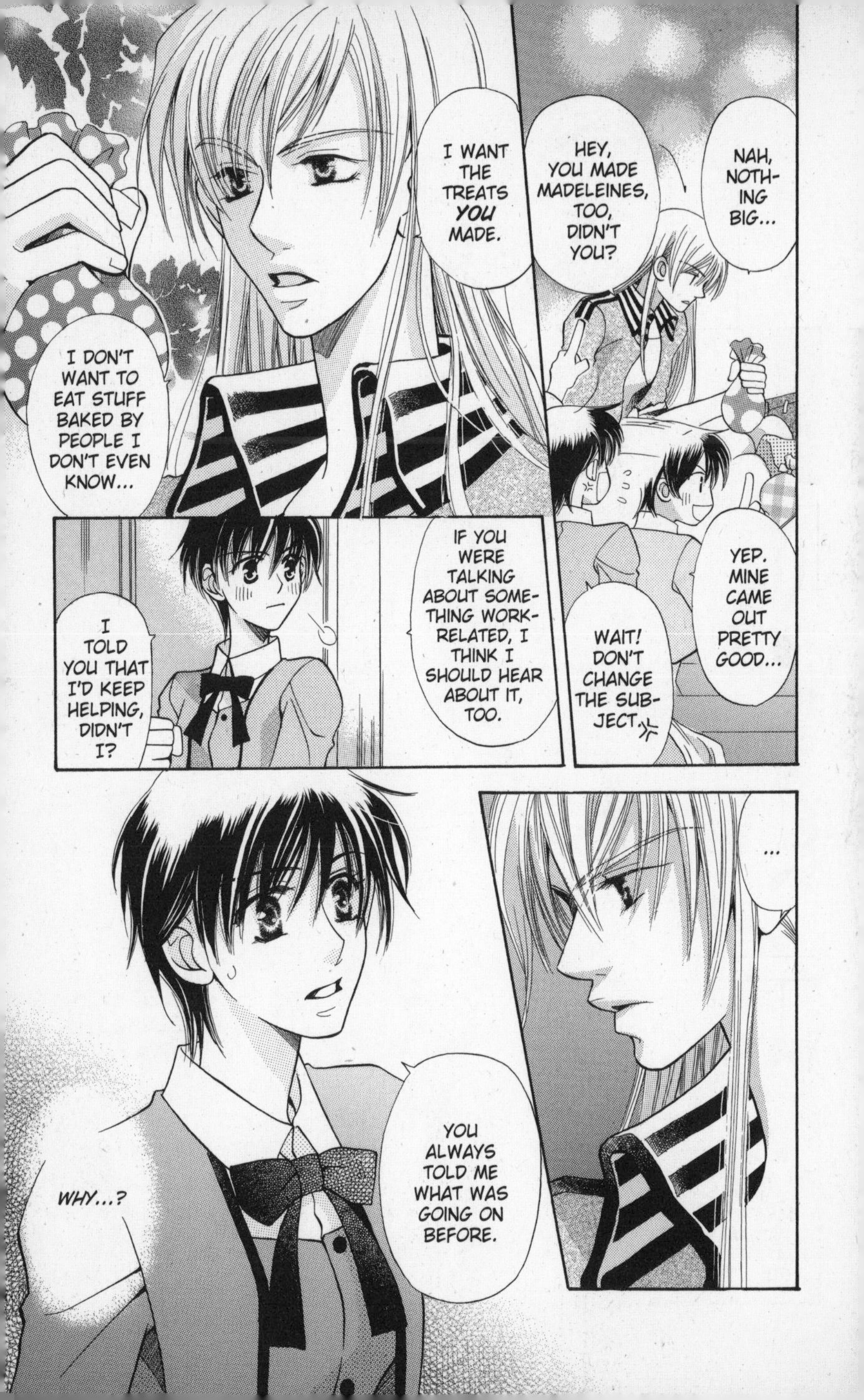
NAH, NOTHING-ING BIG...
HEY, YOU MADE MADELEINES, TOO, DIDN'T YOU?
YEP. MINE CAME OUT PRETTY GOOD...
WAIT! DON'T CHANGE THE SUB-JECT.
I WANT THE TREATS *YOU* MADE.
I DON'T WANT TO EAT STUFF BAKED BY PEOPLE I DON'T EVEN KNOW...
IF YOU WERE TALKING ABOUT SOME-THING WORK-RELATED, I THINK I SHOULD HEAR ABOUT IT, TOO.
I TOLD YOU THAT I'D KEEP HELPING, DIDN'T I?
...
YOU ALWAYS TOLD ME WHAT WAS GOING ON BEFORE.
WHY...?

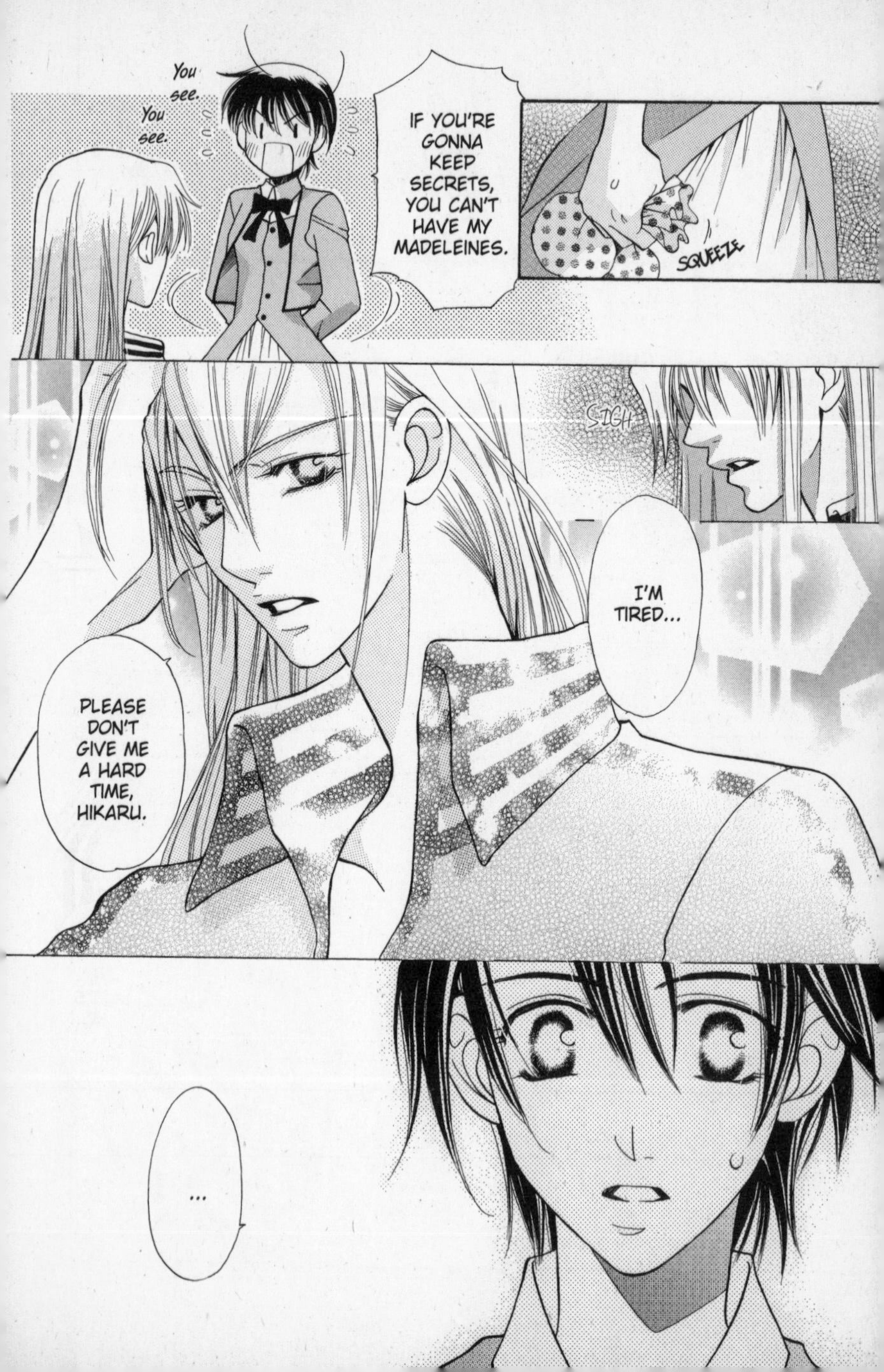
SQUEEZE
IF YOU'RE GONNA KEEP SECRETS, YOU CAN'T HAVE MY MADELEINES.
You see.
You see.
SIGH
I'M TIRED...
PLEASE DON'T GIVE ME A HARD TIME, HIKARU.
...

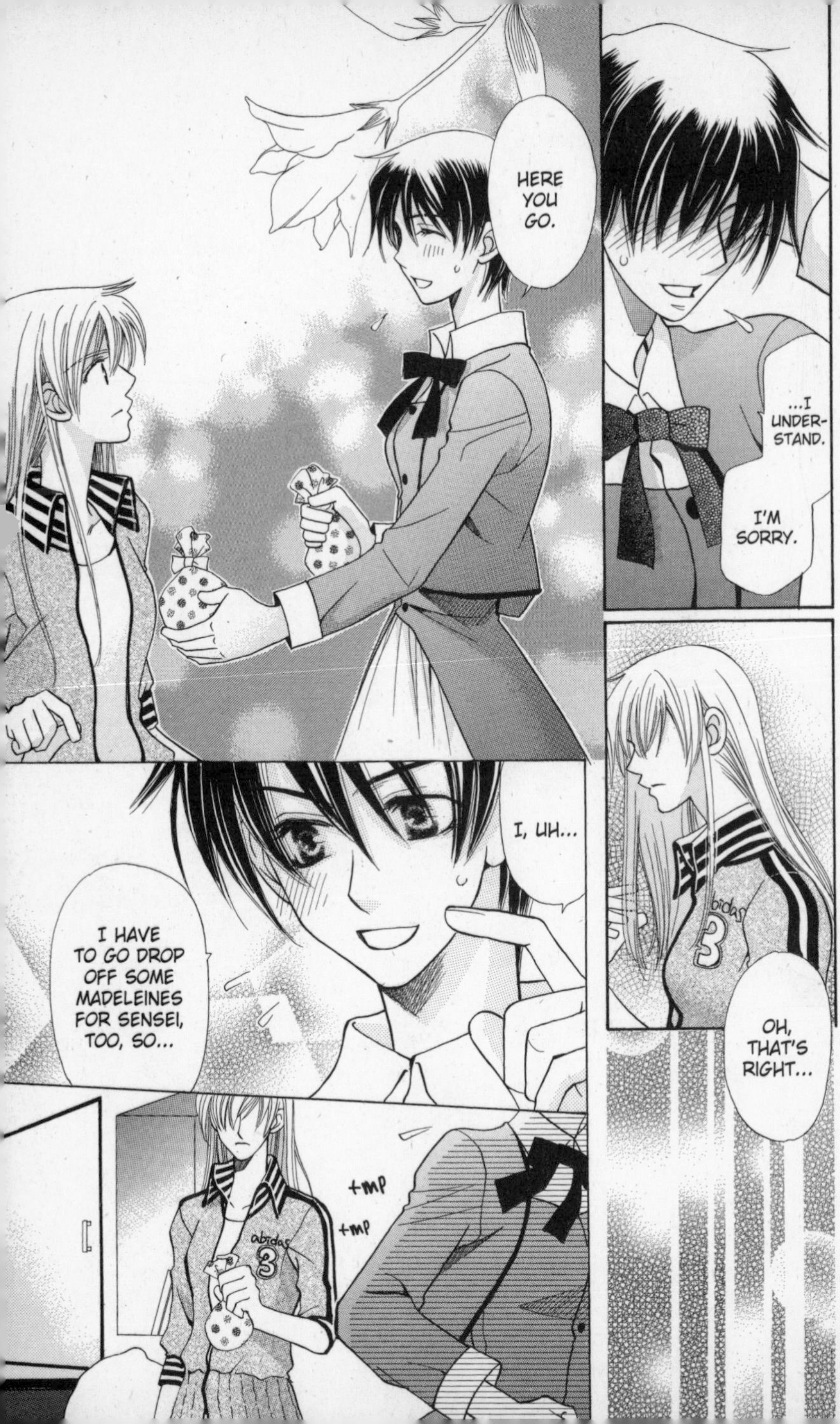
...I UNDERSTAND.
I'M SORRY.
HERE YOU GO.
I, UH...
I HAVE TO GO DROP OFF SOME MADELEINES FOR SENSEI, TOO, SO...
OH, THAT'S RIGHT...
tmp
tmp

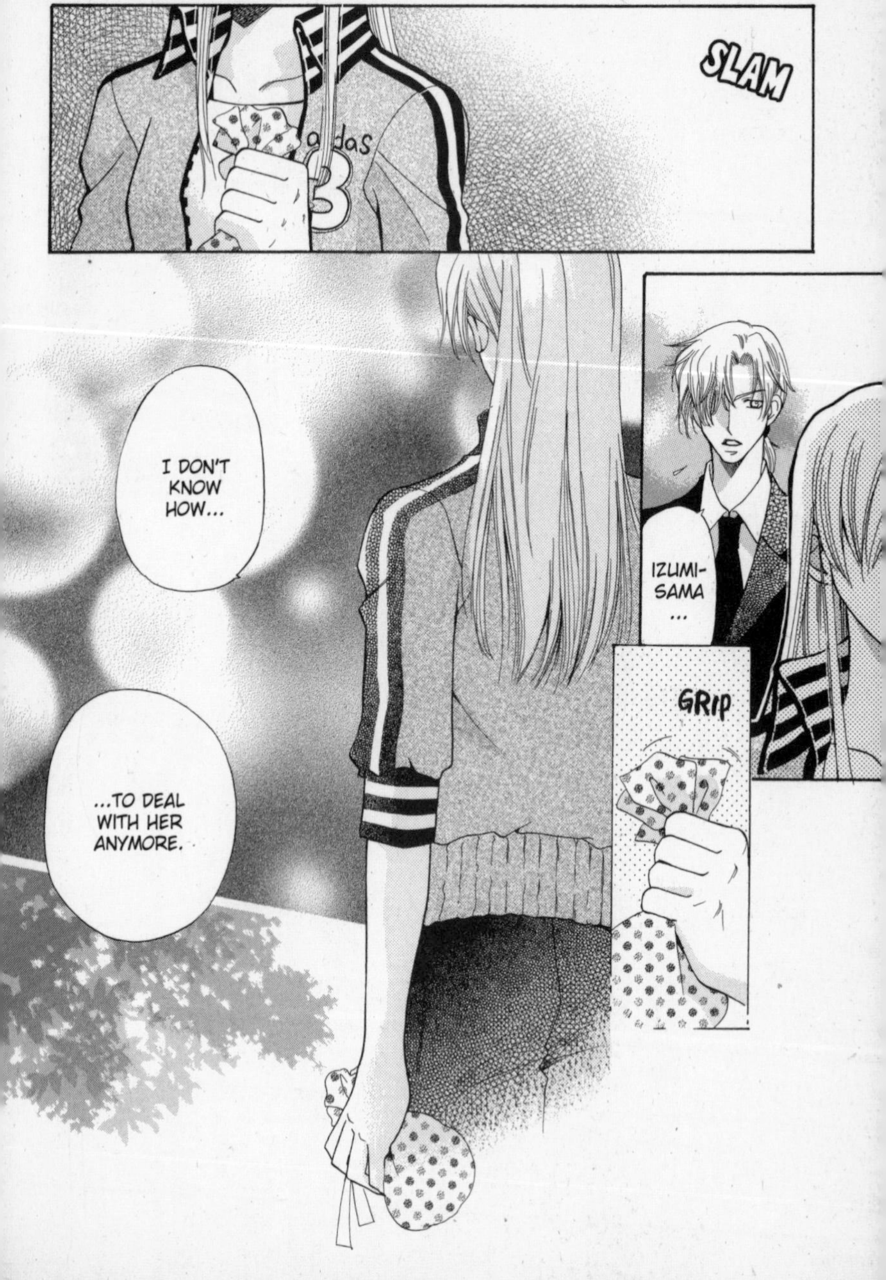
SLAM
IZUMI-SAMA...
GRIP
I DON'T KNOW HOW...
...TO DEAL WITH HER ANYMORE.

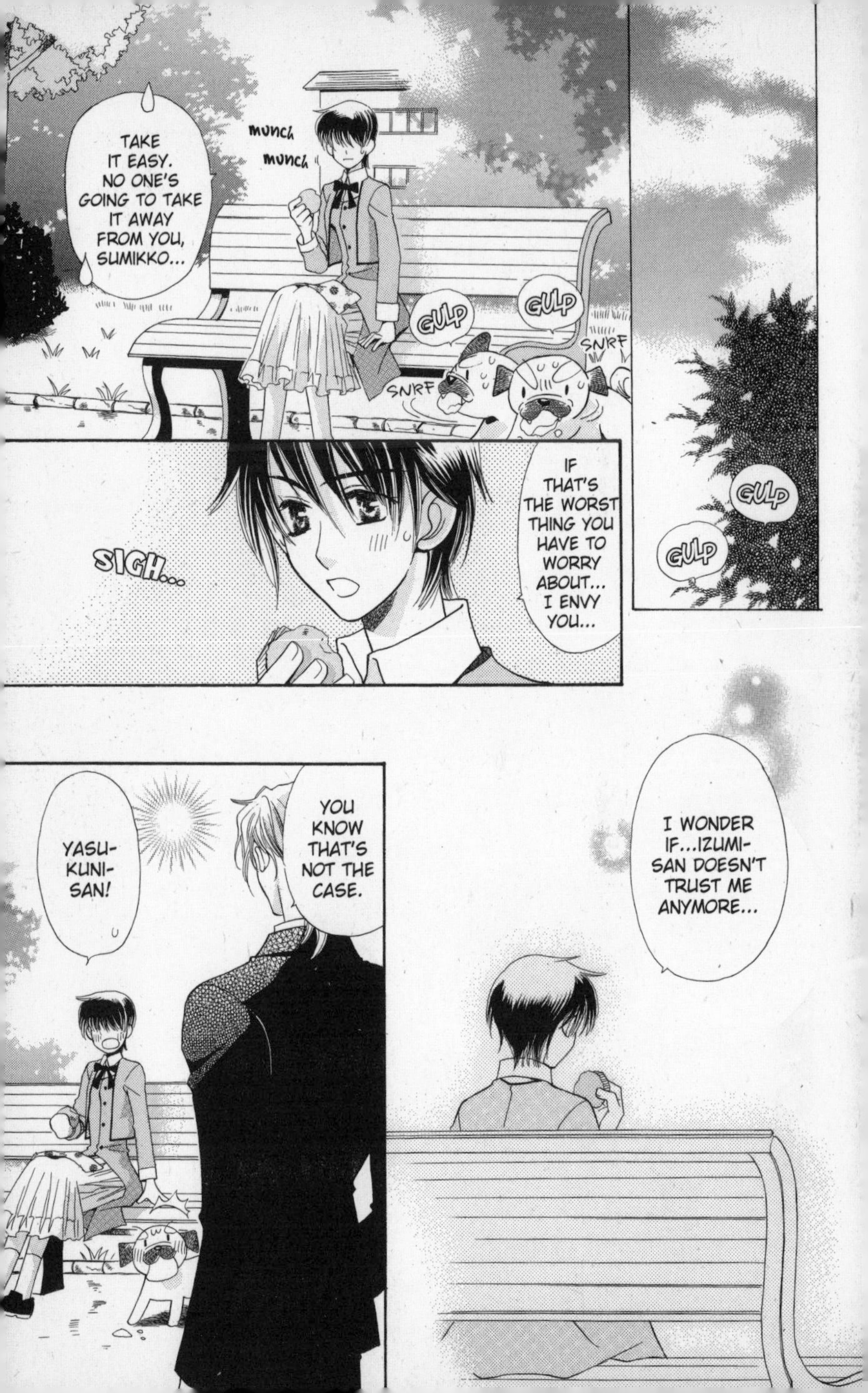
GULP
GULP
munch
munch
TAKE IT EASY. NO ONE'S GOING TO TAKE IT AWAY FROM YOU, SUMIKKO...
GULP
GULP
SNRF
SNRF
IF THAT'S THE WORST THING YOU HAVE TO WORRY ABOUT... I ENVY YOU...
SIGH...
I WONDER IF...IZUMI-SAN DOESN'T TRUST ME ANYMORE...
YOU KNOW THAT'S NOT THE CASE.
YASU-KUNI-SAN!

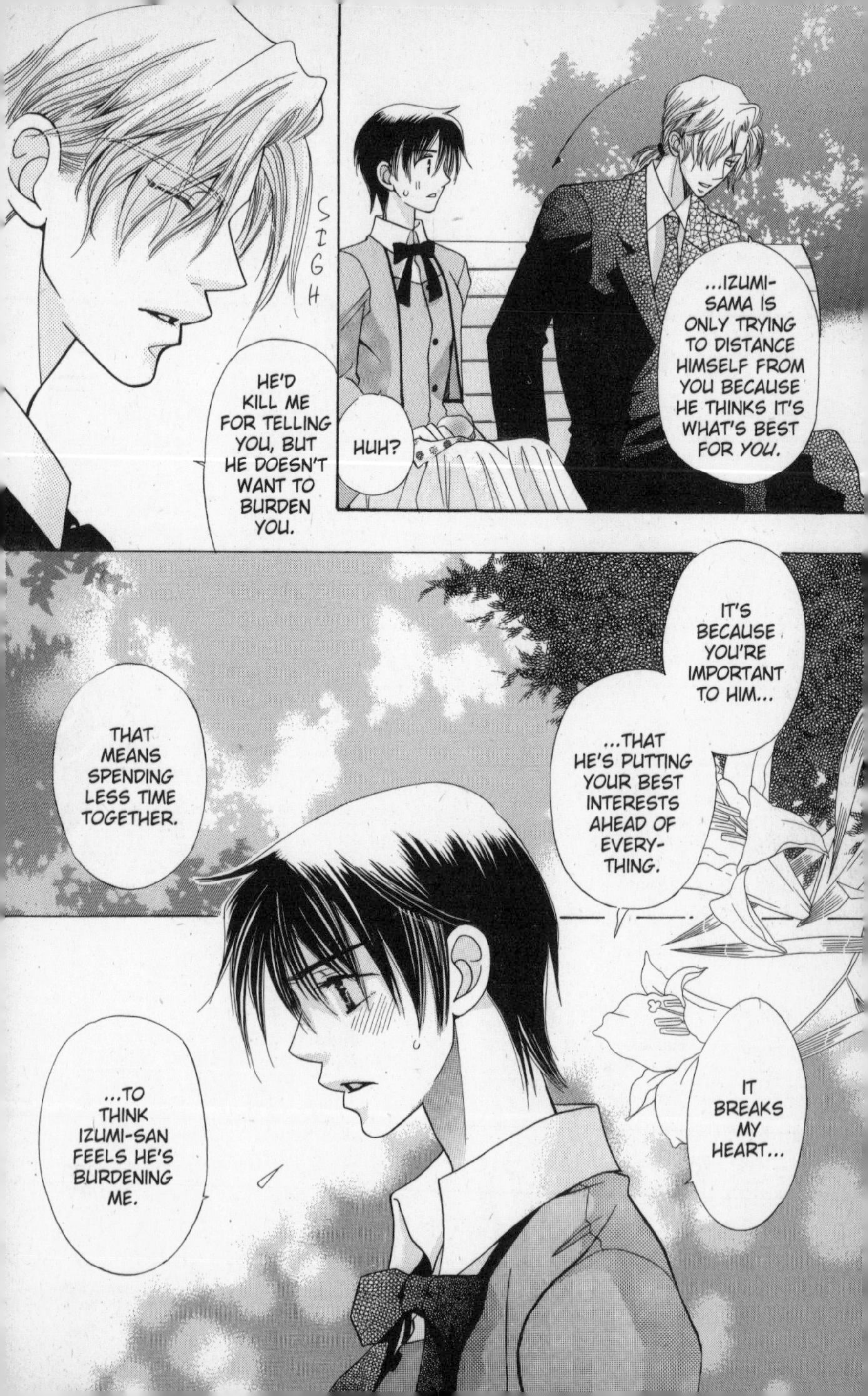
...IZUMI-SAMA IS ONLY TRYING TO DISTANCE HIMSELF FROM YOU BECAUSE HE THINKS IT'S WHAT'S BEST FOR *YOU*.
HUH?
SIGH
HE'D KILL ME FOR TELLING YOU, BUT HE DOESN'T WANT TO BURDEN YOU.
IT'S BECAUSE YOU'RE IMPORTANT TO HIM...
...THAT HE'S PUTTING YOUR BEST INTERESTS AHEAD OF EVERY-THING.
THAT MEANS SPENDING LESS TIME TOGETHER.
IT BREAKS MY HEART...
...TO THINK IZUMI-SAN FEELS HE'S BURDENING ME.

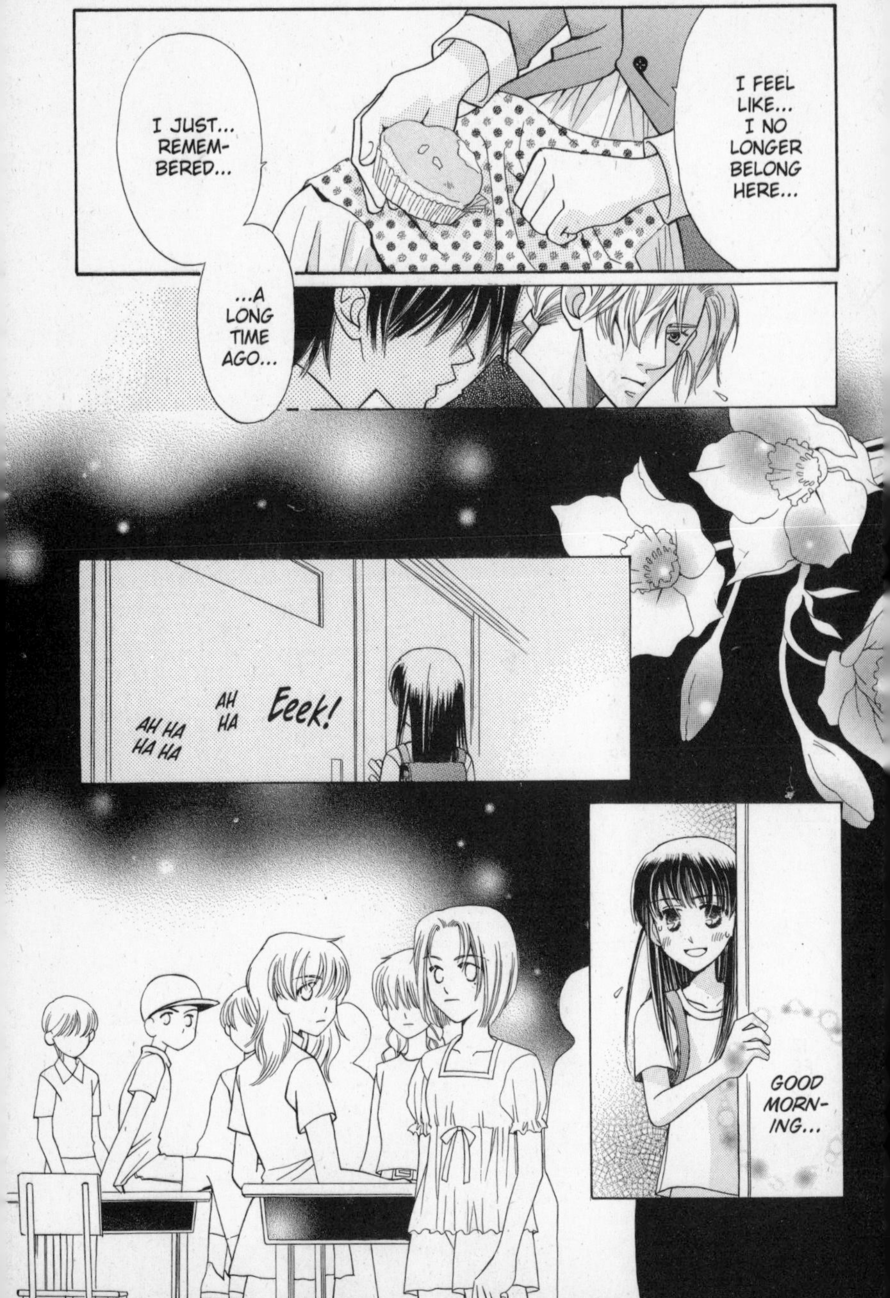
I FEEL LIKE... I NO LONGER BELONG HERE...
I JUST... REMEMBERED...
...A LONG TIME AGO...
Eeek!
AH HA
AH HA HA HA
GOOD MORNING...

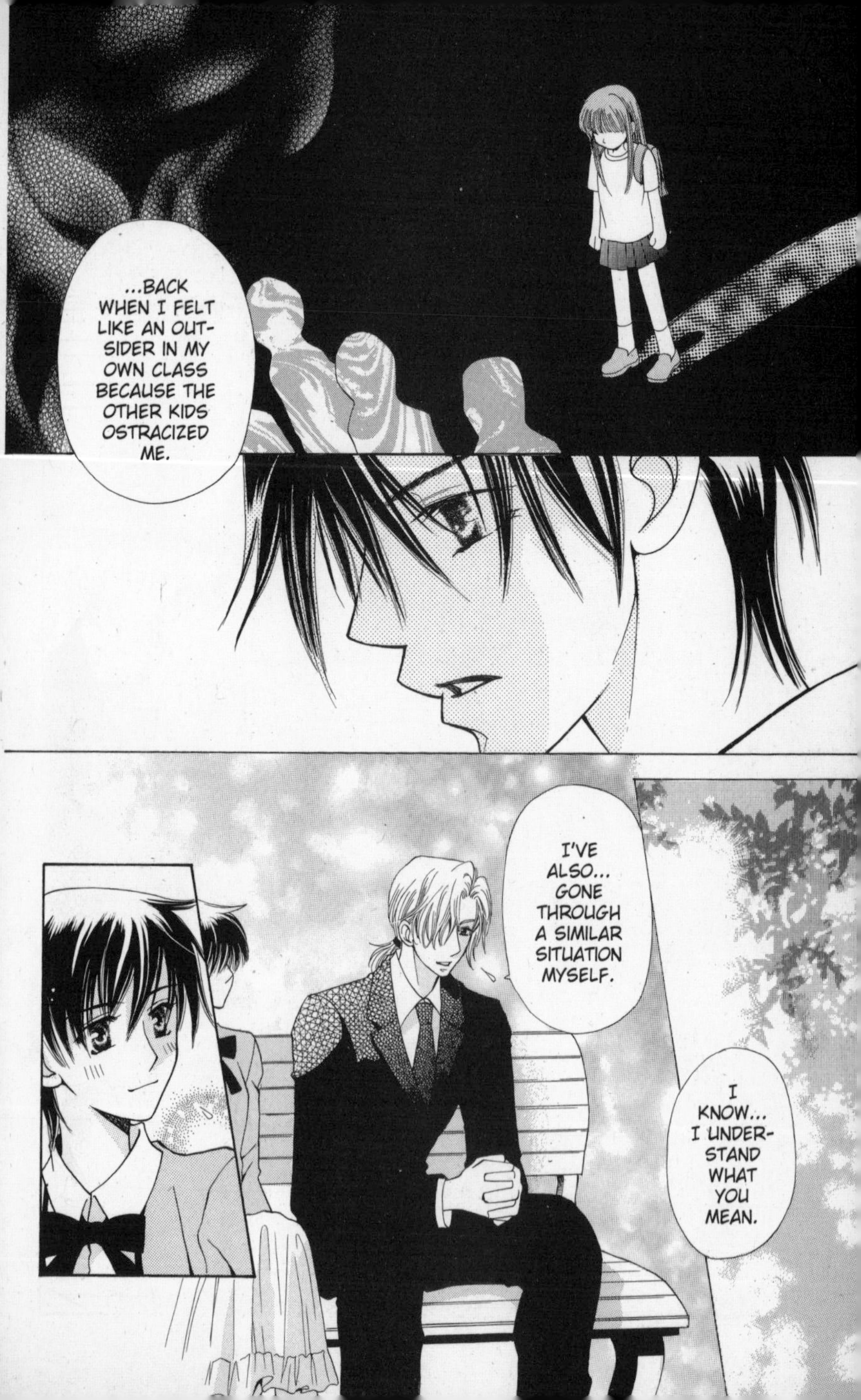
...BACK WHEN I FELT LIKE AN OUTSIDER IN MY OWN CLASS BECAUSE THE OTHER KIDS OSTRACIZED ME.
I KNOW... I UNDERSTAND WHAT YOU MEAN.
I'VE ALSO... GONE THROUGH A SIMILAR SITUATION MYSELF.

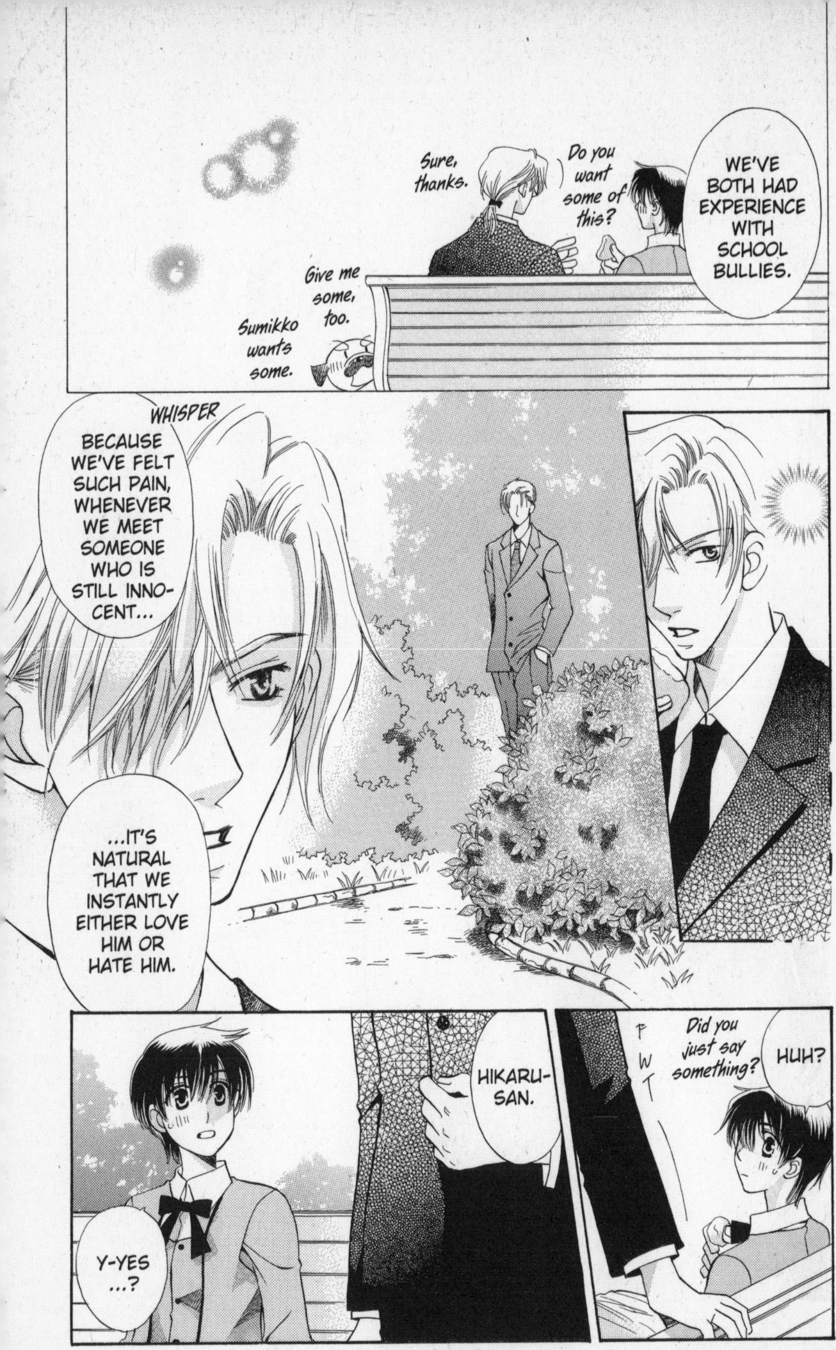
WE'VE BOTH HAD EXPERIENCE WITH SCHOOL BULLIES.
Do you want some of this?
Sure, thanks.
Give me some, too.
Sumikko wants some.
WHISPER
BECAUSE WE'VE FELT SUCH PAIN, WHENEVER WE MEET SOMEONE WHO IS STILL INNO-CENT...
...IT'S NATURAL THAT WE INSTANTLY EITHER LOVE HIM OR HATE HIM.
HUH?
Did you just say something?
PWT
HIKARU-SAN.
Y-YES ...?

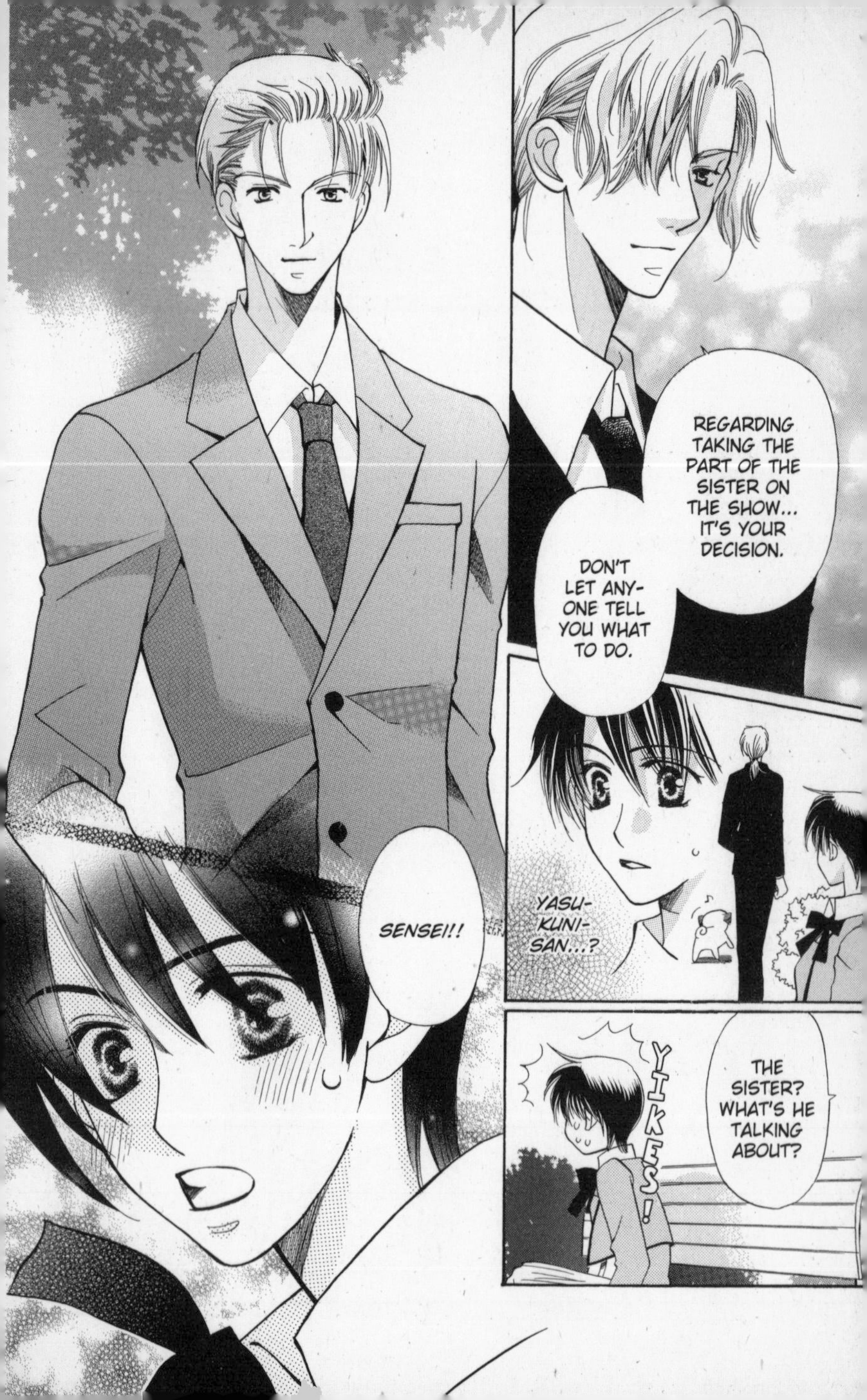
REGARDING TAKING THE PART OF THE SISTER ON THE SHOW... IT'S YOUR DECISION.
DON'T LET ANY-ONE TELL YOU WHAT TO DO.
YASU-KUNI-SAN...?
THE SISTER? WHAT'S HE TALKING ABOUT?
YIKES!
SENSEI!!

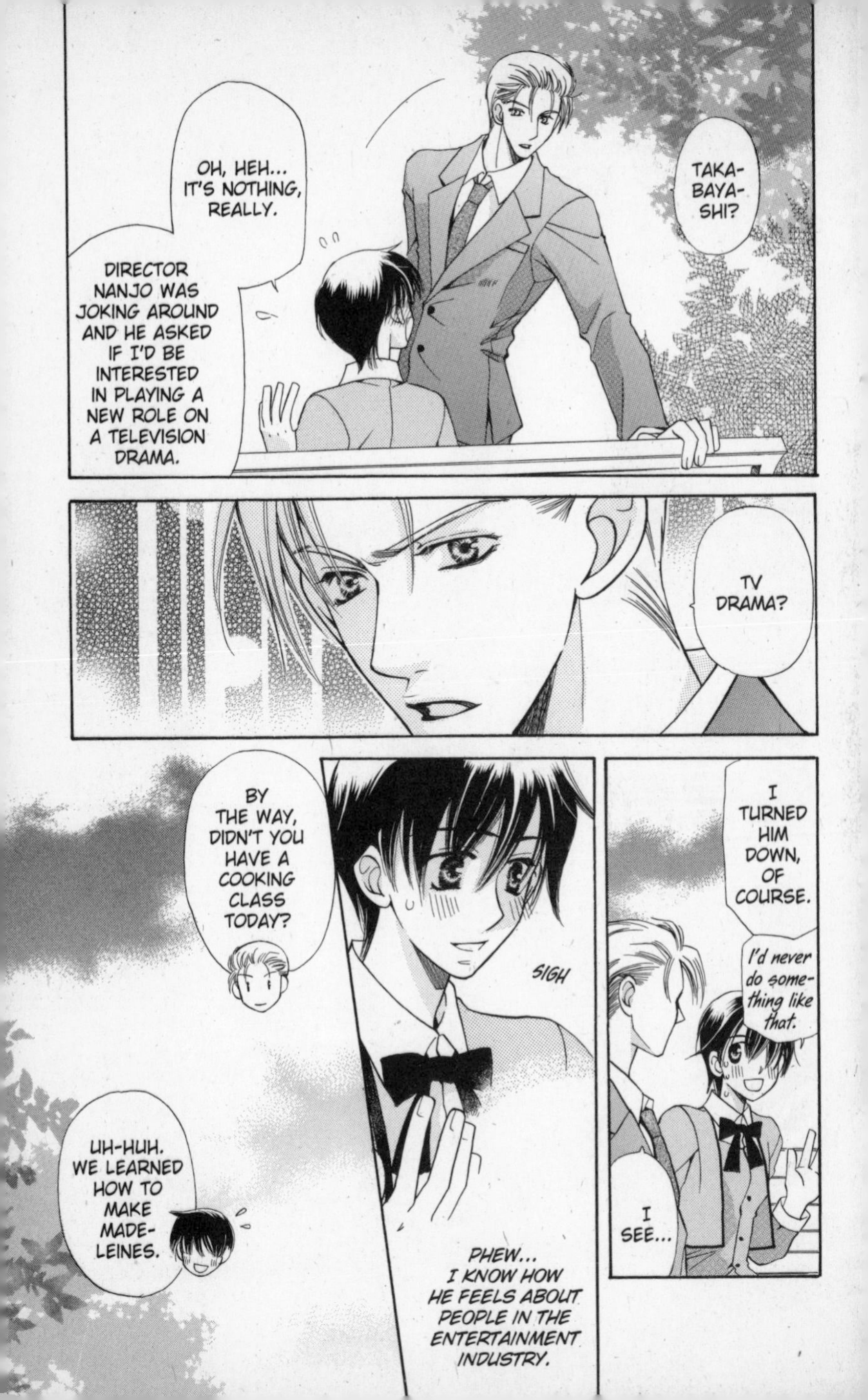
TAKA-BAYASHI?
OH, HEH... IT'S NOTHING, REALLY.
DIRECTOR NANJO WAS JOKING AROUND AND HE ASKED IF I'D BE INTERESTED IN PLAYING A NEW ROLE ON A TELEVISION DRAMA.
TV DRAMA?
I TURNED HIM DOWN, OF COURSE.
I'd never do something like that.
I SEE...
BY THE WAY, DIDN'T YOU HAVE A COOKING CLASS TODAY?
SIGH
UH-HUH. WE LEARNED HOW TO MAKE MADE-LEINES.
PHEW... I KNOW HOW HE FEELS ABOUT PEOPLE IN THE ENTERTAINMENT INDUSTRY.

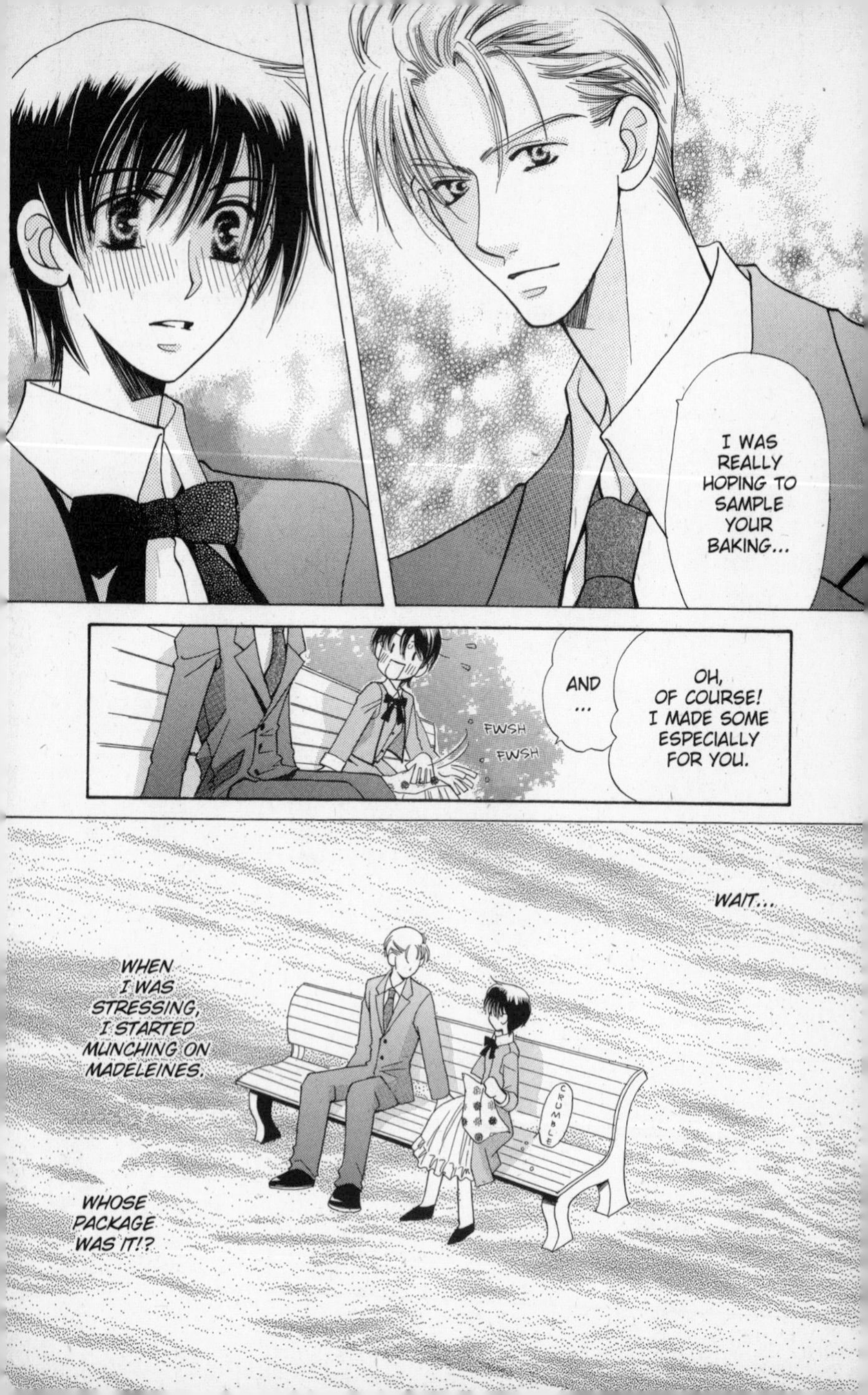
I WAS REALLY HOPING TO SAMPLE YOUR BAKING...
OH, OF COURSE! I MADE SOME ESPECIALLY FOR YOU.
AND ...
FWSH
FWSH
WAIT...
WHEN I WAS STRESSING, I STARTED MUNCHING ON MADELEINES.
CRUMBLE
WHOSE PACKAGE WAS IT!?

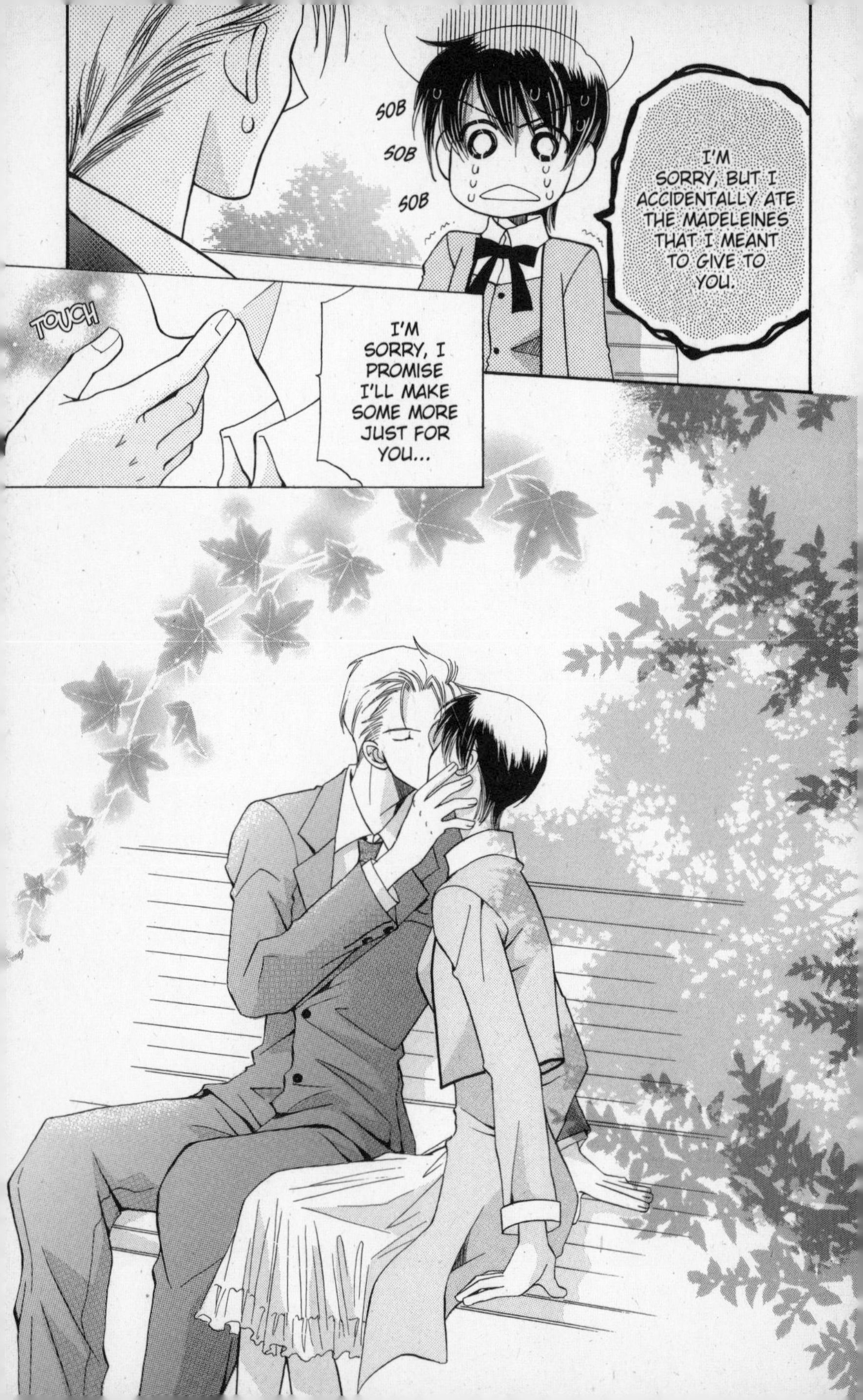
I'M SORRY, BUT I ACCIDENTALLY ATE THE MADELEINES THAT I MEANT TO GIVE TO YOU.
SOB
SOB
SOB
I'M SORRY, I PROMISE I'LL MAKE SOME MORE JUST FOR YOU...
TOUCH

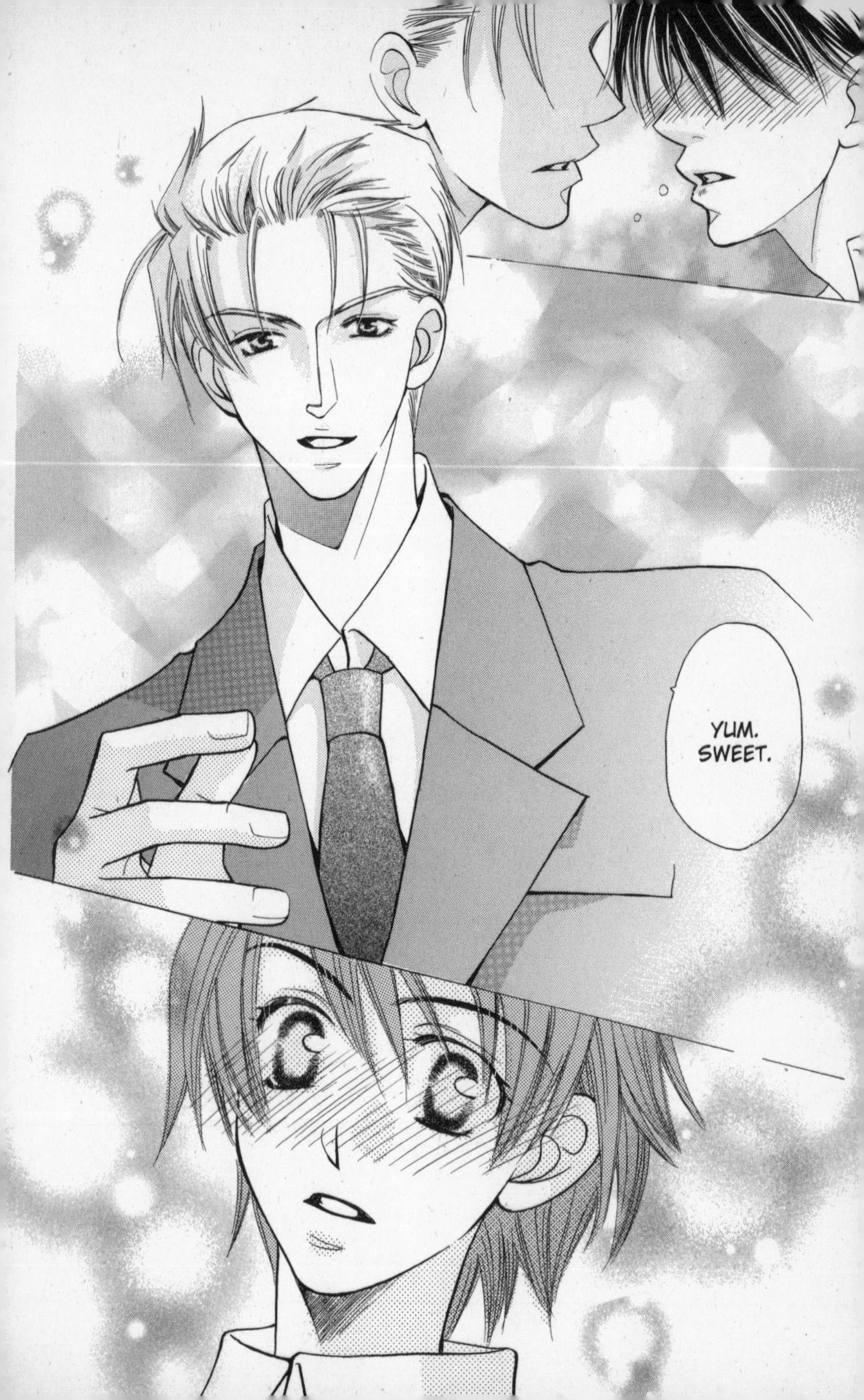
YUM. SWEET.

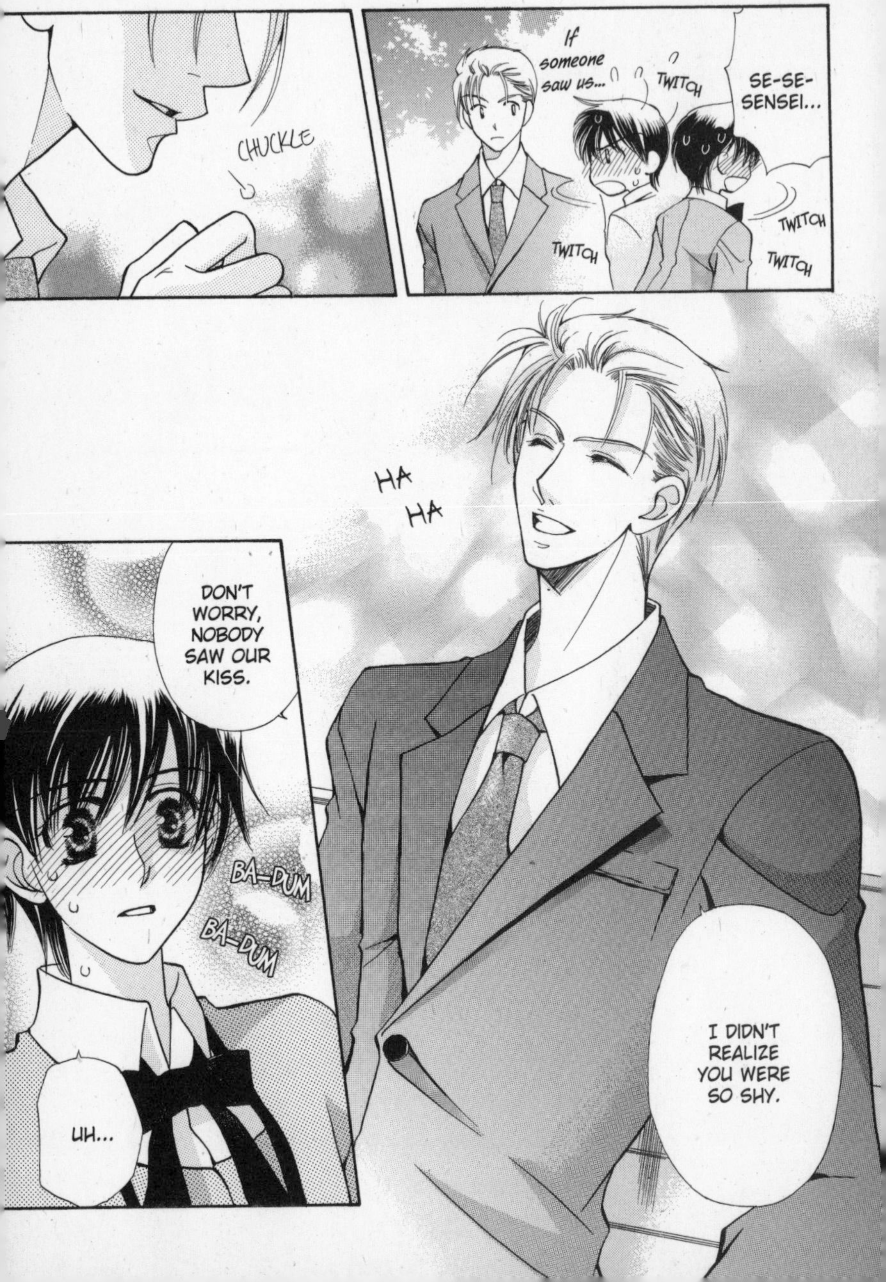
SE-SE-SENSEI...
If someone saw us...
TWITCH
TWITCH
TWITCH
TWITCH
CHUCKLE
HA HA
DON'T WORRY, NOBODY SAW OUR KISS.
BA-DUM
BA-DUM
I DIDN'T REALIZE YOU WERE SO SHY.
UH...

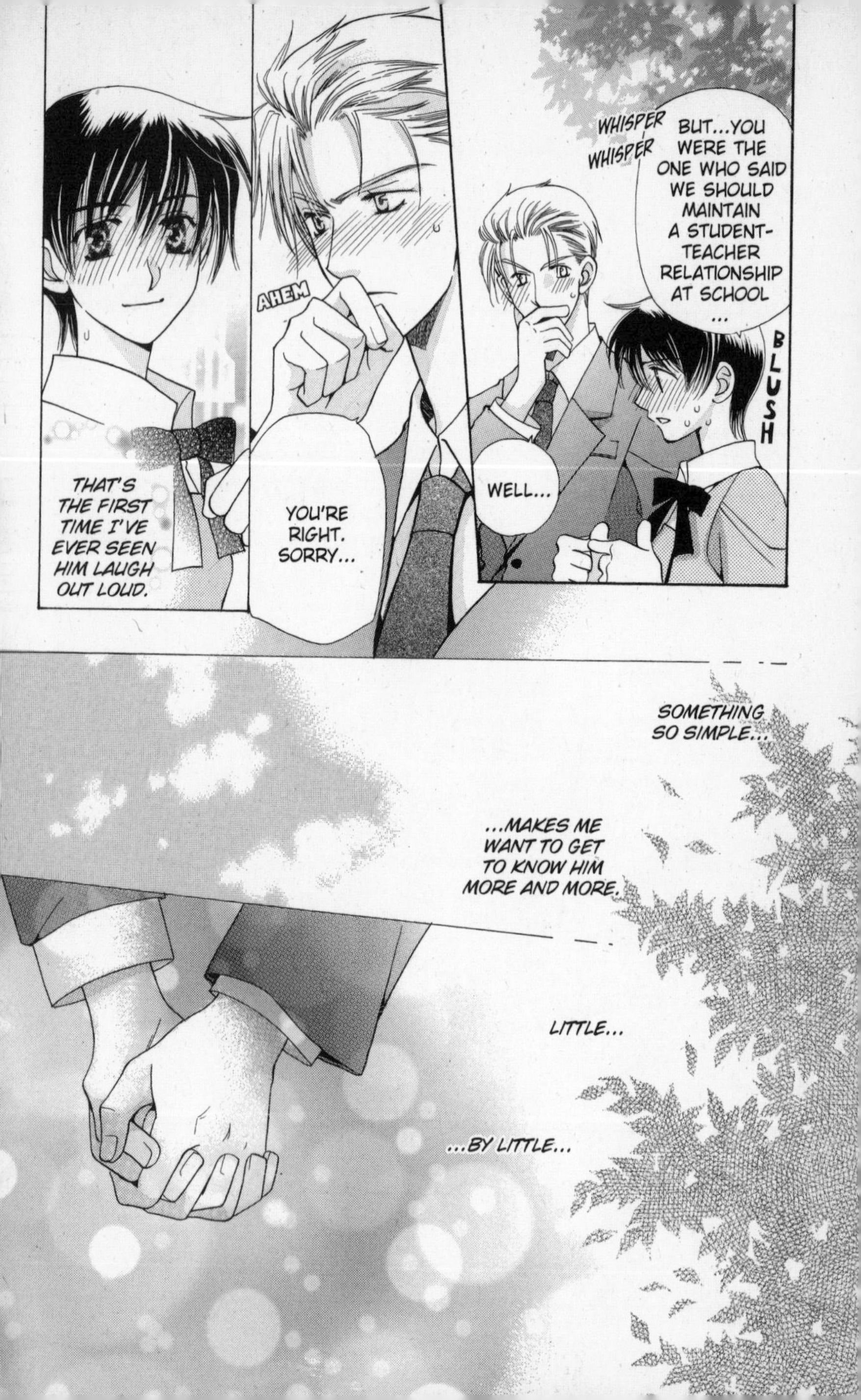
WHISPER WHISPER
BUT...YOU WERE THE ONE WHO SAID WE SHOULD MAINTAIN A STUDENT-TEACHER RELATIONSHIP AT SCHOOL ...
BLUSH
WELL...
AHEM
YOU'RE RIGHT. SORRY...
THAT'S THE FIRST TIME I'VE EVER SEEN HIM LAUGH OUT LOUD.
SOMETHING SO SIMPLE...
...MAKES ME WANT TO GET TO KNOW HIM MORE AND MORE.
LITTLE...
...BY LITTLE...

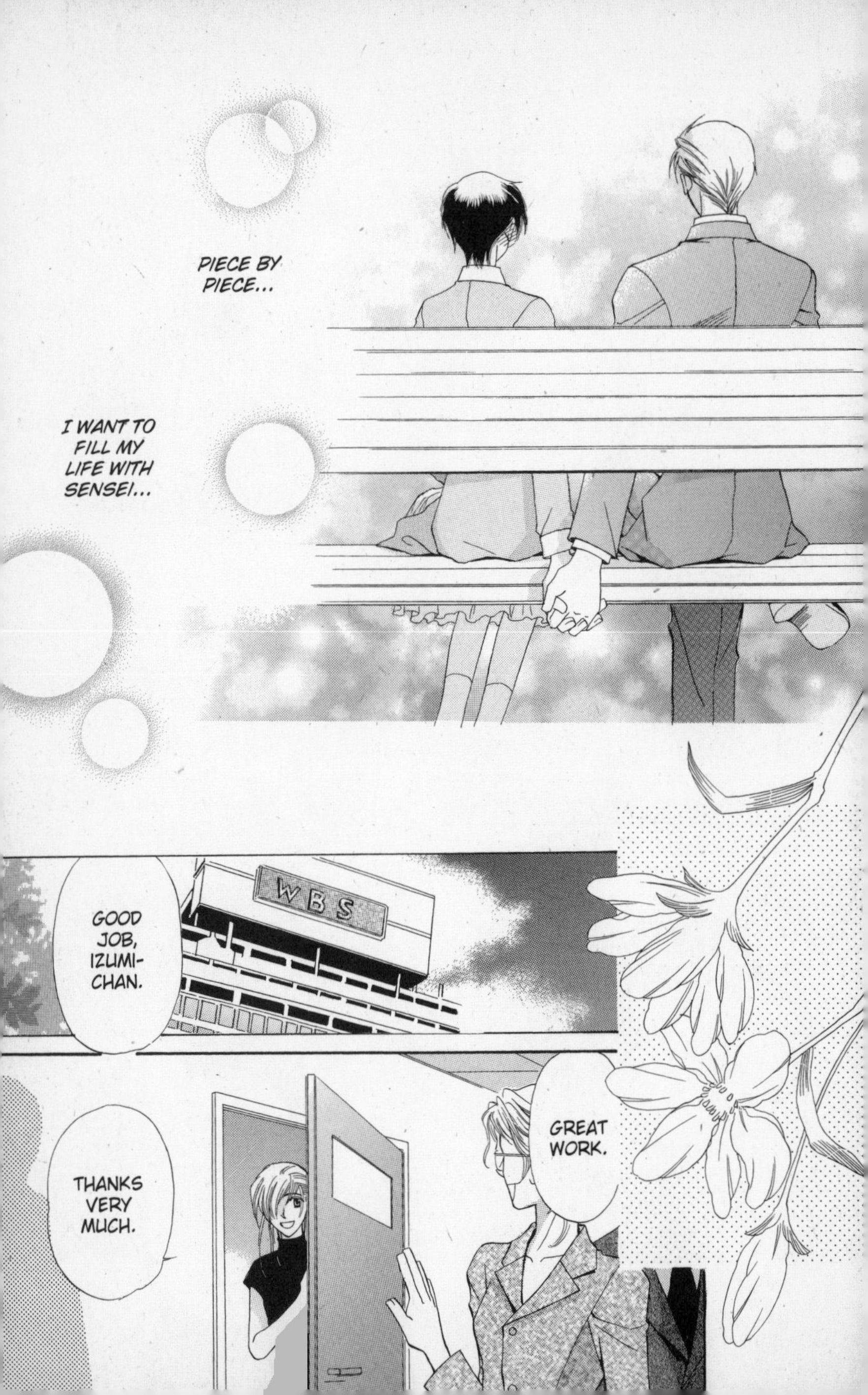
PIECE BY PIECE...
I WANT TO FILL MY LIFE WITH SENSEI...
GOOD JOB, IZUMI-CHAN.
GREAT WORK.
THANKS VERY MUCH.

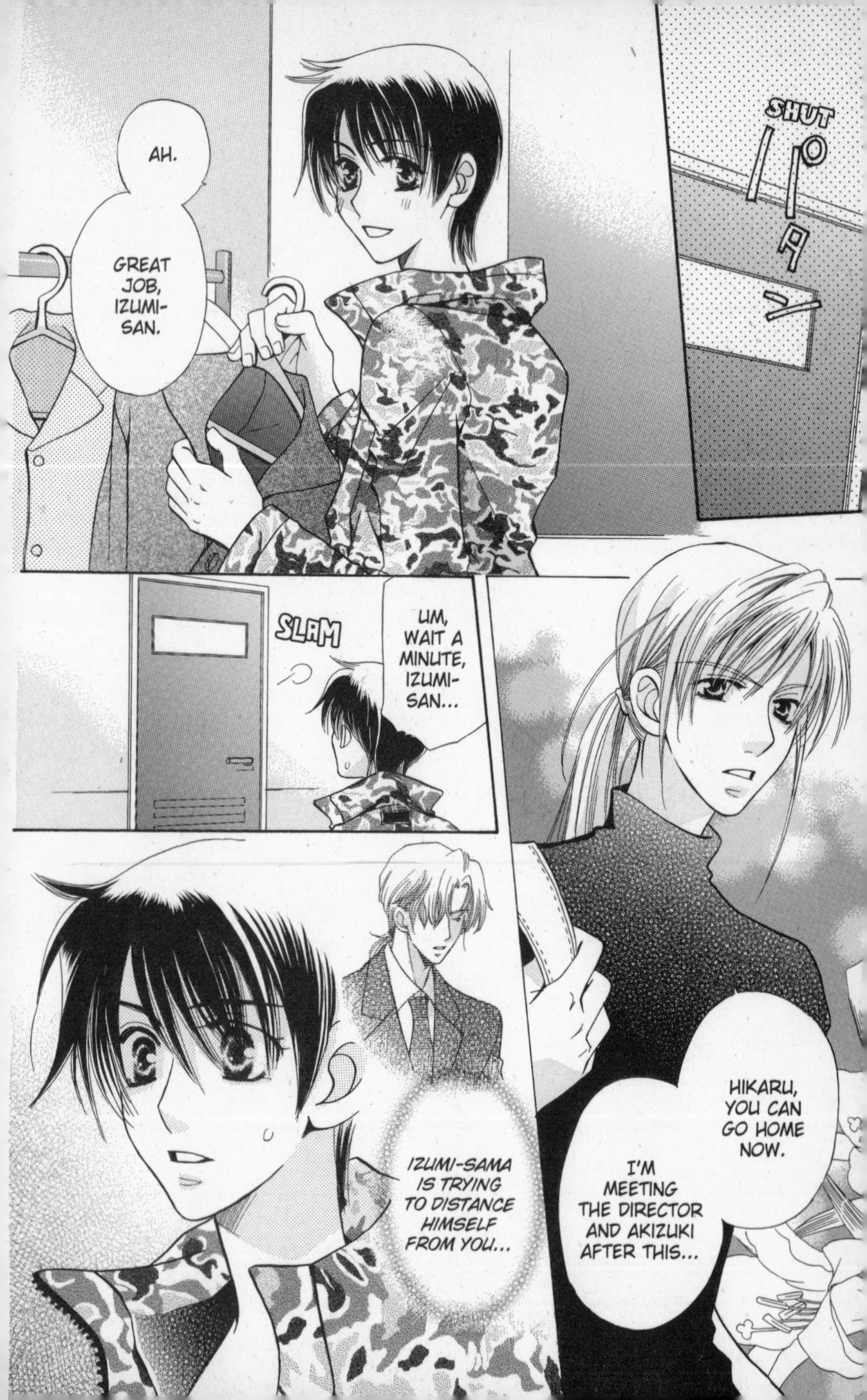
SHUT
AH.
GREAT JOB, IZUMI-SAN.
HIKARU, YOU CAN GO HOME NOW.
I'M MEETING THE DIRECTOR AND AKIZUKI AFTER THIS...
SLAM
UM, WAIT A MINUTE, IZUMI-SAN...
IZUMI-SAMA IS TRYING TO DISTANCE HIMSELF FROM YOU...

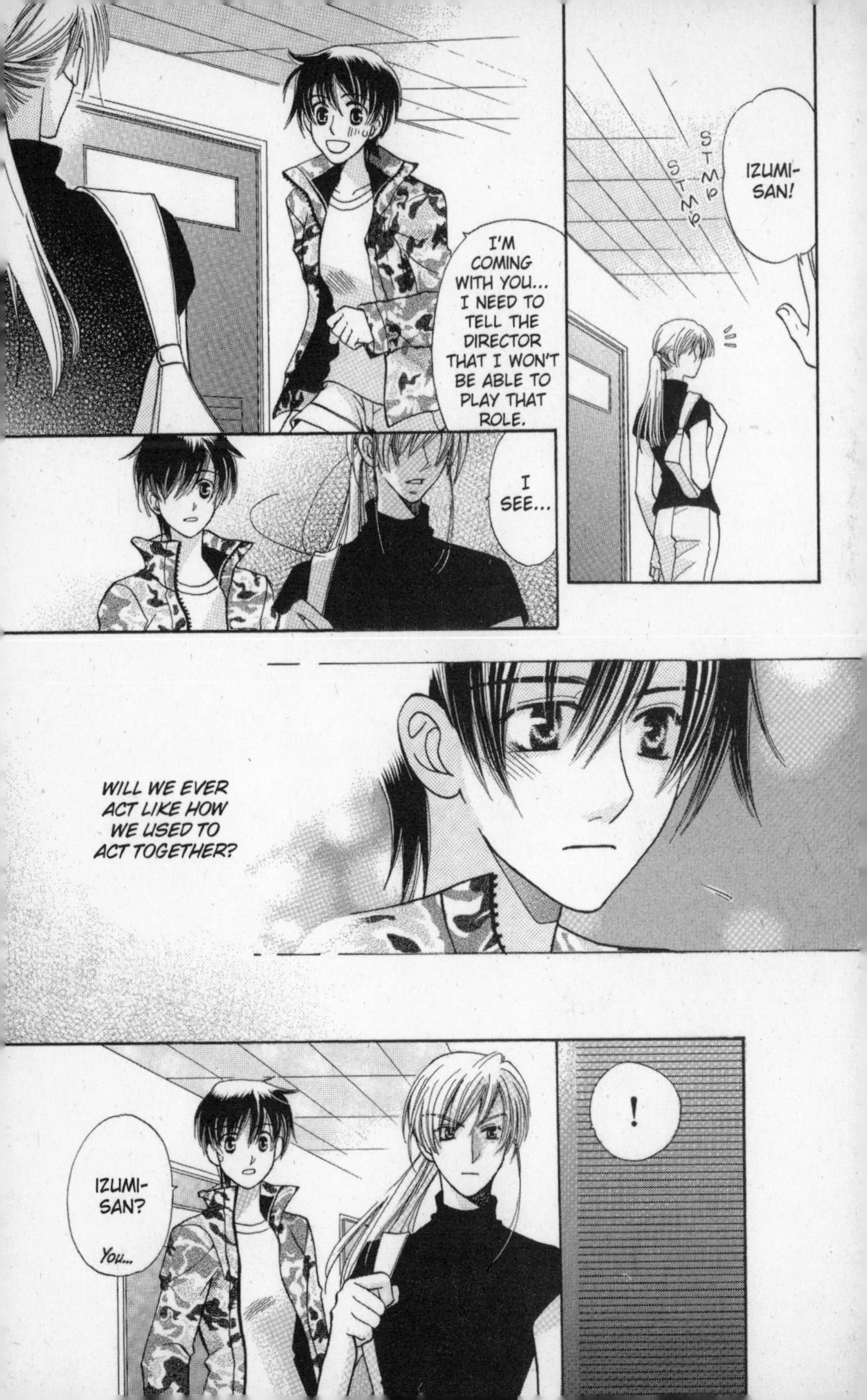
STMP
STMP
IZUMI-SAN!
I'M COMING WITH YOU... I NEED TO TELL THE DIRECTOR THAT I WON'T BE ABLE TO PLAY THAT ROLE.
I SEE...
WILL WE EVER ACT LIKE HOW WE USED TO ACT TOGETHER?
!
IZUMI-SAN?
You...

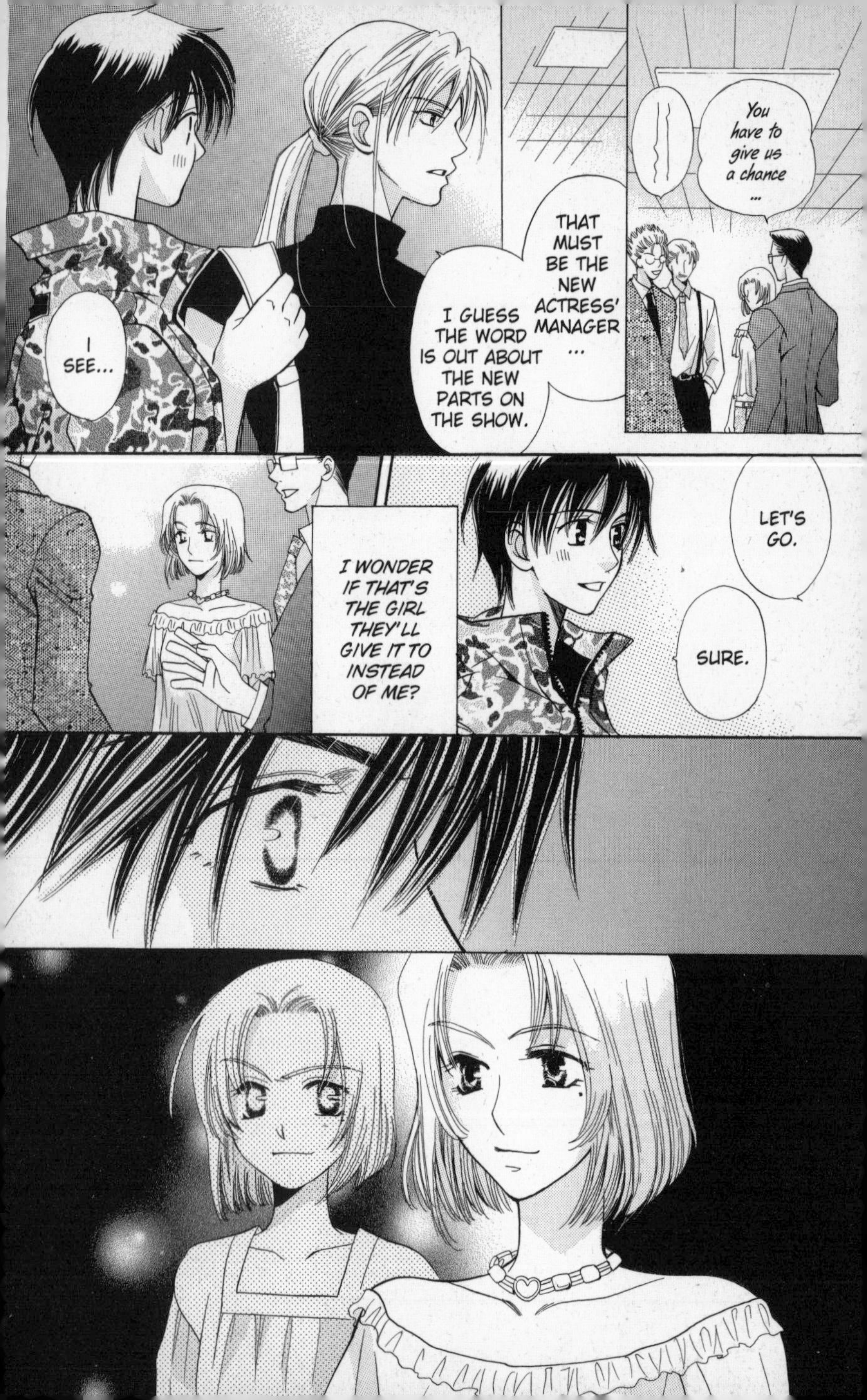
You have to give us a chance ...
THAT MUST BE THE NEW ACTRESS' MANAGER ...
I GUESS THE WORD IS OUT ABOUT THE NEW PARTS ON THE SHOW.
I SEE...
LET'S GO.
SURE.
I WONDER IF THAT'S THE GIRL THEY'LL GIVE IT TO INSTEAD OF ME?

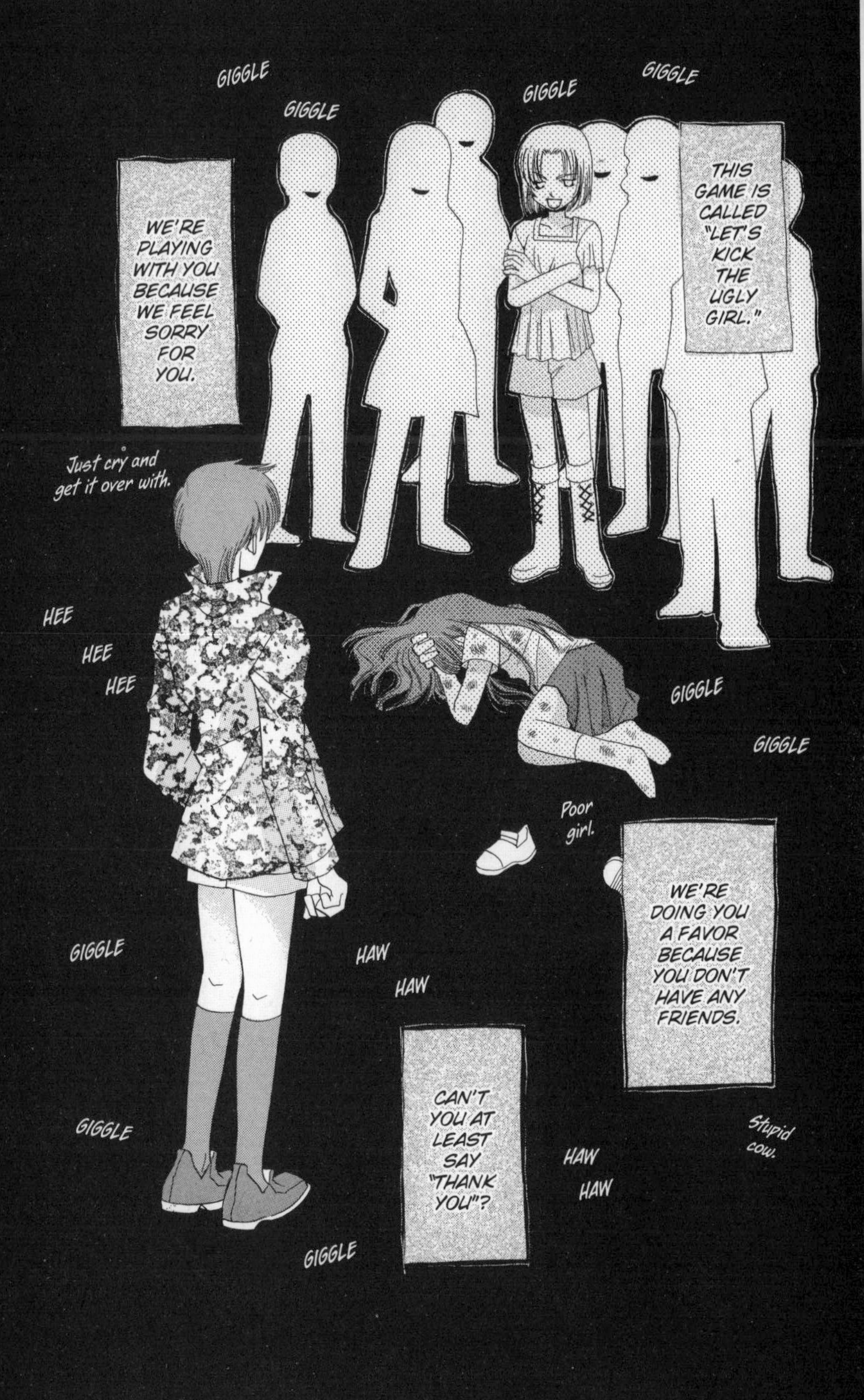
GIGGLE
GIGGLE
GIGGLE
GIGGLE
THIS GAME IS CALLED "LET'S KICK THE UGLY GIRL."
WE'RE PLAYING WITH YOU BECAUSE WE FEEL SORRY FOR YOU.
Just cry and get it over with.
GIGGLE
GIGGLE
HEE
HEE
HEE
Poor girl.
WE'RE DOING YOU A FAVOR BECAUSE YOU DON'T HAVE ANY FRIENDS.
HAW
HAW
GIGGLE
Stupid cow.
CAN'T YOU AT LEAST SAY "THANK YOU"?
HAW
HAW
GIGGLE
GIGGLE

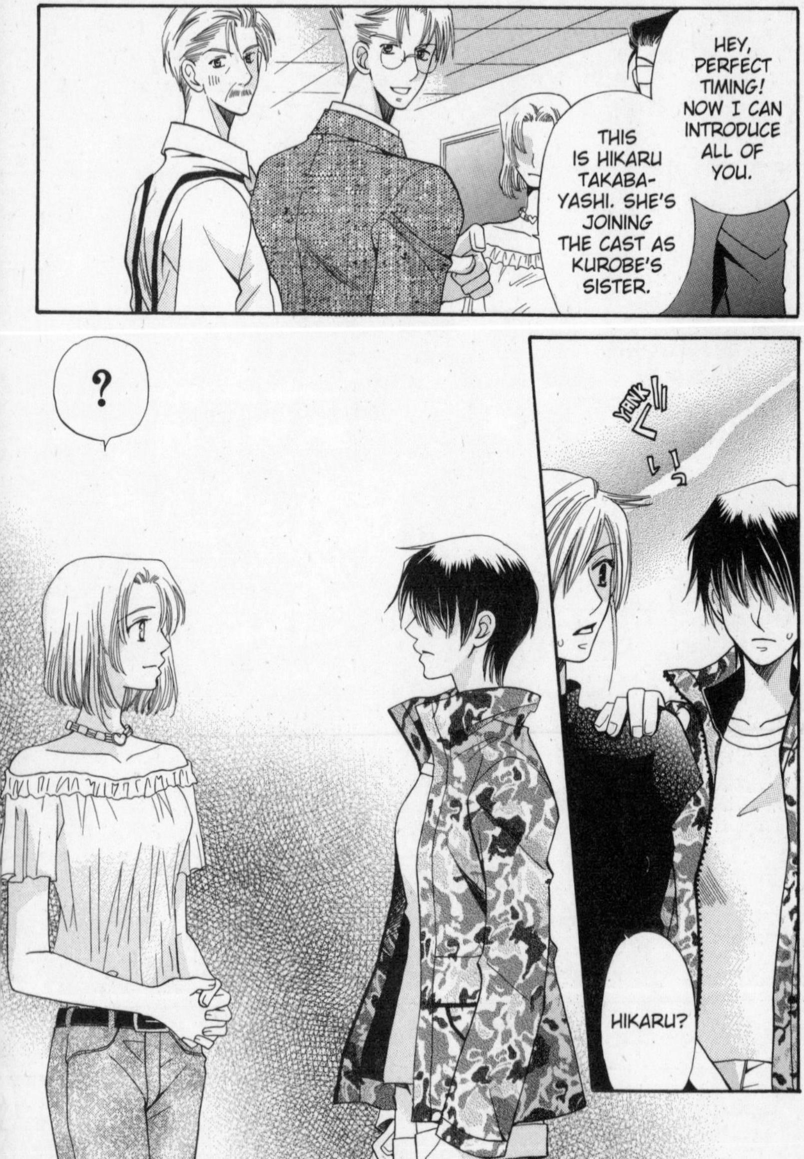
HEY, PERFECT TIMING! NOW I CAN INTRODUCE ALL OF YOU.
THIS IS HIKARU TAKABAYASHI. SHE'S JOINING THE CAST AS KUROBE'S SISTER.
YEINK
HIKARU?
?

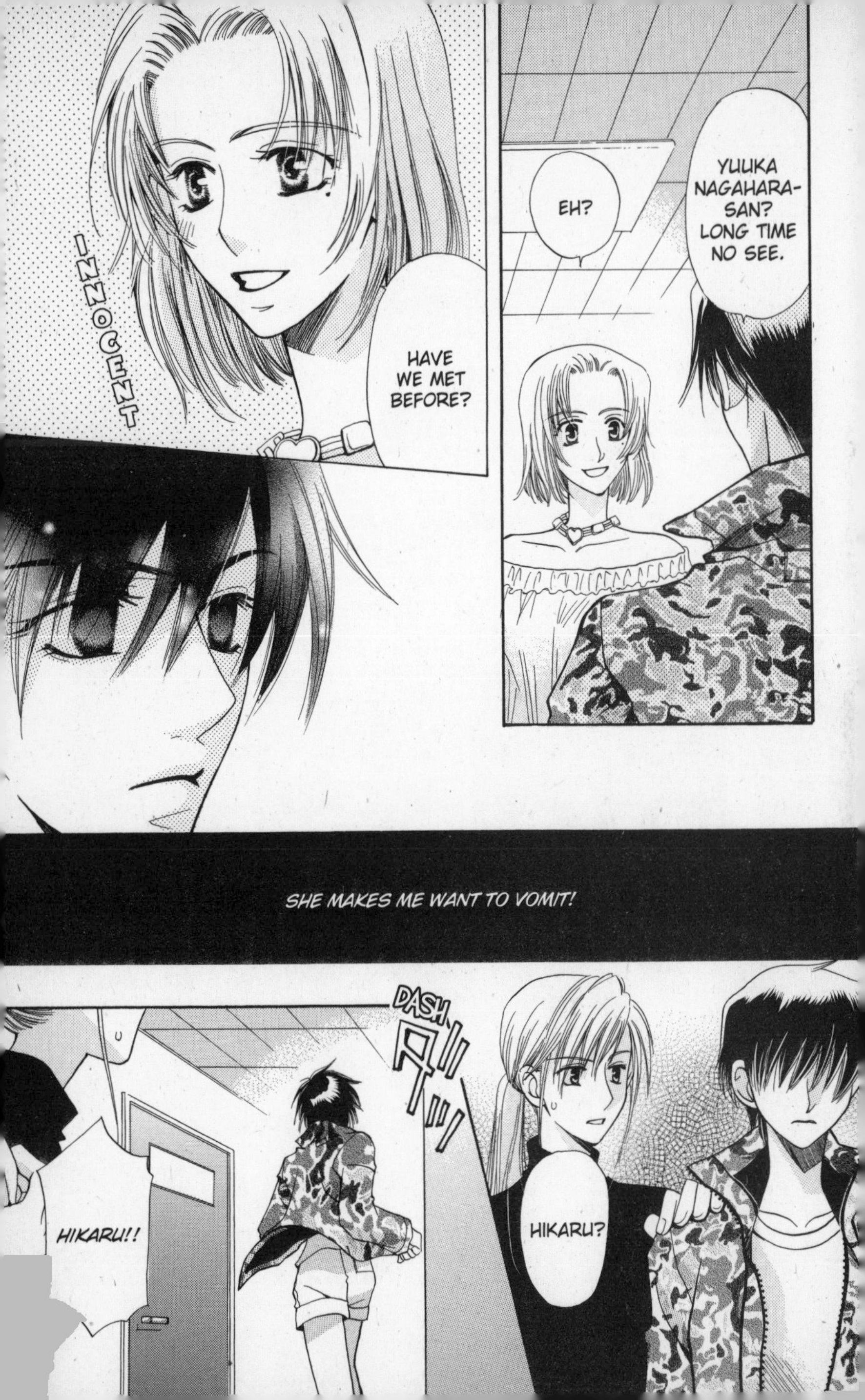
YUUKA NAGAHARA-SAN? LONG TIME NO SEE.
EH?
INNOCENT
HAVE WE MET BEFORE?
SHE MAKES ME WANT TO VOMIT!
HIKARU?
DASH
HIKARU!!

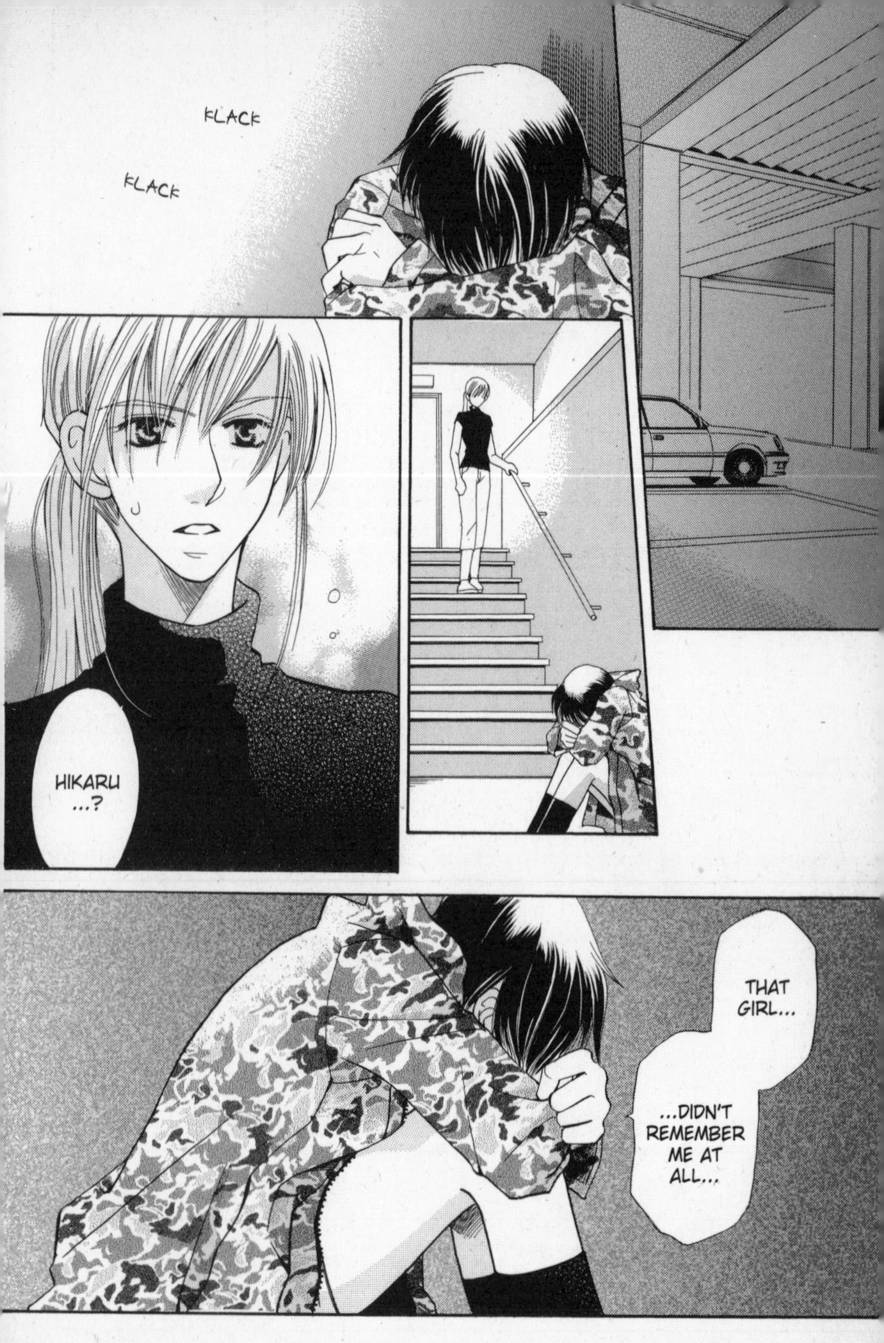
KLACK
KLACK
HIKARU ...?
THAT GIRL...
...DIDN'T REMEMBER ME AT ALL...

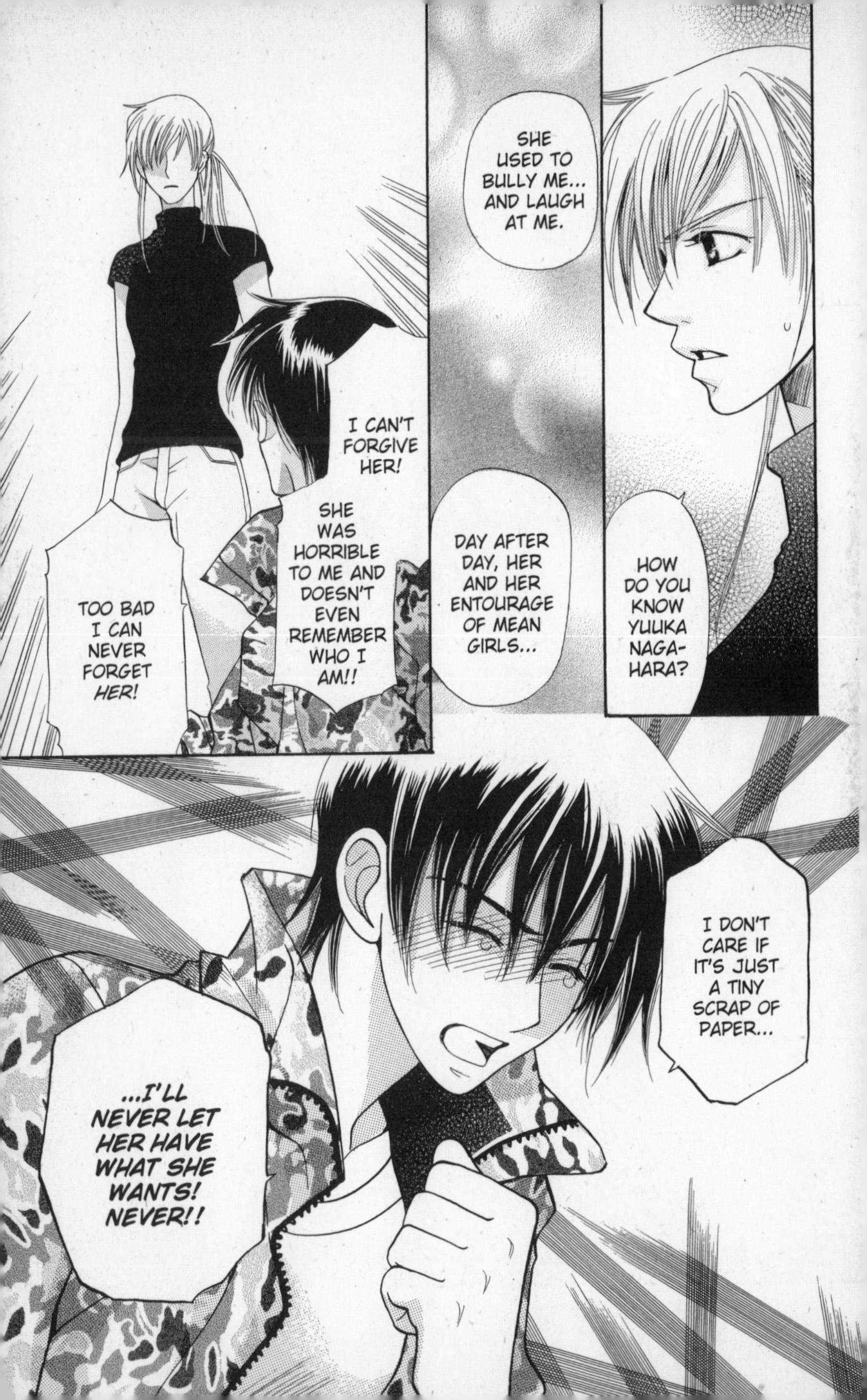
HOW DO YOU KNOW YUUKA NAGA-HARA?
SHE USED TO BULLY ME... AND LAUGH AT ME.
DAY AFTER DAY, HER AND HER ENTOURAGE OF MEAN GIRLS...
I CAN'T FORGIVE HER!
SHE WAS HORRIBLE TO ME AND DOESN'T EVEN REMEMBER WHO I AM!!
TOO BAD I CAN NEVER FORGET HER!
I DON'T CARE IF IT'S JUST A TINY SCRAP OF PAPER...
...I'LL NEVER LET HER HAVE WHAT SHE WANTS! NEVER!!

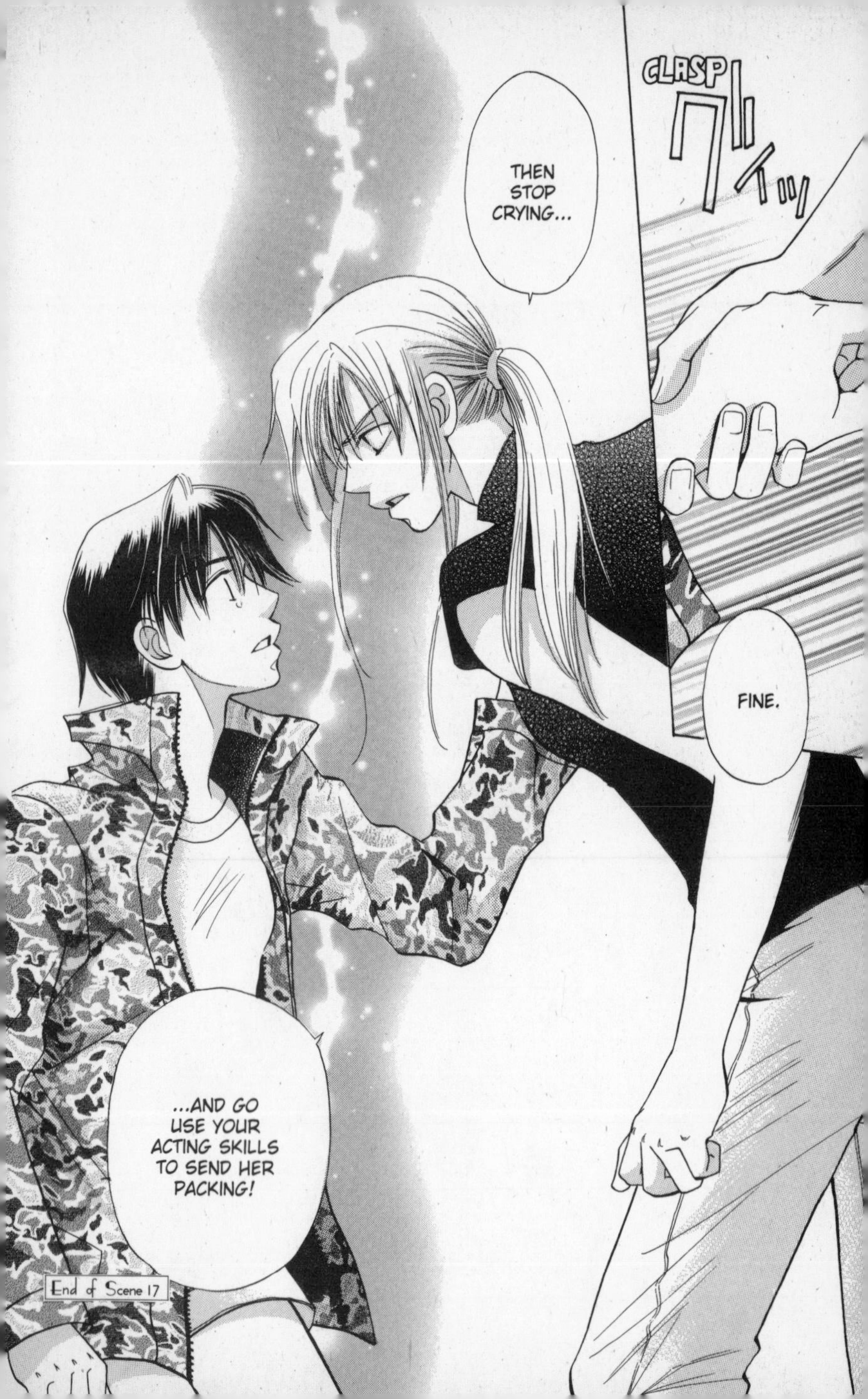
CLASP
FINE.
THEN STOP CRYING...
...AND GO USE YOUR ACTING SKILLS TO SEND HER PACKING!
End of Scene 17

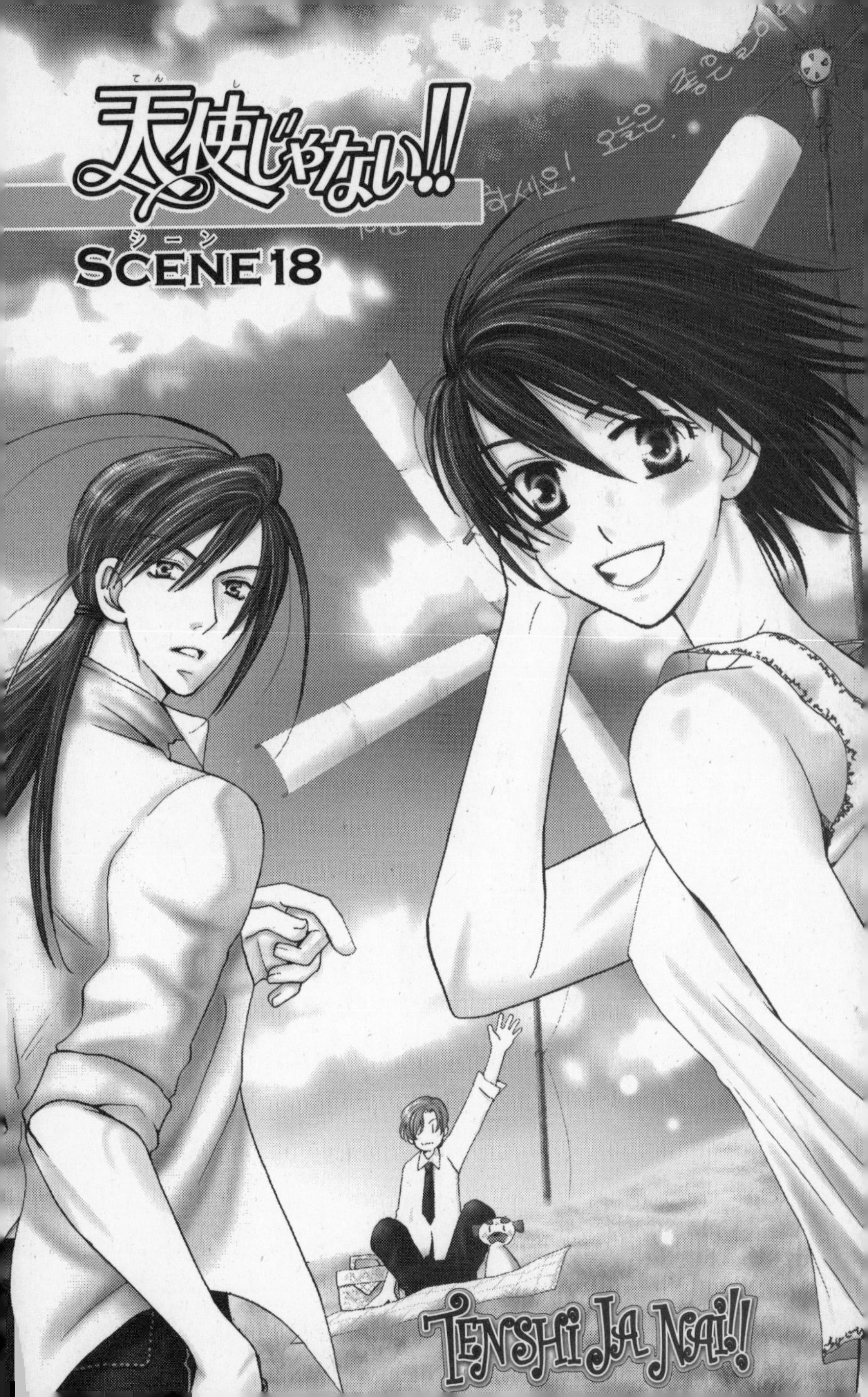
天使じゃない!!
SCENE 18
TENSHI JA NAI!!

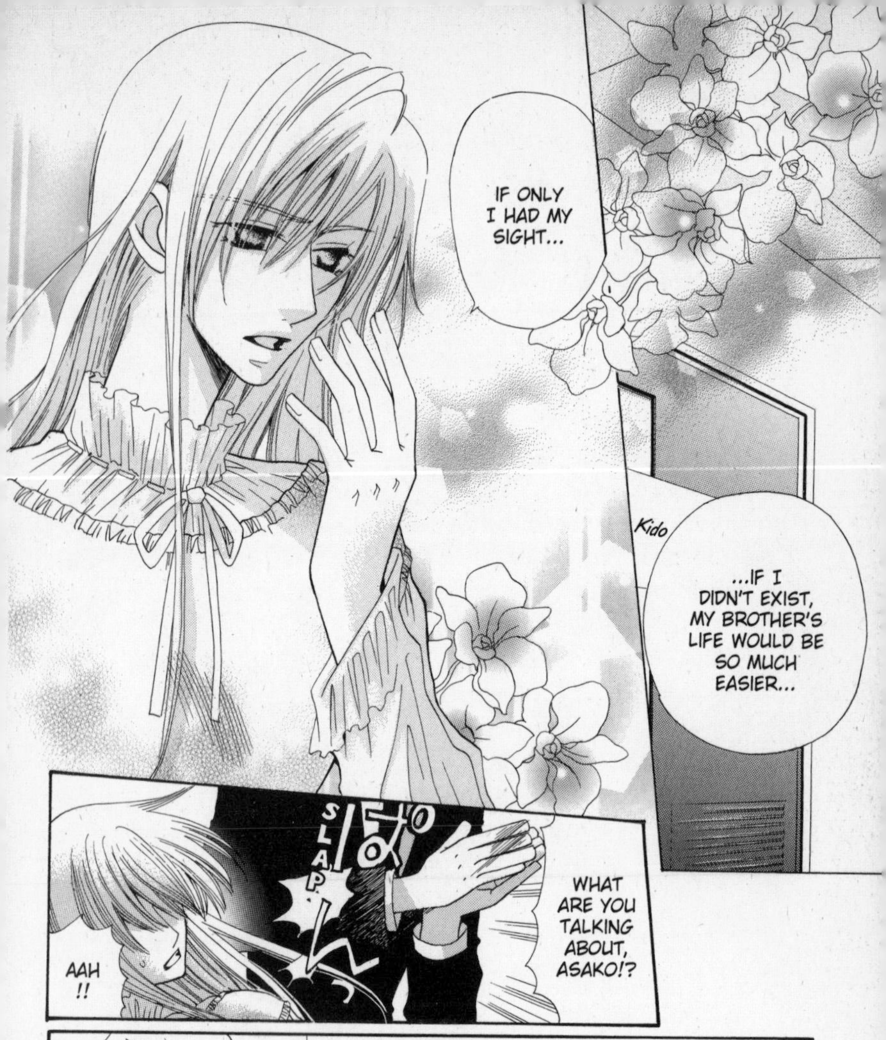
IF ONLY I HAD MY SIGHT...
Kido
...IF I DIDN'T EXIST, MY BROTHER'S LIFE WOULD BE SO MUCH EASIER...
WHAT ARE YOU TALKING ABOUT, ASAKO!?
SLAP
AAH !!

Yuuka Nagahara (Age: 16)

Born on August 21.

Blood type: B

An Izabella type. Well, for some reason, when it comes to a mean girl, the name Izabella always pops into my mind. I wonder why that is...? I wonder if it has anything to do with the influence of the old anime I always watched.

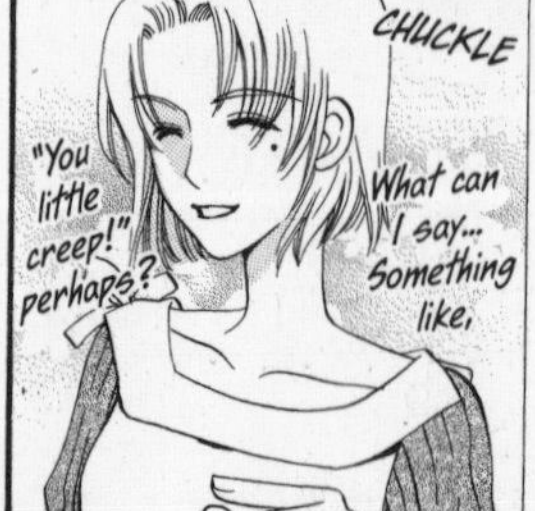
CHUCKLE
What can I say... Something like,
"You little creep!" perhaps?

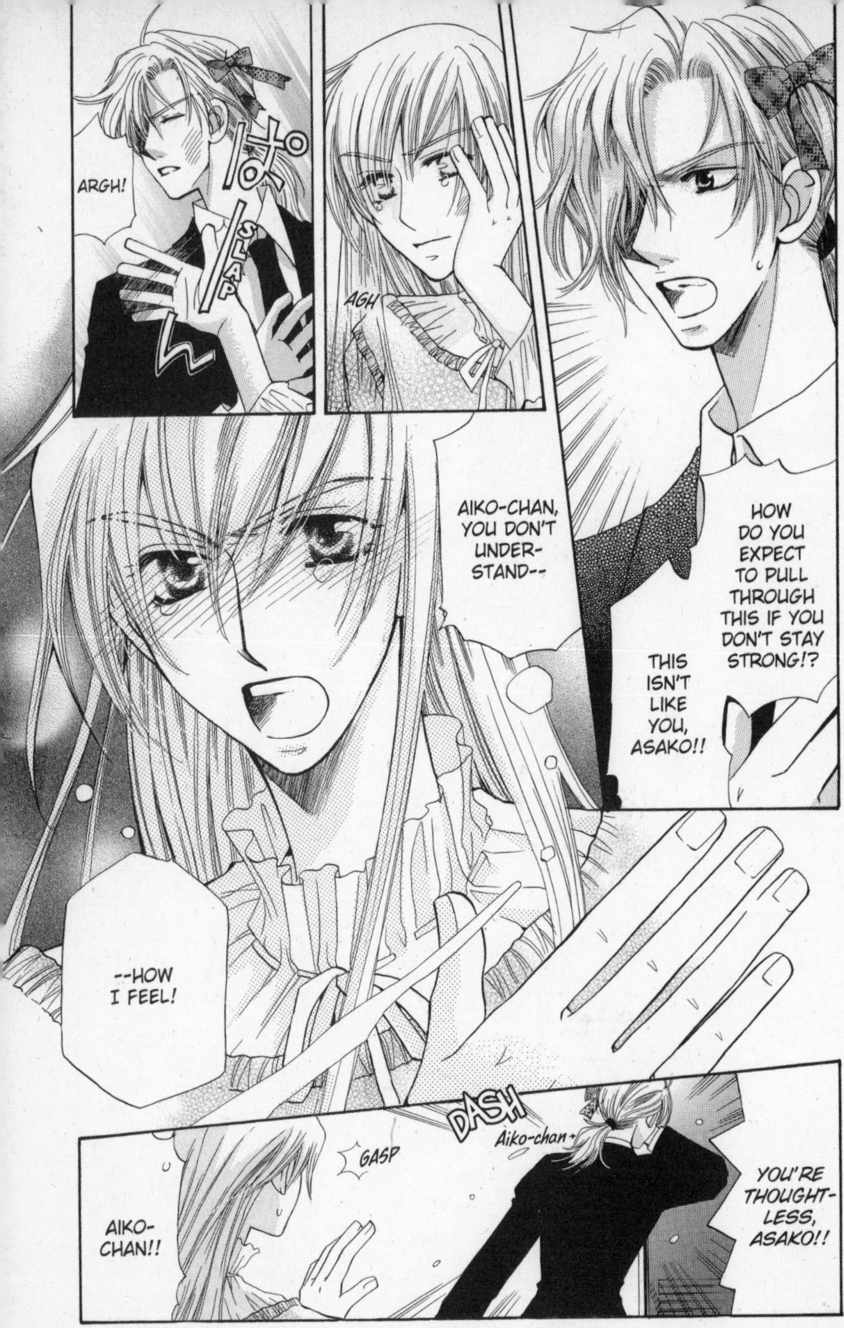
HOW DO YOU EXPECT TO PULL THROUGH THIS IF YOU DON'T STAY STRONG!?
THIS ISN'T LIKE YOU, ASAKO!!
AGH
SLAP
ARGH!
AIKO-CHAN, YOU DON'T UNDER-STAND--
--HOW I FEEL!
YOU'RE THOUGHT-LESS, ASAKO!!
DASH
Aiko-chan
GASP
AIKO-CHAN!!

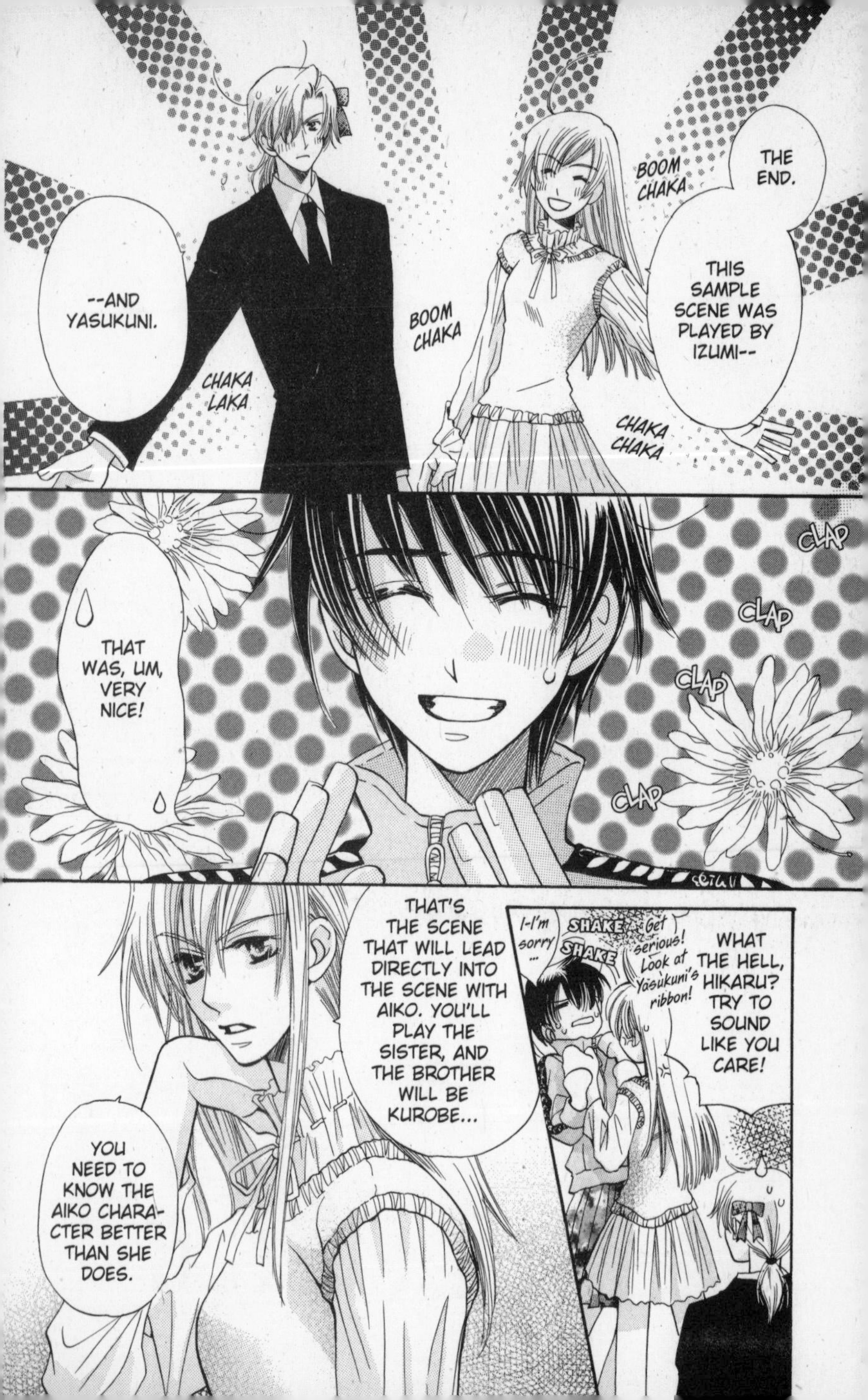
THE END.
BOOM CHAKA
THIS SAMPLE SCENE WAS PLAYED BY IZUMI--
BOOM CHAKA
CHAKA CHAKA
--AND YASUKUNI.
CHAKA LAKA
CLAP
CLAP
CLAP
CLAP
THAT WAS, UM, VERY NICE!
WHAT THE HELL, HIKARU? TRY TO SOUND LIKE YOU CARE!
Get serious! Look at Yasukuni's ribbon!
SHAKE SHAKE
I-I'm sorry ...
THAT'S THE SCENE THAT WILL LEAD DIRECTLY INTO THE SCENE WITH AIKO. YOU'LL PLAY THE SISTER, AND THE BROTHER WILL BE KUROBE...
YOU NEED TO KNOW THE AIKO CHARACTER BETTER THAN SHE DOES.

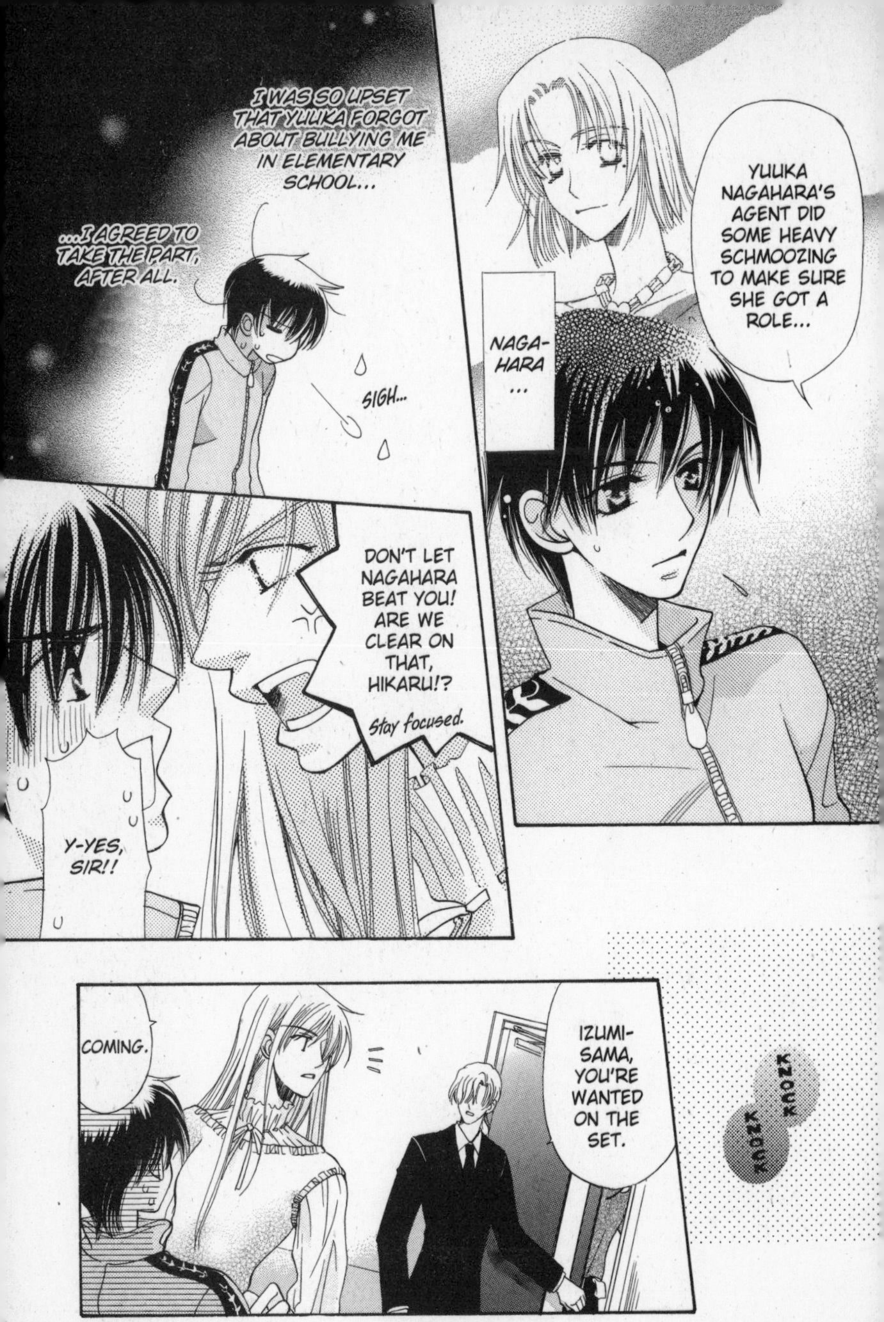
YUUKA NAGAHARA'S AGENT DID SOME HEAVY SCHMOOZING TO MAKE SURE SHE GOT A ROLE...
NAGA-HARA...
I WAS SO UPSET THAT YUUKA FORGOT ABOUT BULLYING ME IN ELEMENTARY SCHOOL...
...I AGREED TO TAKE THE PART, AFTER ALL.
SIGH...
DON'T LET NAGAHARA BEAT YOU! ARE WE CLEAR ON THAT, HIKARU!?
Stay focused.
Y-YES, SIR!!
KNOCK KNOCK
IZUMI-SAMA, YOU'RE WANTED ON THE SET.
COMING.

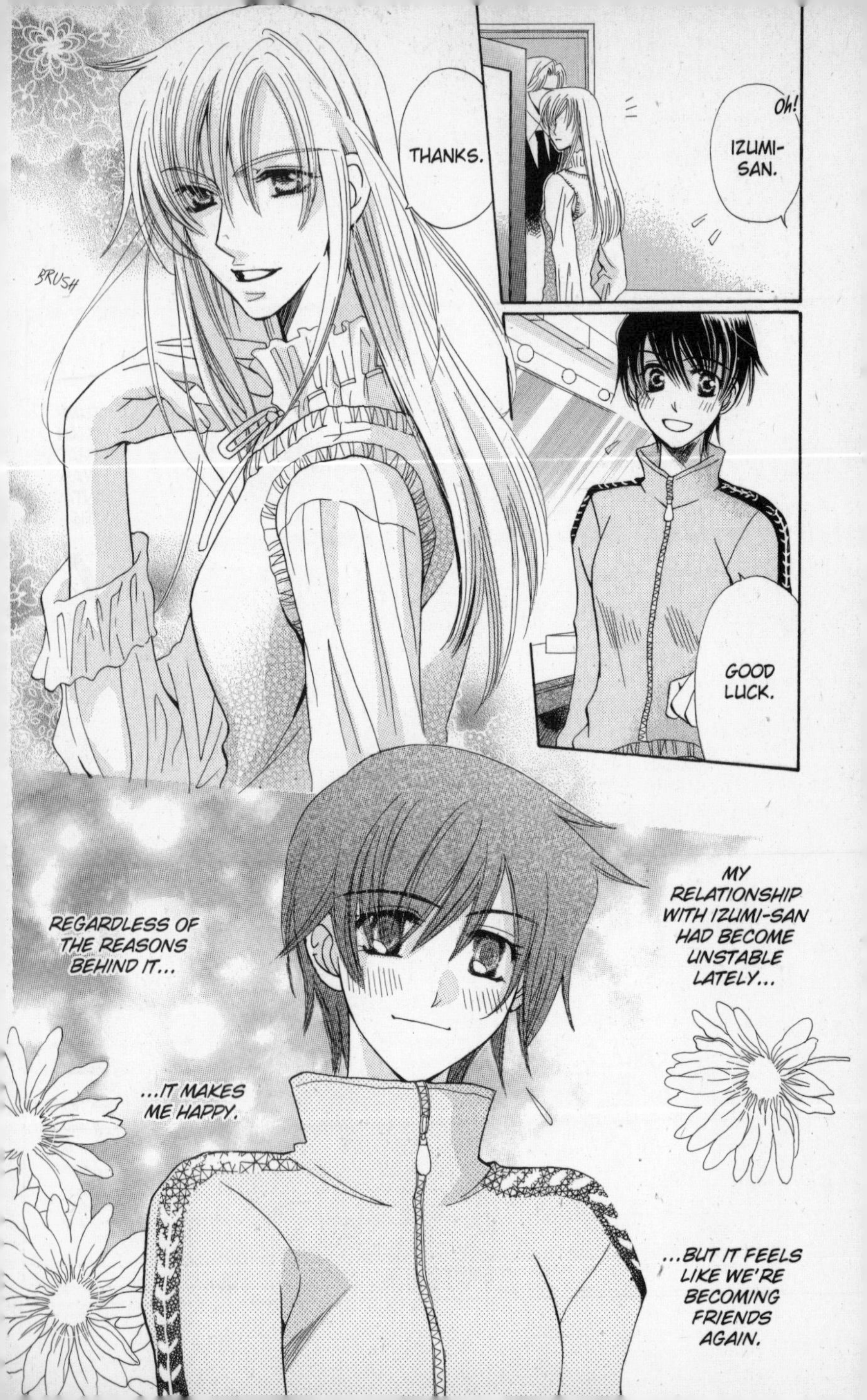
Oh!
IZUMI-SAN.
GOOD LUCK.
THANKS.
BRUSH
MY RELATIONSHIP WITH IZUMI-SAN HAD BECOME UNSTABLE LATELY...
...BUT IT FEELS LIKE WE'RE BECOMING FRIENDS AGAIN.
REGARDLESS OF THE REASONS BEHIND IT...
...IT MAKES ME HAPPY.

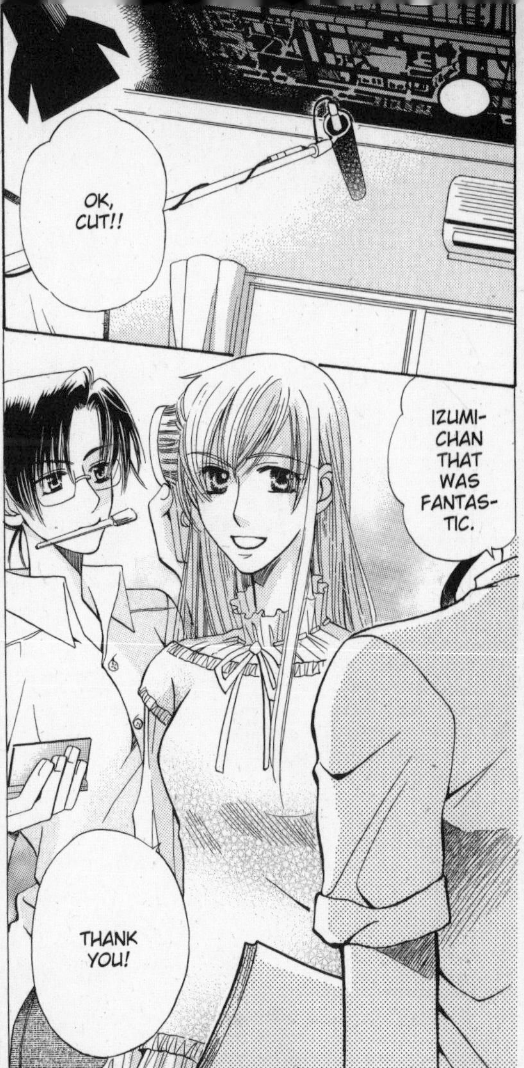

OK, CUT!!
IZUMI-CHAN THAT WAS FANTASTIC.
THANK YOU!
This time we'll shoot from the other angle.
CHATTER
CHATTER
I'll reposition the camera.
DAZED
Script

My Current Addictons #1

I'm a DVD junkie...

What can I say... once I decide I like a movie, if I have to work long hours by myself, I'll play the DVD over and over. Lord of the Rings is one of those movies. I like any movie about people learning magic (laugh). Who knows, pretty soon I might memorize all of the lines (from the film, that is)... Perhaps I should call myself a DVD monkey, as opposed to a DVD junkie? It's sort of simian-like to do the same thing over and over without getting tired of it. (But that's unfair to monkeys.) Sometimes, I even cry during the same scenes...maybe that's how I deal with my stress? (sweat)

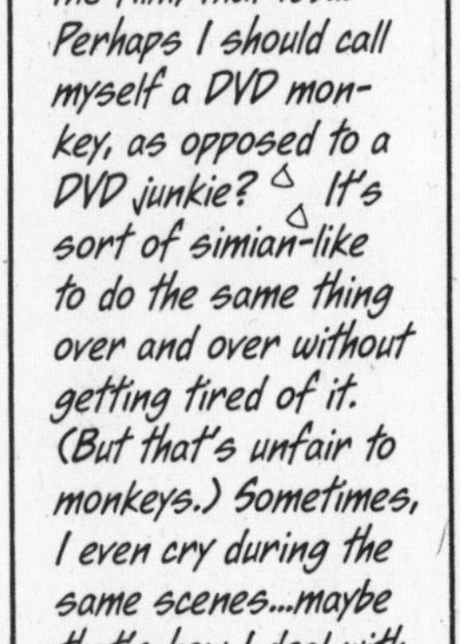

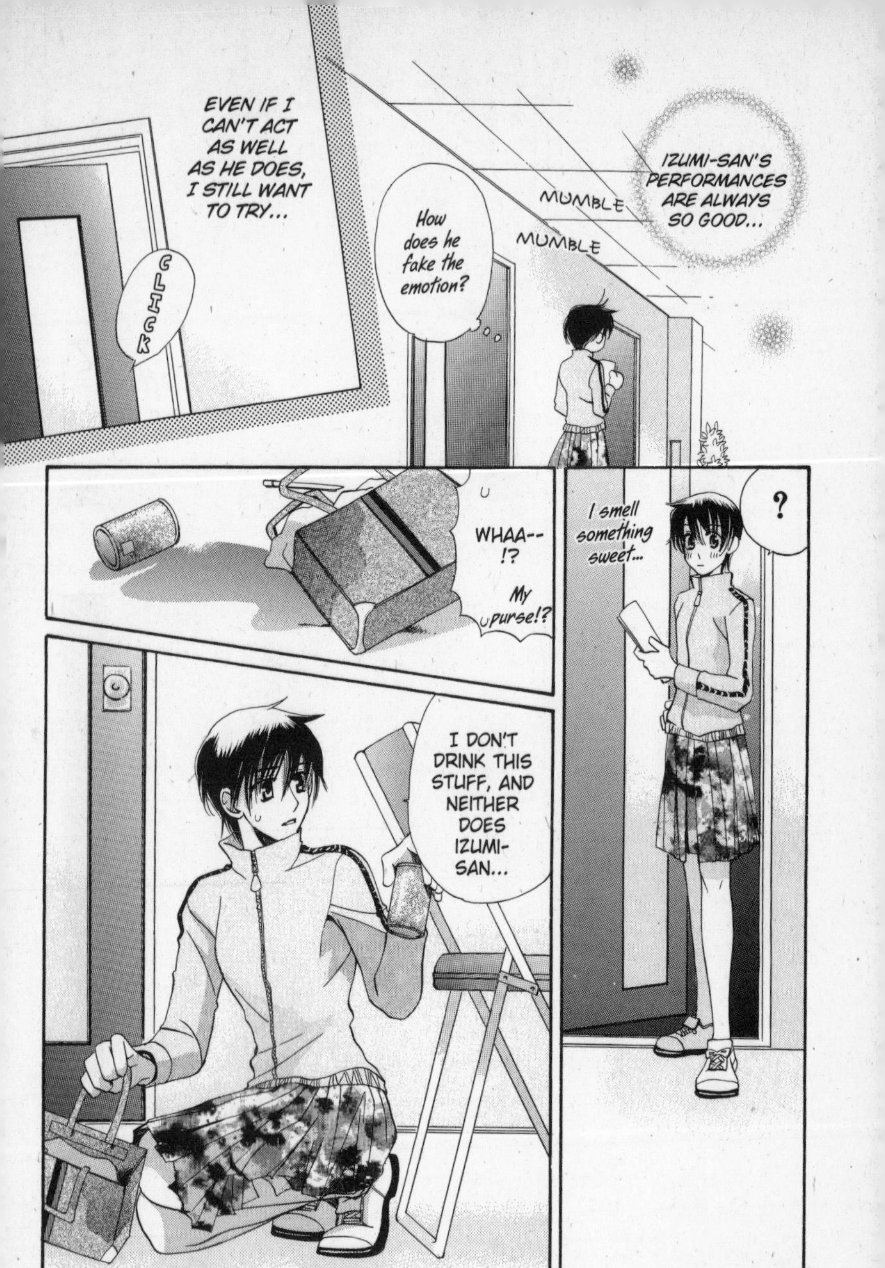
IZUMI-SAN'S PERFORMANCES ARE ALWAYS SO GOOD...
MUMBLE
MUMBLE
How does he fake the emotion?
EVEN IF I CAN'T ACT AS WELL AS HE DOES, I STILL WANT TO TRY...
CLICK
?
I smell something sweet...
WHAA-- !?
My purse!?
I DON'T DRINK THIS STUFF, AND NEITHER DOES IZUMI-SAN...

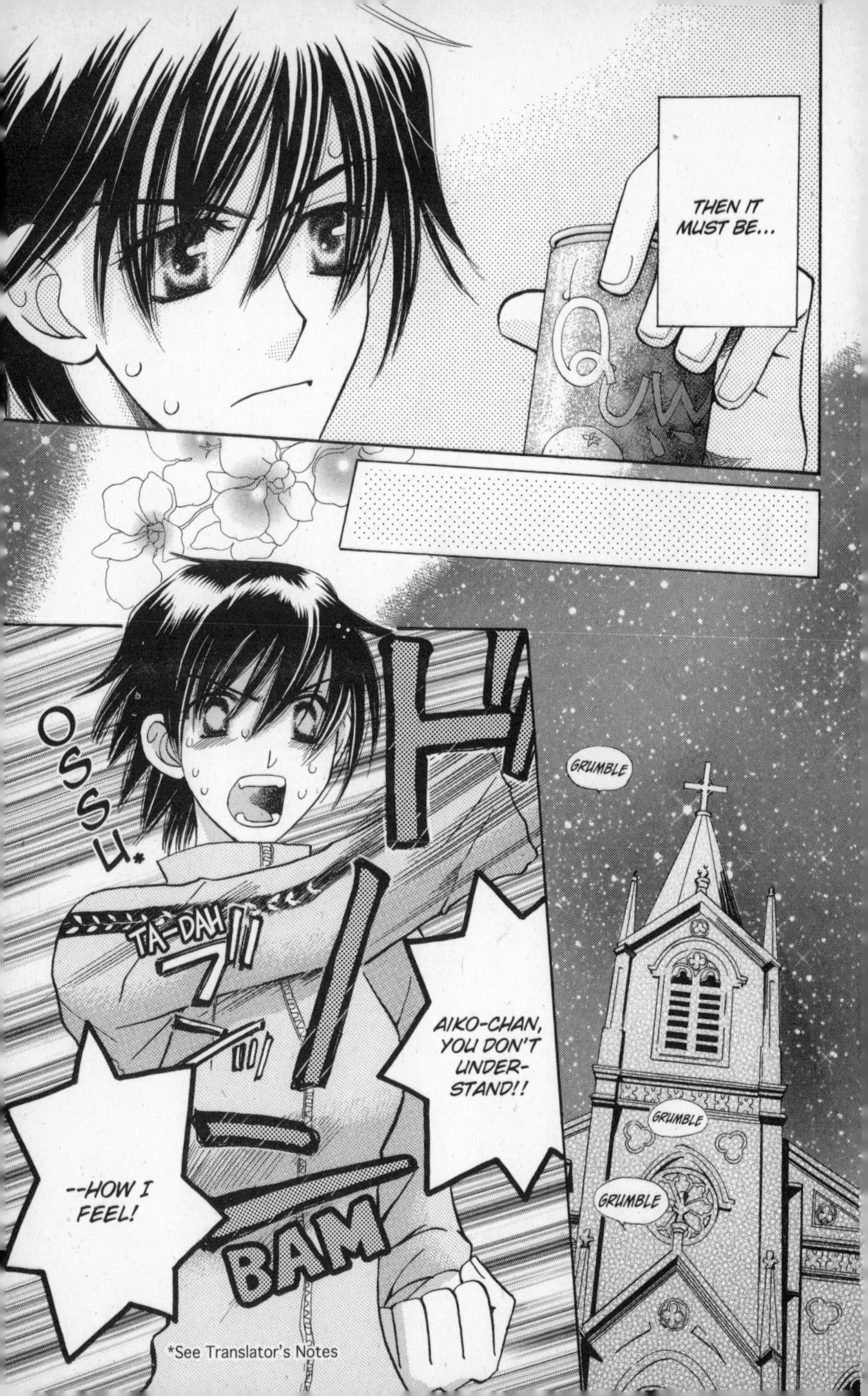
THEN IT MUST BE...
GRUMBLE
GRUMBLE
GRUMBLE
AIKO-CHAN, YOU DON'T UNDER-STAND!!
OSSU.*
TA-DAH
--HOW I FEEL!
BAM
*See Translator's Notes

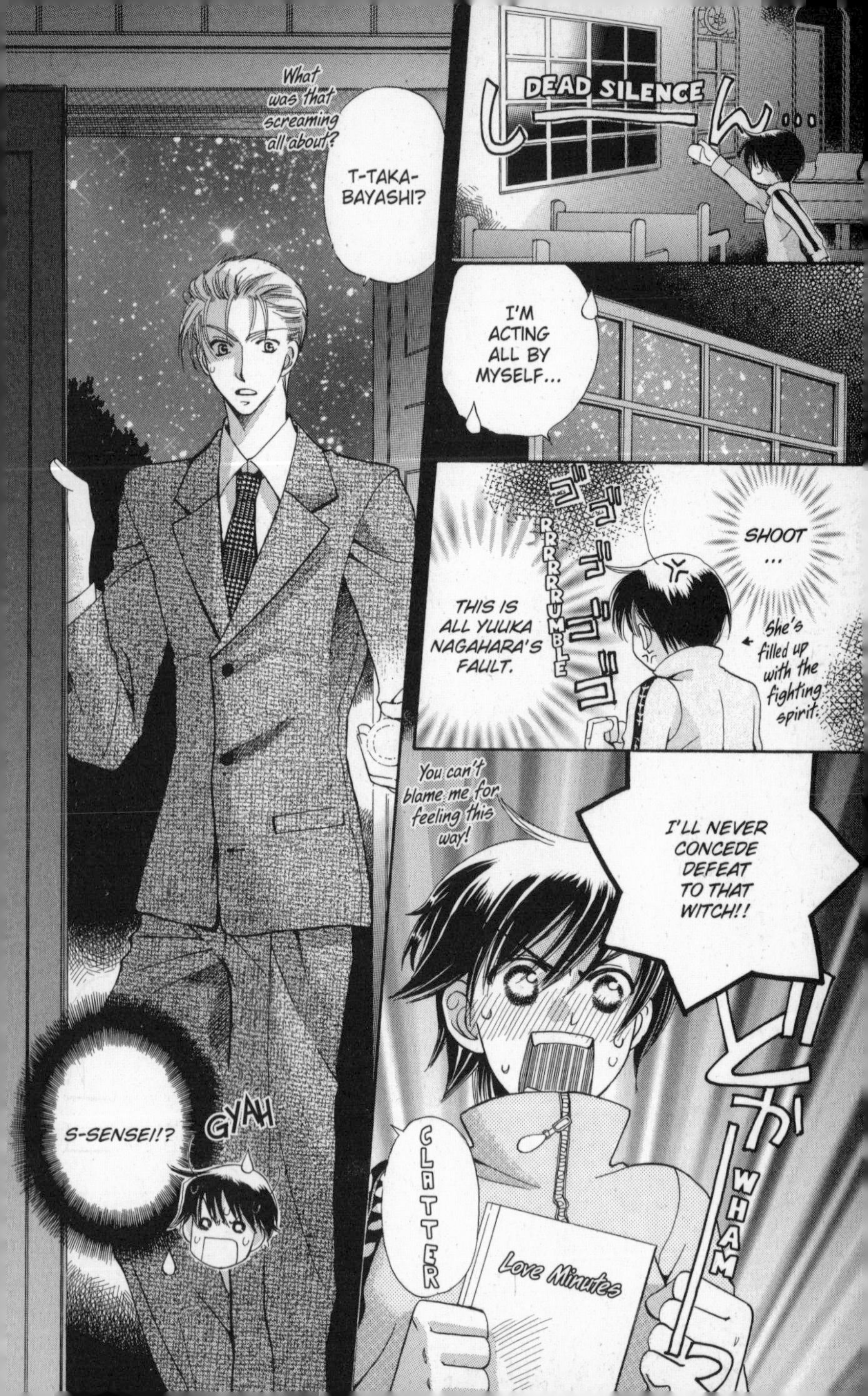
DEAD SILENCE
I'M ACTING ALL BY MYSELF...
SHOOT ...
RRRRRUMBLE
THIS IS ALL YUUKA NAGAHARA'S FAULT.
She's filled up with the fighting spirit.
I'LL NEVER CONCEDE DEFEAT TO THAT WITCH!!
You can't blame me for feeling this way!
WHAM
CLATTER
Love Minutes
What was that screaming all about?
T-TAKA-BAYASHI?
S-SENSEI!?
GYAH

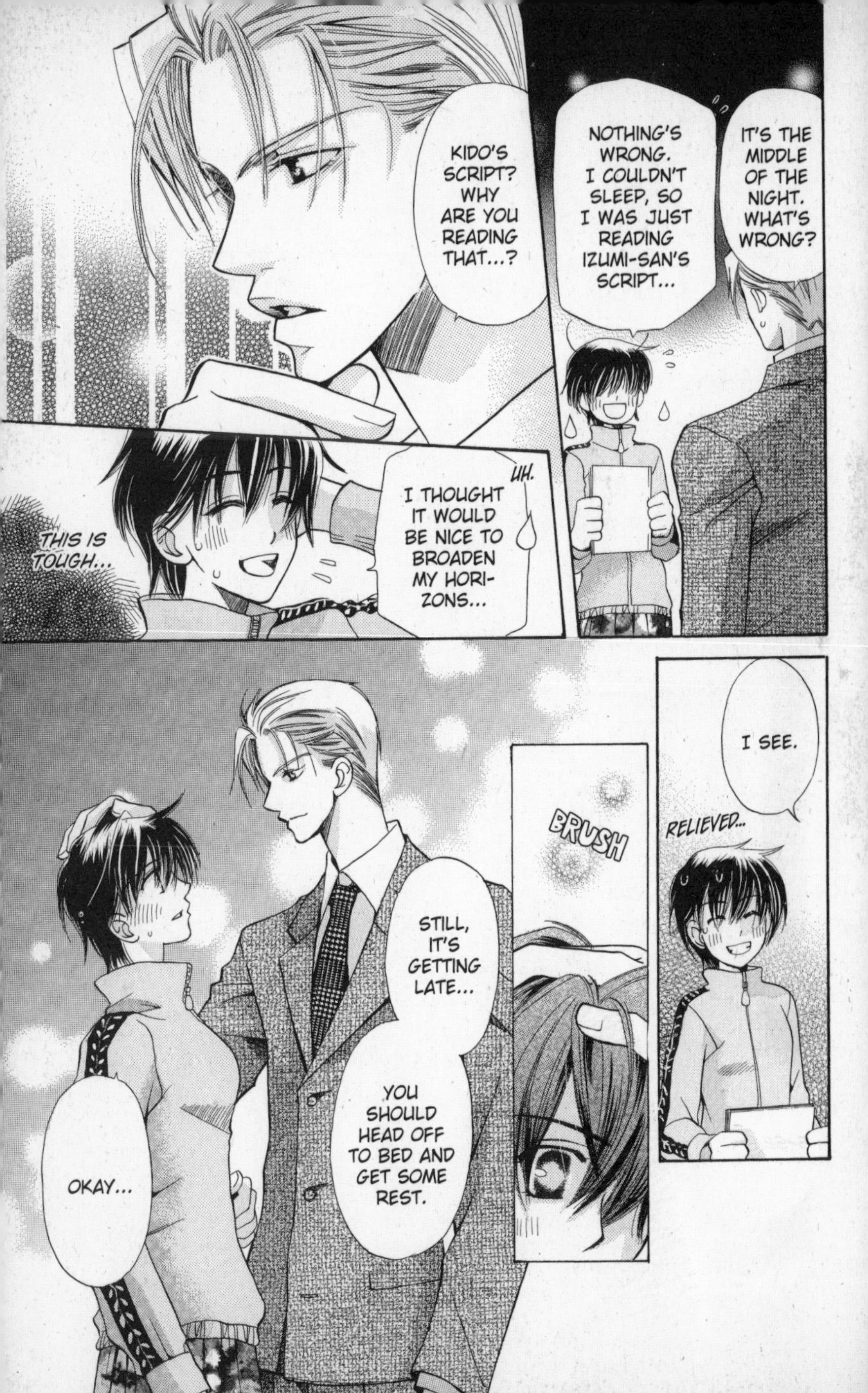
IT'S THE MIDDLE OF THE NIGHT. WHAT'S WRONG?
NOTHING'S WRONG. I COULDN'T SLEEP, SO I WAS JUST READING IZUMI-SAN'S SCRIPT...
KIDO'S SCRIPT? WHY ARE YOU READING THAT...?
UH.
I THOUGHT IT WOULD BE NICE TO BROADEN MY HORI-ZONS...
THIS IS TOUGH...
I SEE.
RELIEVED...
BRUSH
STILL, IT'S GETTING LATE...
YOU SHOULD HEAD OFF TO BED AND GET SOME REST.
OKAY...

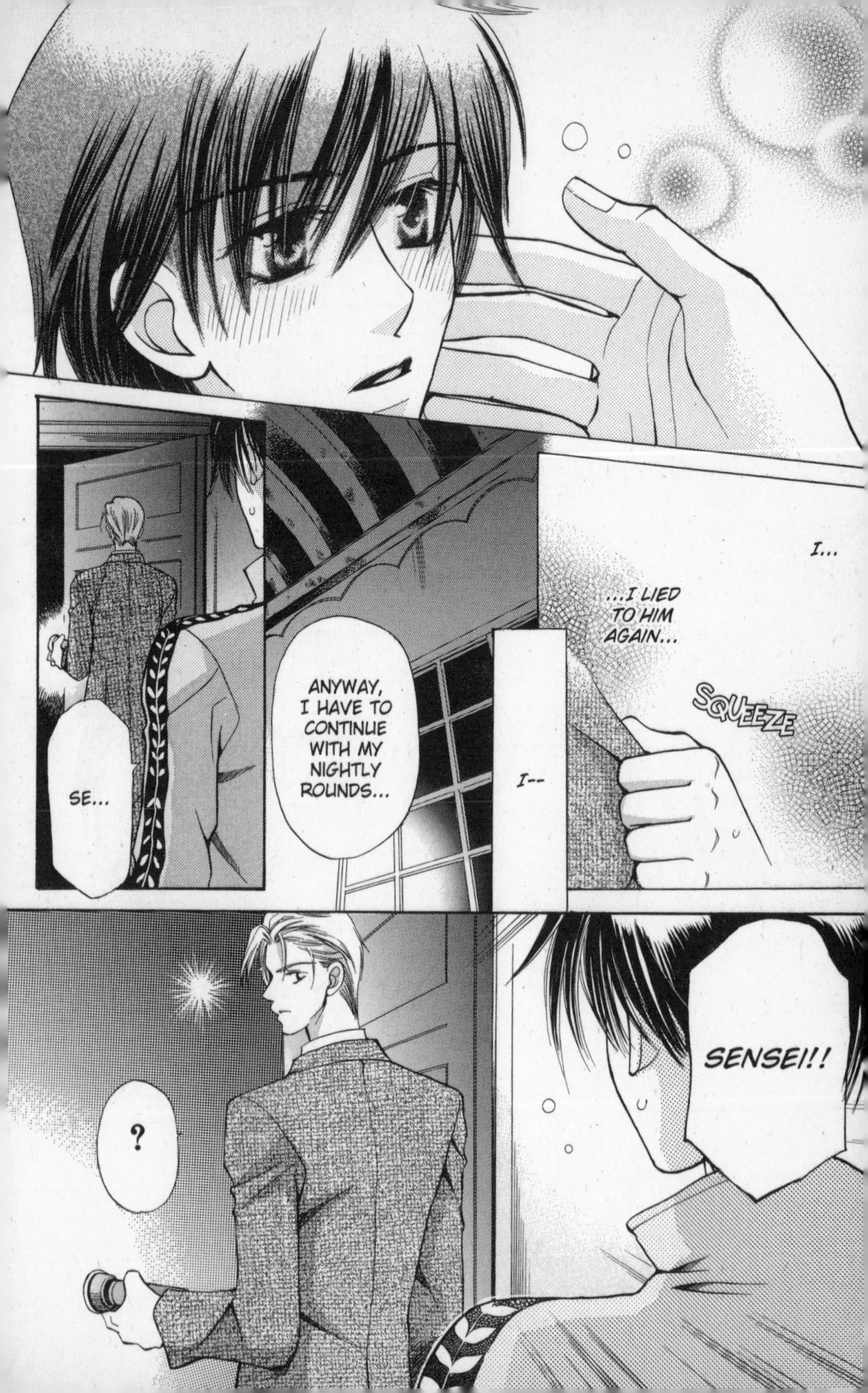
I...
...I LIED TO HIM AGAIN...
SQUEEZE
I--
ANYWAY, I HAVE TO CONTINUE WITH MY NIGHTLY ROUNDS...
SE...
SENSEI!!
?

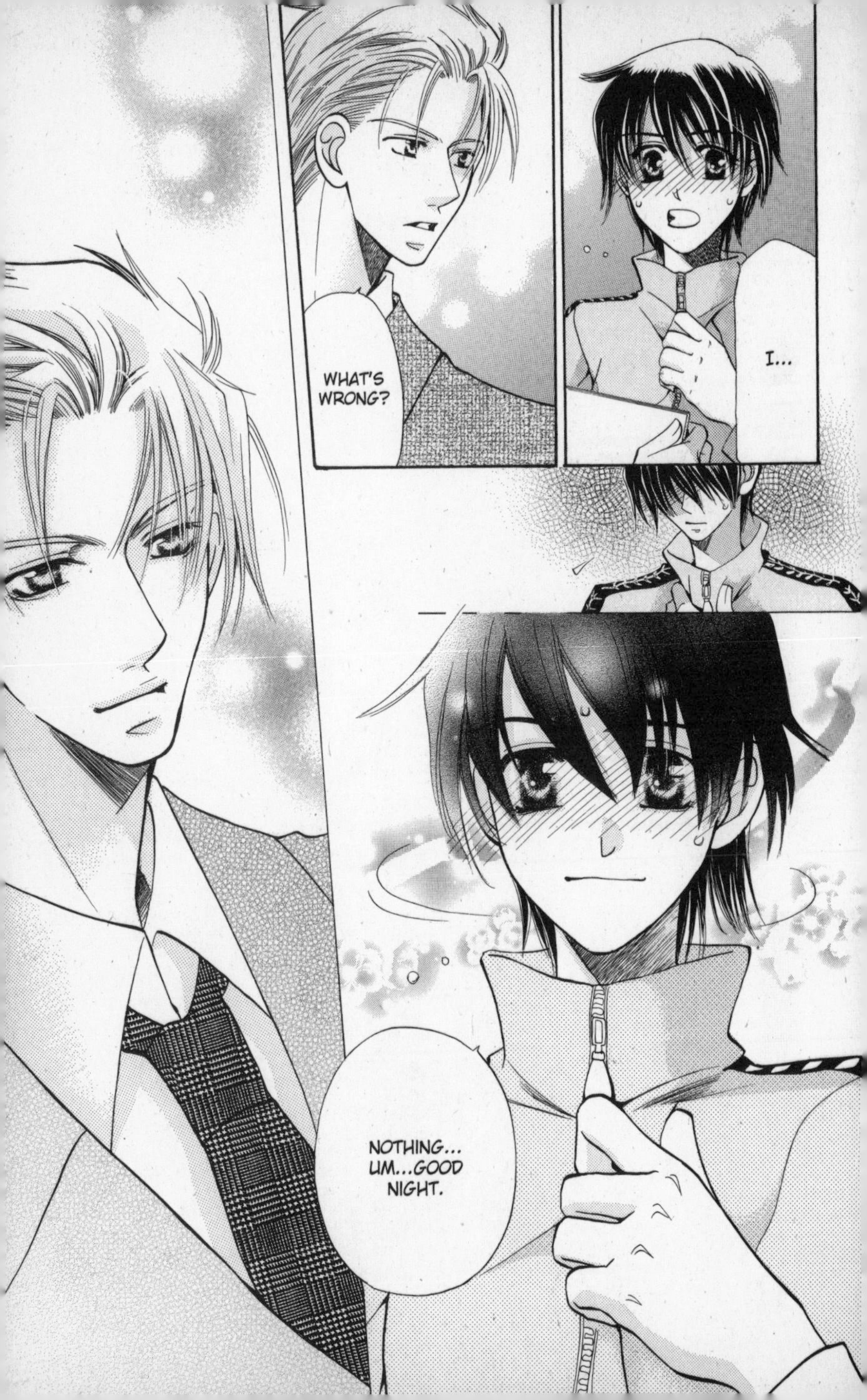
I...
WHAT'S WRONG?
NOTHING... UM...GOOD NIGHT.

NO MATTER HOW MANY SECRETS AND LIES THERE ARE BETWEEN US...
...MY LOVE FOR SENSEI...
...REMAINS THE MOST HONEST THING IN MY LIFE.
SENSEI...
...I HOPE YOU CAN FORGIVE ME.

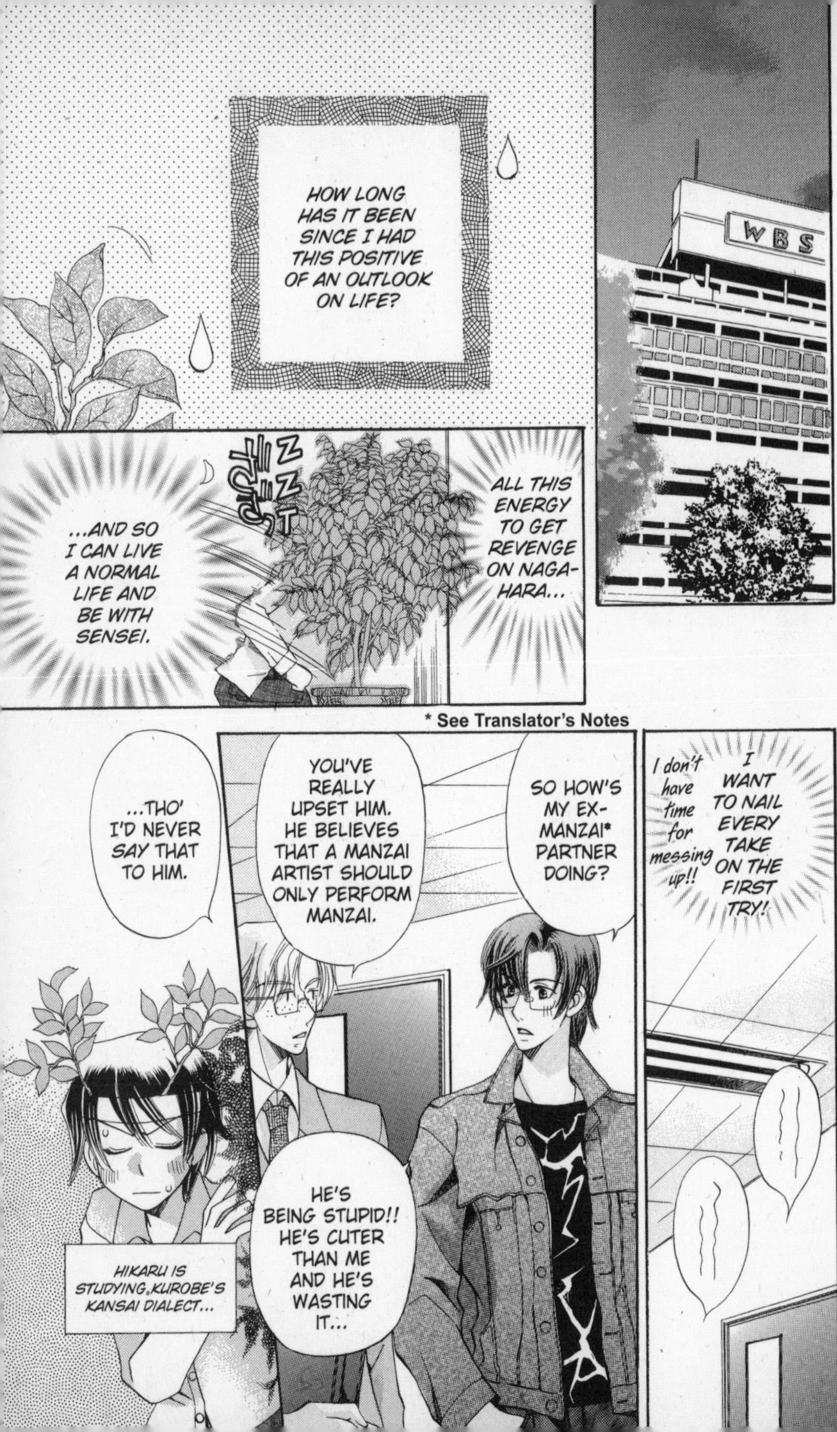
HOW LONG HAS IT BEEN SINCE I HAD THIS POSITIVE OF AN OUTLOOK ON LIFE?
ALL THIS ENERGY TO GET REVENGE ON NAGA-HARA...
...AND SO I CAN LIVE A NORMAL LIFE AND BE WITH SENSEI.
* See Translator's Notes
I WANT TO NAIL EVERY TAKE ON THE FIRST TRY!
I don't have time for messing up!!
SO HOW'S MY EX-MANZAI* PARTNER DOING?
YOU'VE REALLY UPSET HIM. HE BELIEVES THAT A MANZAI ARTIST SHOULD ONLY PERFORM MANZAI.
...THO' I'D NEVER SAY THAT TO HIM.
HE'S BEING STUPID!! HE'S CUTER THAN ME AND HE'S WASTING IT...
HIKARU IS STUDYING KUROBE'S KANSAI DIALECT...

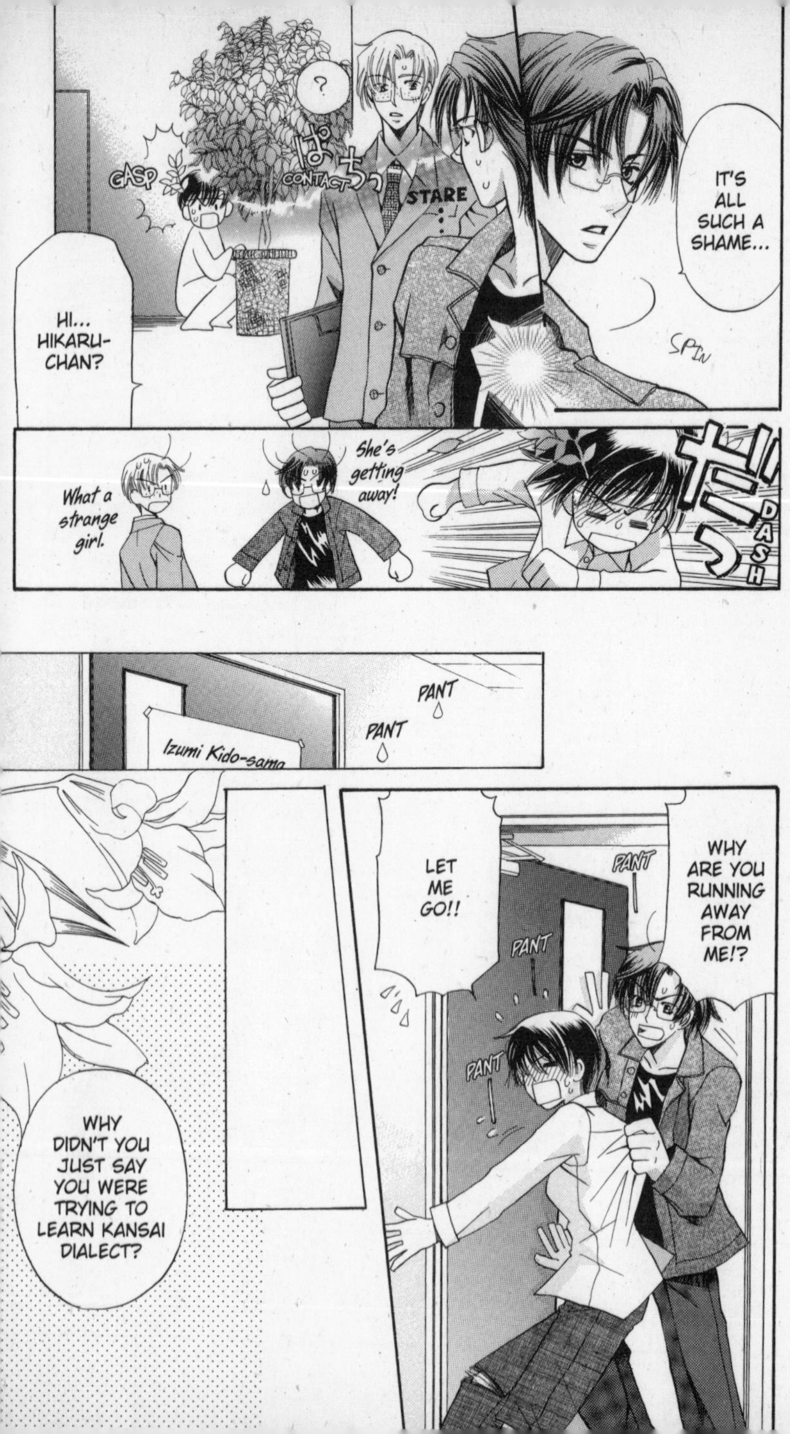
IT'S ALL SUCH A SHAME...
SPIN
STARE
ぱちっ CONTACT
?
GASP
HI... HIKARU-CHAN?
だっ DASH
She's getting away!
What a strange girl.
PANT
PANT
Izumi Kido-sama
WHY ARE YOU RUNNING AWAY FROM ME!?
PANT
LET ME GO!!
PANT
PANT
WHY DIDN'T YOU JUST SAY YOU WERE TRYING TO LEARN KANSAI DIALECT?

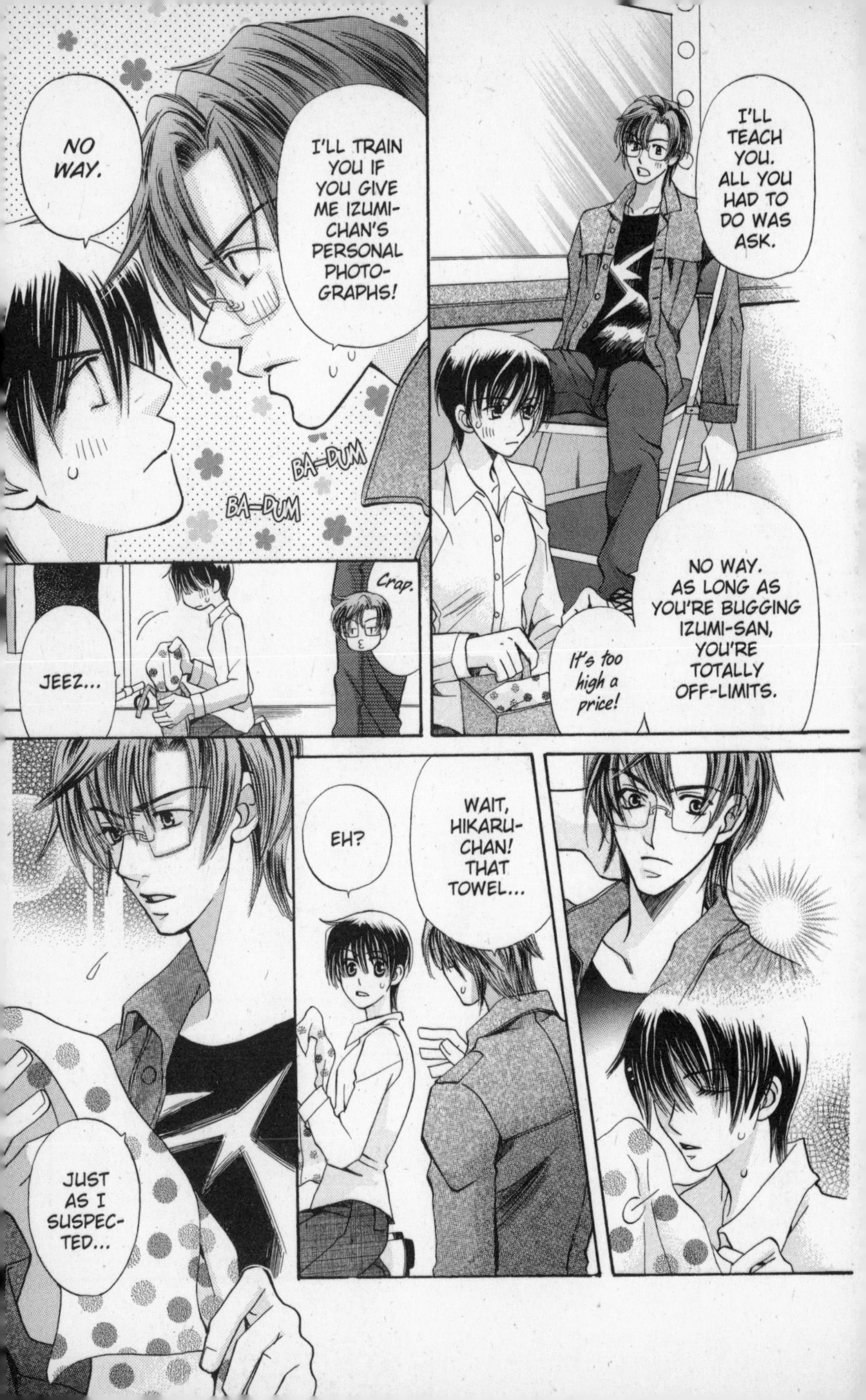
I'LL TEACH YOU. ALL YOU HAD TO DO WAS ASK.
NO WAY. AS LONG AS YOU'RE BUGGING IZUMI-SAN, YOU'RE TOTALLY OFF-LIMITS.
It's too high a price!
I'LL TRAIN YOU IF YOU GIVE ME IZUMI-CHAN'S PERSONAL PHOTOGRAPHS!
NO WAY.
BA-DUM
BA-DUM
Crap.
JEEZ...
WAIT, HIKARU-CHAN! THAT TOWEL...
EH?
JUST AS I SUSPECTED...

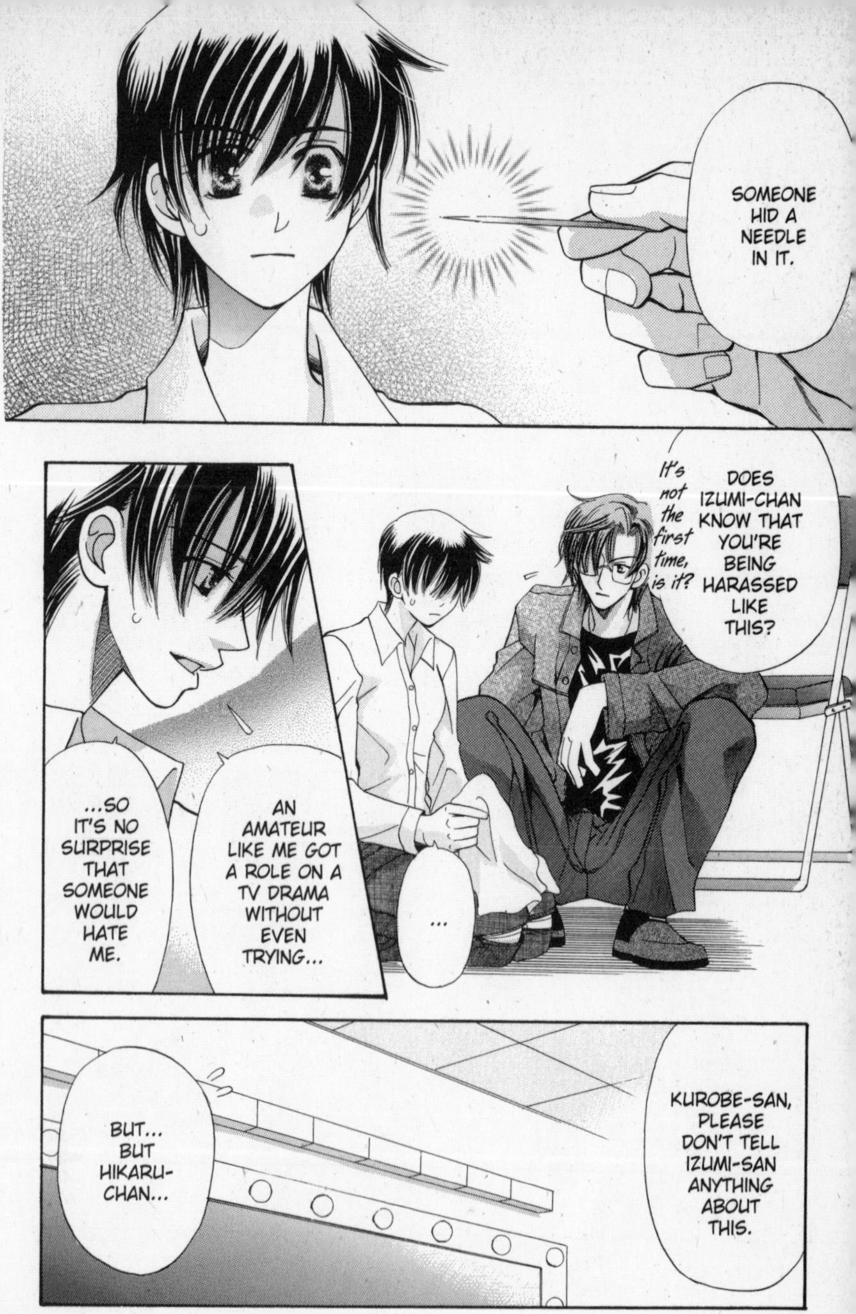
SOMEONE HID A NEEDLE IN IT.
DOES IZUMI-CHAN KNOW THAT YOU'RE BEING HARASSED LIKE THIS?
It's not the first time, is it?
...
AN AMATEUR LIKE ME GOT A ROLE ON A TV DRAMA WITHOUT EVEN TRYING...
...SO IT'S NO SURPRISE THAT SOMEONE WOULD HATE ME.
KUROBE-SAN, PLEASE DON'T TELL IZUMI-SAN ANYTHING ABOUT THIS.
BUT... BUT HIKARU-CHAN...

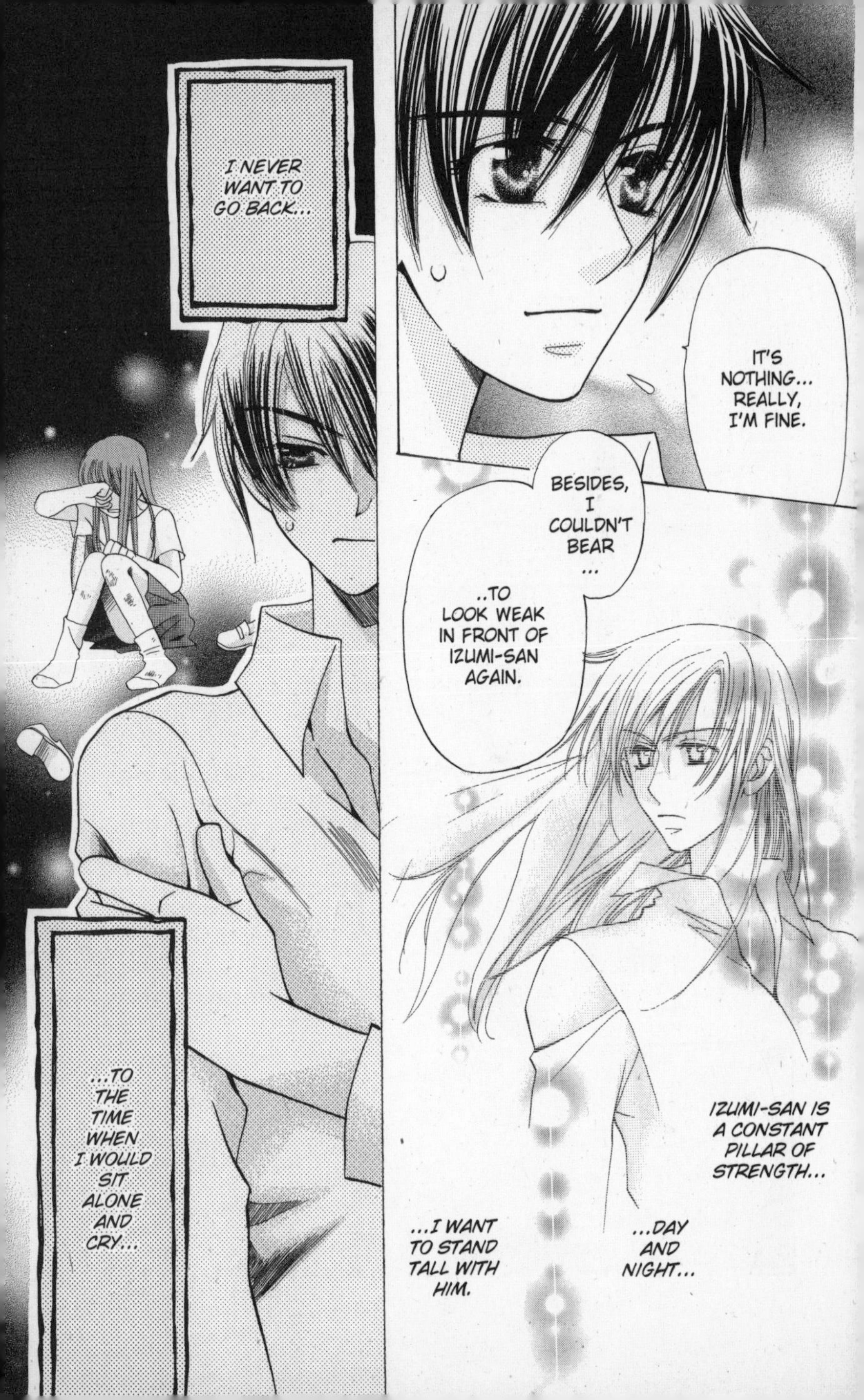
IT'S NOTHING... REALLY, I'M FINE.
BESIDES, I COULDN'T BEAR ...
..TO LOOK WEAK IN FRONT OF IZUMI-SAN AGAIN.
IZUMI-SAN IS A CONSTANT PILLAR OF STRENGTH...
...DAY AND NIGHT...
...I WANT TO STAND TALL WITH HIM.
I NEVER WANT TO GO BACK...
...TO THE TIME WHEN I WOULD SIT ALONE AND CRY...

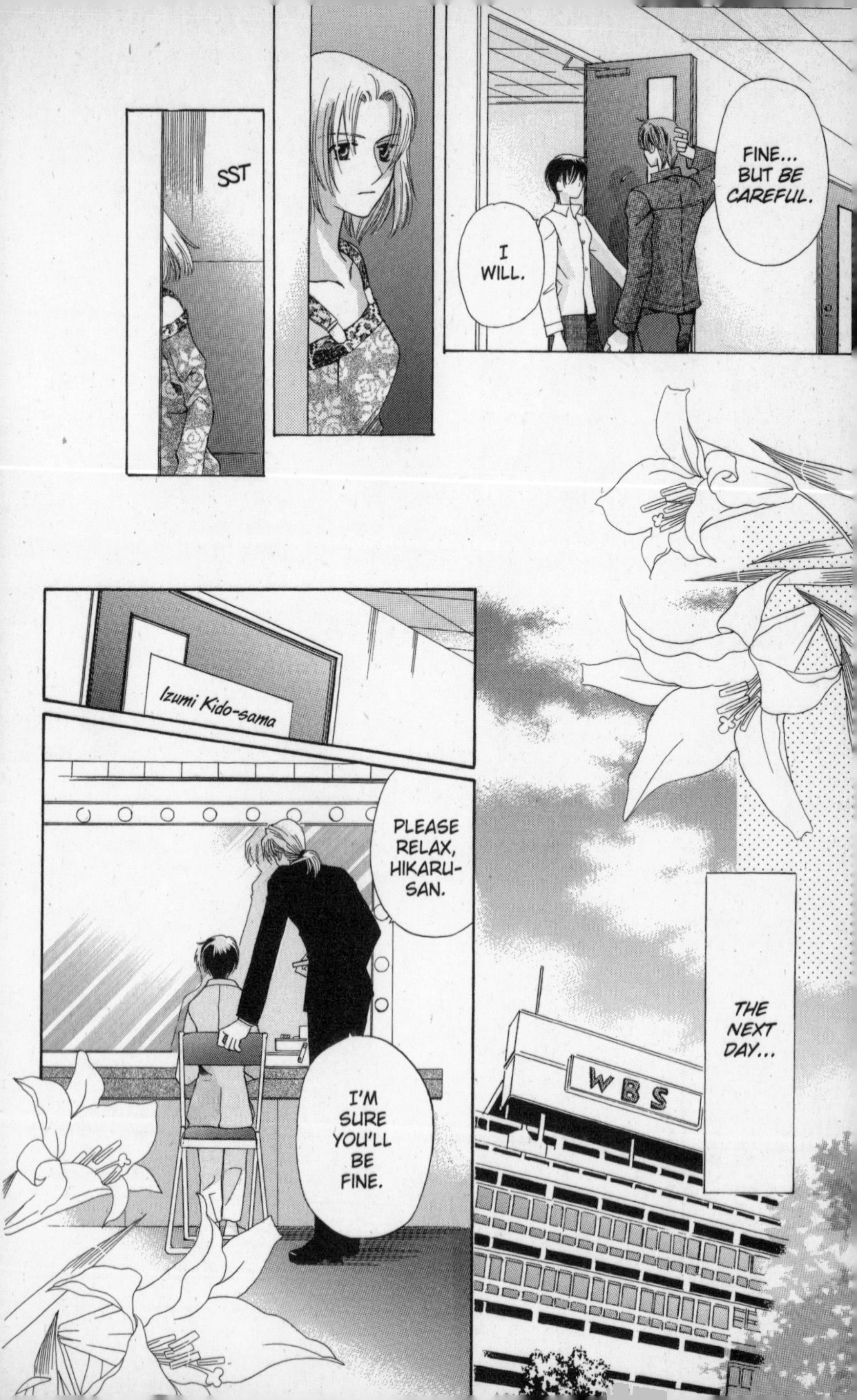
FINE... BUT BE CAREFUL.
I WILL.
SST
THE NEXT DAY...
WBS
Izumi Kido-sama
PLEASE RELAX, HIKARU-SAN.
I'M SURE YOU'LL BE FINE.

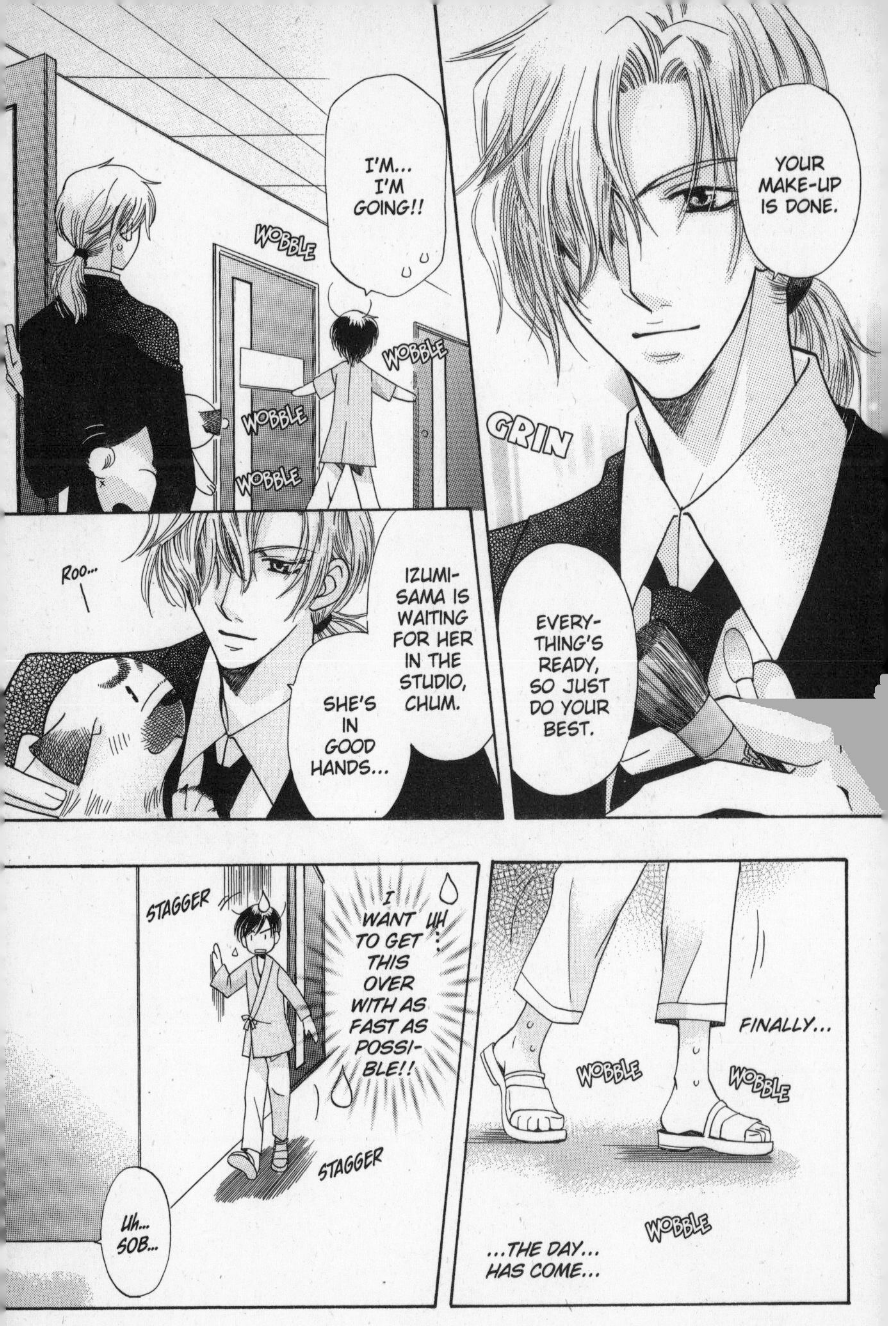
YOUR MAKE-UP IS DONE.
GRIN
EVERY-THING'S READY, SO JUST DO YOUR BEST.
I'M... I'M GOING!!
WOBBLE
WOBBLE
WOBBLE
WOBBLE
IZUMI-SAMA IS WAITING FOR HER IN THE STUDIO, CHUM.
SHE'S IN GOOD HANDS...
Roo...
FINALLY...
WOBBLE
WOBBLE
WOBBLE
...THE DAY... HAS COME...
UH...
I WANT TO GET THIS OVER WITH AS FAST AS POSSI-BLE!!
STAGGER
STAGGER
Uh... SOB...

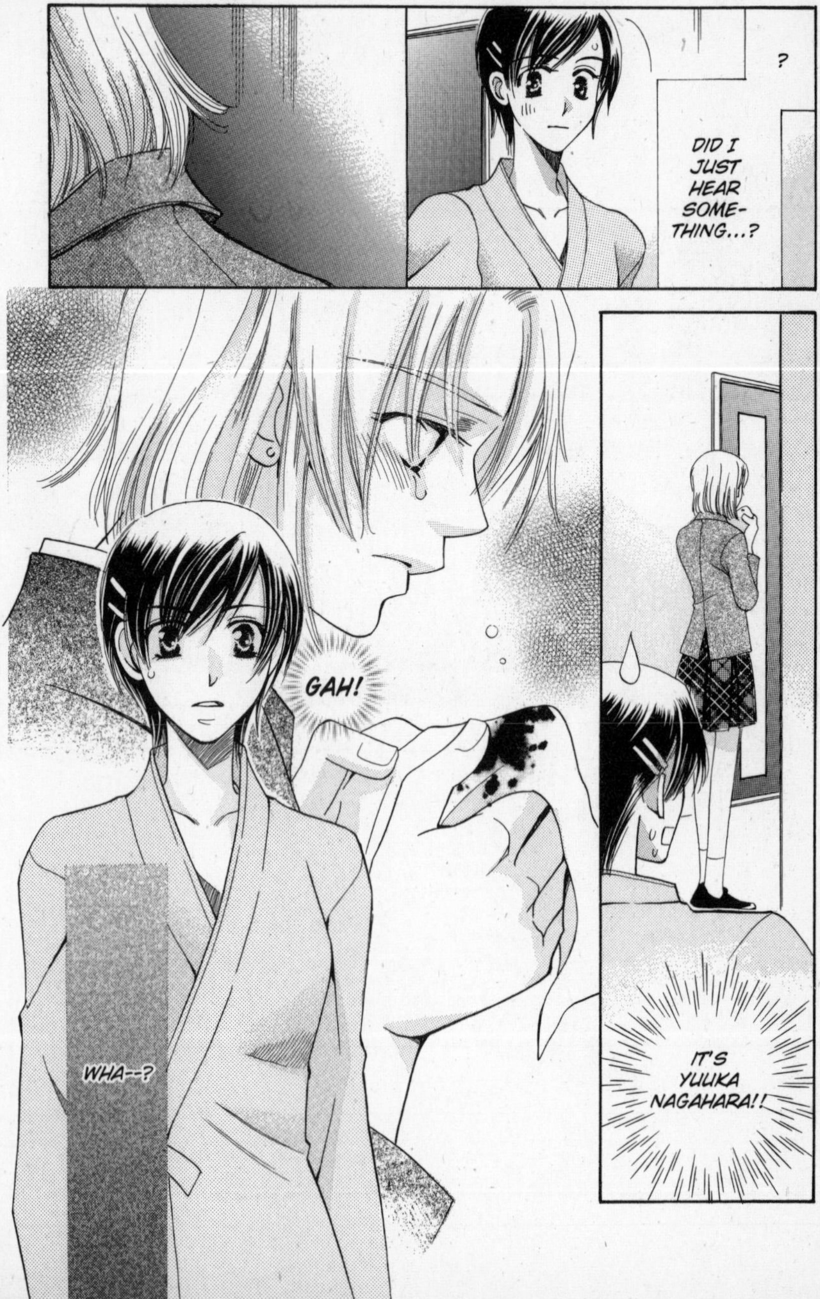
?
DID I JUST HEAR SOME-THING...?
IT'S YUUKA NAGAHARA!!
GAH!
WHA--?

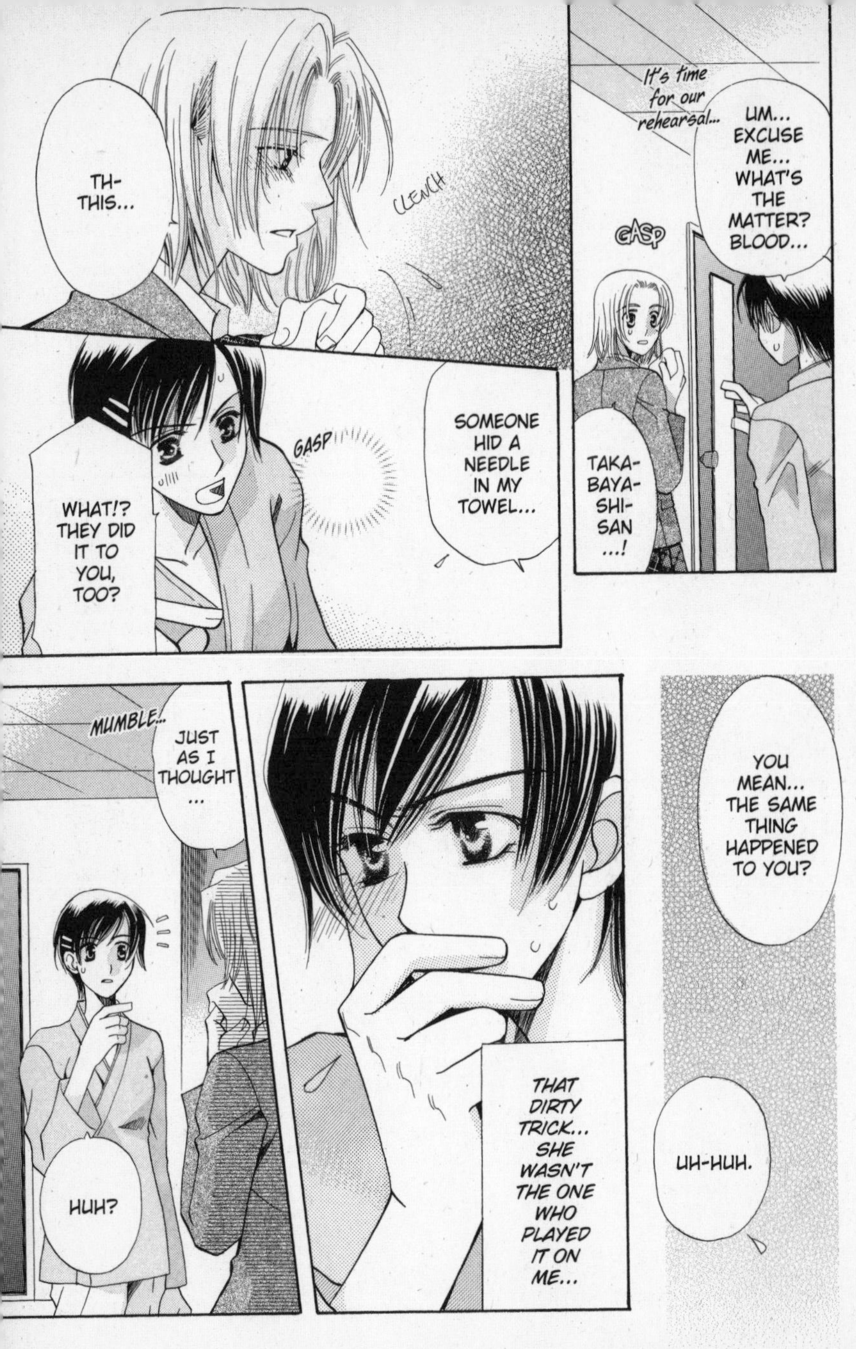
It's time for our rehearsal...
UM... EXCUSE ME... WHAT'S THE MATTER? BLOOD...
GASP
TAKA-BAYA-SHI-SAN ...!
TH- THIS...
CLENCH
SOMEONE HID A NEEDLE IN MY TOWEL...
GASP
WHAT!? THEY DID IT TO YOU, TOO?
YOU MEAN... THE SAME THING HAPPENED TO YOU?
UH-HUH.
THAT DIRTY TRICK... SHE WASN'T THE ONE WHO PLAYED IT ON ME...
MUMBLE...
JUST AS I THOUGHT ...
HUH?

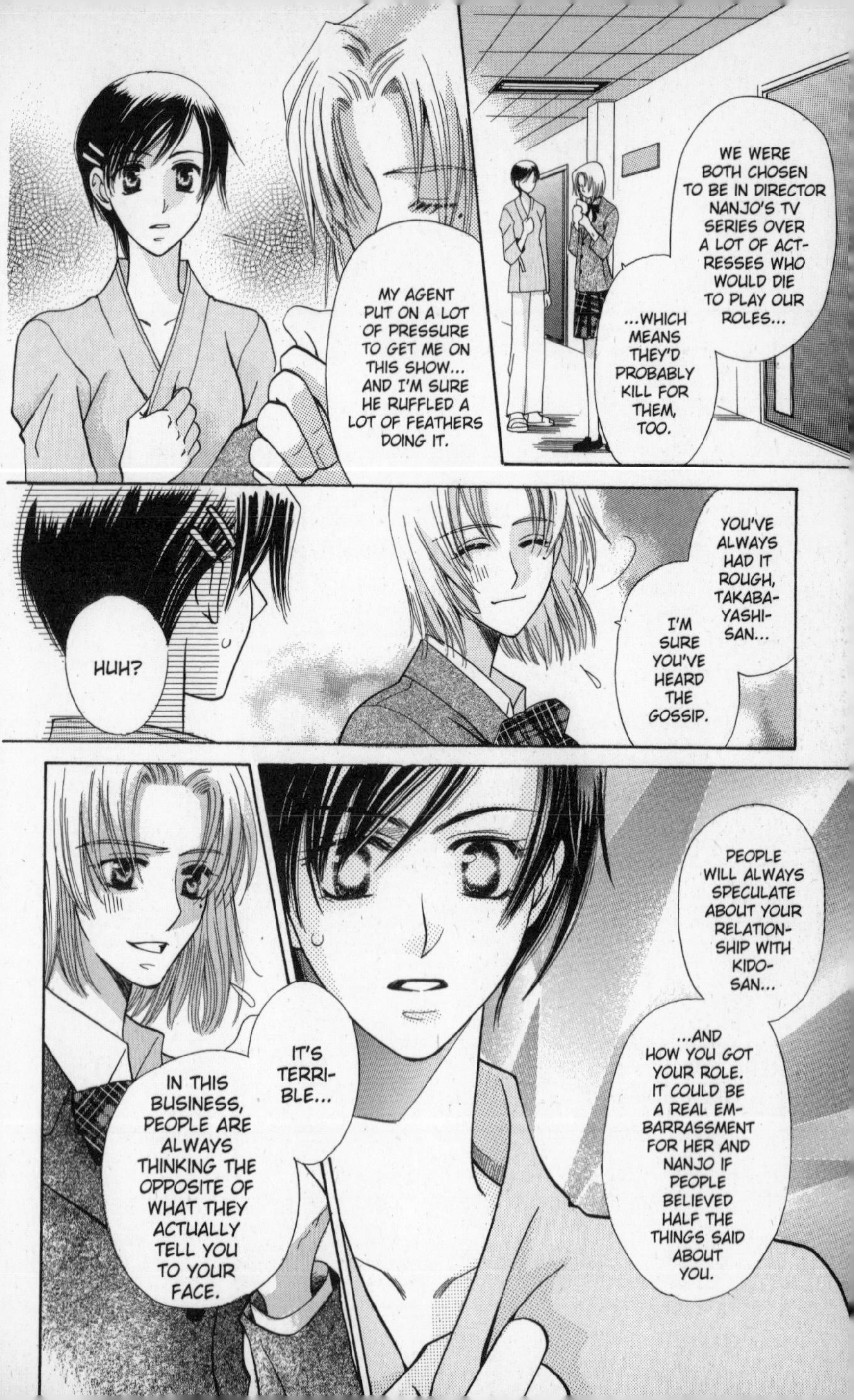
WE WERE BOTH CHOSEN TO BE IN DIRECTOR NANJO'S TV SERIES OVER A LOT OF ACT-RESSES WHO WOULD DIE TO PLAY OUR ROLES...
...WHICH MEANS THEY'D PROBABLY KILL FOR THEM, TOO.
MY AGENT PUT ON A LOT OF PRESSURE TO GET ME ON THIS SHOW... AND I'M SURE HE RUFFLED A LOT OF FEATHERS DOING IT.
YOU'VE ALWAYS HAD IT ROUGH, TAKABA-YASHI-SAN...
I'M SURE YOU'VE HEARD THE GOSSIP.
HUH?
PEOPLE WILL ALWAYS SPECULATE ABOUT YOUR RELATION-SHIP WITH KIDO-SAN...
...AND HOW YOU GOT YOUR ROLE. IT COULD BE A REAL EM-BARRASSMENT FOR HER AND NANJO IF PEOPLE BELIEVED HALF THE THINGS SAID ABOUT YOU.
IT'S TERRI-BLE...
IN THIS BUSINESS, PEOPLE ARE ALWAYS THINKING THE OPPOSITE OF WHAT THEY ACTUALLY TELL YOU TO YOUR FACE.

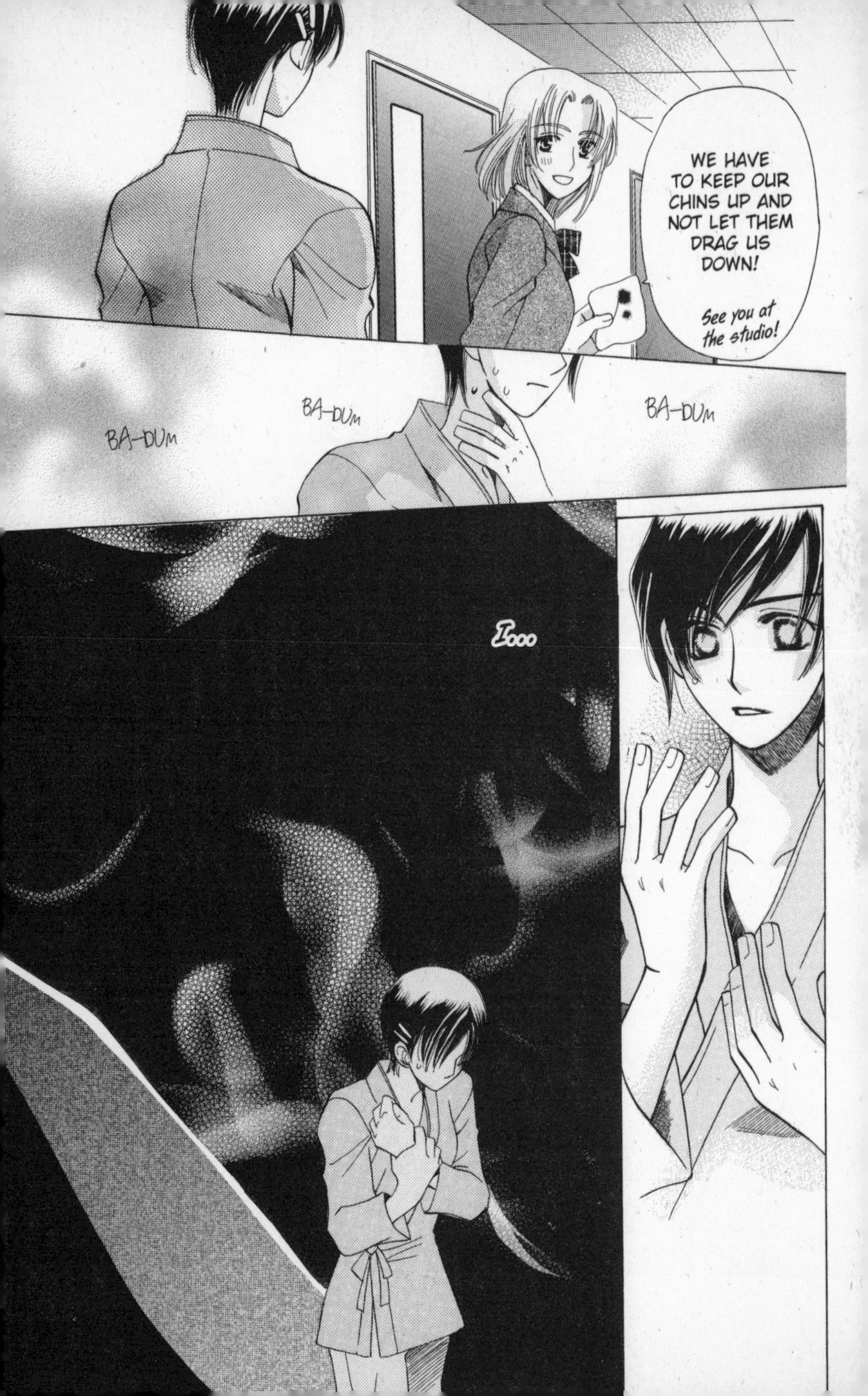

WE HAVE TO KEEP OUR CHINS UP AND NOT LET THEM DRAG US DOWN!
See you at the studio!
BA-DUM
BA-DUM
BA-DUM
Iooo

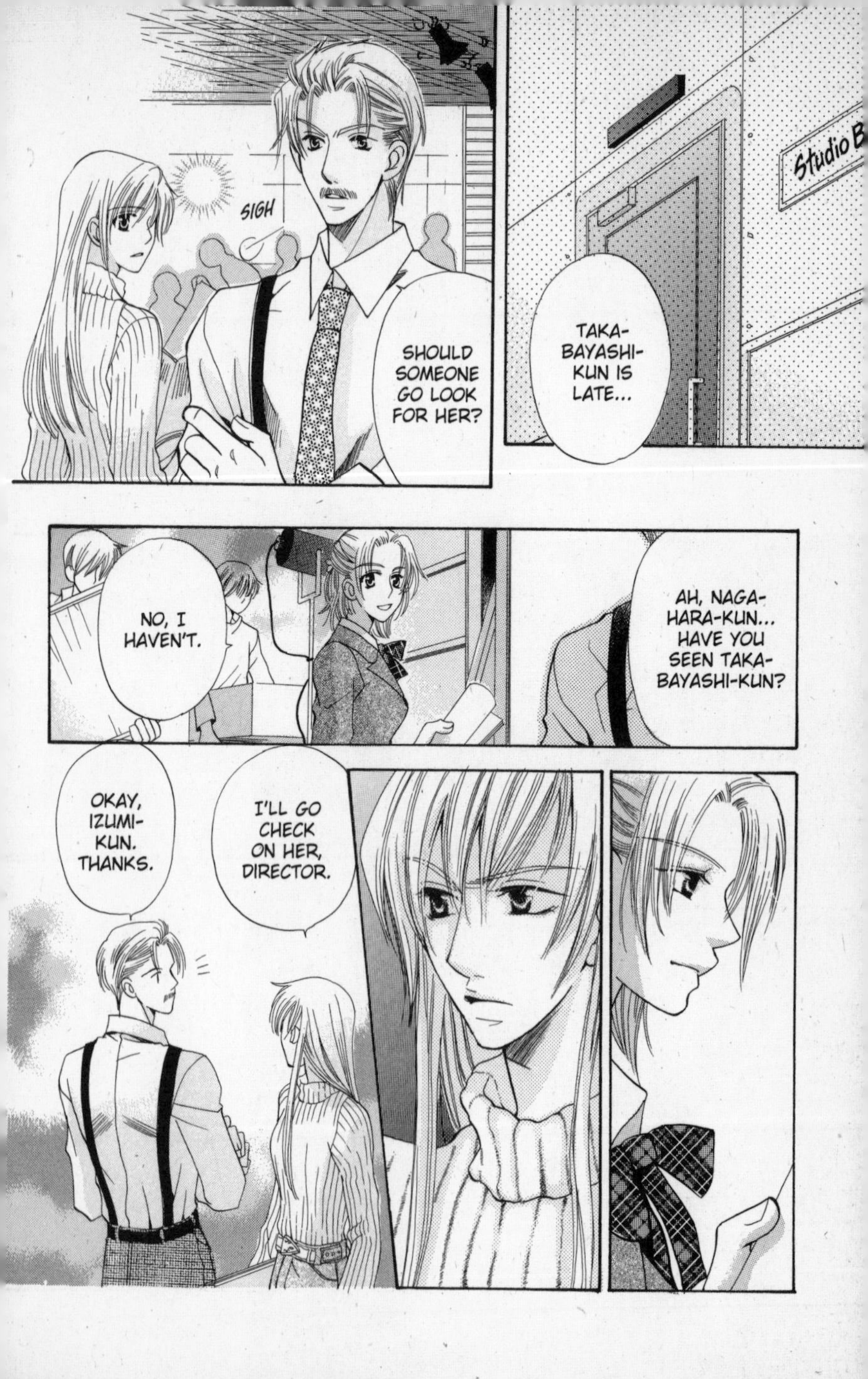
Studio B
TAKA-BAYASHI-KUN IS LATE...
SIGH
SHOULD SOMEONE GO LOOK FOR HER?
AH, NAGA-HARA-KUN... HAVE YOU SEEN TAKA-BAYASHI-KUN?
NO, I HAVEN'T.
I'LL GO CHECK ON HER, DIRECTOR.
OKAY, IZUMI-KUN. THANKS.

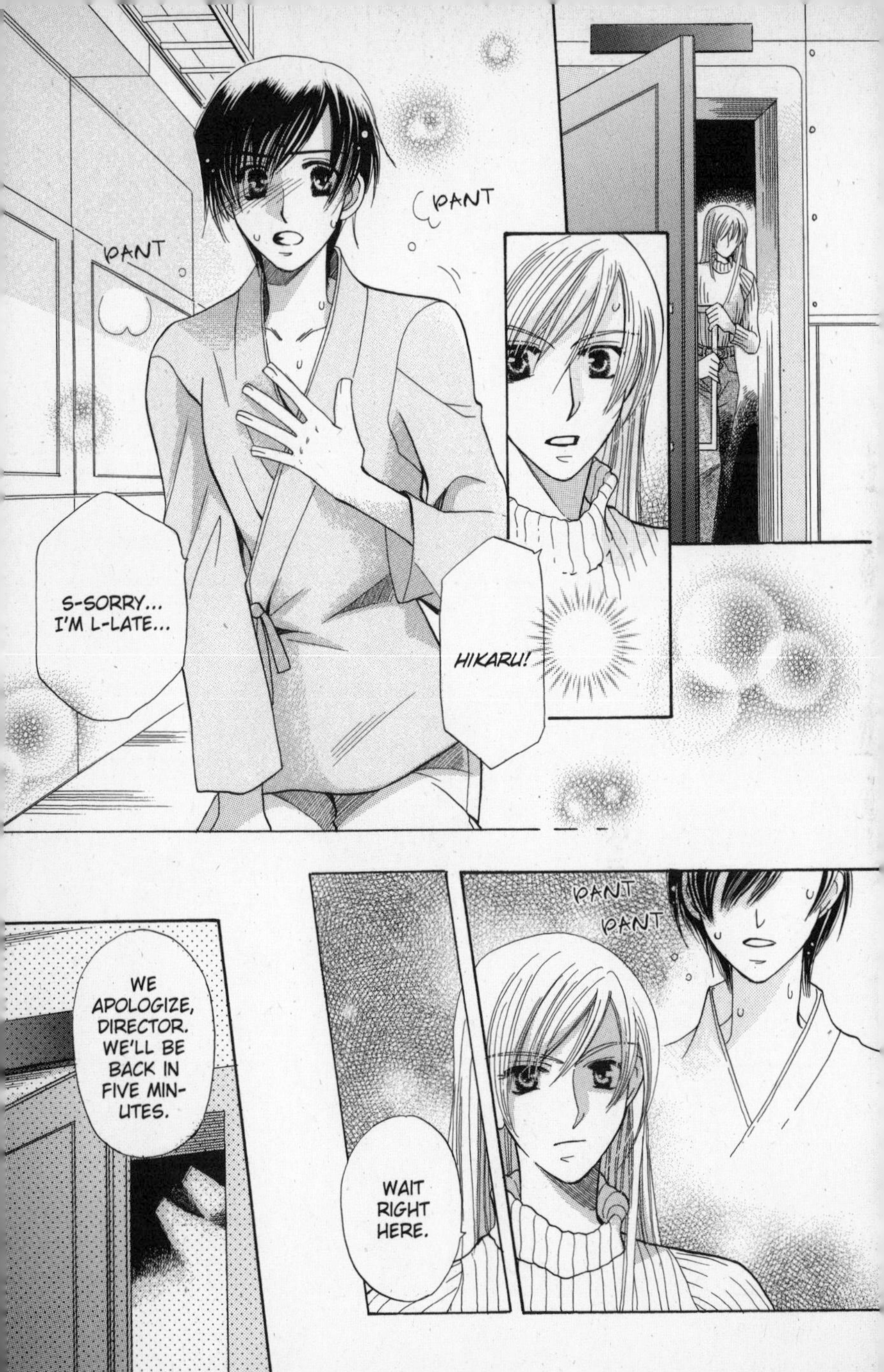
HIKARU!
PANT
PANT
S-SORRY... I'M L-LATE...
PANT
PANT
WAIT RIGHT HERE.
WE APOLOGIZE, DIRECTOR. WE'LL BE BACK IN FIVE MIN-UTES.

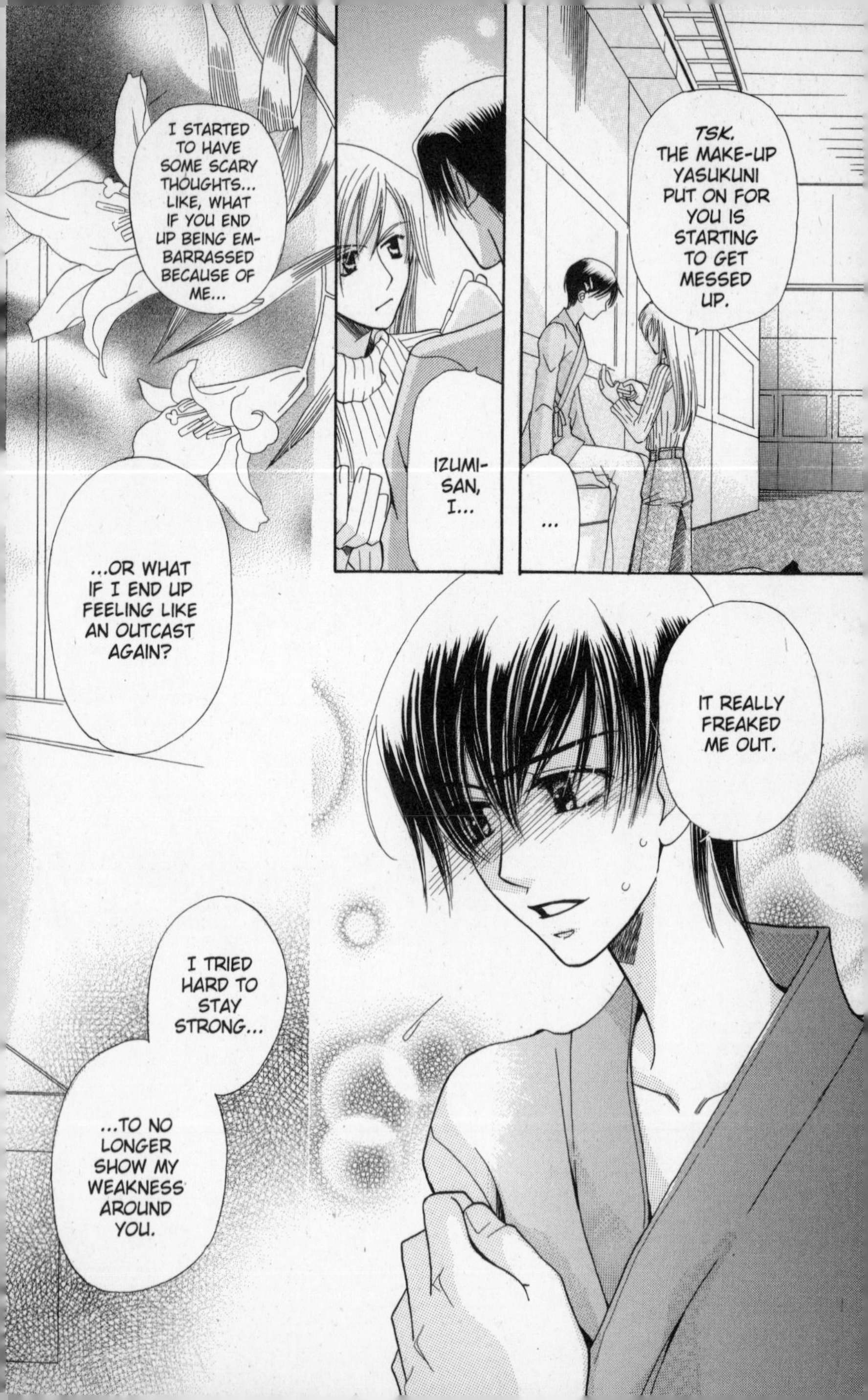
TSK. THE MAKE-UP YASUKUNI PUT ON FOR YOU IS STARTING TO GET MESSED UP.
...
IZUMI-SAN, I...
I STARTED TO HAVE SOME SCARY THOUGHTS... LIKE, WHAT IF YOU END UP BEING EM-BARRASSED BECAUSE OF ME...
...OR WHAT IF I END UP FEELING LIKE AN OUTCAST AGAIN?
IT REALLY FREAKED ME OUT.
I TRIED HARD TO STAY STRONG...
...TO NO LONGER SHOW MY WEAKNESS AROUND YOU.

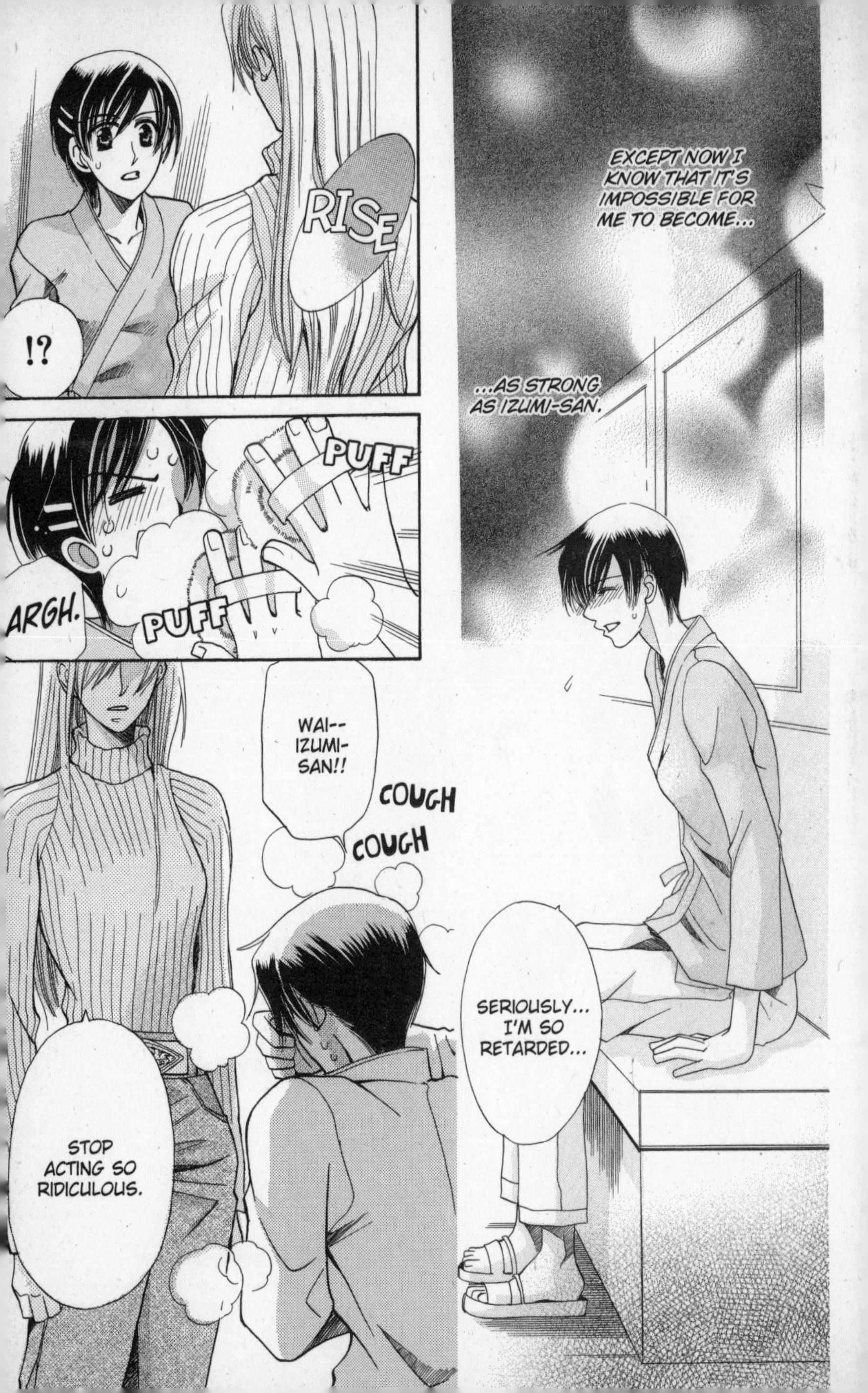
EXCEPT NOW I KNOW THAT IT'S IMPOSSIBLE FOR ME TO BECOME...
...AS STRONG AS IZUMI-SAN.
SERIOUSLY... I'M SO RETARDED...
RISE
!?
PUFF
PUFF
ARGH.
WAI-- IZUMI-SAN!!
COUGH
COUGH
STOP ACTING SO RIDICULOUS.

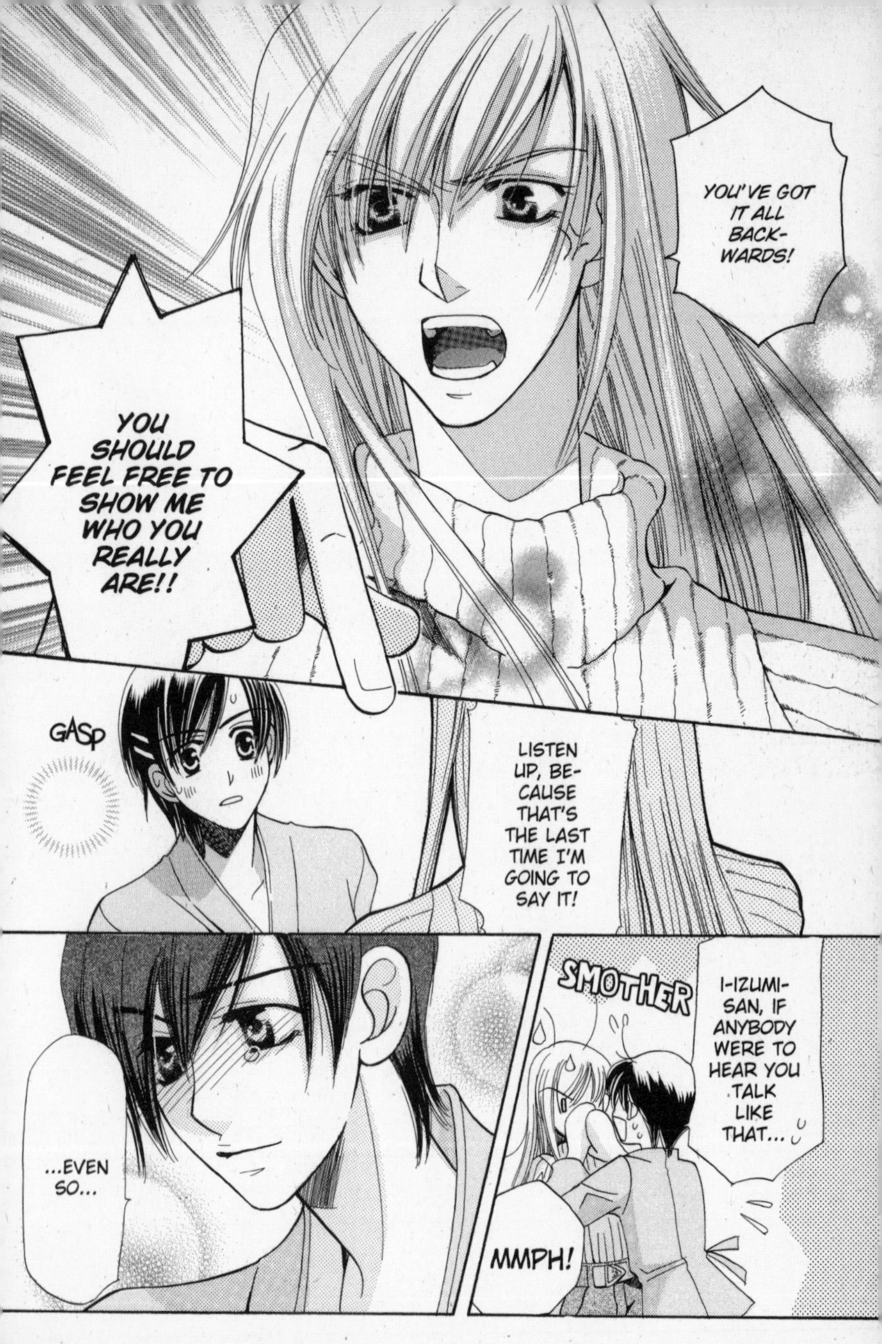
YOU'VE GOT IT ALL BACK-WARDS!
YOU SHOULD FEEL FREE TO SHOW ME WHO YOU REALLY ARE!!
LISTEN UP, BE-CAUSE THAT'S THE LAST TIME I'M GOING TO SAY IT!
GASP
SMOTHER
I-IZUMI-SAN, IF ANYBODY WERE TO HEAR YOU TALK LIKE THAT...
MMPH!
...EVEN SO...

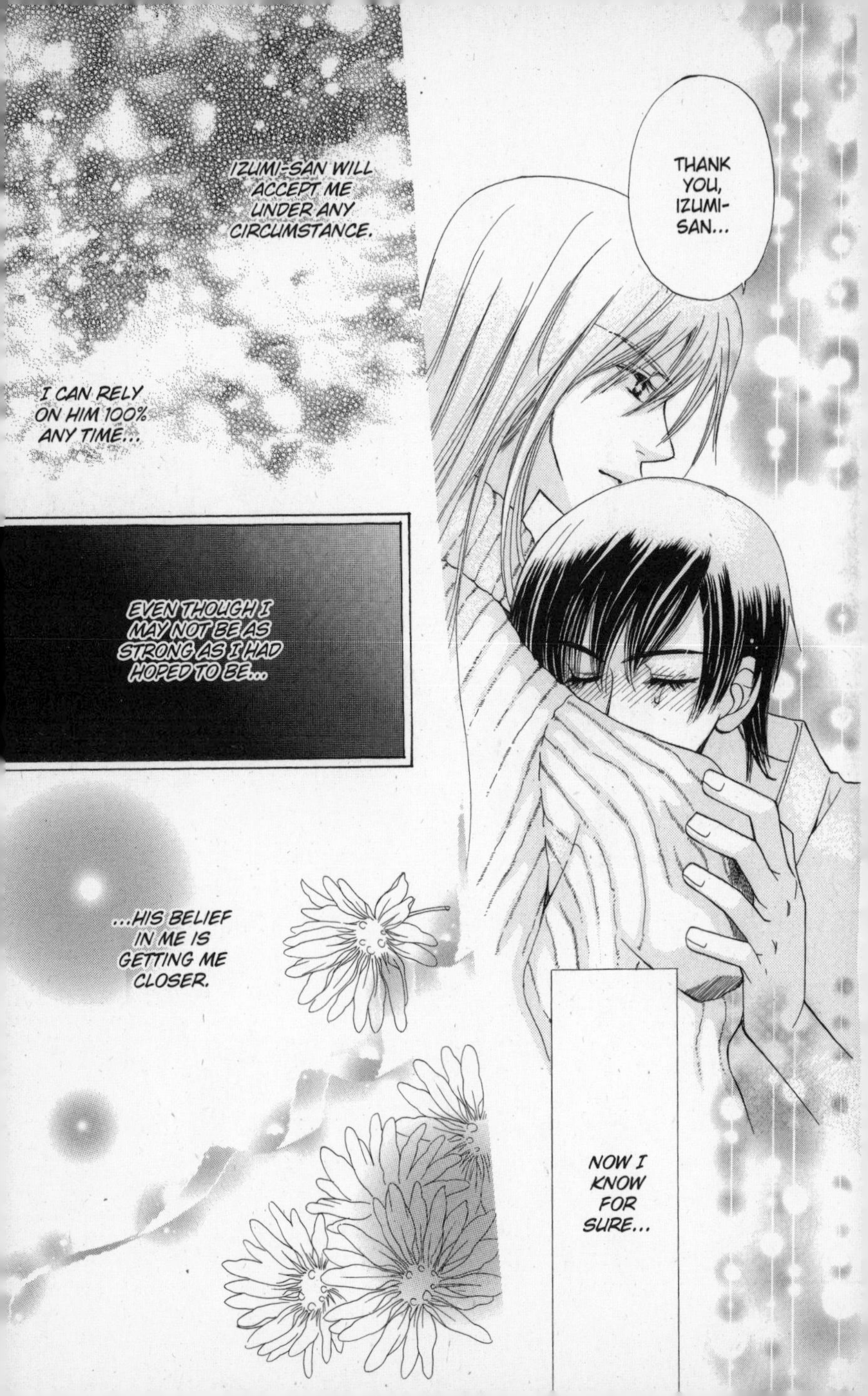
THANK YOU, IZUMI-SAN...
NOW I KNOW FOR SURE...
IZUMI-SAN WILL ACCEPT ME UNDER ANY CIRCUMSTANCE.
I CAN RELY ON HIM 100% ANY TIME...
EVEN THOUGH I MAY NOT BE AS STRONG AS I HAD HOPED TO BE...
...HIS BELIEF IN ME IS GETTING ME CLOSER.

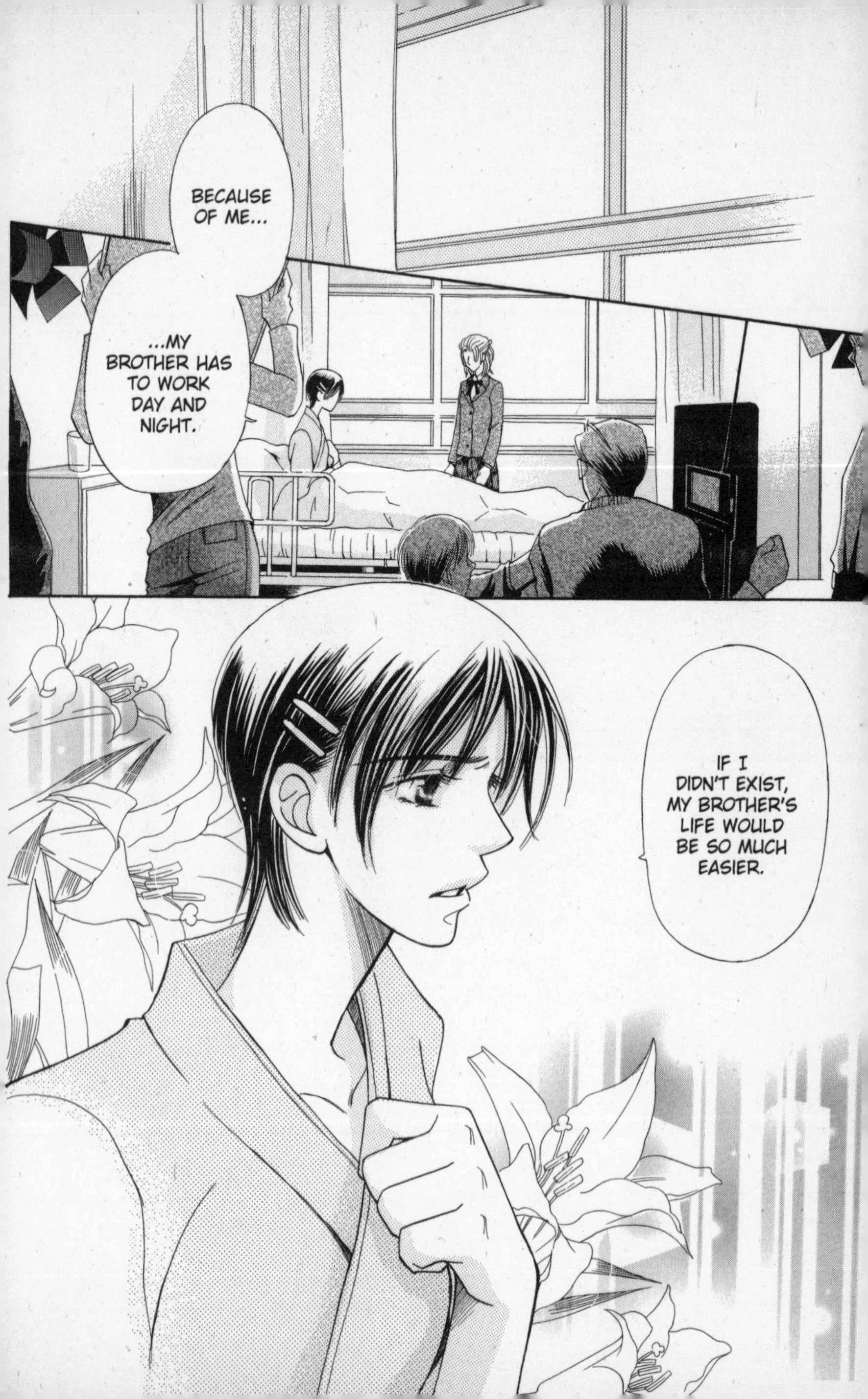

BECAUSE OF ME...
...MY BROTHER HAS TO WORK DAY AND NIGHT.
IF I DIDN'T EXIST, MY BROTHER'S LIFE WOULD BE SO MUCH EASIER.

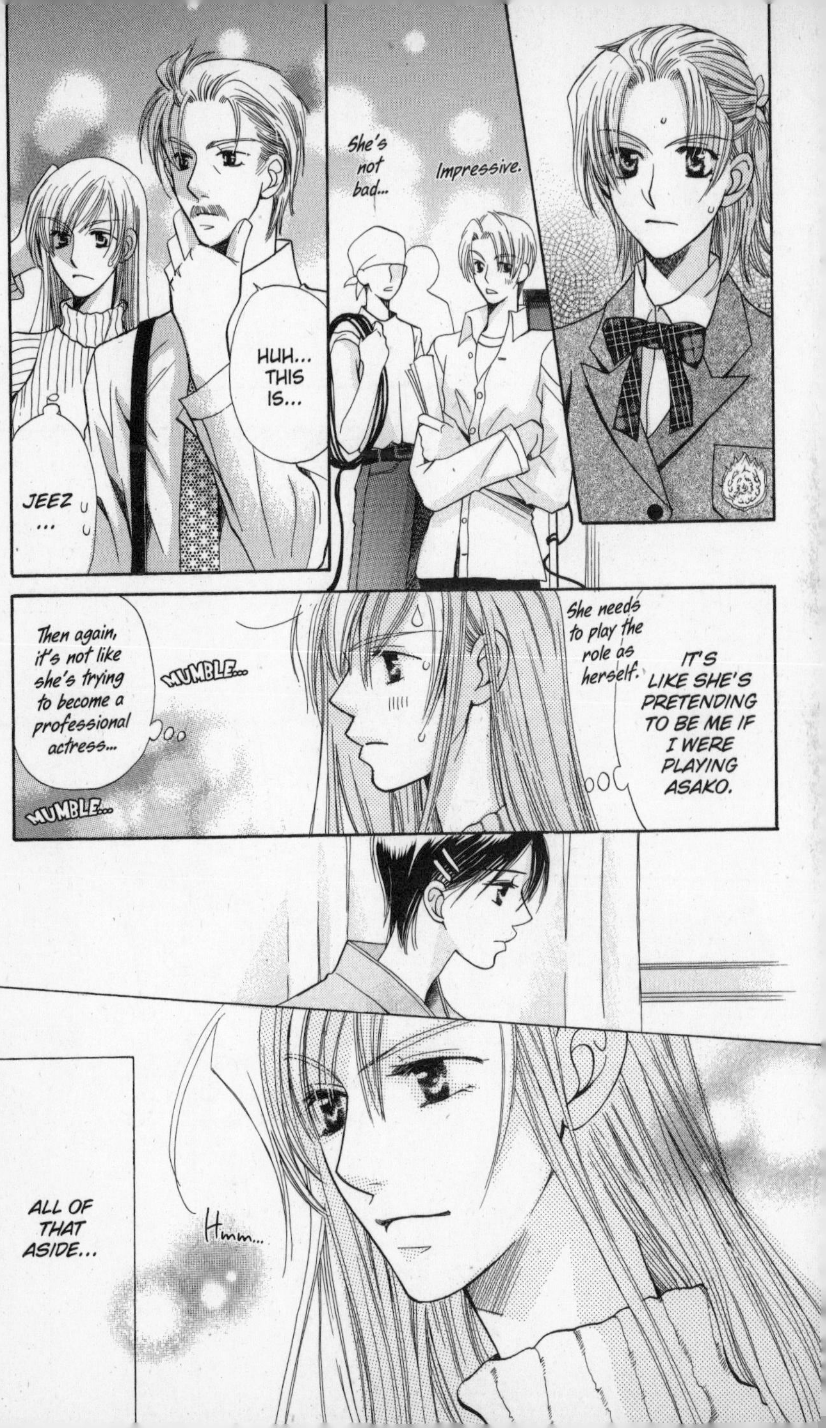
Impressive.
She's not bad...
HUH... THIS IS...
JEEZ...
IT'S LIKE SHE'S PRETENDING TO BE ME IF I WERE PLAYING ASAKO.
She needs to play the role as herself.
MUMBLE...
Then again, it's not like she's trying to become a professional actress...
MUMBLE...
Hmm...
ALL OF THAT ASIDE...

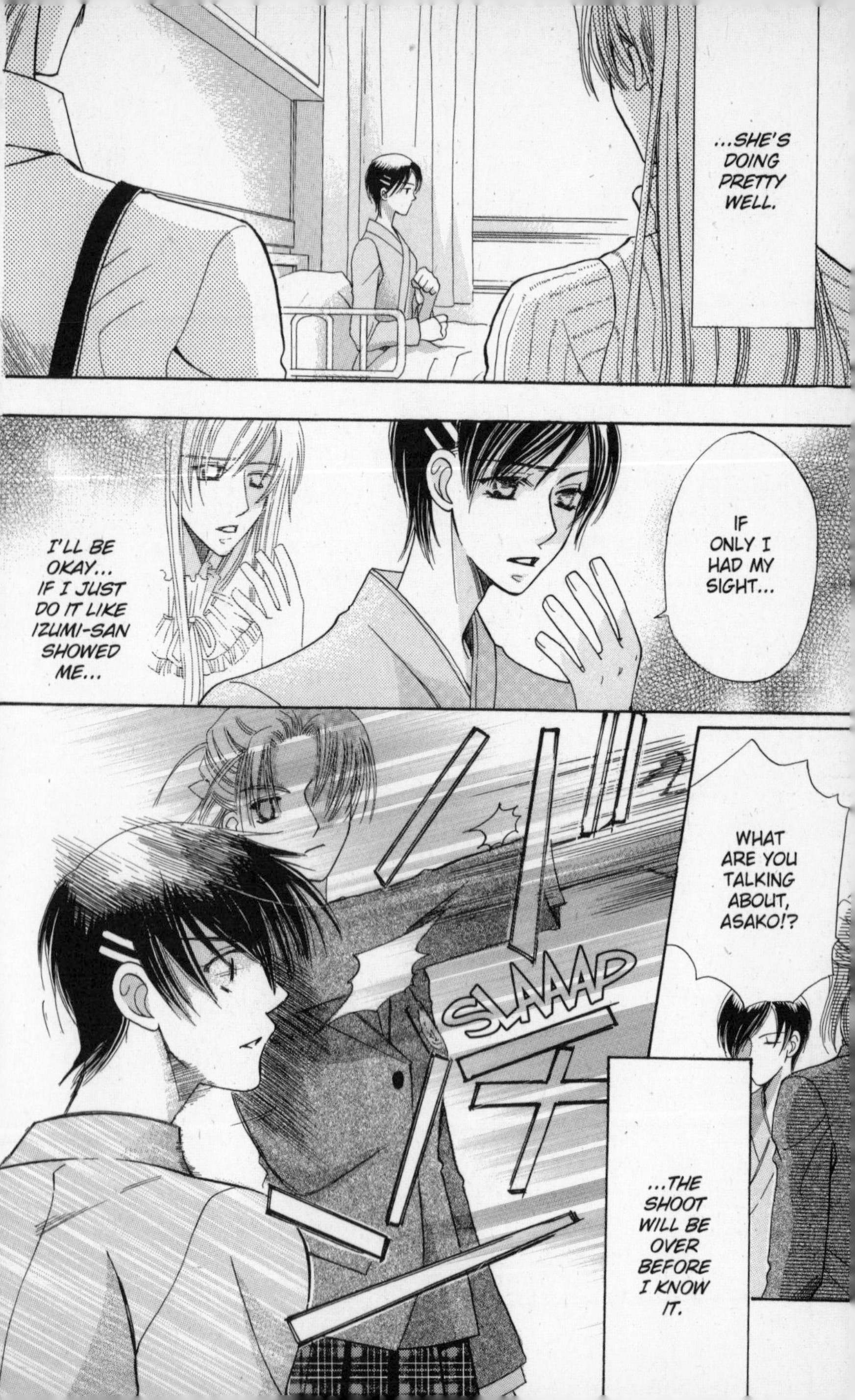
...SHE'S DOING PRETTY WELL.
IF ONLY I HAD MY SIGHT...
I'LL BE OKAY... IF I JUST DO IT LIKE IZUMI-SAN SHOWED ME...
WHAT ARE YOU TALKING ABOUT, ASAKO!?
SLAAAP
...THE SHOOT WILL BE OVER BEFORE I KNOW IT.

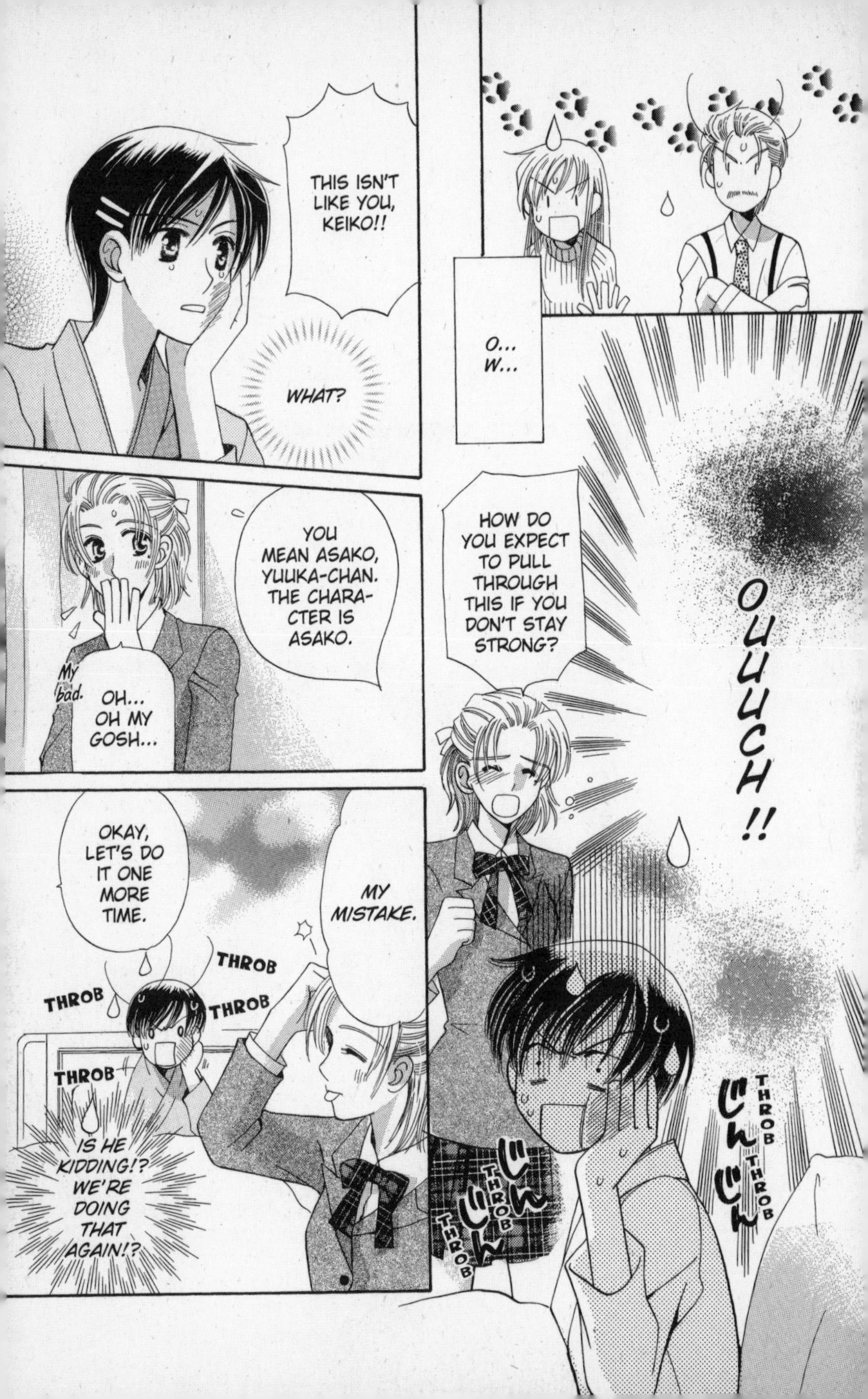

HOW DO YOU EXPECT TO PULL THROUGH THIS IF YOU DON'T STAY STRONG?
OUUUCH!!
THROB THROB
THROB THROB
O... W...
THIS ISN'T LIKE YOU, KEIKO!!
WHAT?
YOU MEAN ASAKO, YUUKA-CHAN. THE CHARACTER IS ASAKO.
My bad.
OH... OH MY GOSH...
MY MISTAKE.
OKAY, LET'S DO IT ONE MORE TIME.
THROB
THROB
THROB
THROB
IS HE KIDDING!? WE'RE DOING THAT AGAIN!?

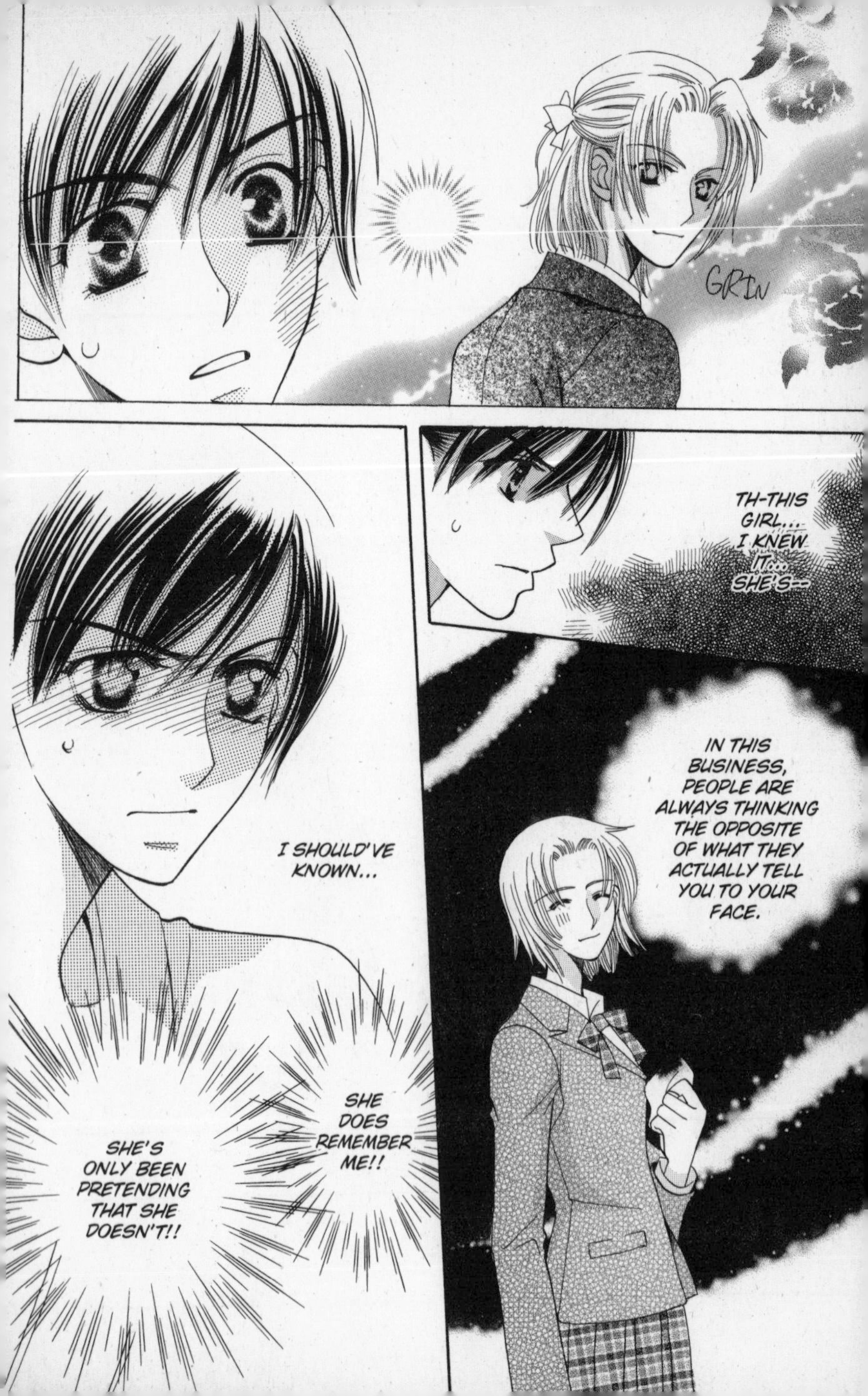
GRIN
TH-THIS GIRL... I KNEW IT... SHE'S--
IN THIS BUSINESS, PEOPLE ARE ALWAYS THINKING THE OPPOSITE OF WHAT THEY ACTUALLY TELL YOU TO YOUR FACE.
I SHOULD'VE KNOWN...
SHE DOES REMEMBER ME!!
SHE'S ONLY BEEN PRETENDING THAT SHE DOESN'T!!

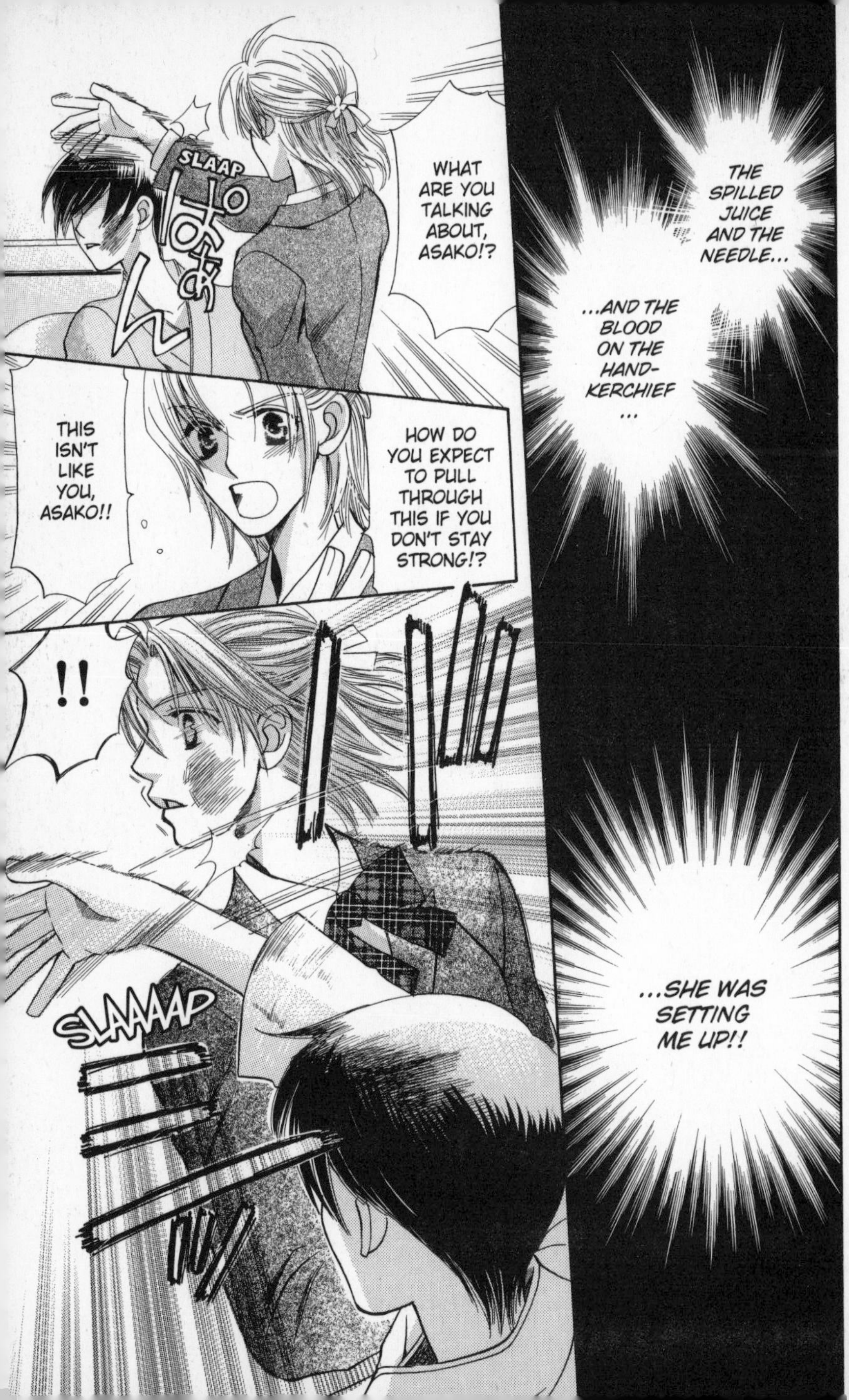
THE SPILLED JUICE AND THE NEEDLE...
...AND THE BLOOD ON THE HAND-KERCHIEF...
...SHE WAS SETTING ME UP!!
WHAT ARE YOU TALKING ABOUT, ASAKO!?
SLAAP
ぱぁん
HOW DO YOU EXPECT TO PULL THROUGH THIS IF YOU DON'T STAY STRONG!?
THIS ISN'T LIKE YOU, ASAKO!!
!!
SLAAAAP

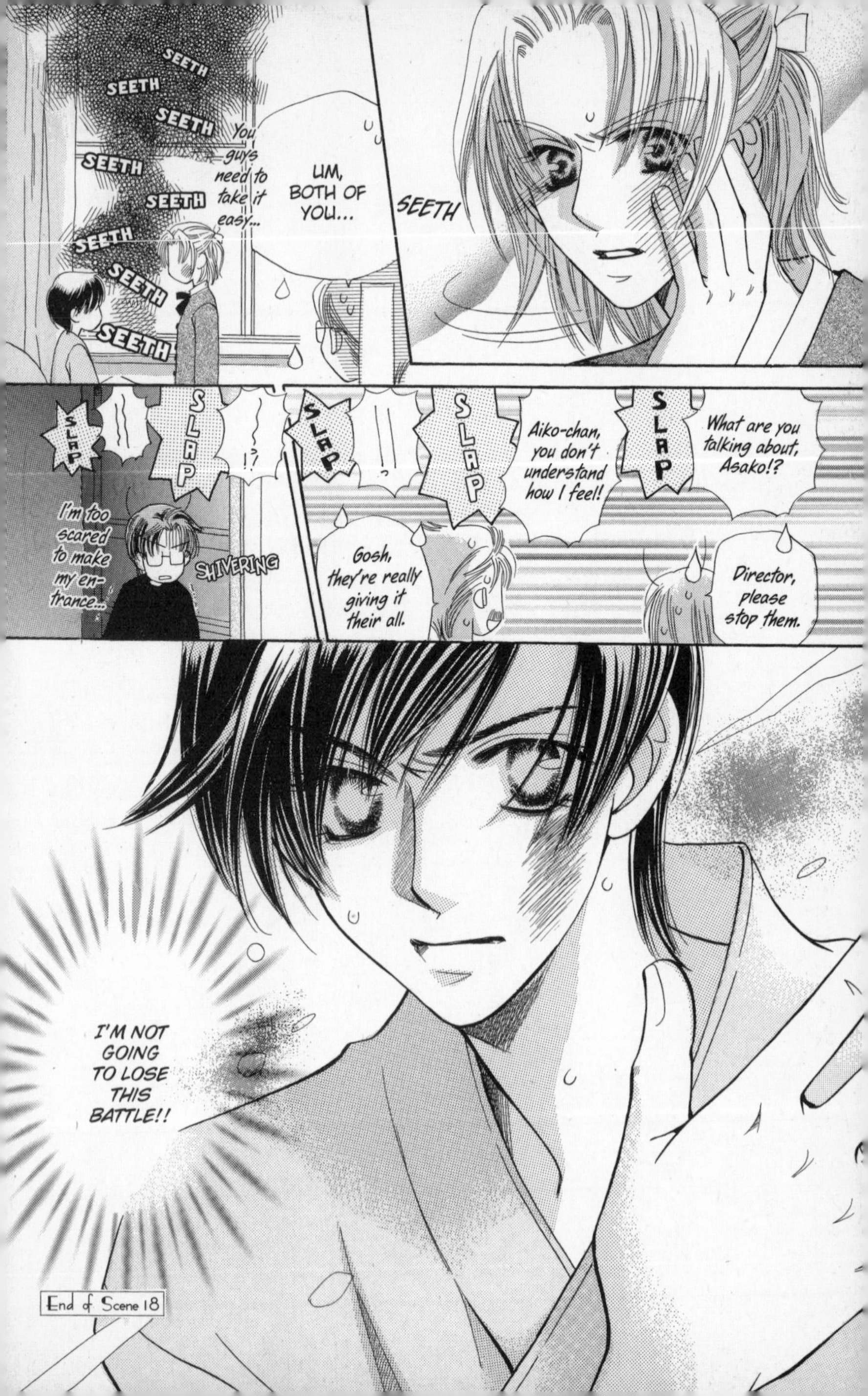
SEETH
UM, BOTH OF YOU...
You guys need to take it easy...
SEETH
SEETH
SEETH
SEETH
SEETH
SEETH
SEETH
SEETH
SLAP
What are you talking about, Asako!?
SLAP
Aiko-chan, you don't understand how I feel!
SLAP
Director, please stop them.
Gosh, they're really giving it their all.
!?
SLAP
SLAP
I'm too scared to make my entrance...
SHIVERING
I'M NOT GOING TO LOSE THIS BATTLE!!
End of Scene 18

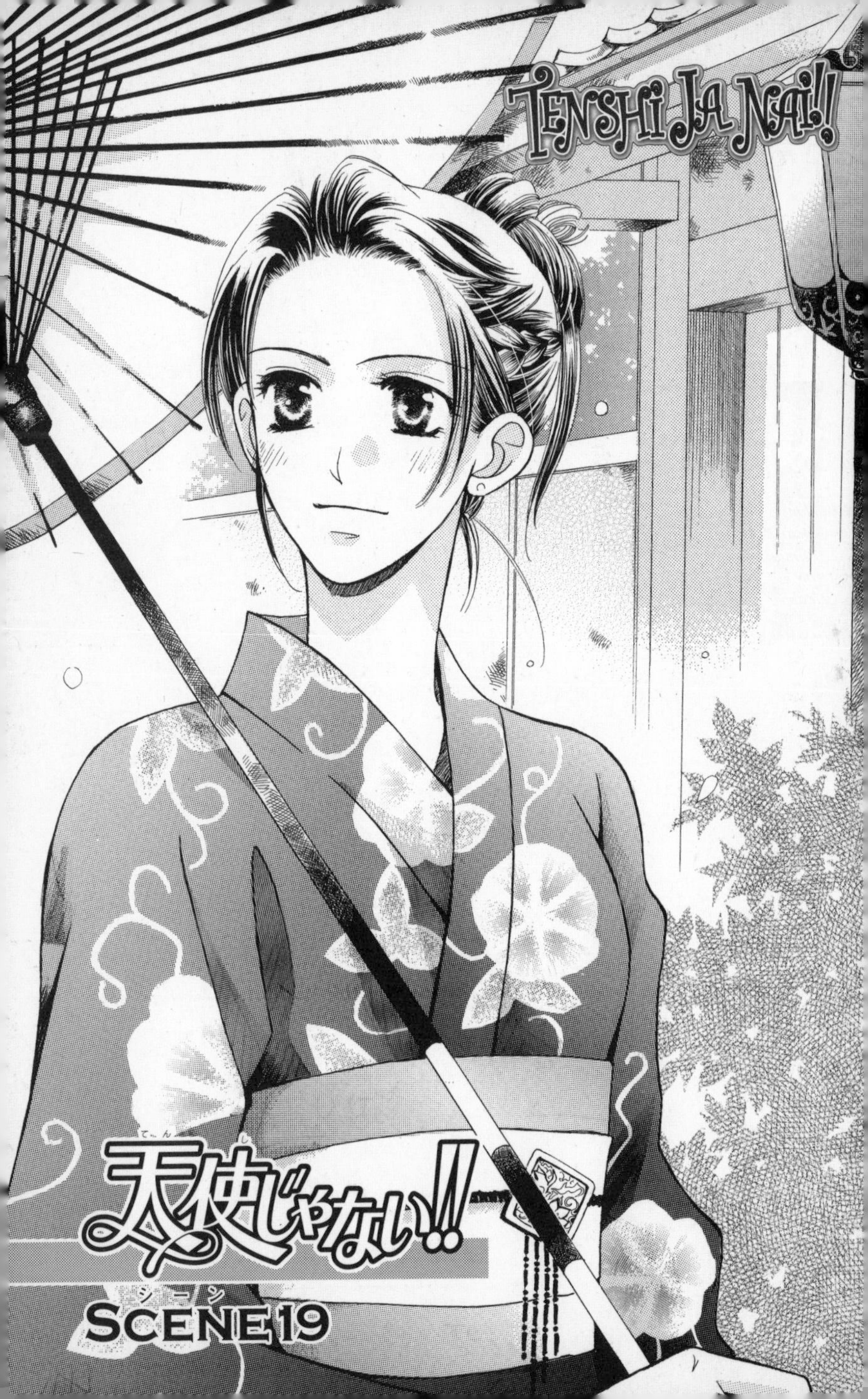
TENSHI JA NAI!!
天使じゃない!!
SCENE 19

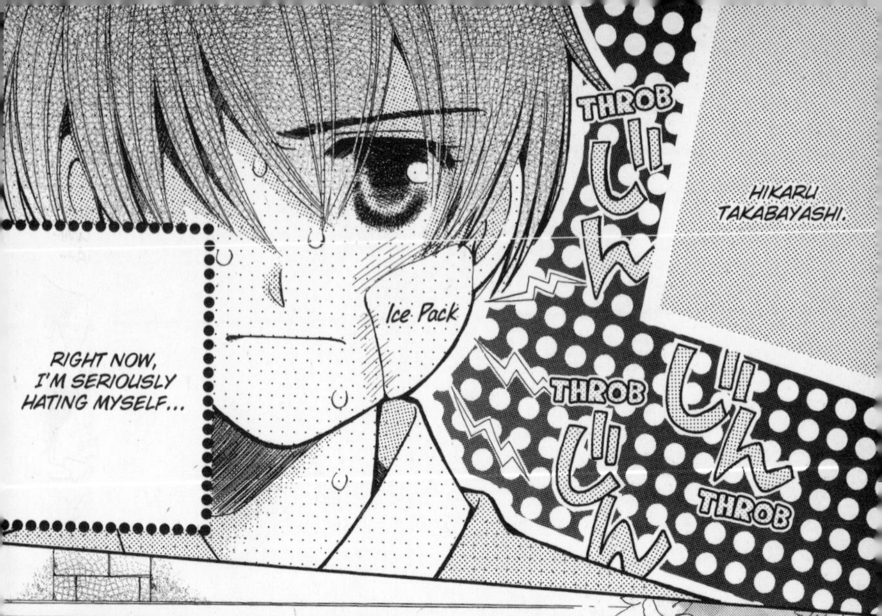
HIKARU TAKABAYASHI.
THROB
じん
THROB
じん
じん
THROB
Ice Pack
RIGHT NOW, I'M SERIOUSLY HATING MYSELF...
I TOLD YOU TO BEAT HER AT HER GAME...
SLUG
SLUG
SLUG
...BUT I DIDN'T TELL YOU TO GET INTO A SLAP FIGHT!

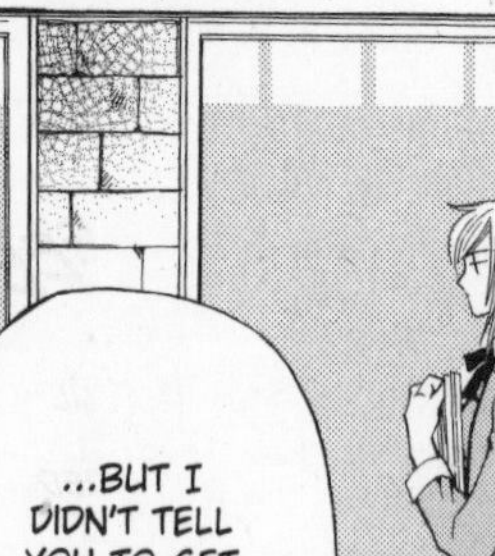

Sumikko (8 years old), Female
Born on June 10.
Dog type (naturally): Pug.
She's Hikaru's oasis. She sees Izumi as a rival. And she's in love with Yasukuni...

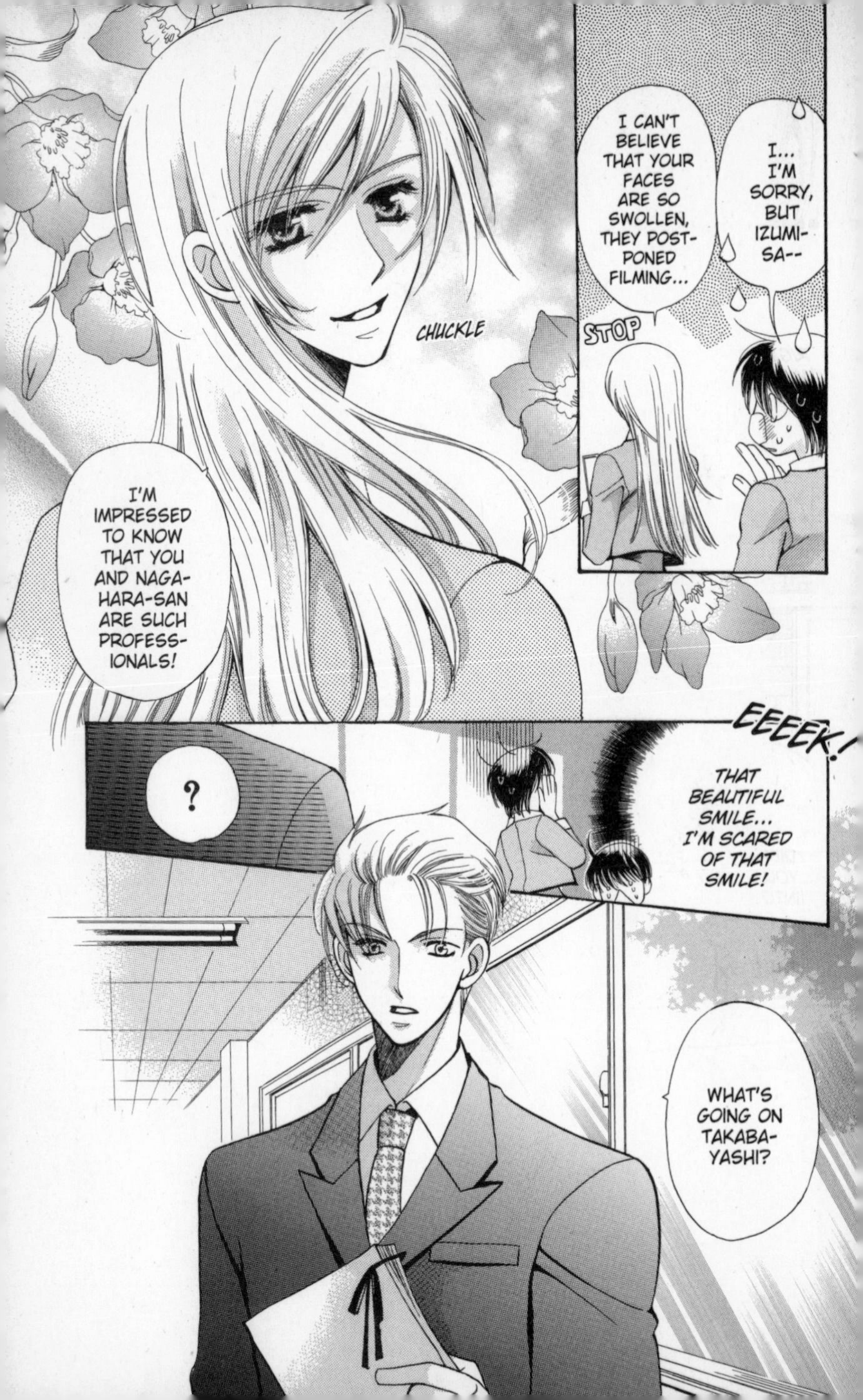
I... I'M SORRY, BUT IZUMI-SA--
I CAN'T BELIEVE THAT YOUR FACES ARE SO SWOLLEN, THEY POST-PONED FILMING...
STOP
CHUCKLE
I'M IMPRESSED TO KNOW THAT YOU AND NAGA-HARA-SAN ARE SUCH PROFESS-IONALS!
EEEEK!
THAT BEAUTIFUL SMILE... I'M SCARED OF THAT SMILE!
?
WHAT'S GOING ON TAKABA-YASHI?

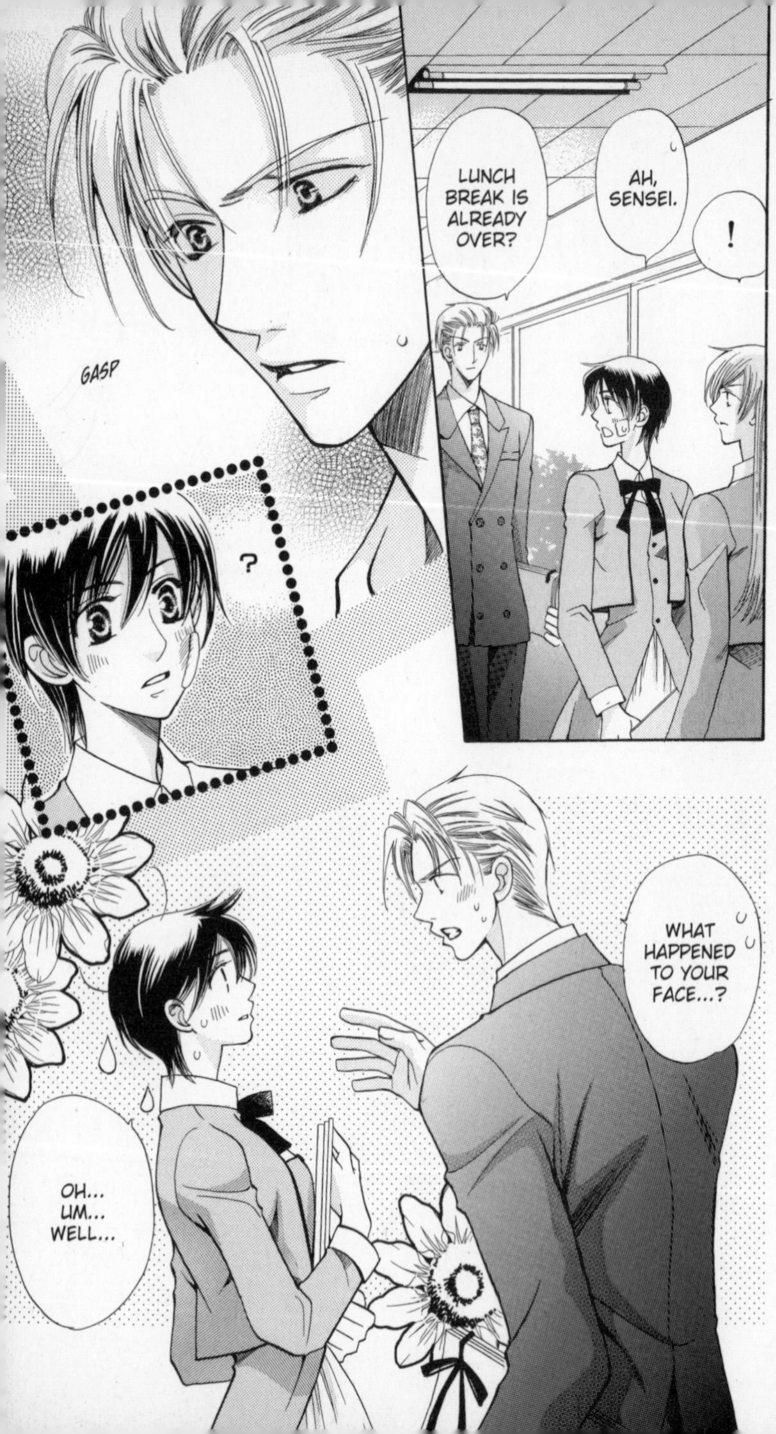
!
AH, SENSEI.
LUNCH BREAK IS ALREADY OVER?
GASP
?
WHAT HAPPENED TO YOUR FACE...?
OH... UM... WELL...

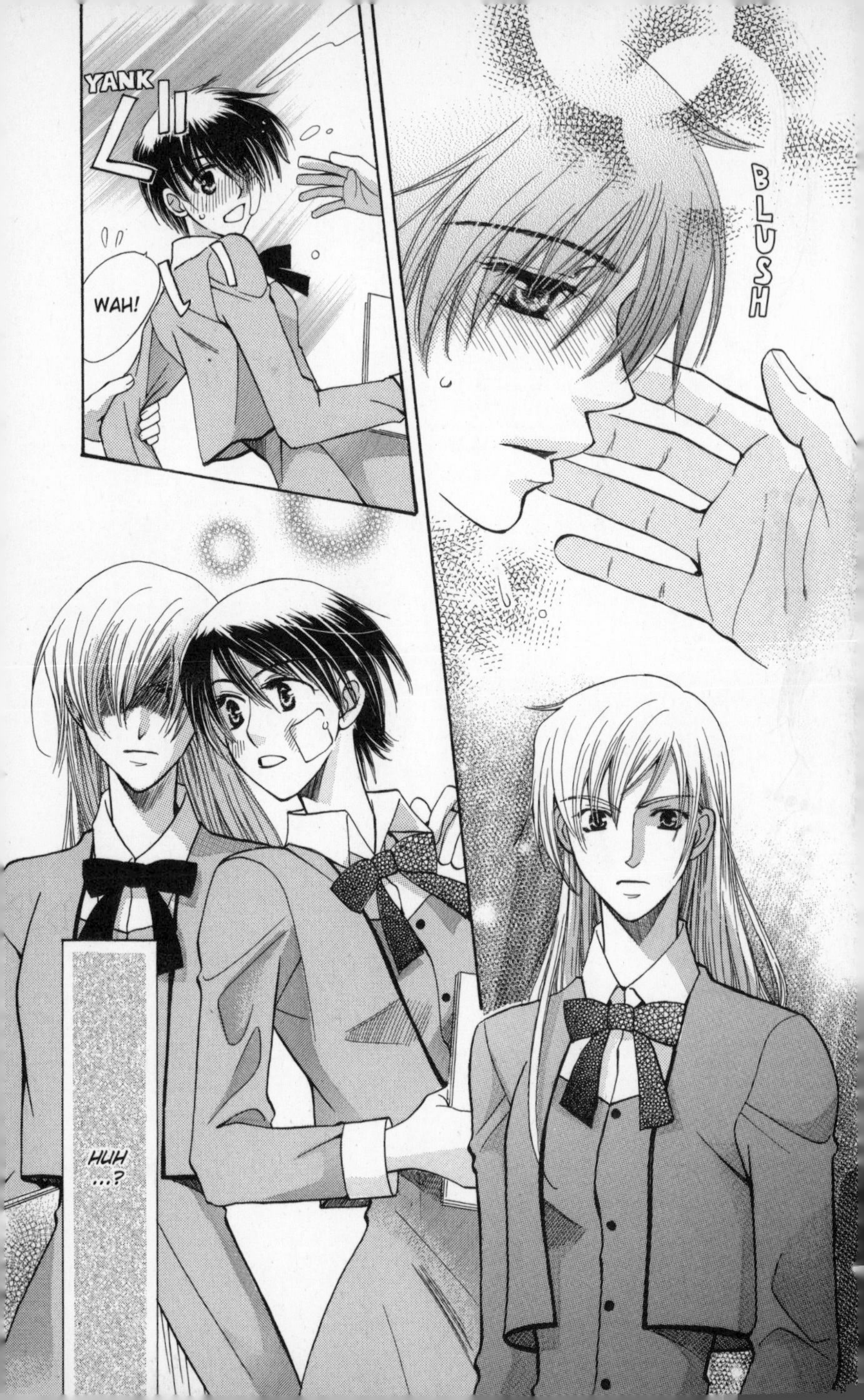
BLUSH
YANK
WAH!
HUH ...?

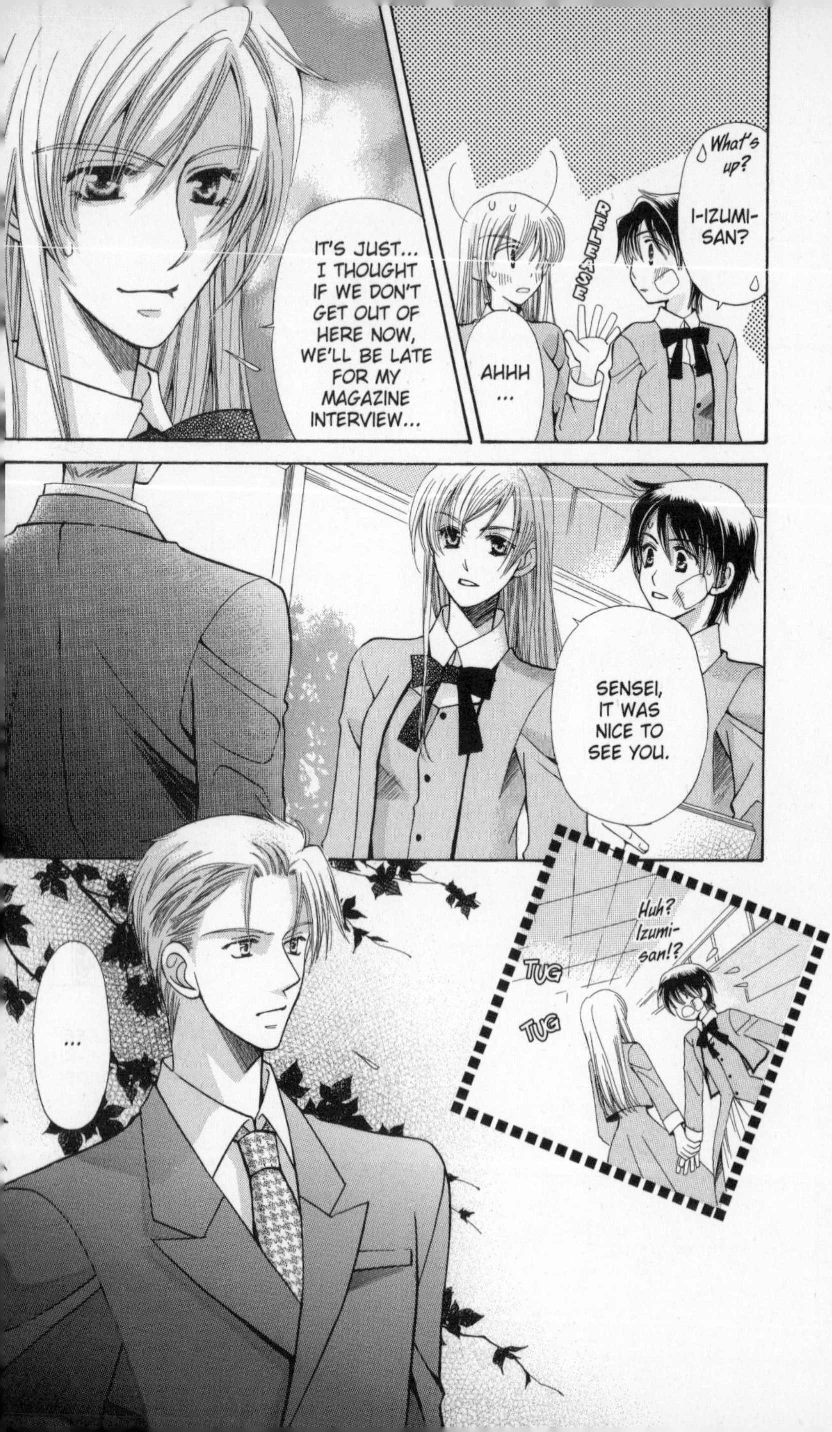
What's up?
I-IZUMI-SAN?
RELEASE
AHHH ...
IT'S JUST... I THOUGHT IF WE DON'T GET OUT OF HERE NOW, WE'LL BE LATE FOR MY MAGAZINE INTERVIEW...
SENSEI, IT WAS NICE TO SEE YOU.
Huh? Izumi-san!?
TUG
TUG
...

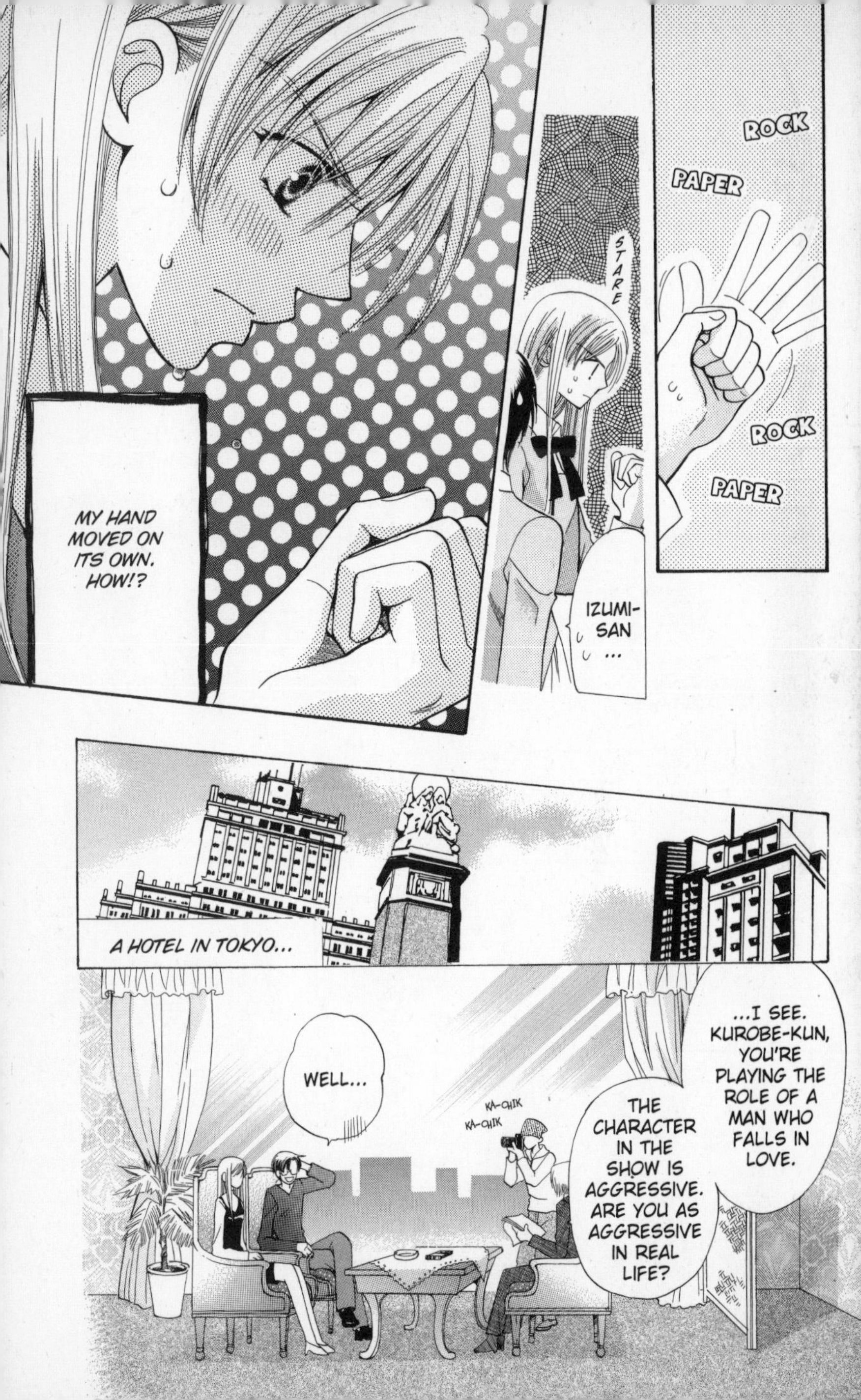
ROCK
PAPER
ROCK
PAPER
STARE
IZUMI-SAN...
MY HAND MOVED ON ITS OWN. HOW!?
A HOTEL IN TOKYO...
...I SEE. KUROBE-KUN, YOU'RE PLAYING THE ROLE OF A MAN WHO FALLS IN LOVE.
THE CHARACTER IN THE SHOW IS AGGRESSIVE. ARE YOU AS AGGRESSIVE IN REAL LIFE?
KA-CHIK
KA-CHIK
WELL...

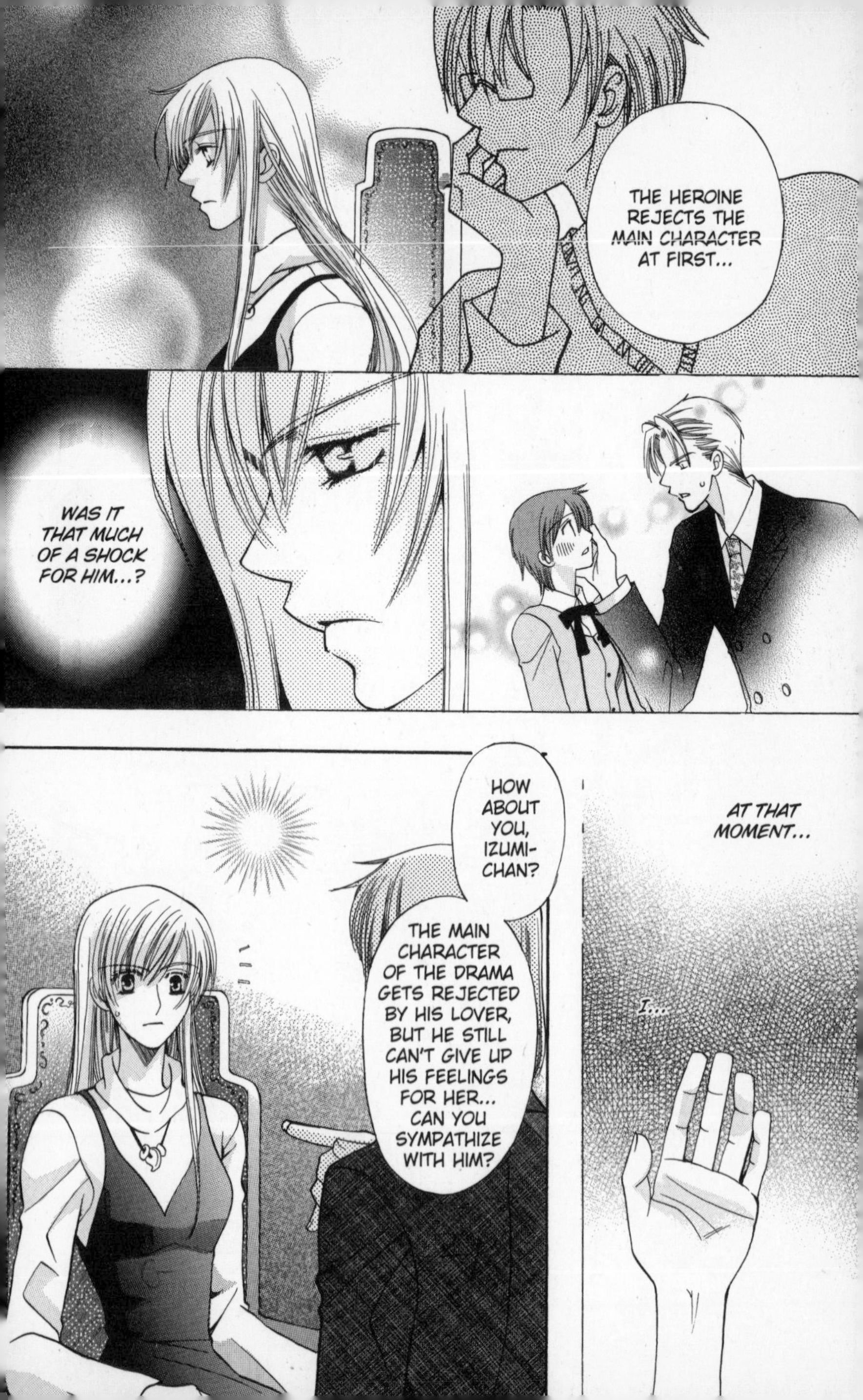
THE HEROINE REJECTS THE MAIN CHARACTER AT FIRST...
WAS IT THAT MUCH OF A SHOCK FOR HIM...?
AT THAT MOMENT...
I...
HOW ABOUT YOU, IZUMI-CHAN?
THE MAIN CHARACTER OF THE DRAMA GETS REJECTED BY HIS LOVER, BUT HE STILL CAN'T GIVE UP HIS FEELINGS FOR HER... CAN YOU SYMPATHIZE WITH HIM?

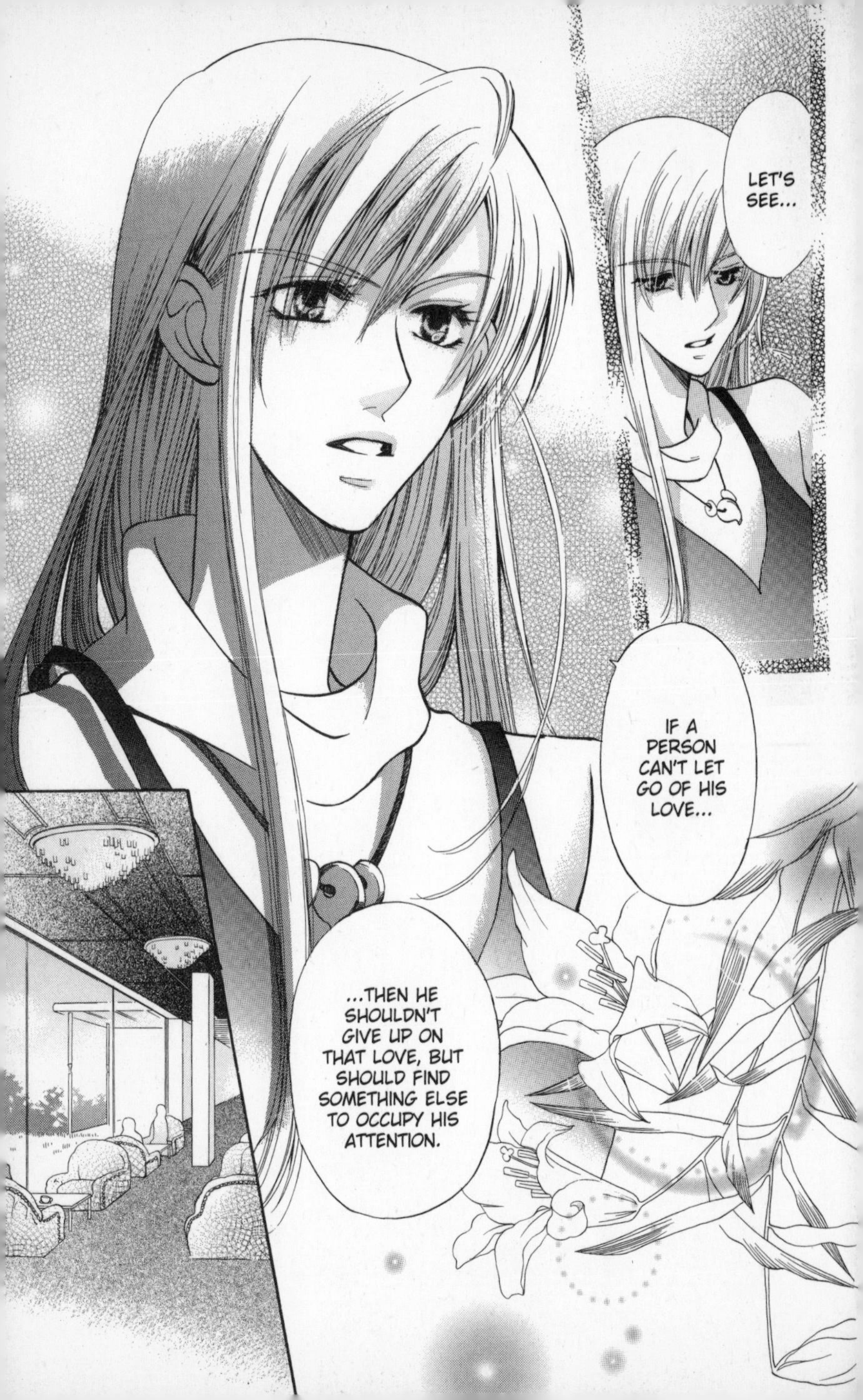
LET'S SEE...
IF A PERSON CAN'T LET GO OF HIS LOVE...
...THEN HE SHOULDN'T GIVE UP ON THAT LOVE, BUT SHOULD FIND SOMETHING ELSE TO OCCUPY HIS ATTENTION.

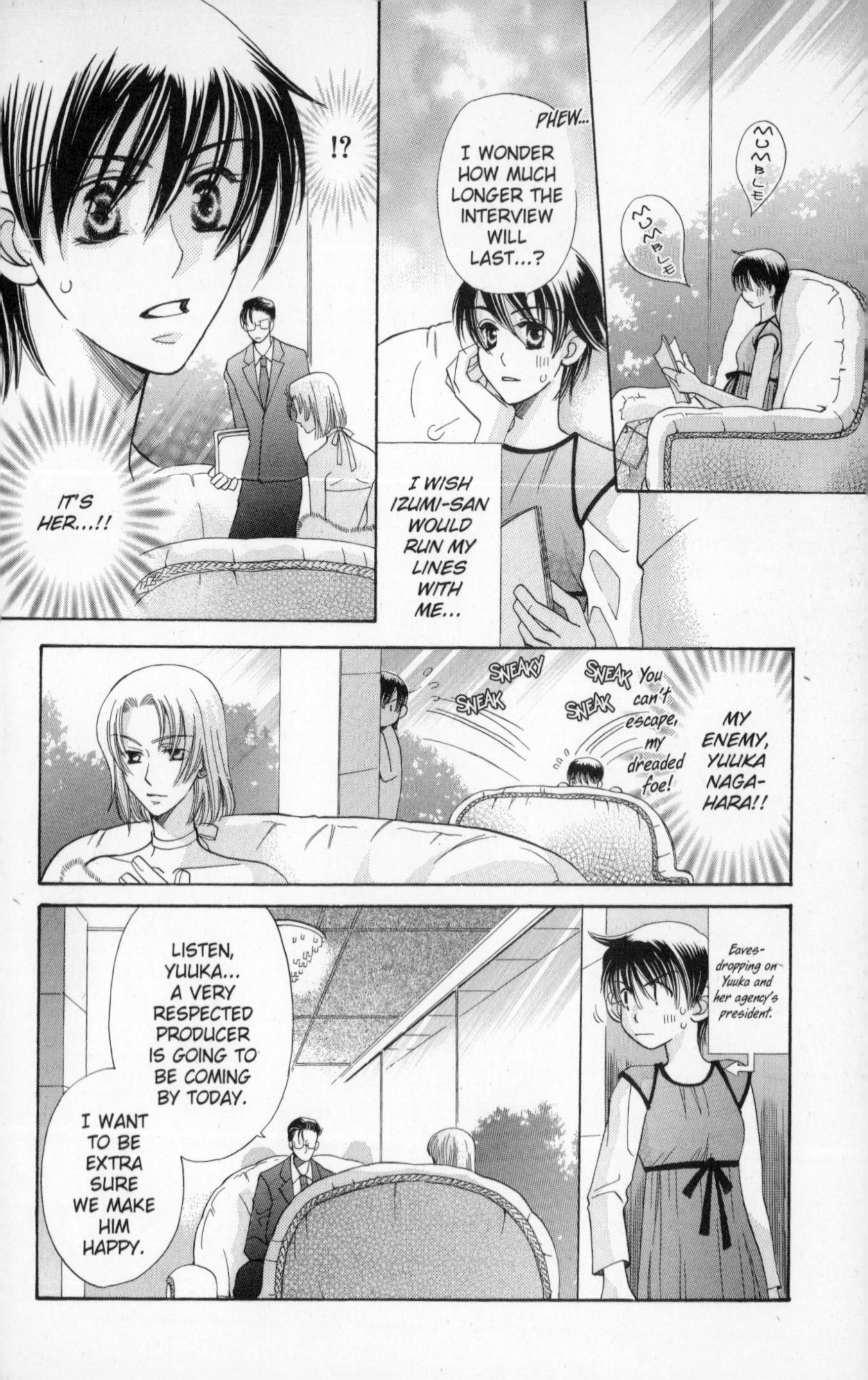
MUMBLE
MUMBLE
PHEW...
I WONDER HOW MUCH LONGER THE INTERVIEW WILL LAST...?
I WISH IZUMI-SAN WOULD RUN MY LINES WITH ME...
!?
IT'S HER...!!
MY ENEMY, YUUKA NAGAHARA!!
You can't escape, my dreaded foe!
SNEAK
SNEAK
SNEAKY
SNEAK
Eaves-dropping on Yuuka and her agency's president.
LISTEN, YUUKA... A VERY RESPECTED PRODUCER IS GOING TO BE COMING BY TODAY.
I WANT TO BE EXTRA SURE WE MAKE HIM HAPPY.

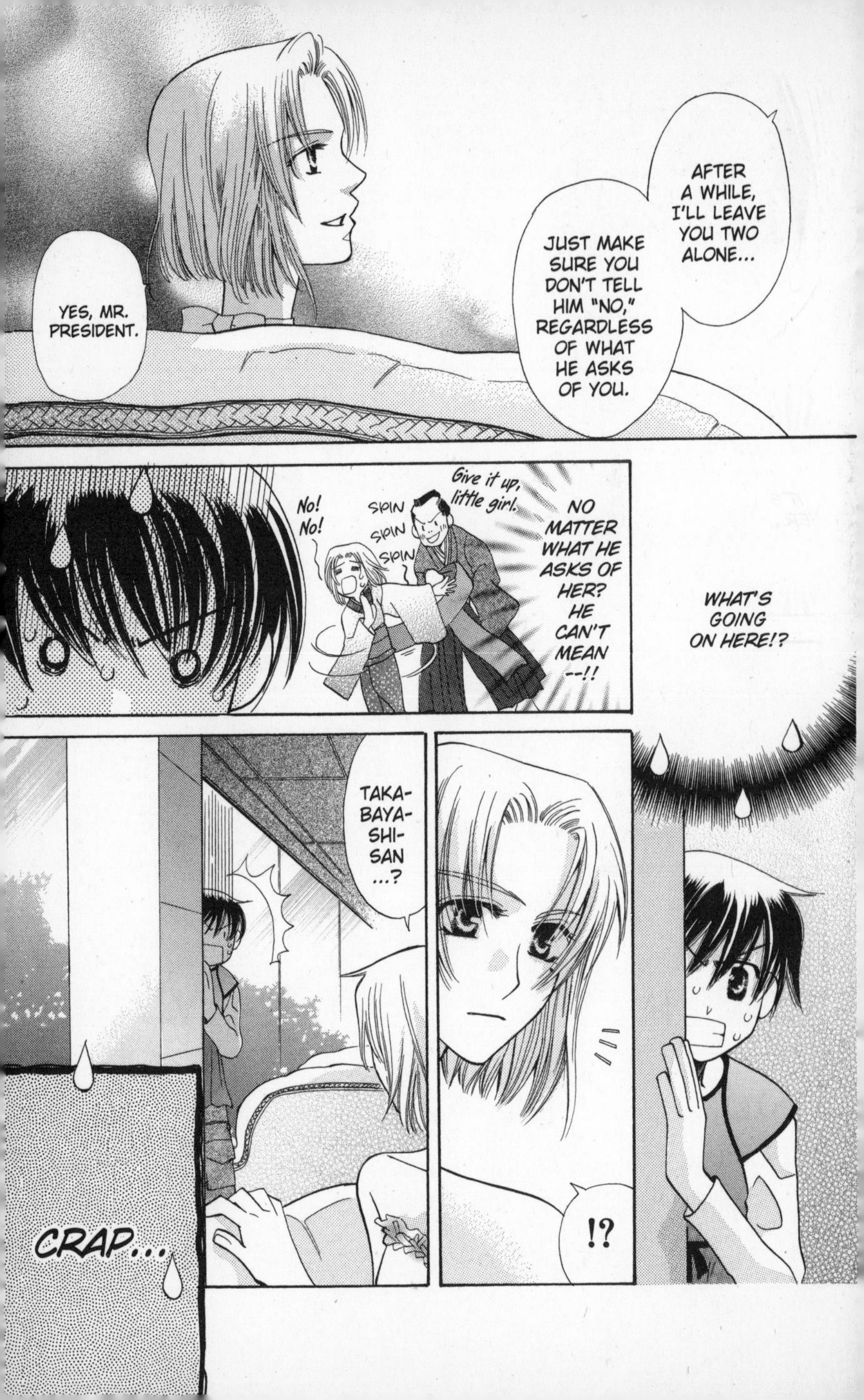
AFTER A WHILE, I'LL LEAVE YOU TWO ALONE...
JUST MAKE SURE YOU DON'T TELL HIM "NO," REGARDLESS OF WHAT HE ASKS OF YOU.
YES, MR. PRESIDENT.
WHAT'S GOING ON HERE!?
NO MATTER WHAT HE ASKS OF HER? HE CAN'T MEAN --!!
Give it up, little girl.
SPIN SPIN SPIN
No! No!
!?
TAKA-BAYA-SHI-SAN ...?
CRAP...

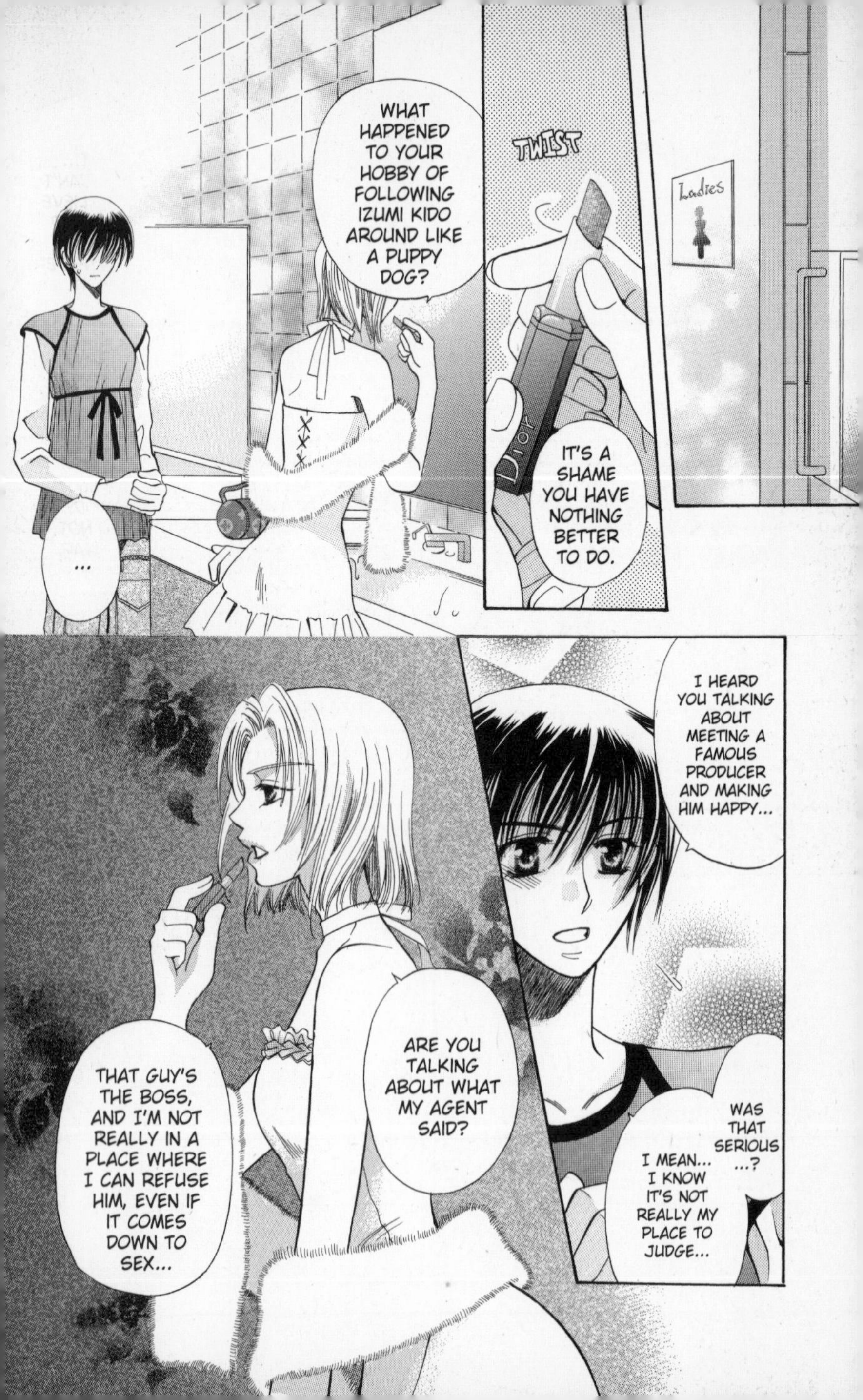
TWIST
Ladies
Dior
IT'S A SHAME YOU HAVE NOTHING BETTER TO DO.
WHAT HAPPENED TO YOUR HOBBY OF FOLLOWING IZUMI KIDO AROUND LIKE A PUPPY DOG?
...
I HEARD YOU TALKING ABOUT MEETING A FAMOUS PRODUCER AND MAKING HIM HAPPY...
WAS THAT SERIOUS ...?
I MEAN... I KNOW IT'S NOT REALLY MY PLACE TO JUDGE...
ARE YOU TALKING ABOUT WHAT MY AGENT SAID?
THAT GUY'S THE BOSS, AND I'M NOT REALLY IN A PLACE WHERE I CAN REFUSE HIM, EVEN IF IT COMES DOWN TO SEX...

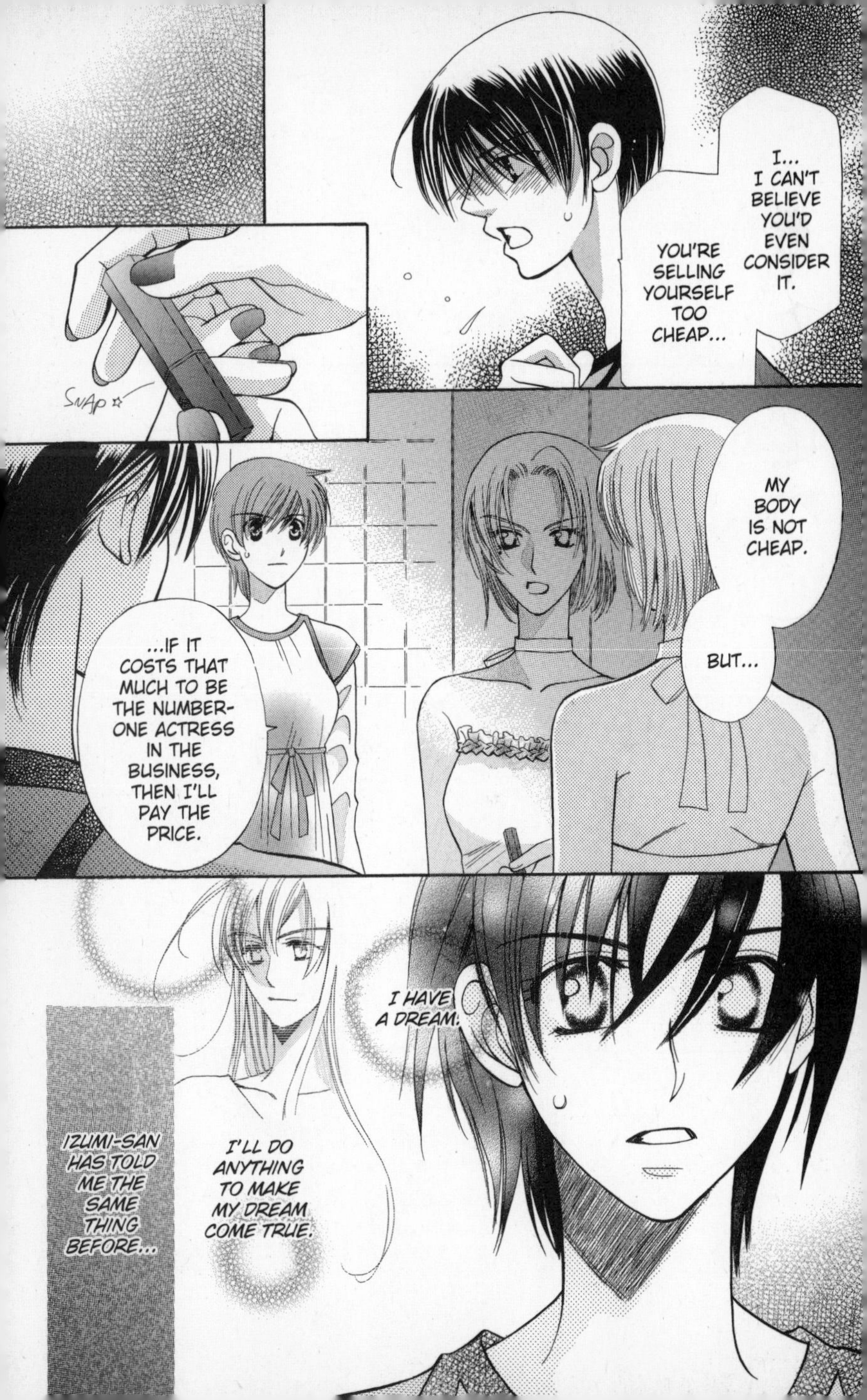
I... I CAN'T BELIEVE YOU'D EVEN CONSIDER IT.
YOU'RE SELLING YOURSELF TOO CHEAP...
SNAP
MY BODY IS NOT CHEAP.
BUT...
...IF IT COSTS THAT MUCH TO BE THE NUMBER-ONE ACTRESS IN THE BUSINESS, THEN I'LL PAY THE PRICE.
I HAVE A DREAM.
I'LL DO ANYTHING TO MAKE MY DREAM COME TRUE.
IZUMI-SAN HAS TOLD ME THE SAME THING BEFORE...

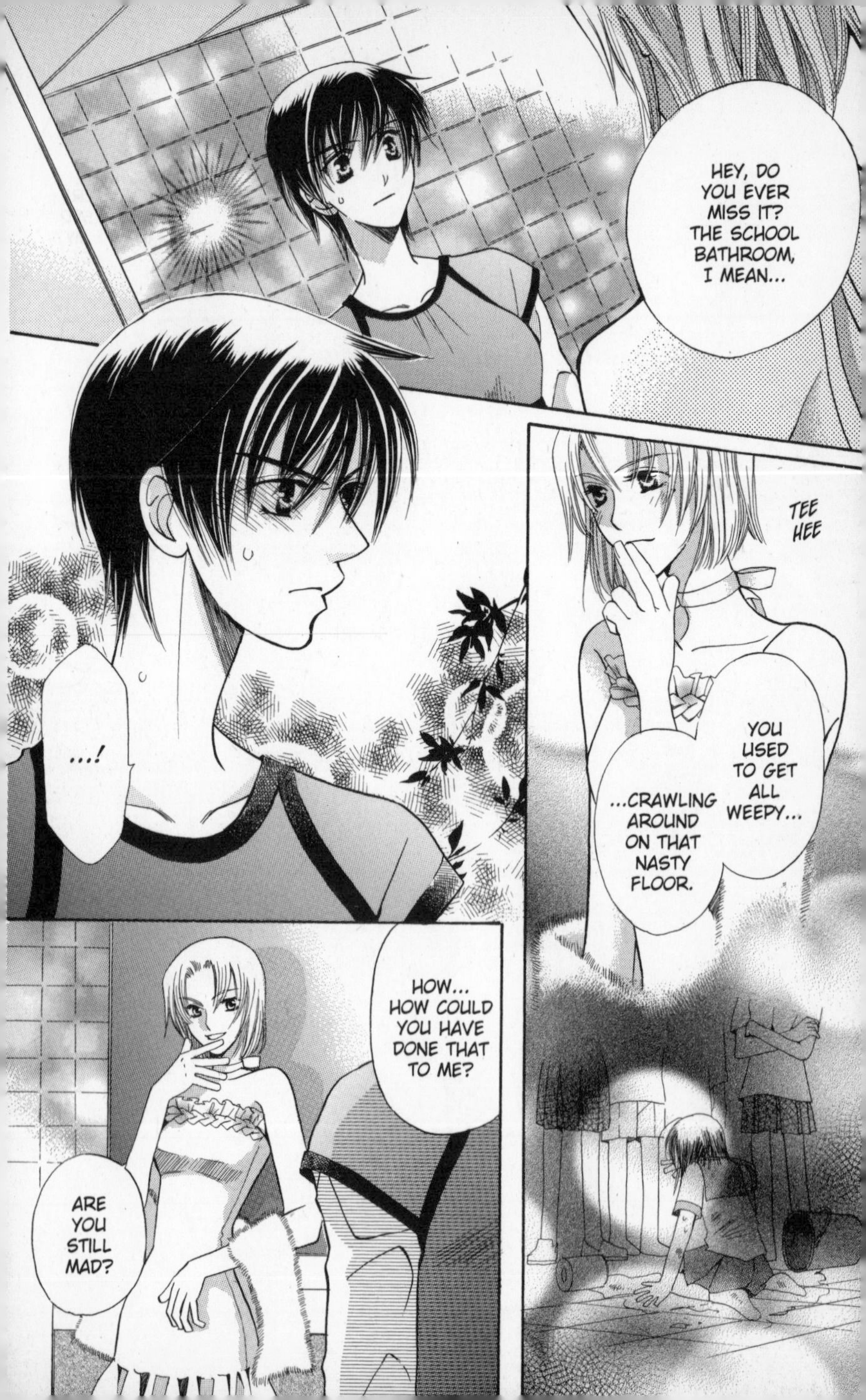
HEY, DO YOU EVER MISS IT? THE SCHOOL BATHROOM, I MEAN...
TEE HEE
YOU USED TO GET ALL WEEPY...
...CRAWLING AROUND ON THAT NASTY FLOOR.
...!
HOW... HOW COULD YOU HAVE DONE THAT TO ME?
ARE YOU STILL MAD?

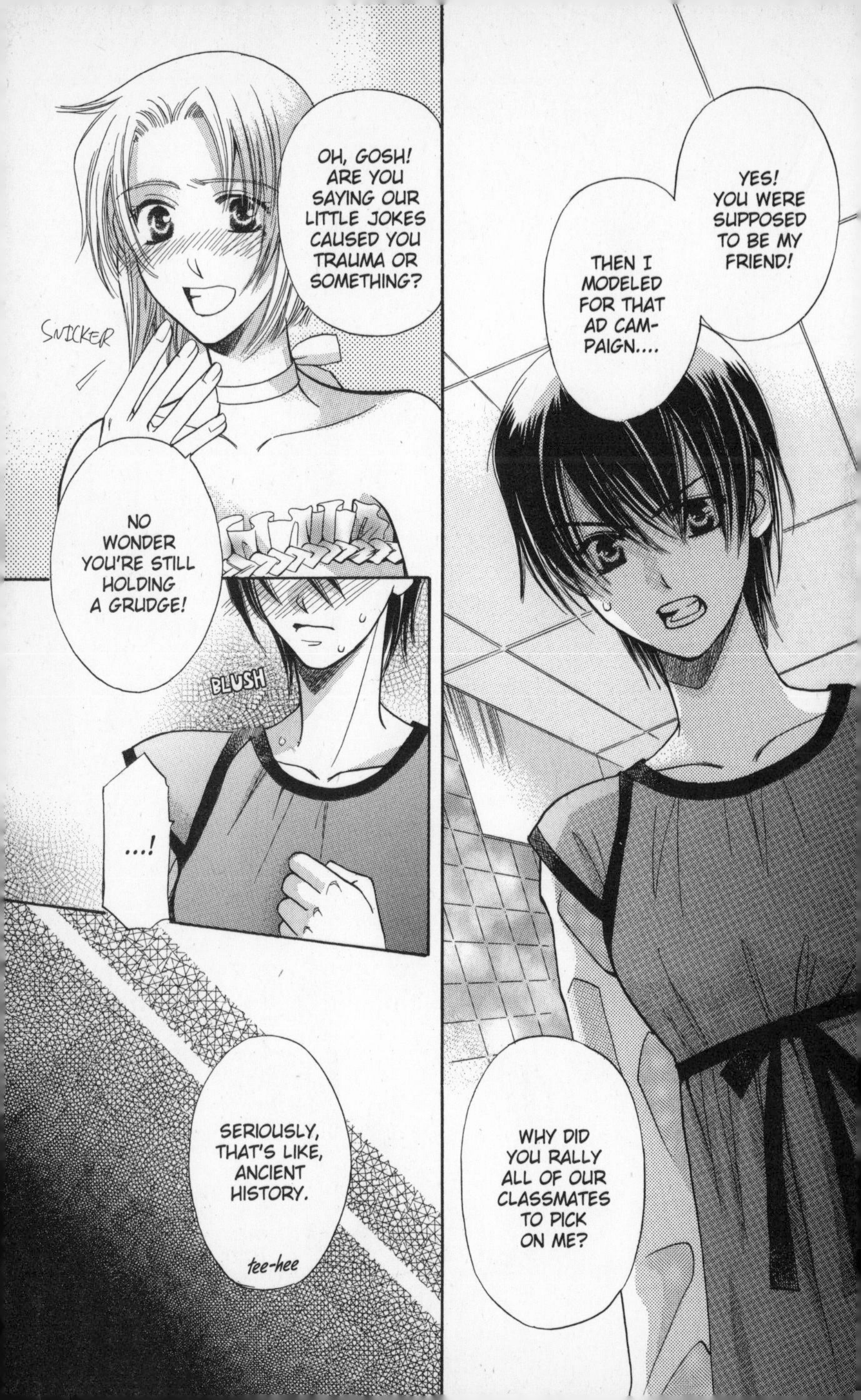
YES! YOU WERE SUPPOSED TO BE MY FRIEND!
THEN I MODELED FOR THAT AD CAM-PAIGN....
WHY DID YOU RALLY ALL OF OUR CLASSMATES TO PICK ON ME?
OH, GOSH! ARE YOU SAYING OUR LITTLE JOKES CAUSED YOU TRAUMA OR SOMETHING?
SNICKER
NO WONDER YOU'RE STILL HOLDING A GRUDGE!
BLUSH
...!
SERIOUSLY, THAT'S LIKE, ANCIENT HISTORY.
tee-hee

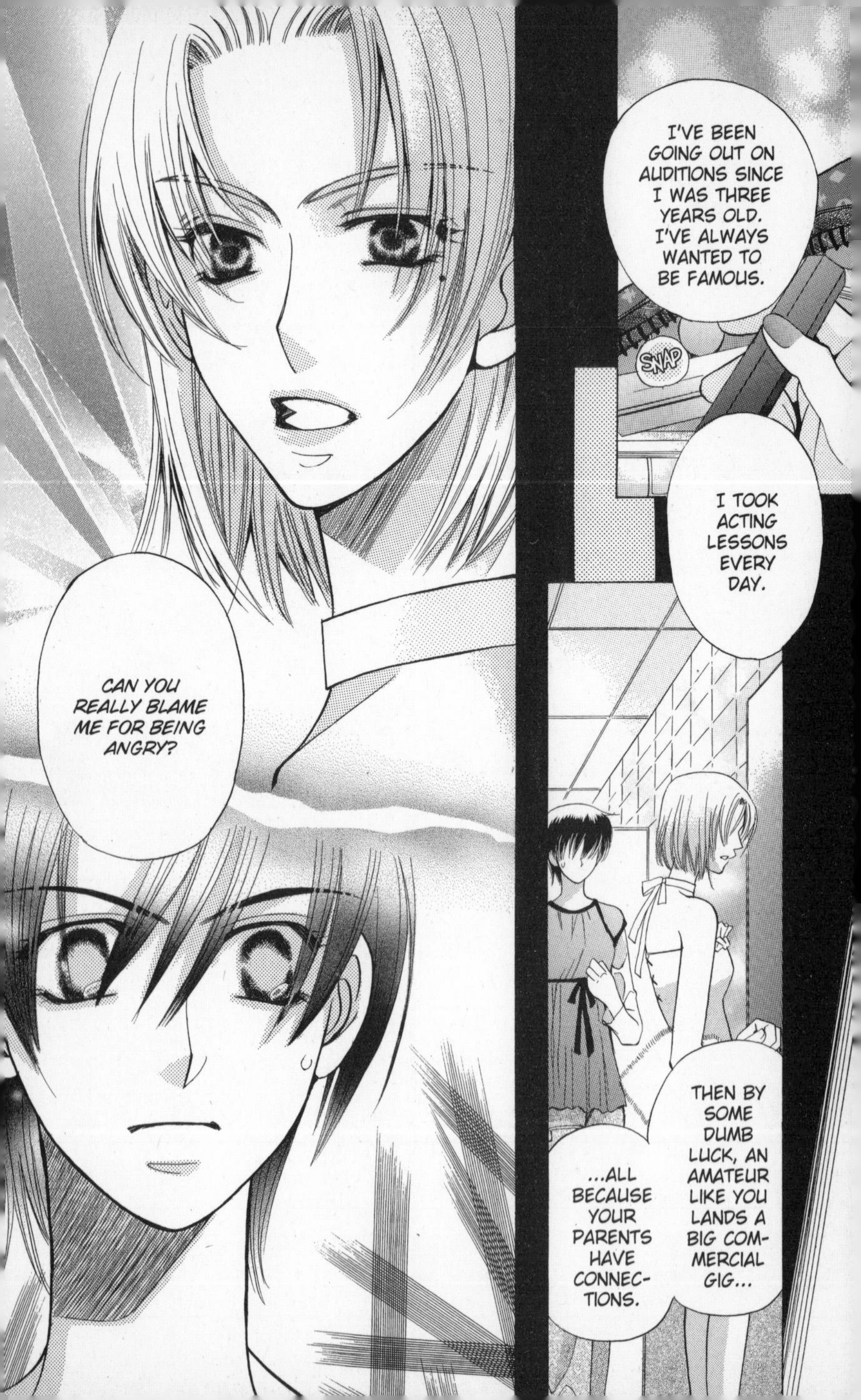
I'VE BEEN GOING OUT ON AUDITIONS SINCE I WAS THREE YEARS OLD. I'VE ALWAYS WANTED TO BE FAMOUS.
SNAP
I TOOK ACTING LESSONS EVERY DAY.
THEN BY SOME DUMB LUCK, AN AMATEUR LIKE YOU LANDS A BIG COMMERCIAL GIG...
...ALL BECAUSE YOUR PARENTS HAVE CONNECTIONS.
CAN YOU REALLY BLAME ME FOR BEING ANGRY?

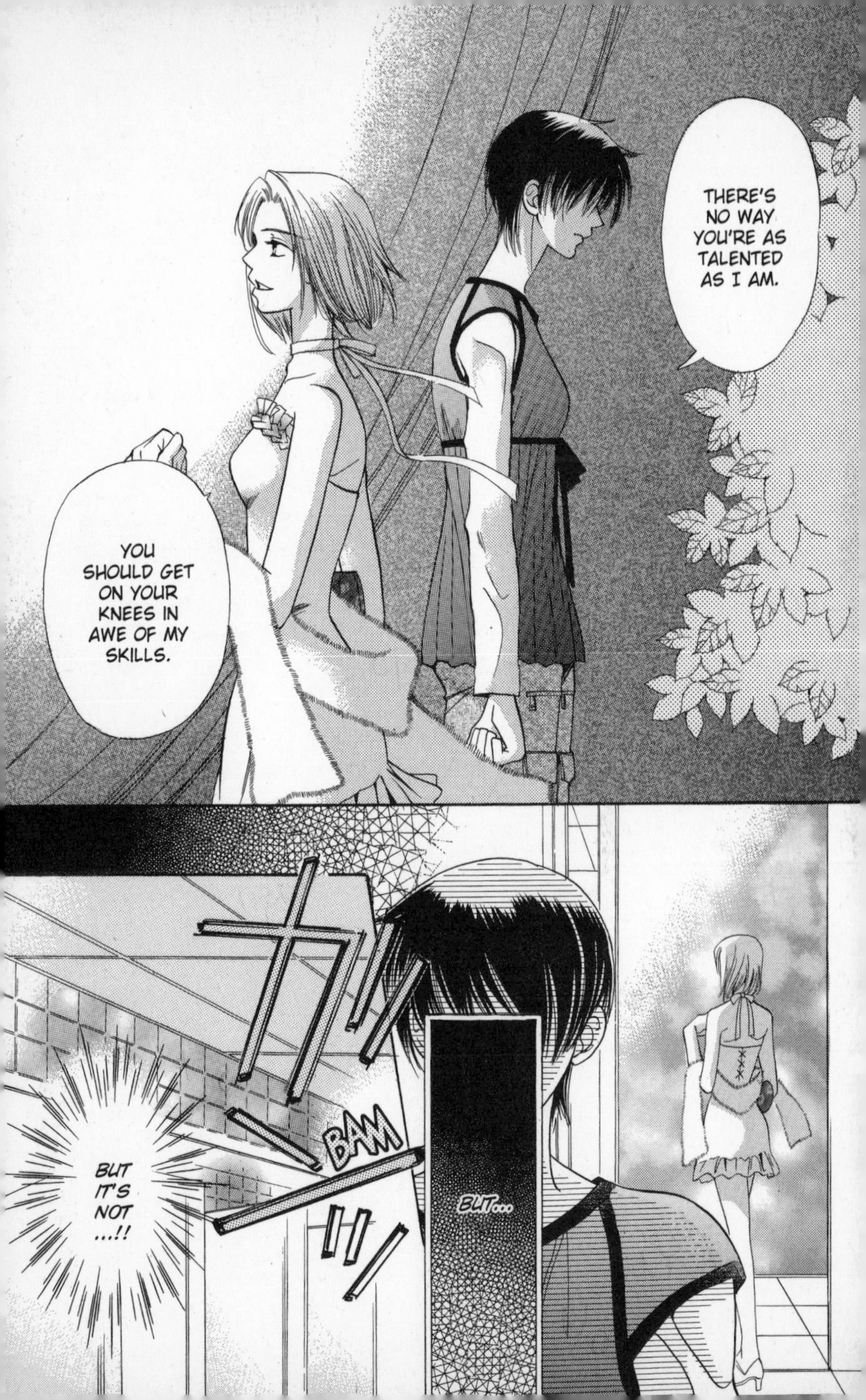
THERE'S NO WAY YOU'RE AS TALENTED AS I AM.
YOU SHOULD GET ON YOUR KNEES IN AWE OF MY SKILLS.
BUT...
BAM
BUT IT'S NOT ...!!

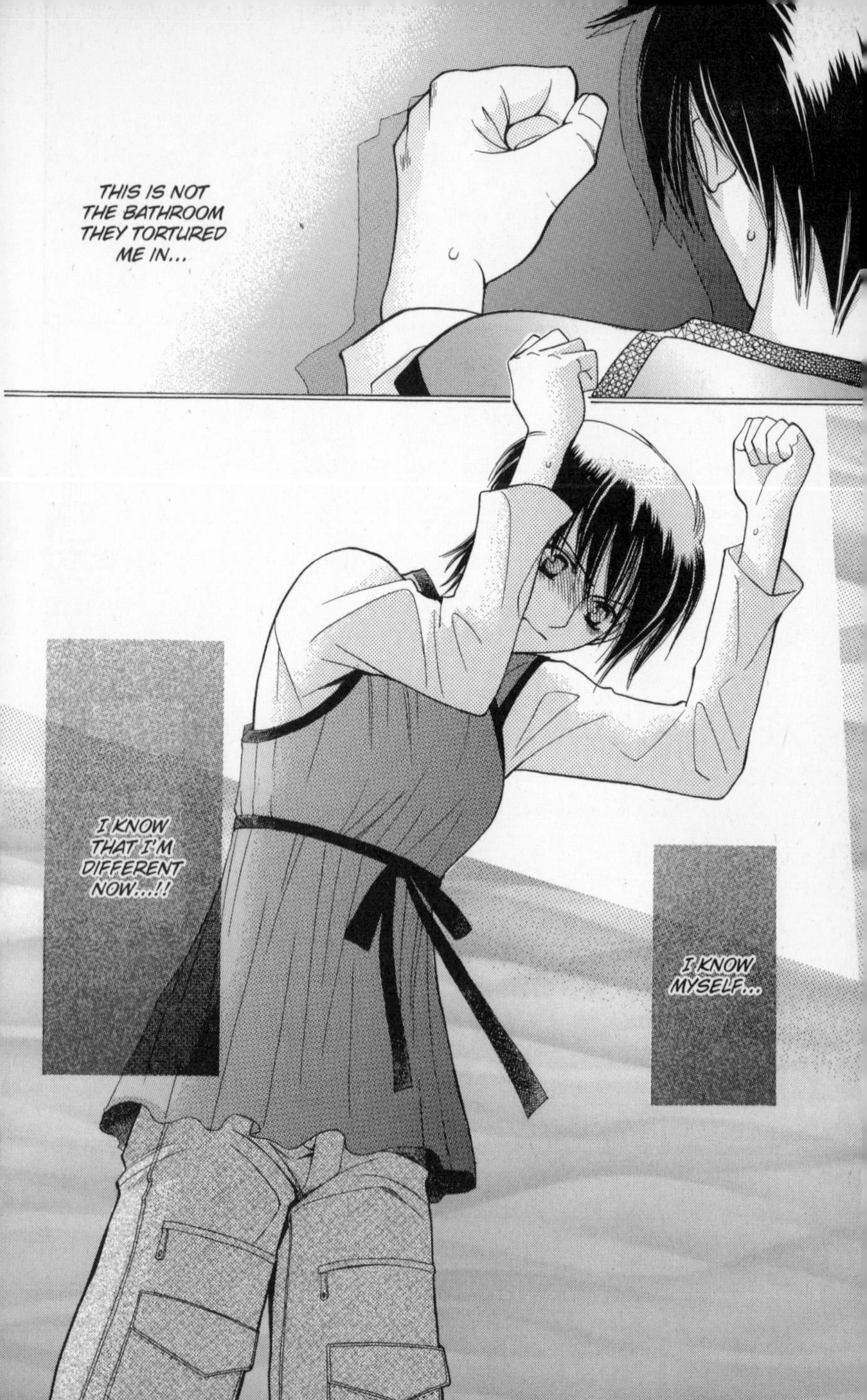
THIS IS NOT THE BATHROOM THEY TORTURED ME IN...
I KNOW THAT I'M DIFFERENT NOW...!!
I KNOW MYSELF...

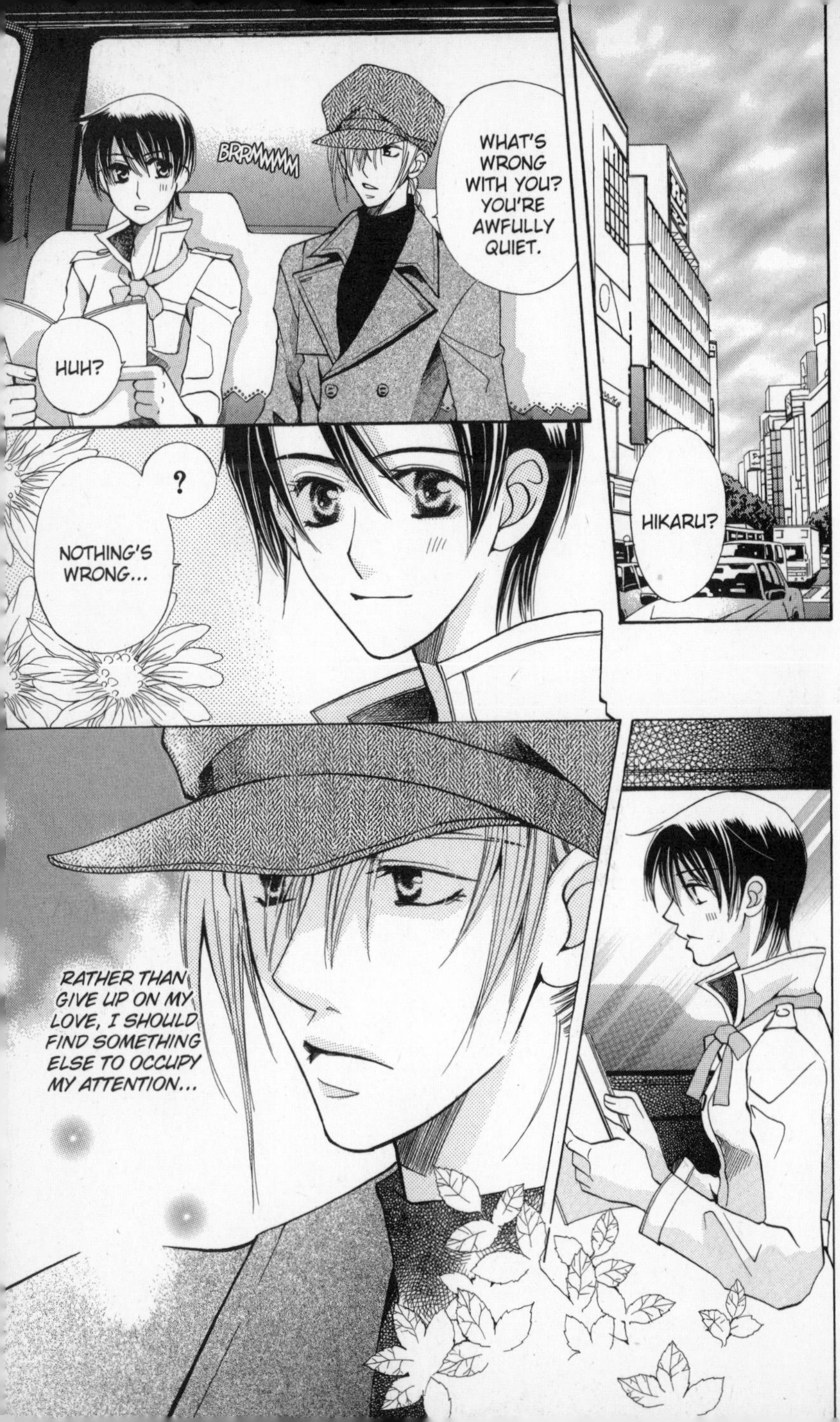
HIKARU?
WHAT'S WRONG WITH YOU? YOU'RE AWFULLY QUIET.
BRRMMMM
HUH?
?
NOTHING'S WRONG...
RATHER THAN GIVE UP ON MY LOVE, I SHOULD FIND SOMETHING ELSE TO OCCUPY MY ATTENTION...

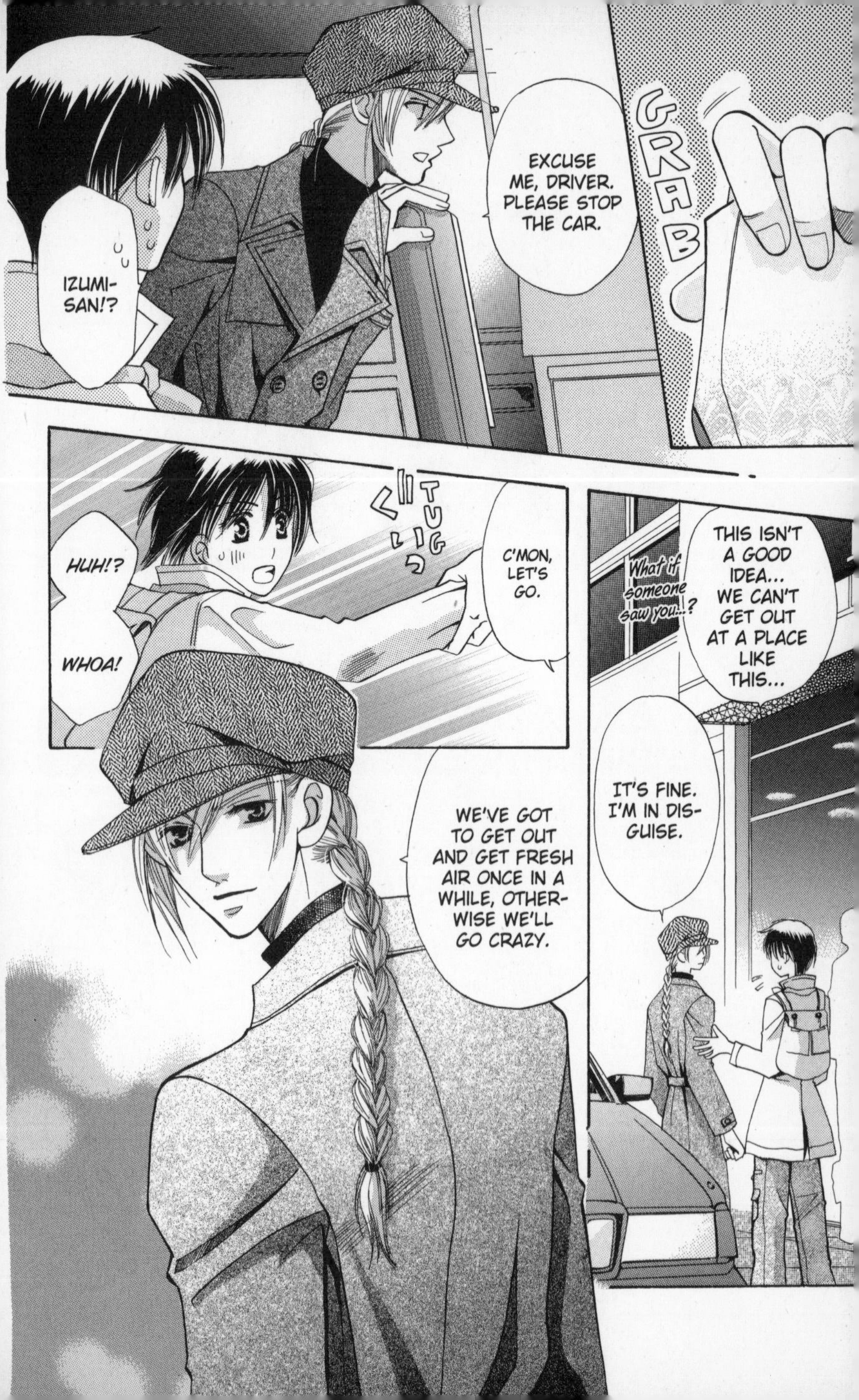
GRAB
EXCUSE ME, DRIVER. PLEASE STOP THE CAR.
IZUMI-SAN!?
THIS ISN'T A GOOD IDEA... WE CAN'T GET OUT AT A PLACE LIKE THIS...
What if someone saw you...?
IT'S FINE. I'M IN DISGUISE.
TUG
C'MON, LET'S GO.
HUH!?
WHOA!
WE'VE GOT TO GET OUT AND GET FRESH AIR ONCE IN A WHILE, OTHER-WISE WE'LL GO CRAZY.

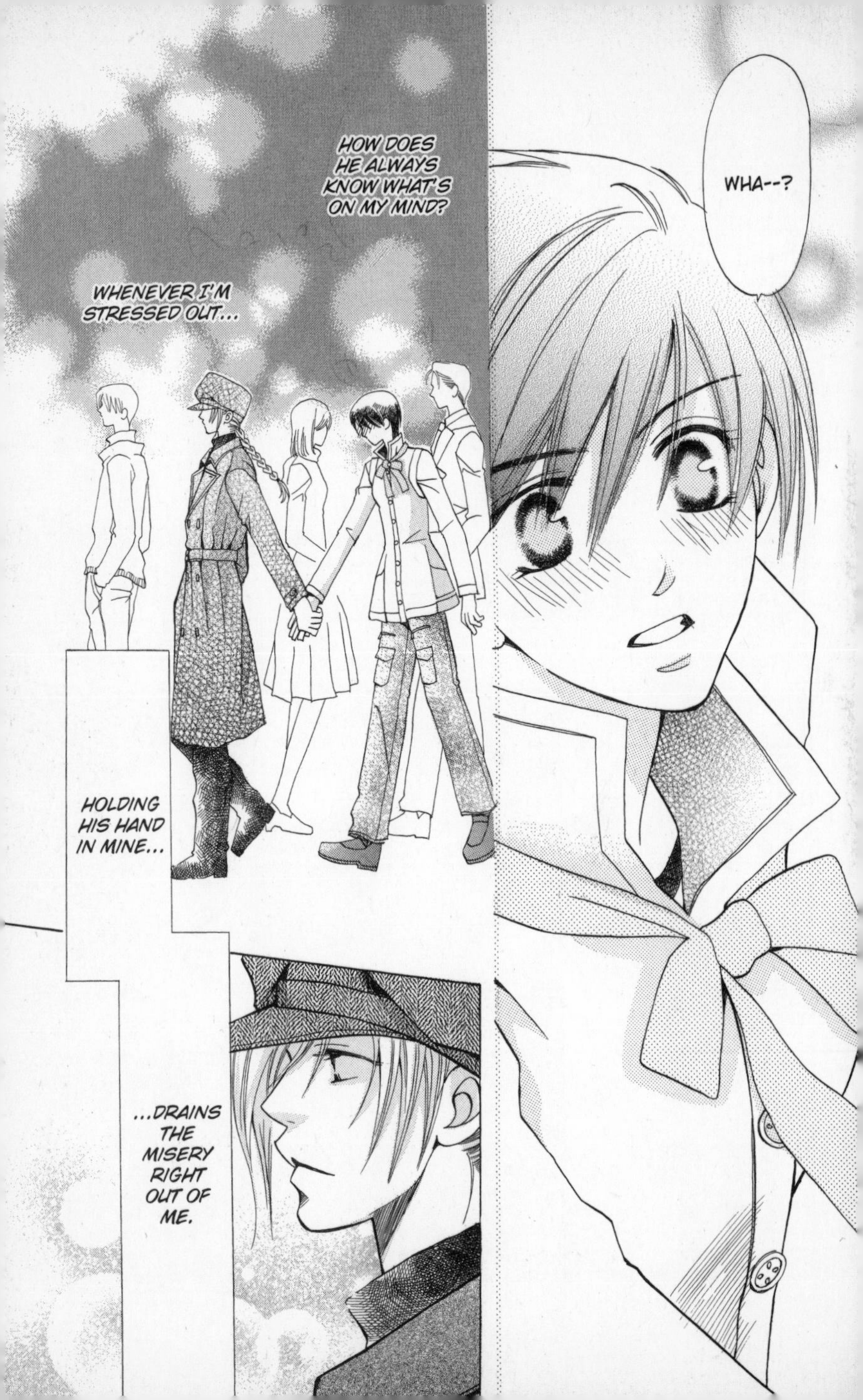
WHA--?
HOW DOES HE ALWAYS KNOW WHAT'S ON MY MIND?
WHENEVER I'M STRESSED OUT...
HOLDING HIS HAND IN MINE...
...DRAINS THE MISERY RIGHT OUT OF ME.

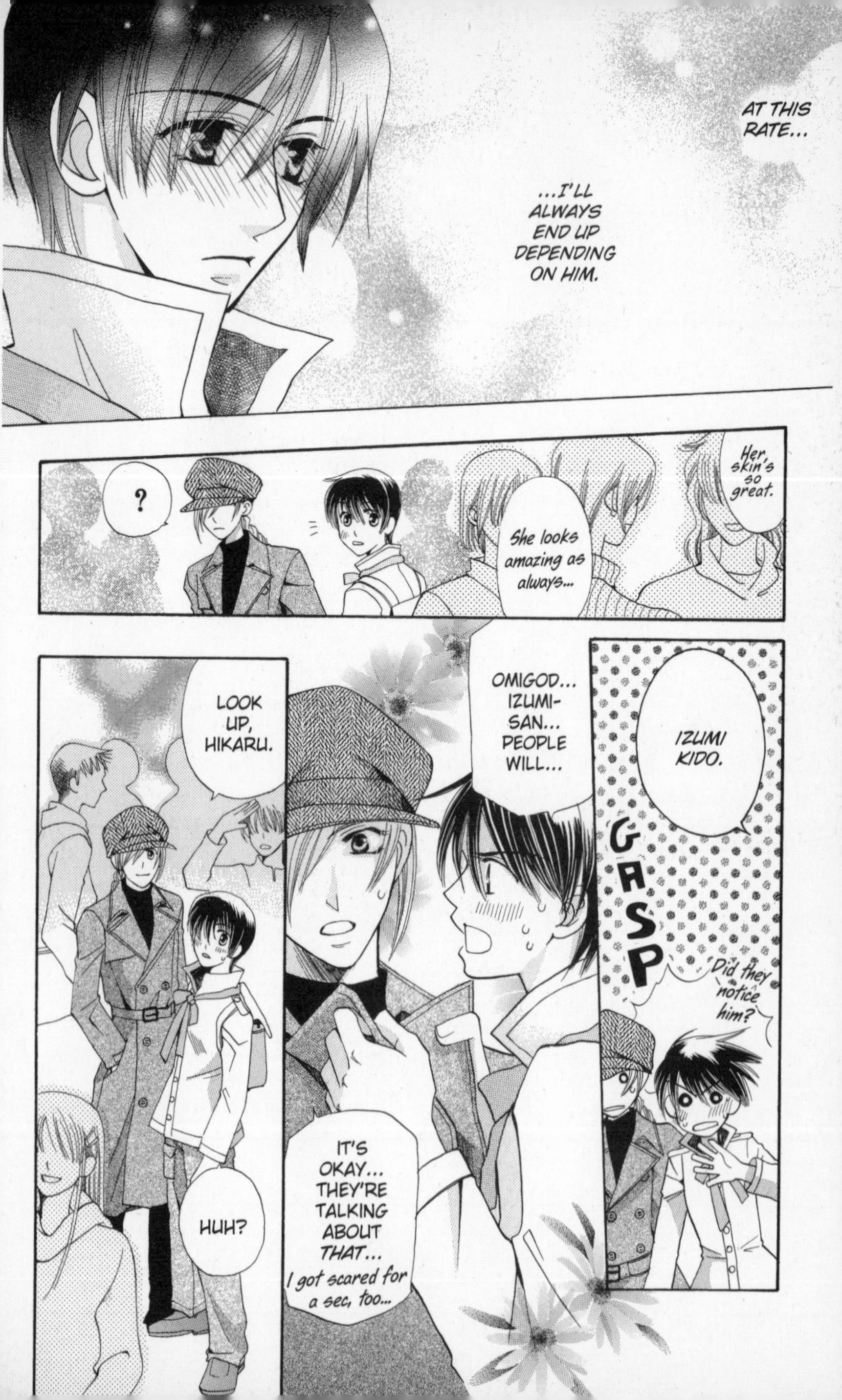
AT THIS RATE…
…I'LL ALWAYS END UP DEPENDING ON HIM.
Her skin's so great.
She looks amazing as always…
?
IZUMI KIDO.
GASP
Did they notice him?
OMIGOD… IZUMI-SAN… PEOPLE WILL…
IT'S OKAY… THEY'RE TALKING ABOUT THAT… I got scared for a sec, too…
LOOK UP, HIKARU.
HUH?

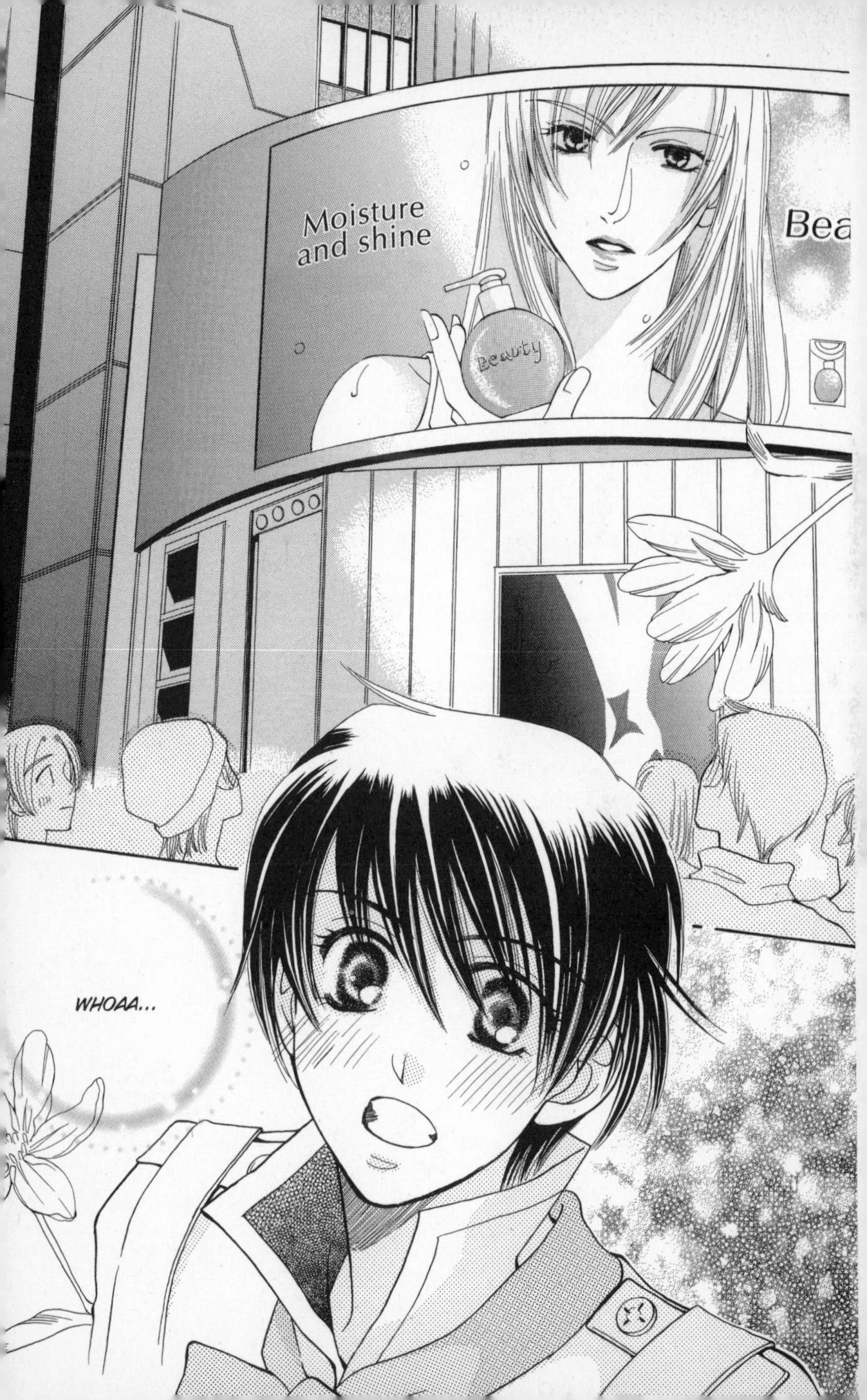
Moisture and shine
Beauty
Bea
WHOAA...

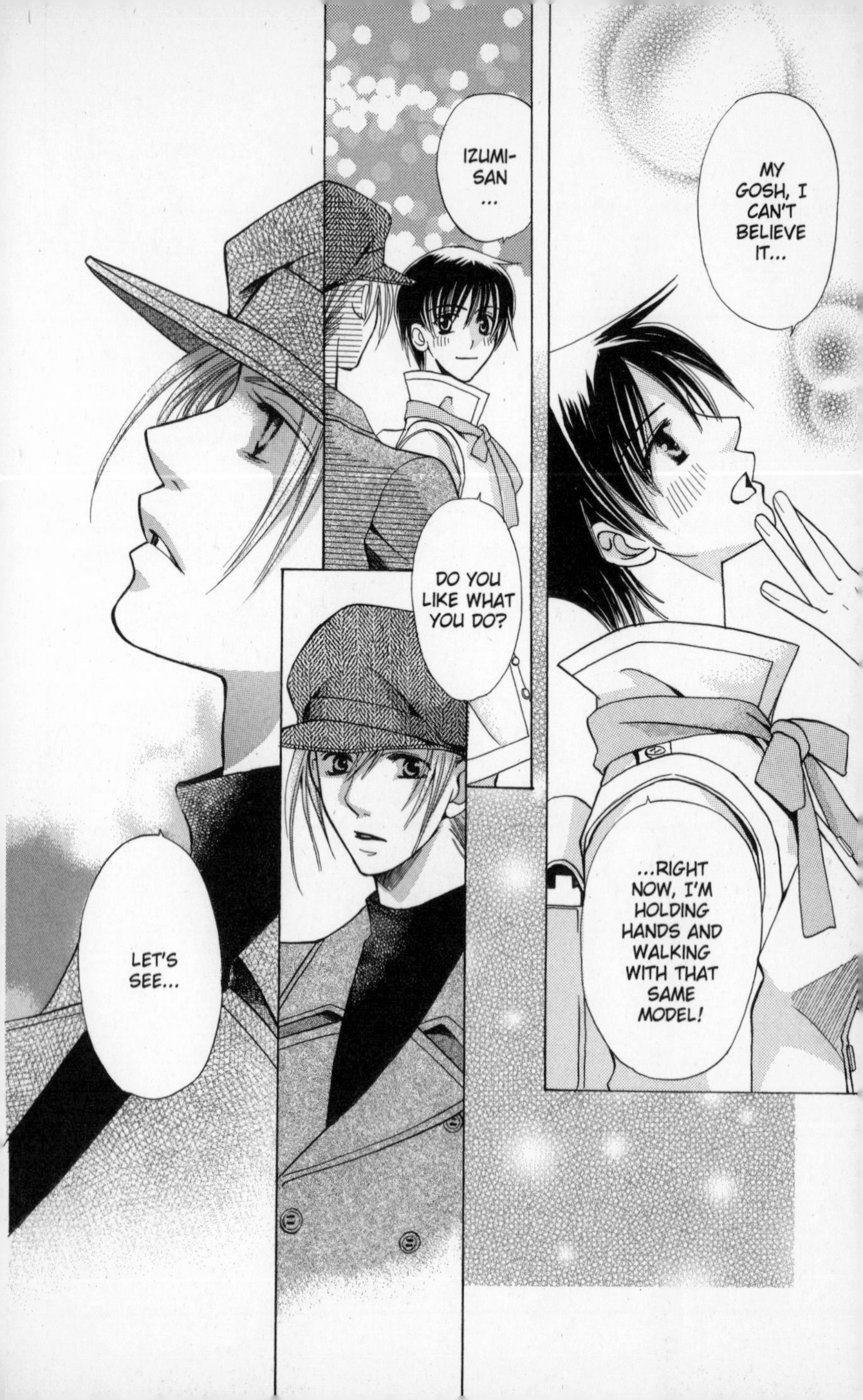
MY GOSH, I CAN'T BELIEVE IT...
...RIGHT NOW, I'M HOLDING HANDS AND WALKING WITH THAT SAME MODEL!
IZUMI-SAN ...
DO YOU LIKE WHAT YOU DO?
LET'S SEE...

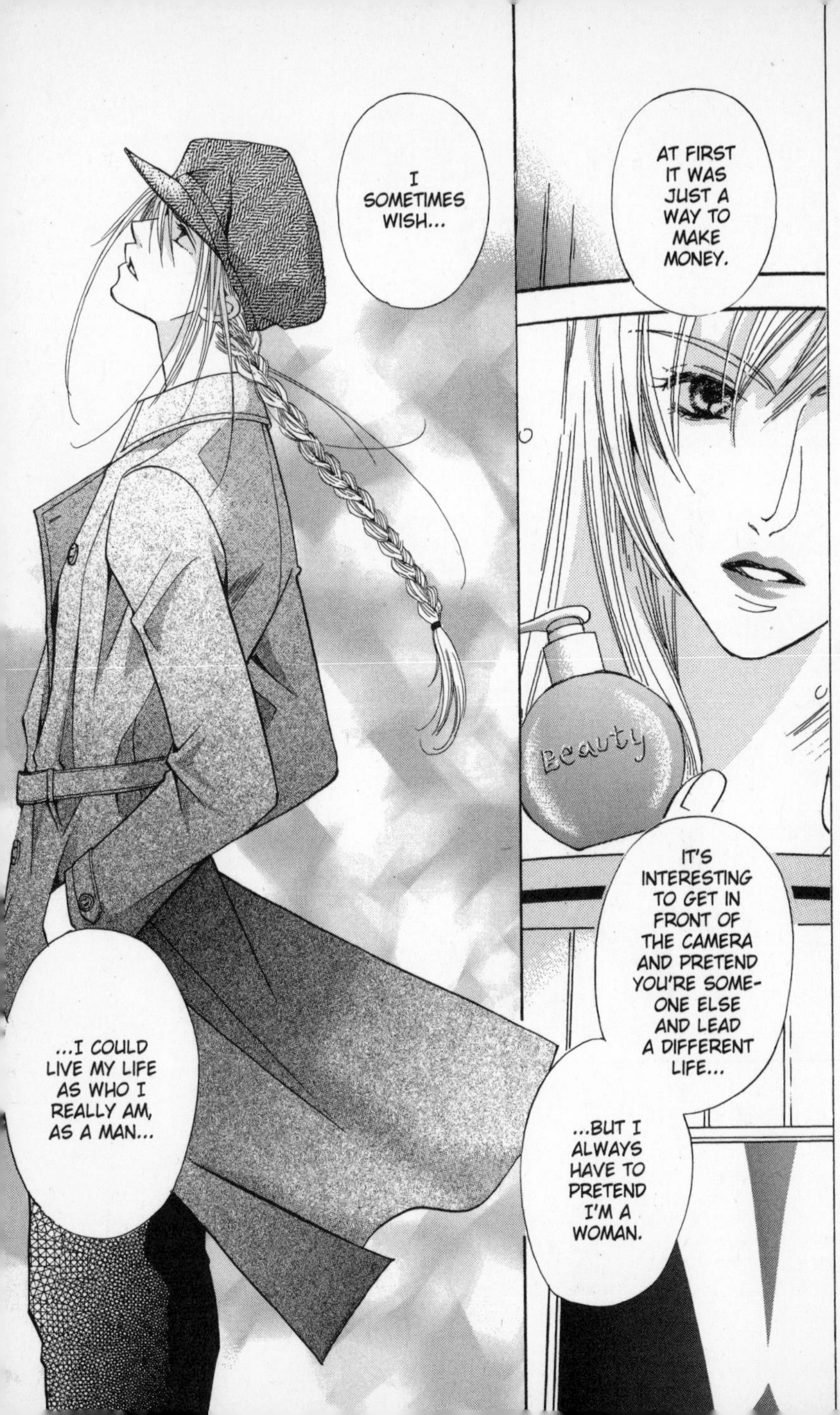
AT FIRST IT WAS JUST A WAY TO MAKE MONEY.
Beauty
IT'S INTERESTING TO GET IN FRONT OF THE CAMERA AND PRETEND YOU'RE SOME-ONE ELSE AND LEAD A DIFFERENT LIFE...
...BUT I ALWAYS HAVE TO PRETEND I'M A WOMAN.
I SOMETIMES WISH...
...I COULD LIVE MY LIFE AS WHO I REALLY AM, AS A MAN...

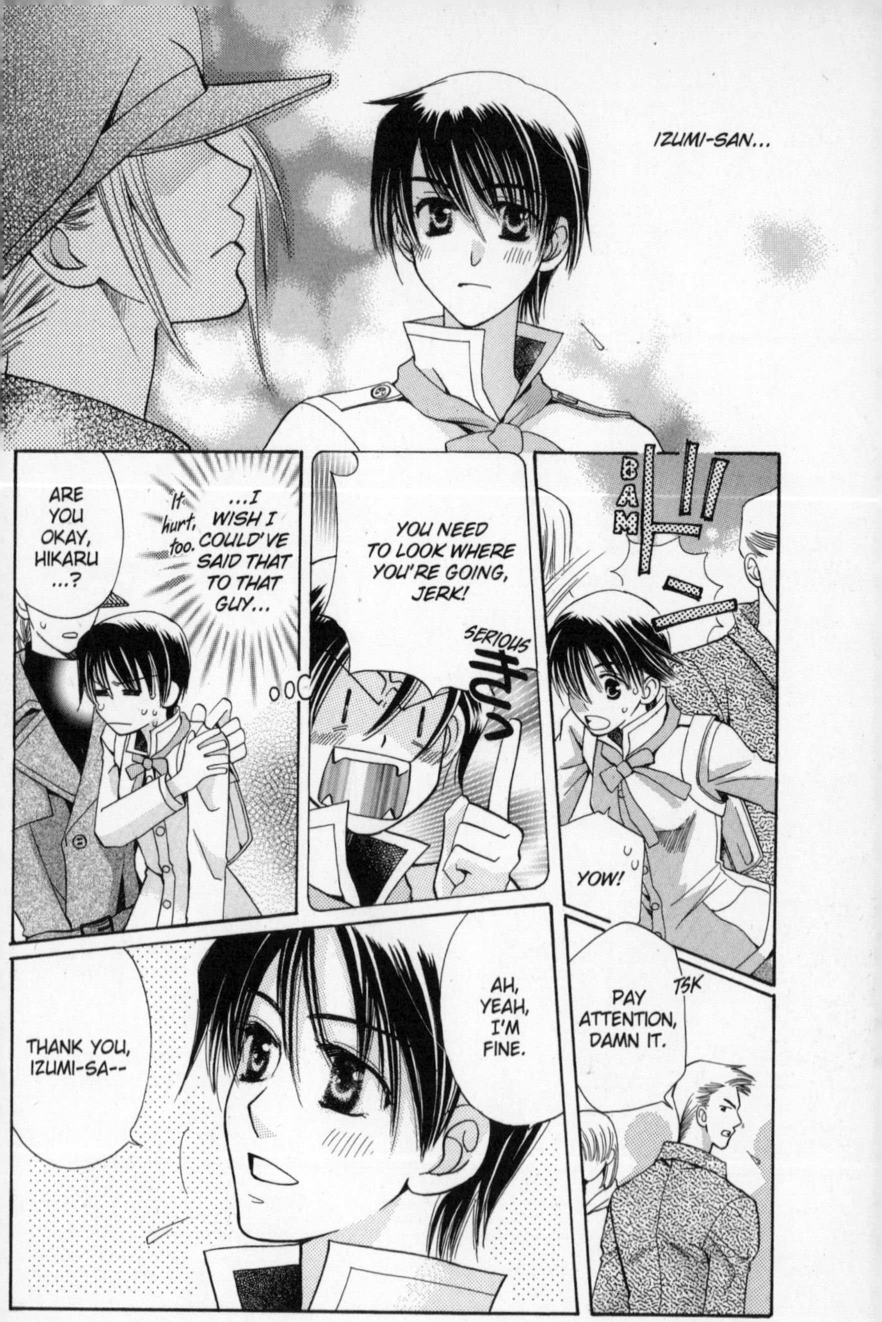
IZUMI-SAN...
BAM
YOW!
YOU NEED TO LOOK WHERE YOU'RE GOING, JERK!
SERIOUS
...I WISH I COULD'VE SAID THAT TO THAT GUY...
It hurt, too.
ARE YOU OKAY, HIKARU...?
TSK
PAY ATTENTION, DAMN IT.
AH, YEAH, I'M FINE.
THANK YOU, IZUMI-SA--

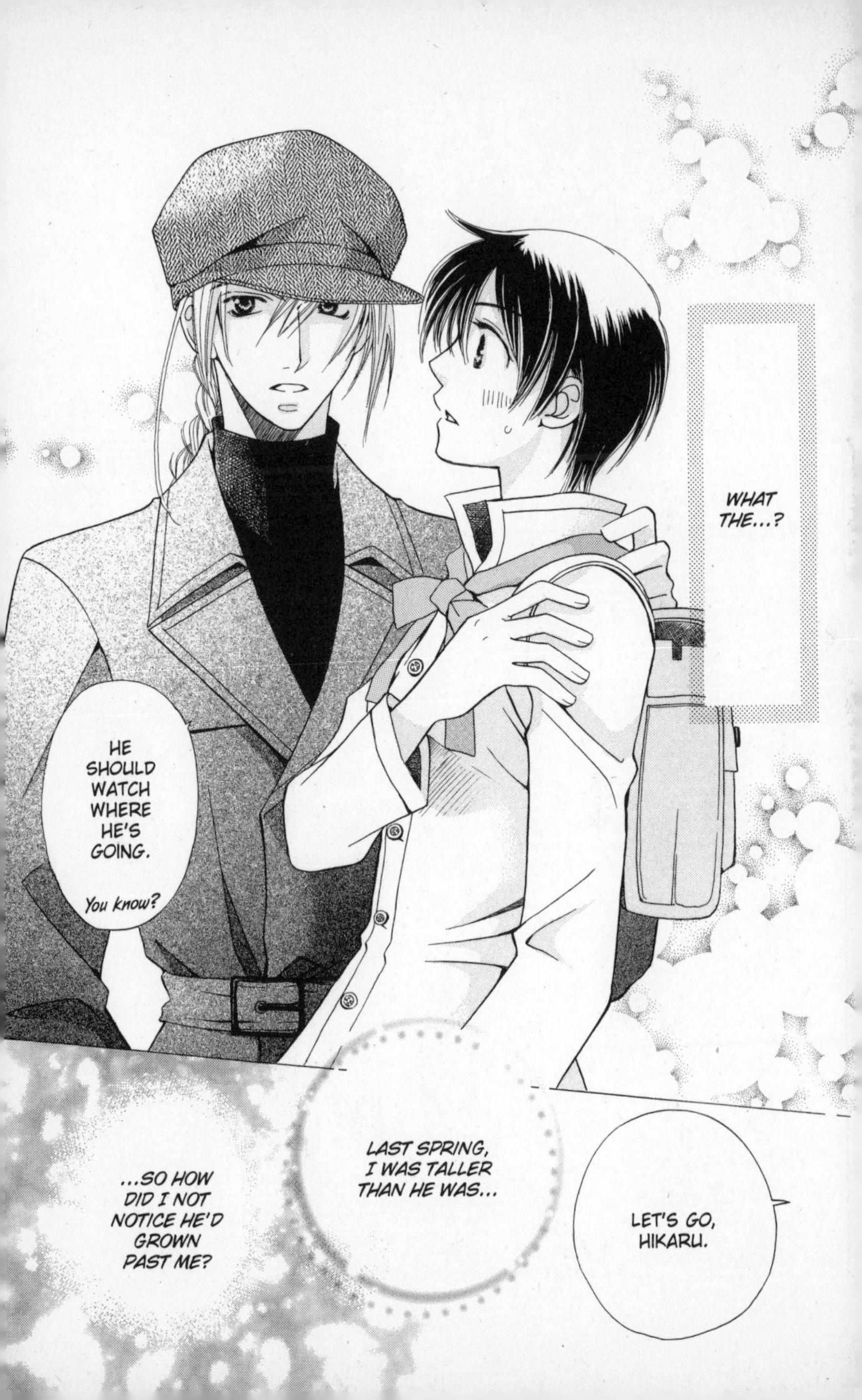
WHAT THE...?
HE SHOULD WATCH WHERE HE'S GOING.
You know?
LET'S GO, HIKARU.
LAST SPRING, I WAS TALLER THAN HE WAS...
...SO HOW DID I NOT NOTICE HE'D GROWN PAST ME?

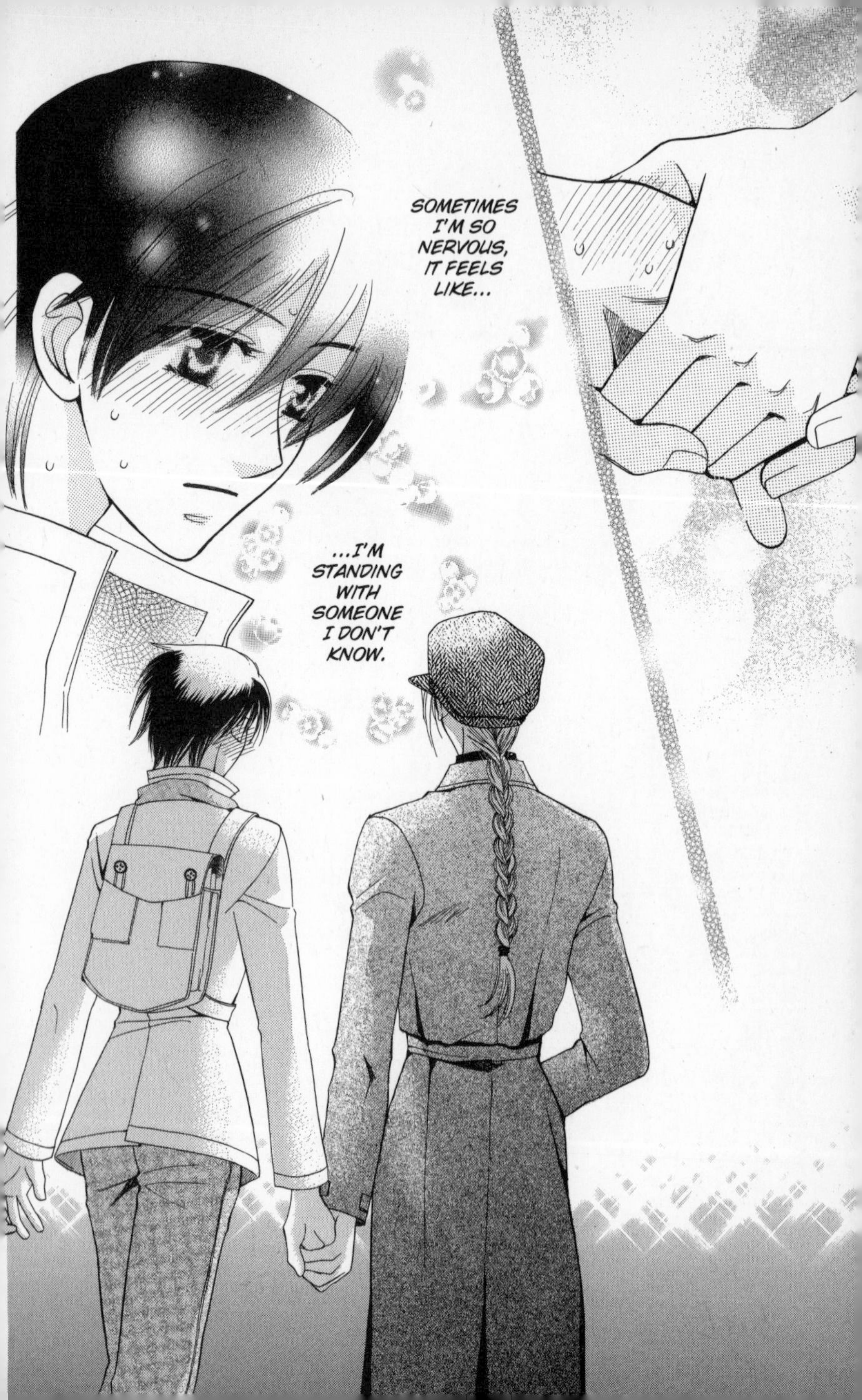
SOMETIMES I'M SO NERVOUS, IT FEELS LIKE...
...I'M STANDING WITH SOMEONE I DON'T KNOW.

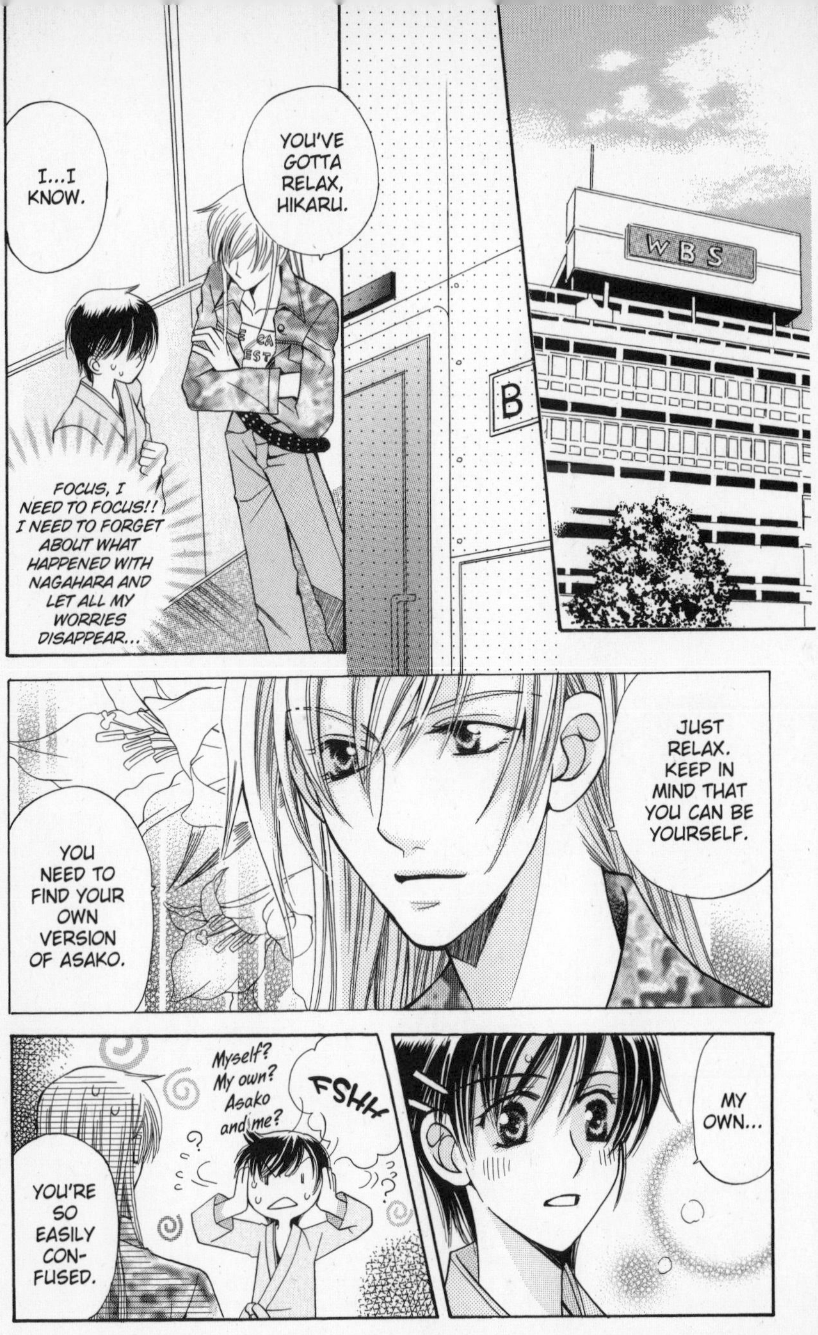
YOU'VE GOTTA RELAX, HIKARU.
I...I KNOW.
FOCUS, I NEED TO FOCUS!! I NEED TO FORGET ABOUT WHAT HAPPENED WITH NAGAHARA AND LET ALL MY WORRIES DISAPPEAR...
JUST RELAX. KEEP IN MIND THAT YOU CAN BE YOURSELF.
YOU NEED TO FIND YOUR OWN VERSION OF ASAKO.
MY OWN...
Myself? My own? Asako and me?
FSHH
YOU'RE SO EASILY CON-FUSED.

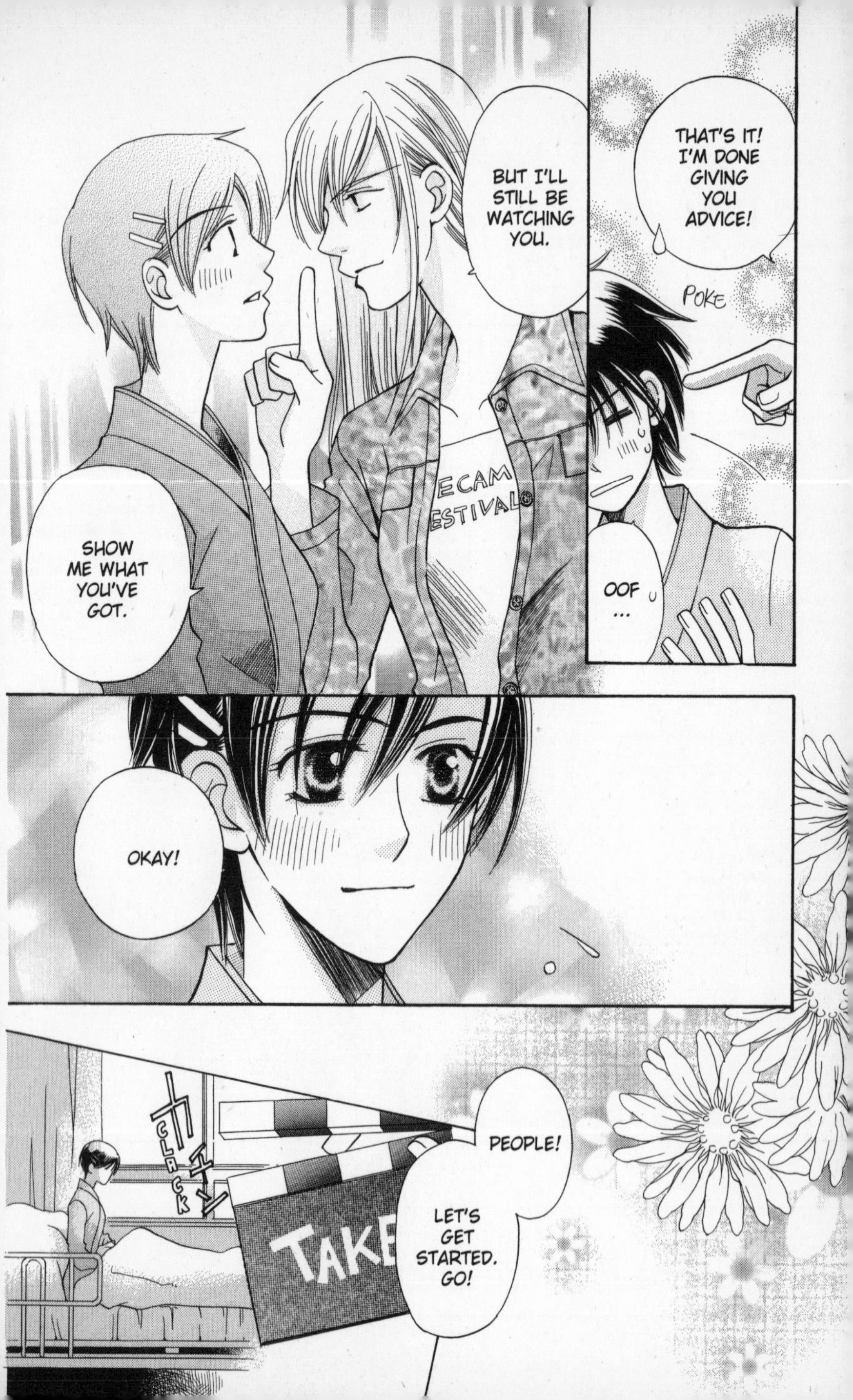
THAT'S IT! I'M DONE GIVING YOU ADVICE!
POKE
OOF ...
BUT I'LL STILL BE WATCHING YOU.
SHOW ME WHAT YOU'VE GOT.
OKAY!
PEOPLE!
LET'S GET STARTED. GO!
CLACK
TAKE

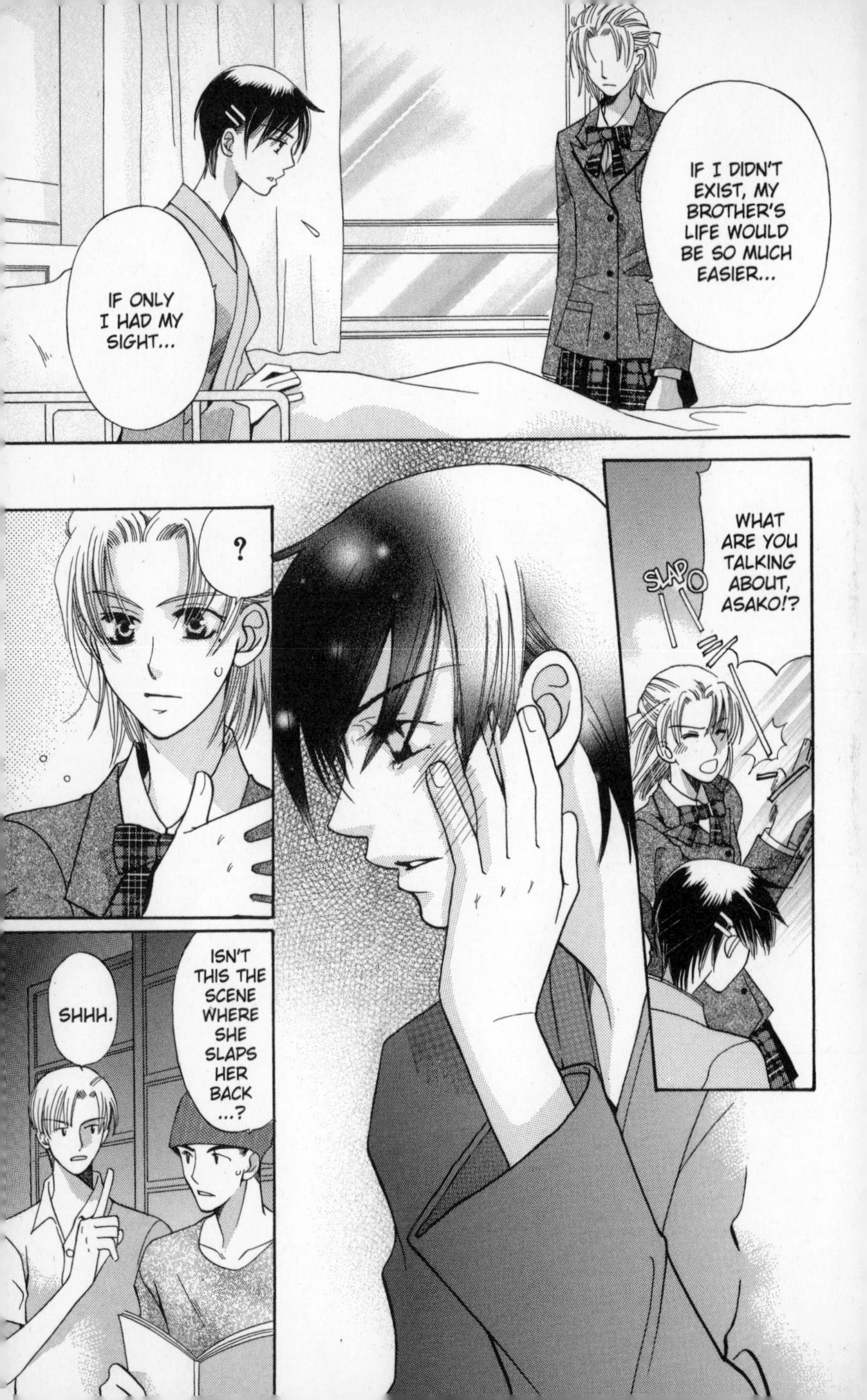
IF I DIDN'T EXIST, MY BROTHER'S LIFE WOULD BE SO MUCH EASIER...
IF ONLY I HAD MY SIGHT...
WHAT ARE YOU TALKING ABOUT, ASAKO!?
SLAP
?
ISN'T THIS THE SCENE WHERE SHE SLAPS HER BACK ...?
SHHH.

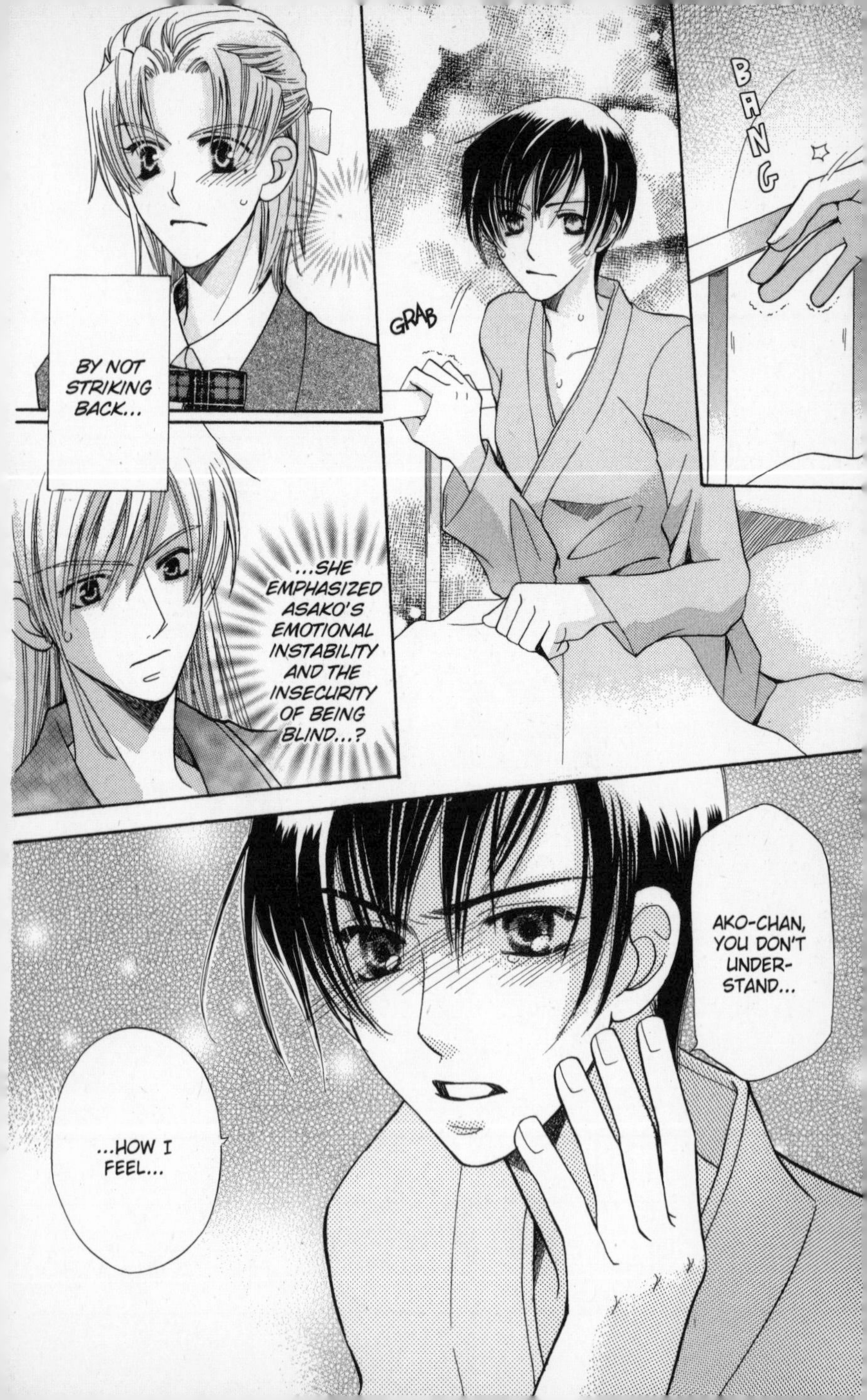
BANG
GRAB
BY NOT STRIKING BACK...
...SHE EMPHASIZED ASAKO'S EMOTIONAL INSTABILITY AND THE INSECURITY OF BEING BLIND...?
AKO-CHAN, YOU DON'T UNDER-STAND...
...HOW I FEEL...

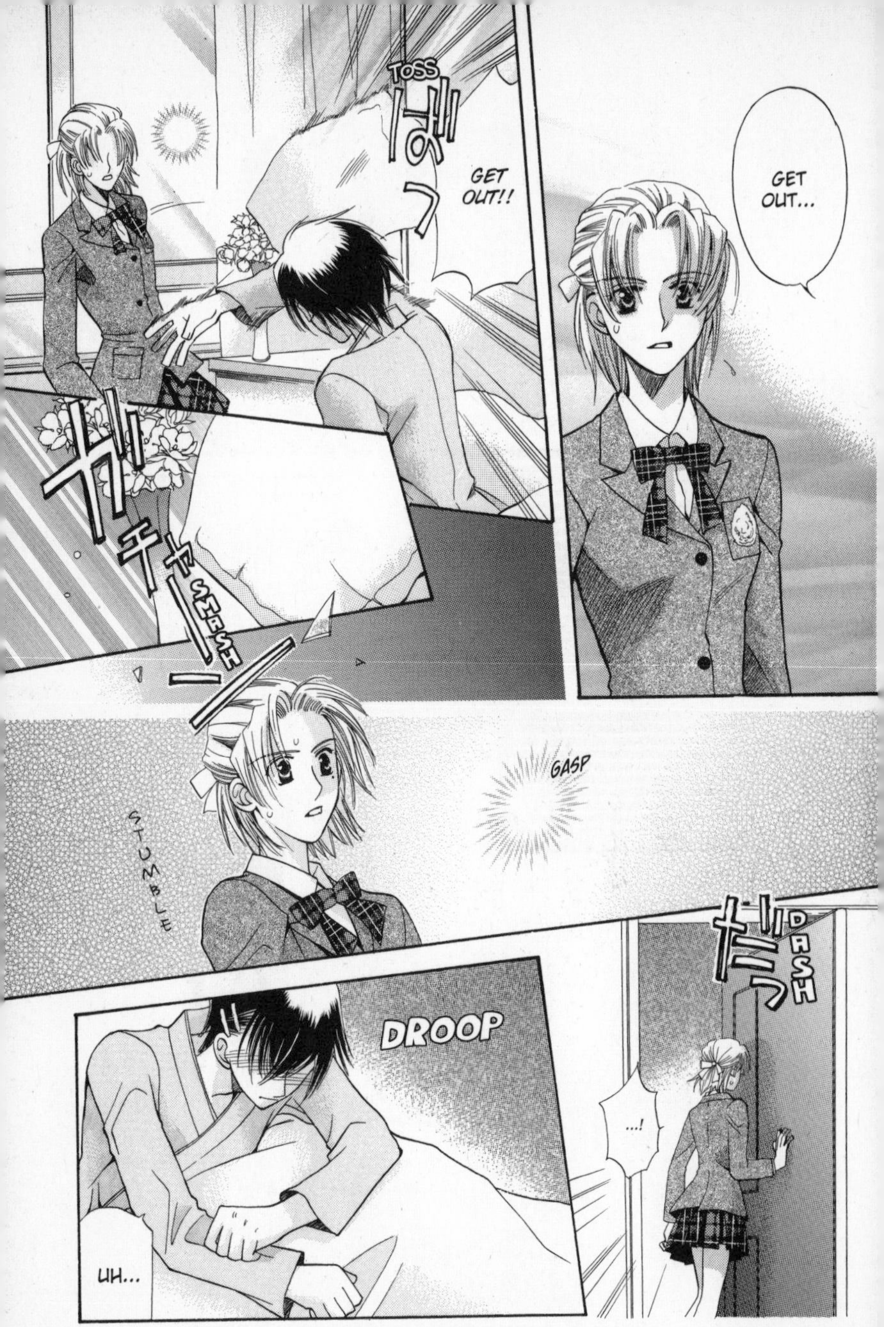
GET OUT...
TOSS
ばっ
GET OUT!!
ガチャー
SMASH
GASP
STUMBLE
たっ
DASH
...!
DROOP
UH...

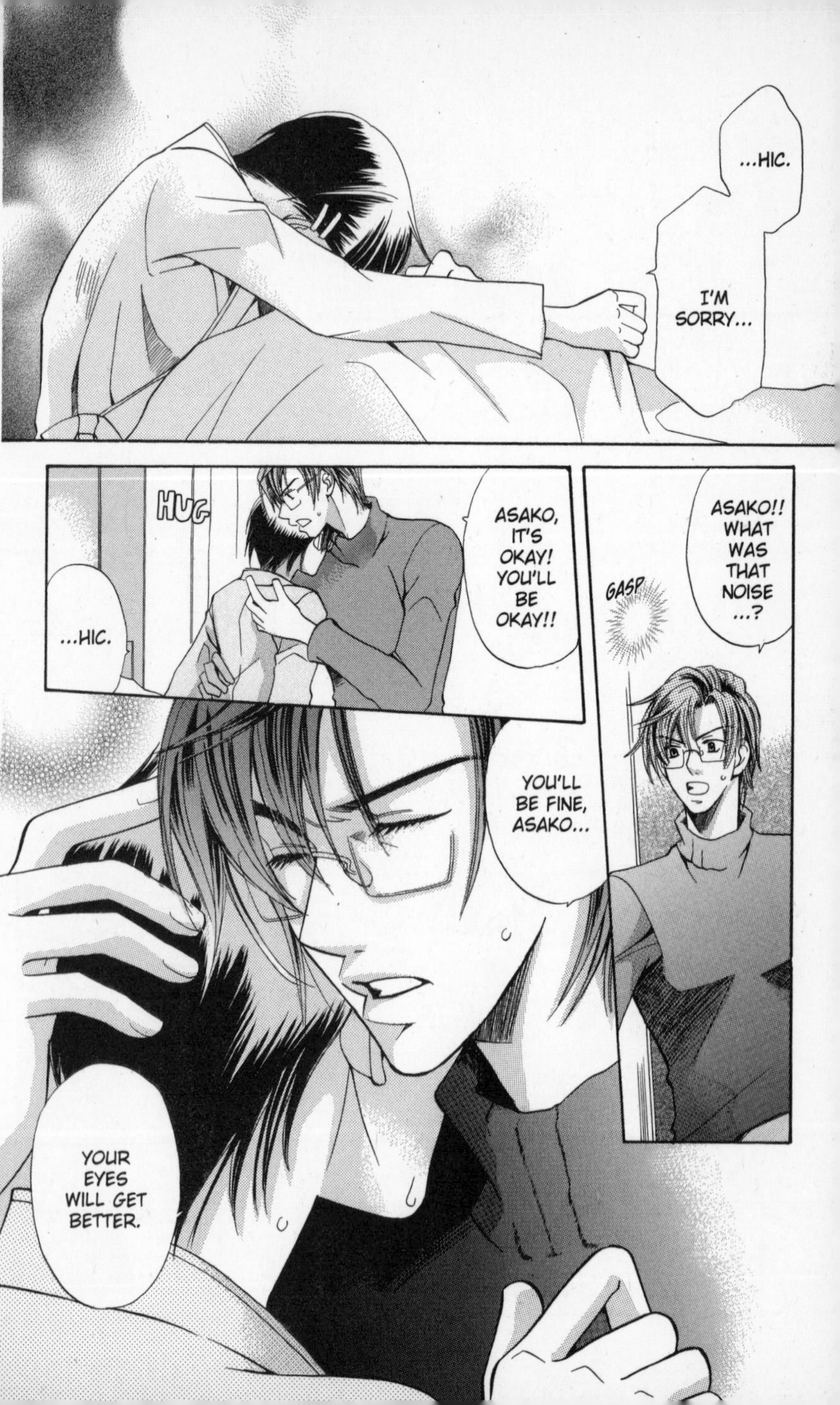
...HIC.
I'M SORRY...
ASAKO!! WHAT WAS THAT NOISE ...?
GASP
ASAKO, IT'S OKAY! YOU'LL BE OKAY!!
HUG
...HIC.
YOU'LL BE FINE, ASAKO...
YOUR EYES WILL GET BETTER.

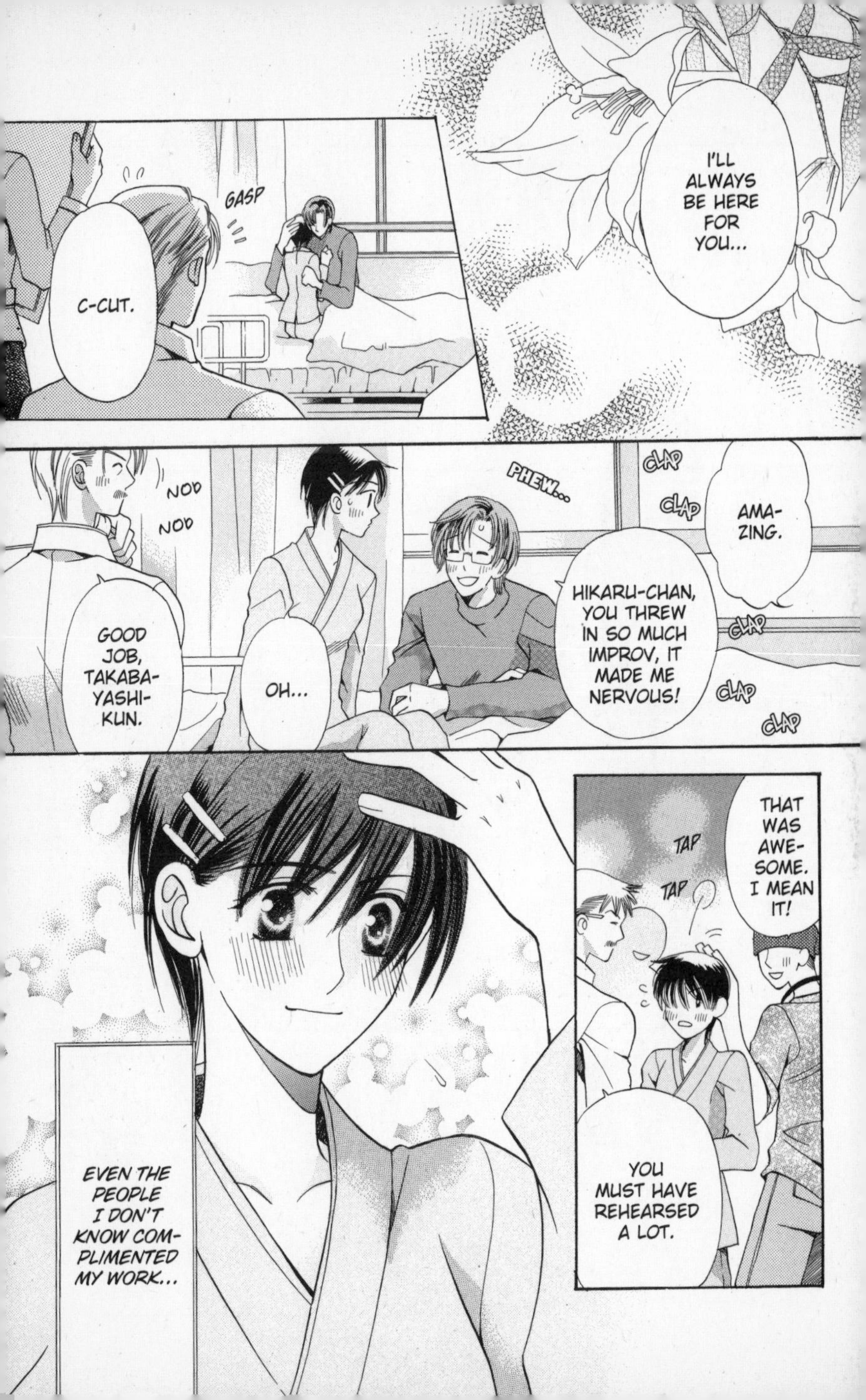

I'LL ALWAYS BE HERE FOR YOU...
GASP
C-CUT.
CLAP
CLAP
AMAZING.
PHEW...
HIKARU-CHAN, YOU THREW IN SO MUCH IMPROV, IT MADE ME NERVOUS!
CLAP
CLAP
CLAP
OH...
NOD
NOD
GOOD JOB, TAKABAYASHI-KUN.
THAT WAS AWESOME. I MEAN IT!
TAP
TAP
YOU MUST HAVE REHEARSED A LOT.
EVEN THE PEOPLE I DON'T KNOW COMPLIMENTED MY WORK...

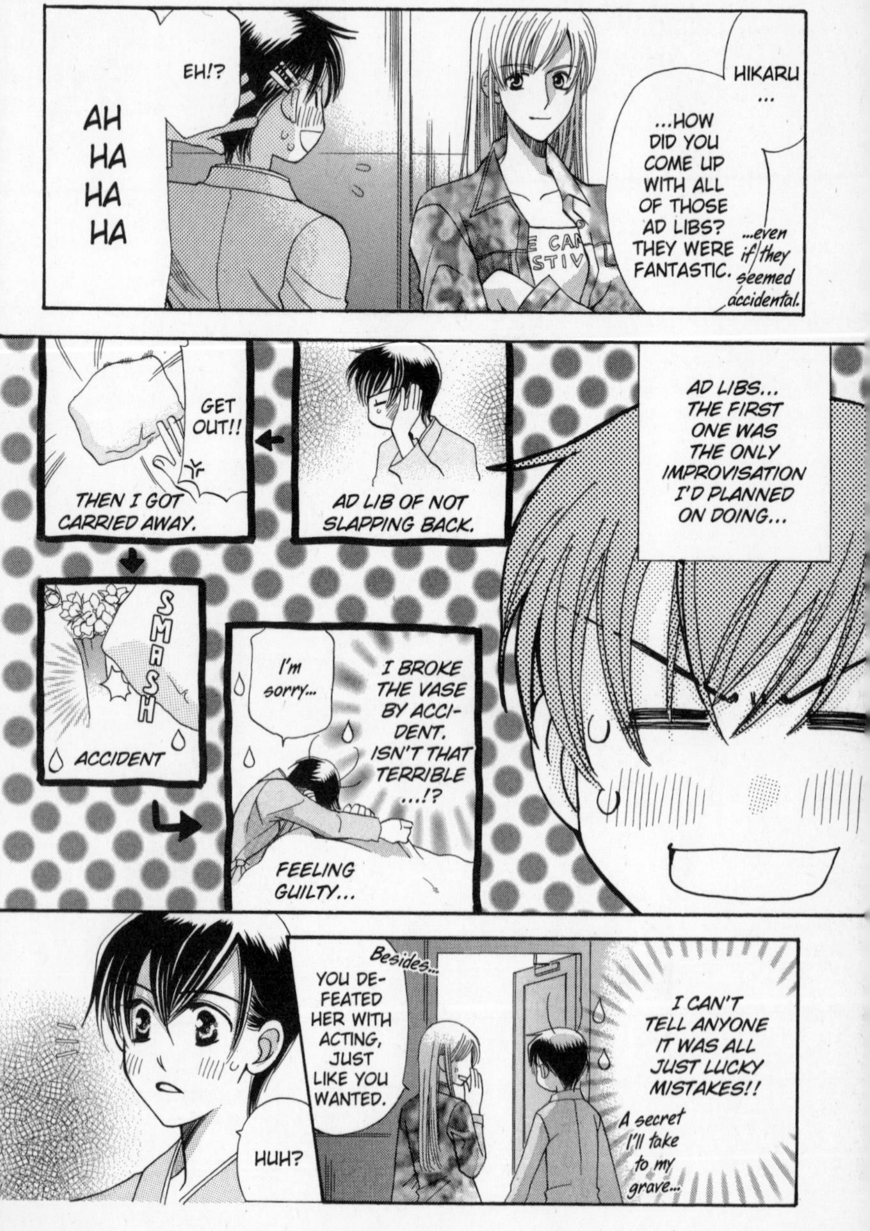
HIKARU ...
...HOW DID YOU COME UP WITH ALL OF THOSE AD LIBS? THEY WERE FANTASTIC.
...even if they seemed accidental.
EH!?
AH HA HA HA
AD LIBS... THE FIRST ONE WAS THE ONLY IMPROVISATION I'D PLANNED ON DOING...
AD LIB OF NOT SLAPPING BACK.
GET OUT!!
THEN I GOT CARRIED AWAY.
SMASH
ACCIDENT
I'm sorry...
I BROKE THE VASE BY ACCIDENT. ISN'T THAT TERRIBLE ...!?
FEELING GUILTY...
I CAN'T TELL ANYONE IT WAS ALL JUST LUCKY MISTAKES!!
A secret I'll take to my grave...
Besides...
YOU DEFEATED HER WITH ACTING, JUST LIKE YOU WANTED.
HUH?

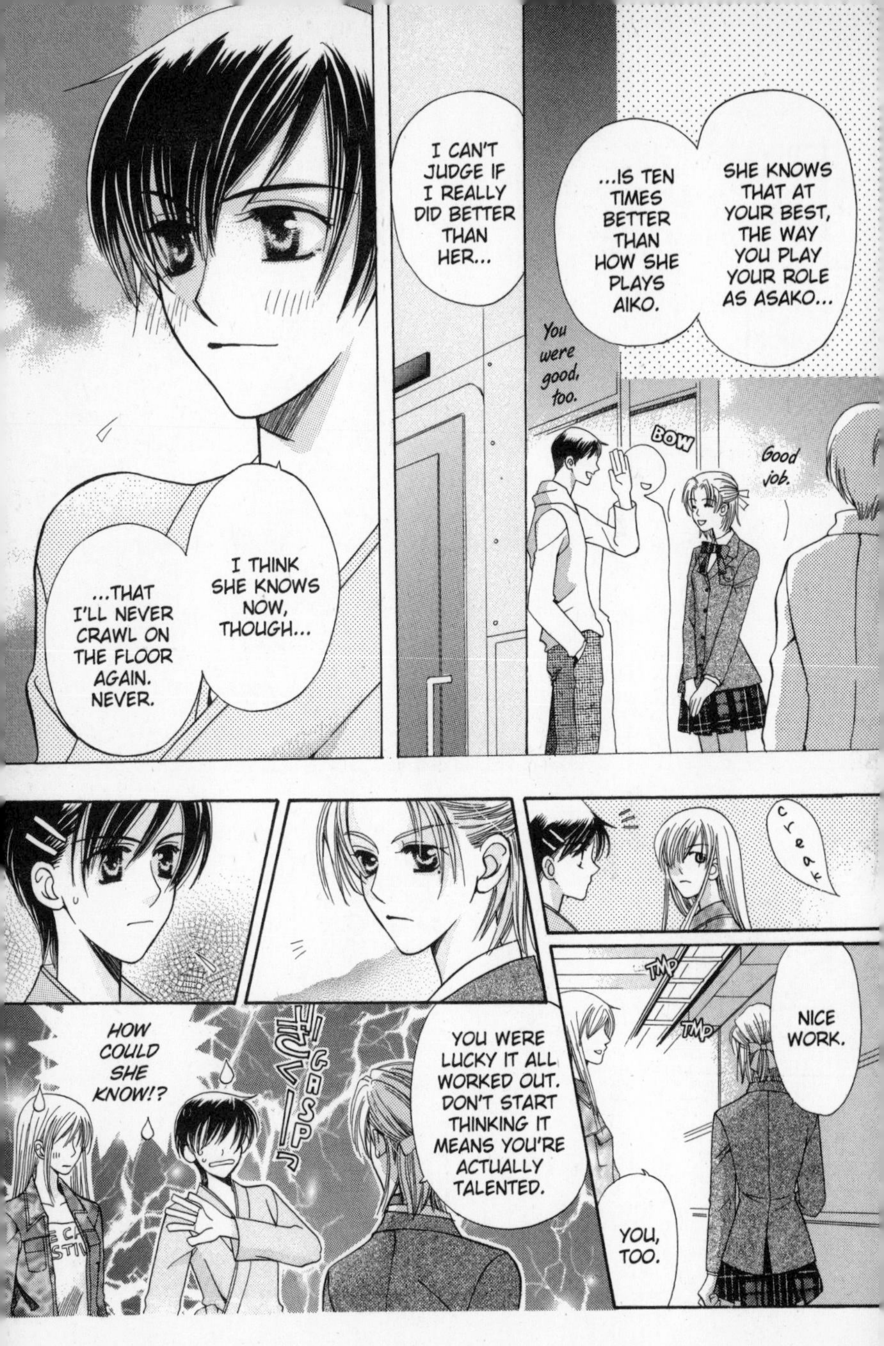
SHE KNOWS THAT AT YOUR BEST, THE WAY YOU PLAY YOUR ROLE AS ASAKO...
...IS TEN TIMES BETTER THAN HOW SHE PLAYS AIKO.
I CAN'T JUDGE IF I REALLY DID BETTER THAN HER...
Good job.
BOW
You were good, too.
I THINK SHE KNOWS NOW, THOUGH...
...THAT I'LL NEVER CRAWL ON THE FLOOR AGAIN. NEVER.
creak
TMP
TMP
NICE WORK.
YOU, TOO.
YOU WERE LUCKY IT ALL WORKED OUT. DON'T START THINKING IT MEANS YOU'RE ACTUALLY TALENTED.
GASP
HOW COULD SHE KNOW!?

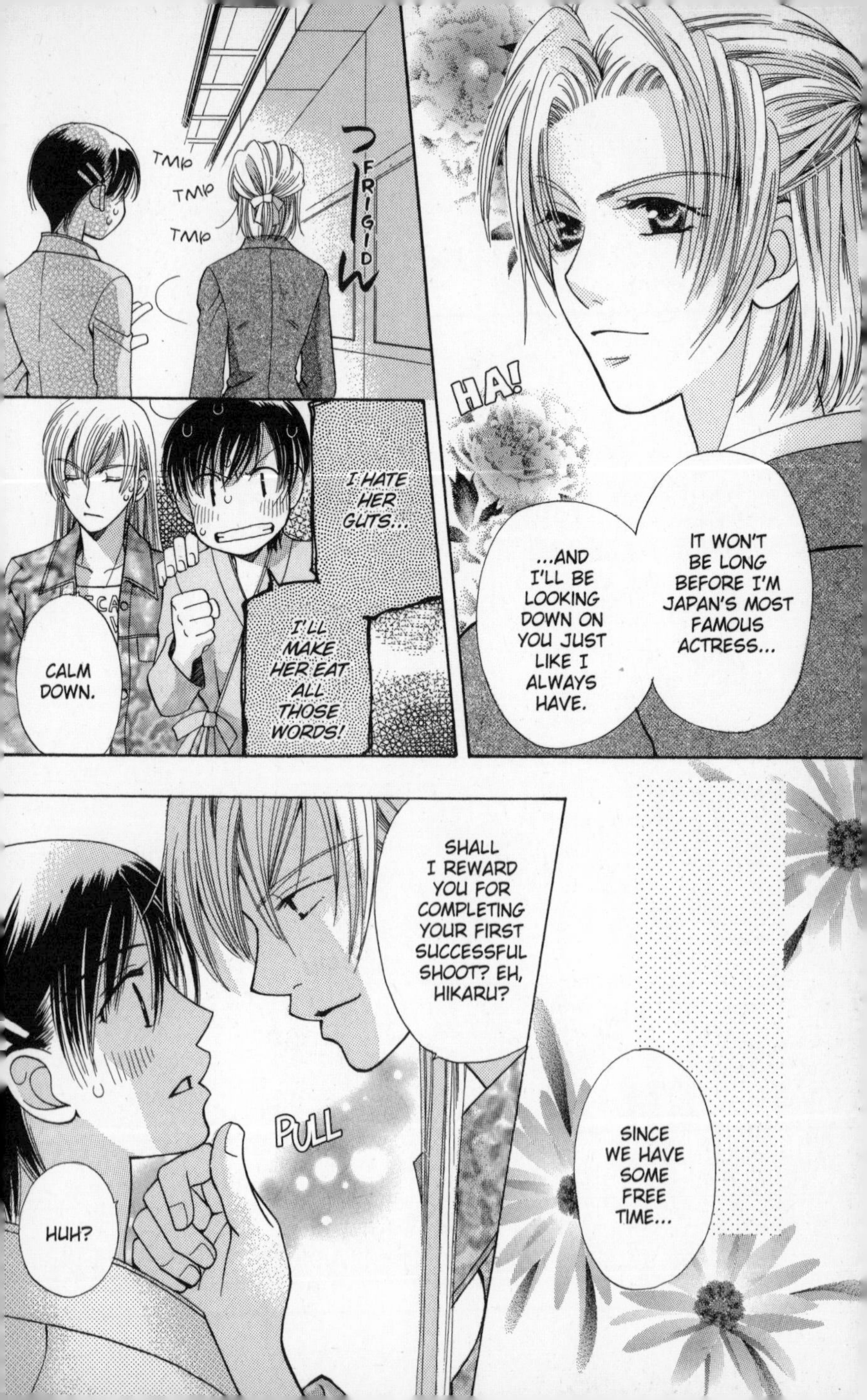
HA!
IT WON'T BE LONG BEFORE I'M JAPAN'S MOST FAMOUS ACTRESS...
...AND I'LL BE LOOKING DOWN ON YOU JUST LIKE I ALWAYS HAVE.
FRIGID
TMP
TMP
TMP
I HATE HER GUTS...
I'LL MAKE HER EAT ALL THOSE WORDS!
CALM DOWN.
SINCE WE HAVE SOME FREE TIME...
SHALL I REWARD YOU FOR COMPLETING YOUR FIRST SUCCESSFUL SHOOT? EH, HIKARU?
PULL
HUH?

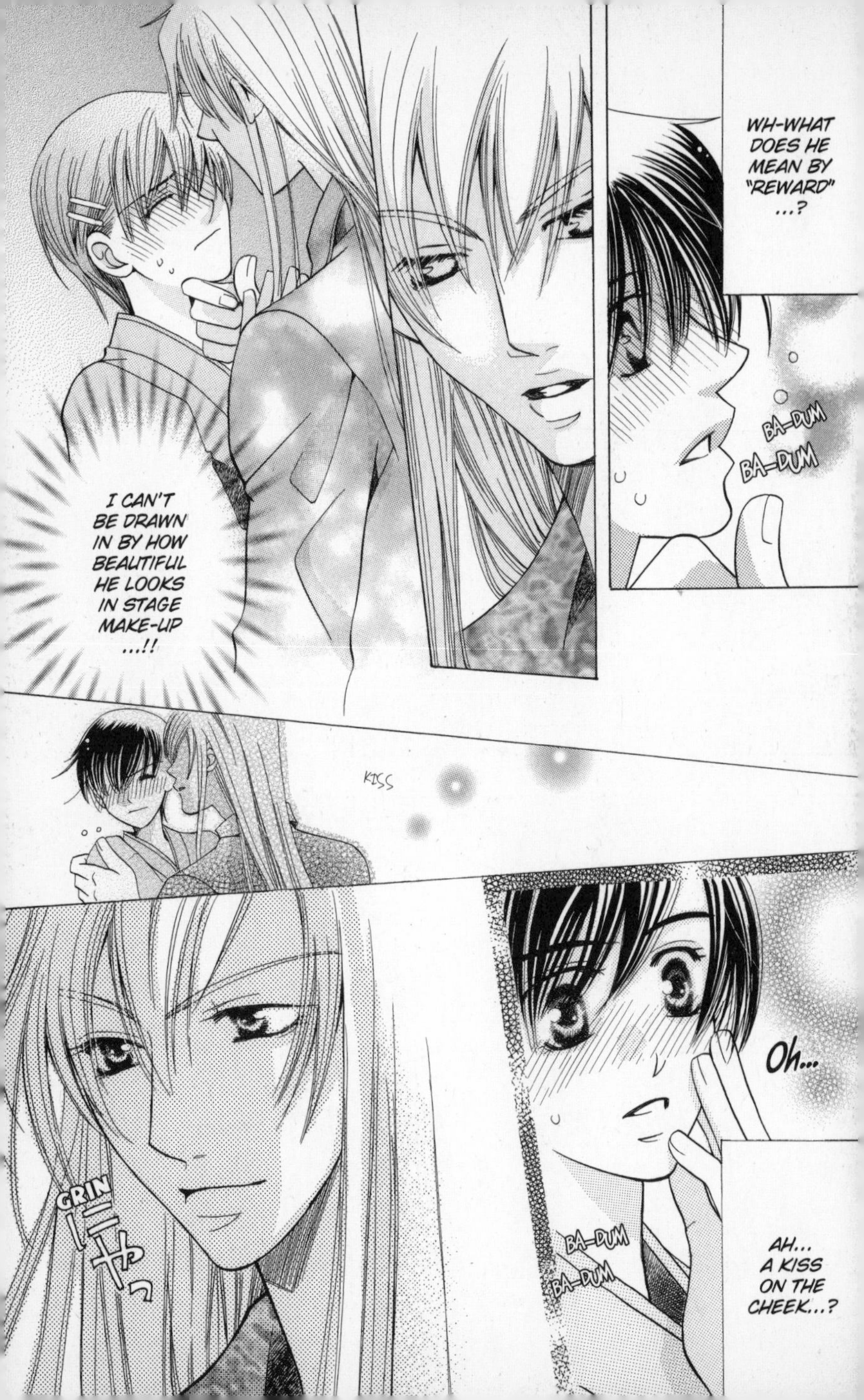
WH-WHAT DOES HE MEAN BY "REWARD" ...?
BA-DUM
BA-DUM
I CAN'T BE DRAWN IN BY HOW BEAUTIFUL HE LOOKS IN STAGE MAKE-UP ...!!
KISS
Oh...
BA-DUM
BA-DUM
AH... A KISS ON THE CHEEK...?
GRIN

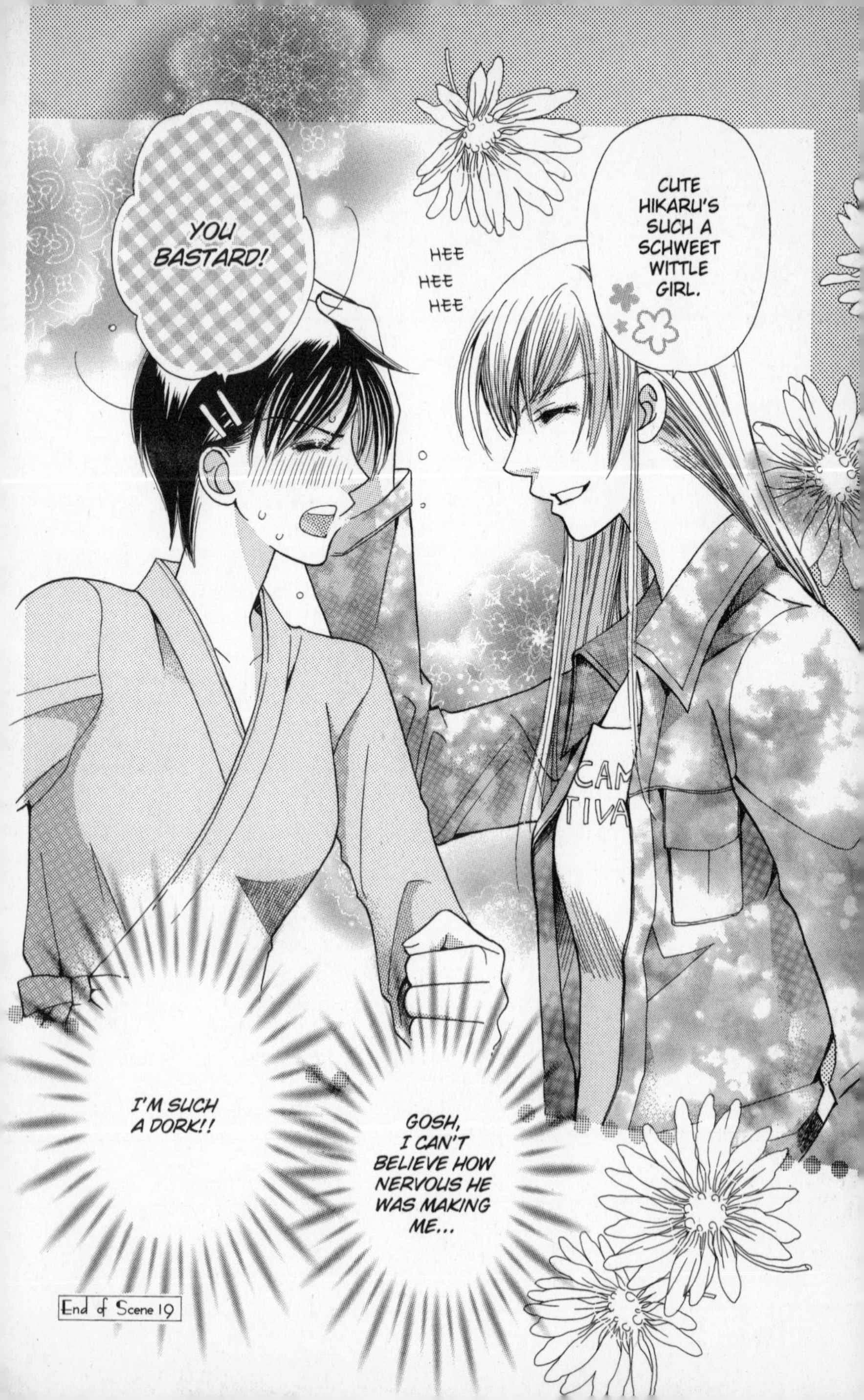
CUTE HIKARU'S SUCH A SCHWEET WITTLE GIRL.
HEE HEE HEE
YOU BASTARD!
GOSH, I CAN'T BELIEVE HOW NERVOUS HE WAS MAKING ME...
I'M SUCH A DORK!!
CAM TIVA
End of Scene 19

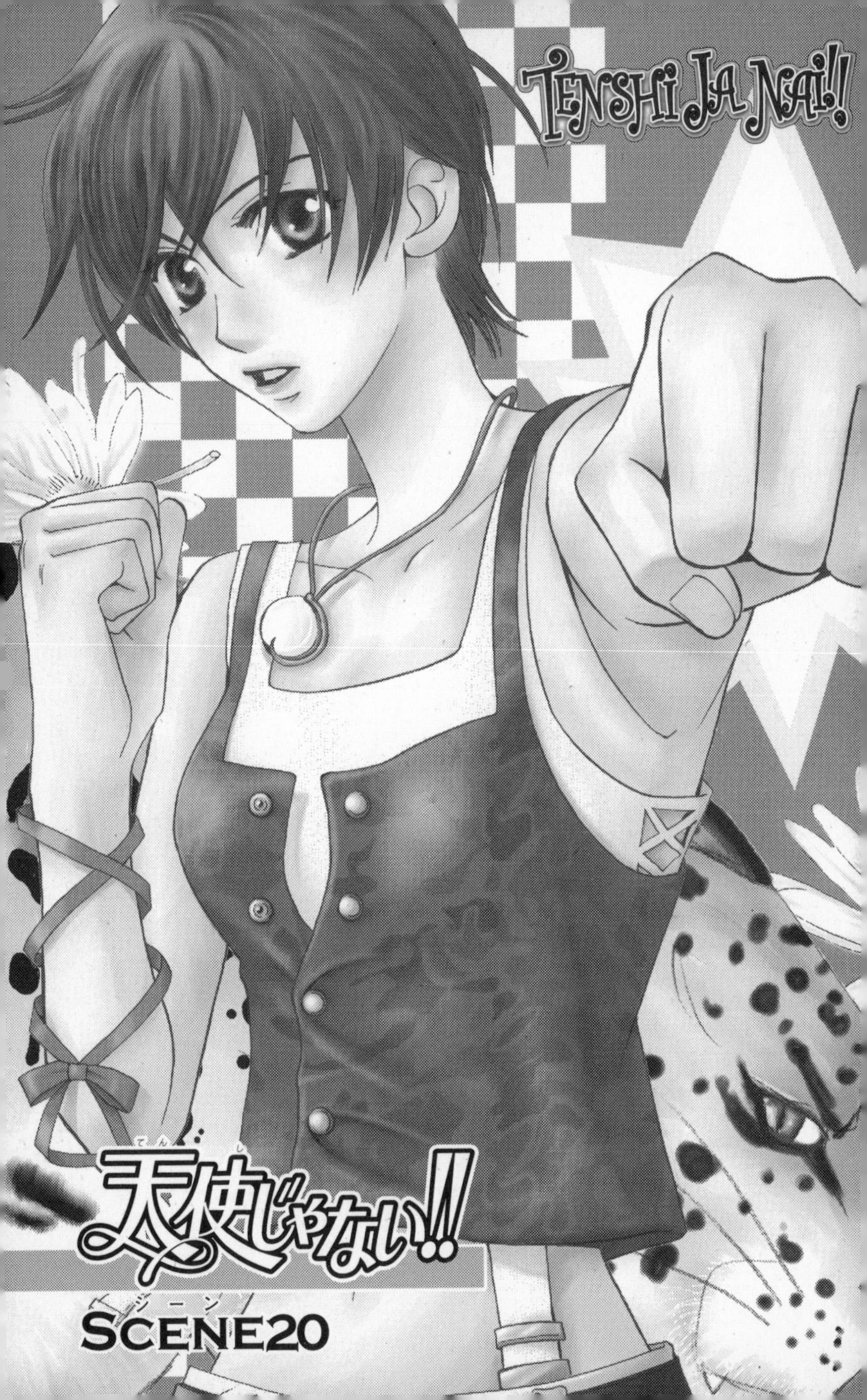
TENSHI JA NAI!!
天使じゃない!!
てん し
シーン
SCENE20

IT'S ONLY BEEN SIX WEEKS SINCE I STARTED DATING SENSEI.
I KNOW I NEED TO TELL HIM THAT I WAS ON THAT TV SHOW, AND THAT I KEPT IT A SECRET FROM HIM...
...BUT I'M SCARED THAT HE'LL HATE ME FOR IT.

INHALE
EXHALE
SQUEEZE
INHALE
EXHALE

My Current Addictions #2

Sour Kimchi...ard rare candies I have to place a special order for...etc...

Because I sit all day, every day to do my work, I'm worried about gaining weight. So, I've started exercising in my room and am trying to get ripping six packs...but I have a long way to go!

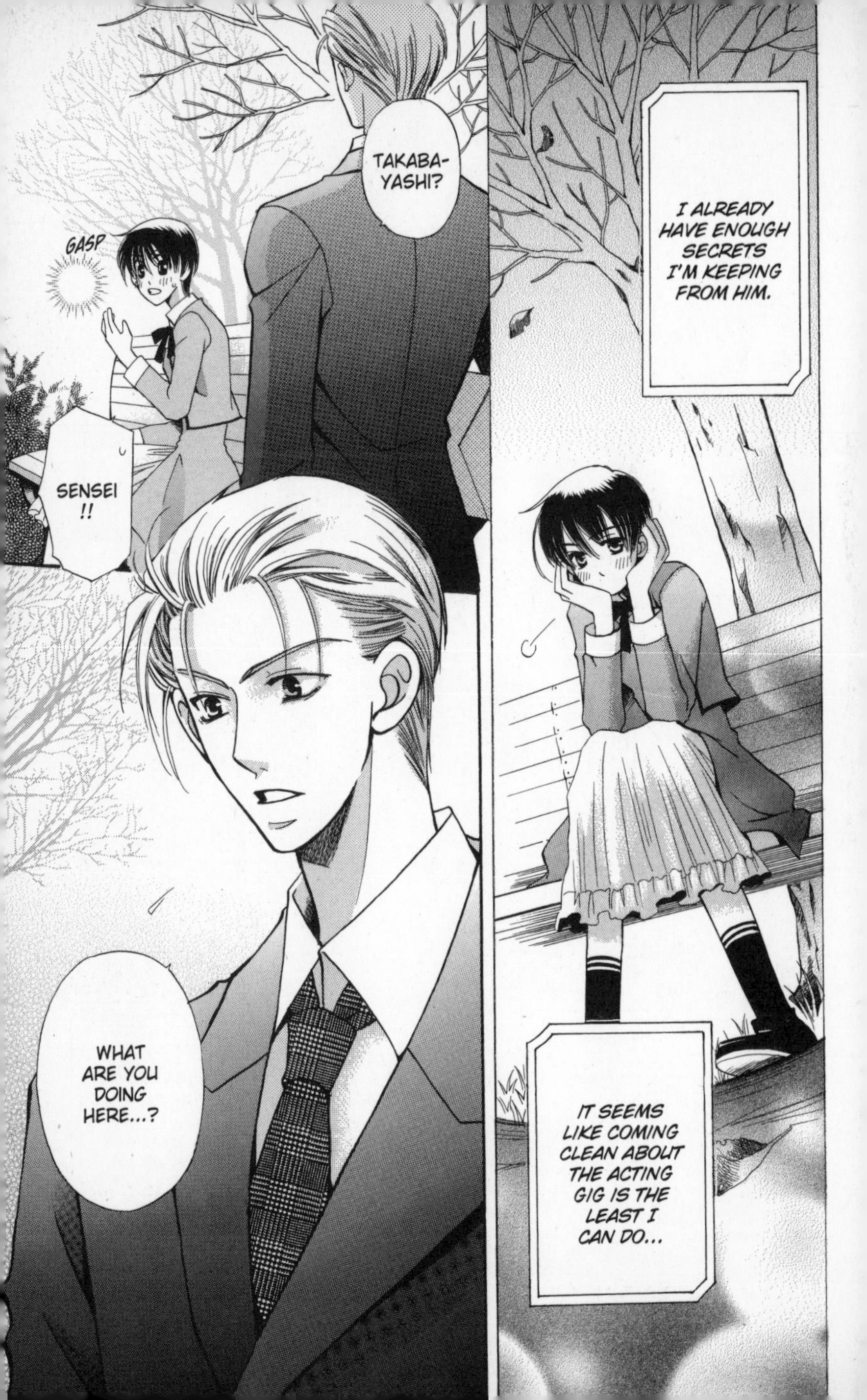
I ALREADY HAVE ENOUGH SECRETS I'M KEEPING FROM HIM.
IT SEEMS LIKE COMING CLEAN ABOUT THE ACTING GIG IS THE LEAST I CAN DO...
TAKABA-YASHI?
GASP
SENSEI !!
WHAT ARE YOU DOING HERE...?

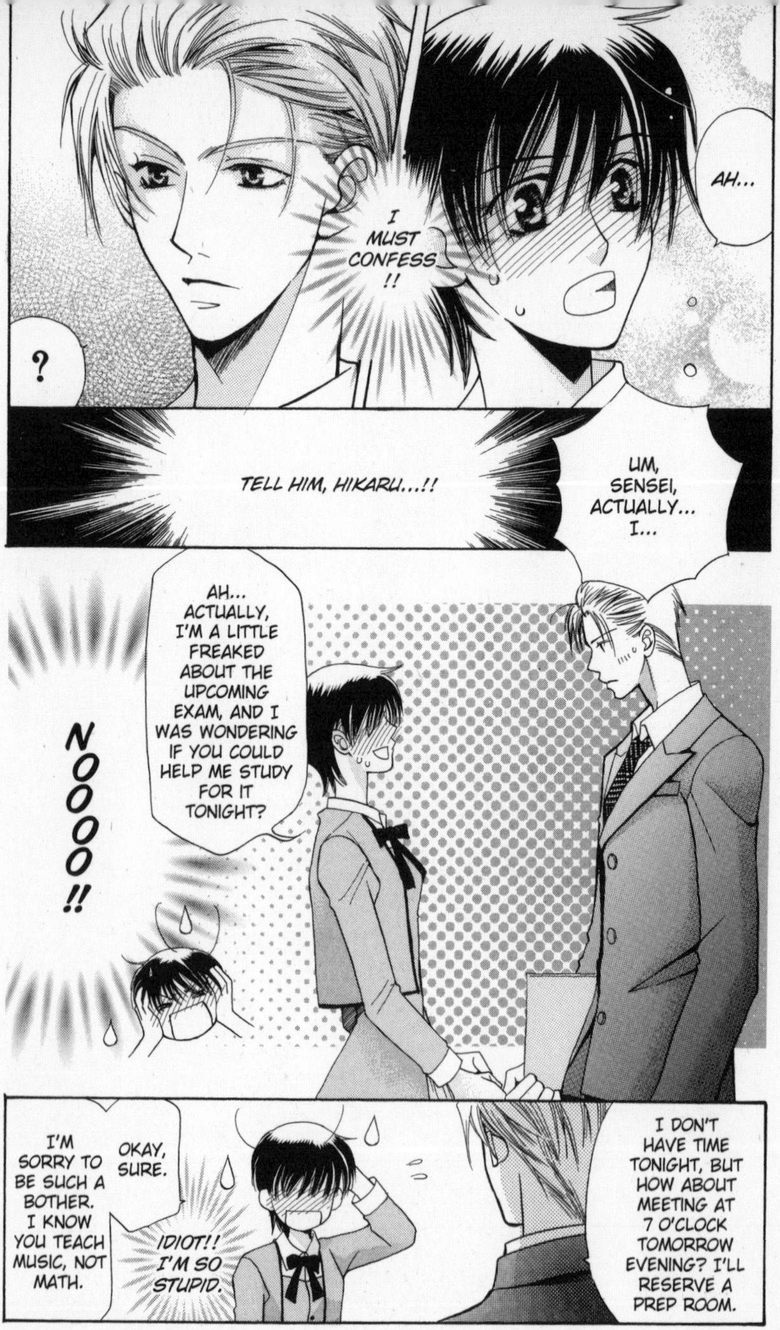
AH...
I MUST CONFESS!!
?
UM, SENSEI, ACTUALLY... I...
TELL HIM, HIKARU...!!
AH... ACTUALLY, I'M A LITTLE FREAKED ABOUT THE UPCOMING EXAM, AND I WAS WONDERING IF YOU COULD HELP ME STUDY FOR IT TONIGHT?
NOOOOO!!
I DON'T HAVE TIME TONIGHT, BUT HOW ABOUT MEETING AT 7 O'CLOCK TOMORROW EVENING? I'LL RESERVE A PREP ROOM.
OKAY, SURE.
I'M SORRY TO BE SUCH A BOTHER. I KNOW YOU TEACH MUSIC, NOT MATH.
IDIOT!! I'M SO STUPID.

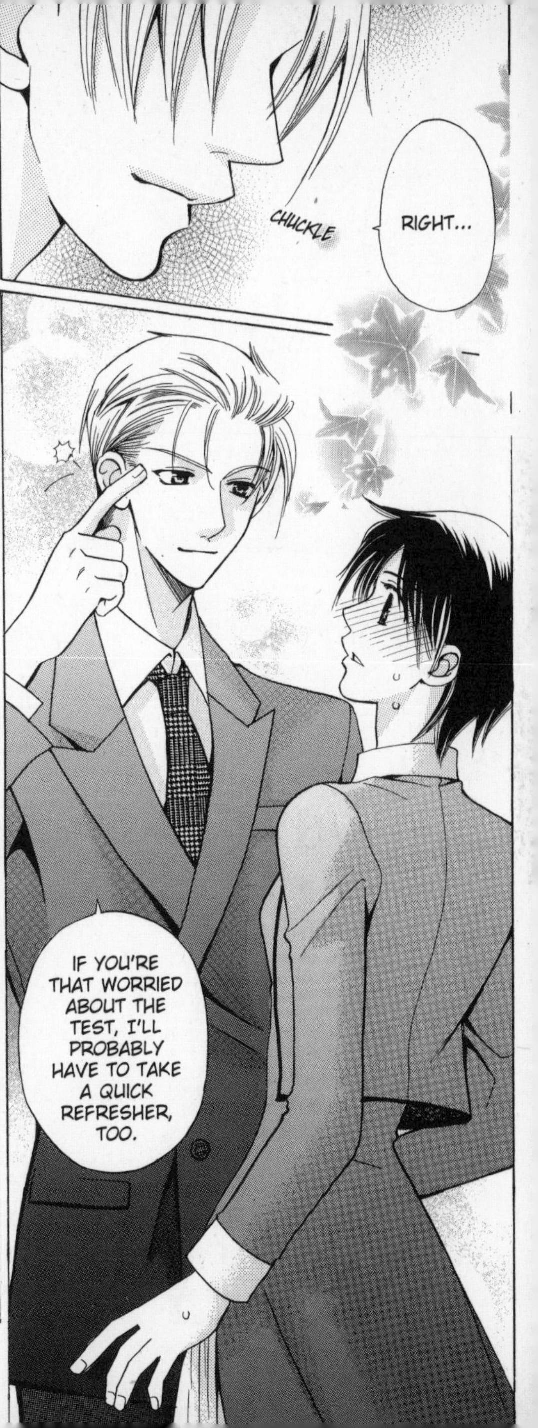
CHUCKLE
RIGHT...
IF YOU'RE THAT WORRIED ABOUT THE TEST, I'LL PROBABLY HAVE TO TAKE A QUICK REFRESHER, TOO.

My Current Addictions #3

While I'm working, if I'm working with my assistants, sometimes we play a game of "Let's remember old anime songs!" The three of us get together, and we all try to remember opening and ending theme songs of anime we used to watch as kids, going for full lyrics and choruses... We play this game while we create manga, and it can get really tough. In an effort to avoid accepting that our brains are deteriorating, we're not allowed to give up.

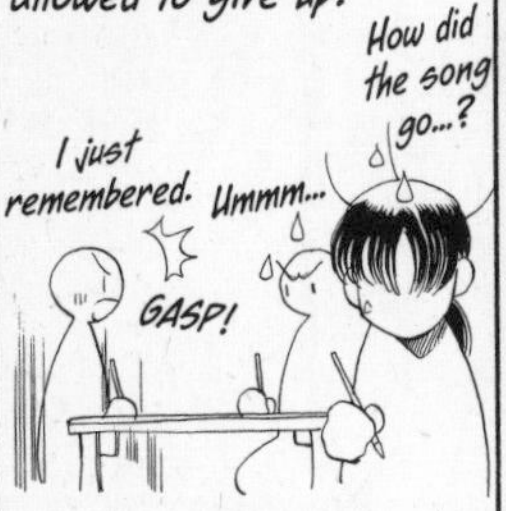
How did the song go...?
I just remembered.
Ummm...
GASP!

If we can't remember for a while, it gets frustrating, but once we figure it out, it makes us feel good, so...it's an addictive experience.

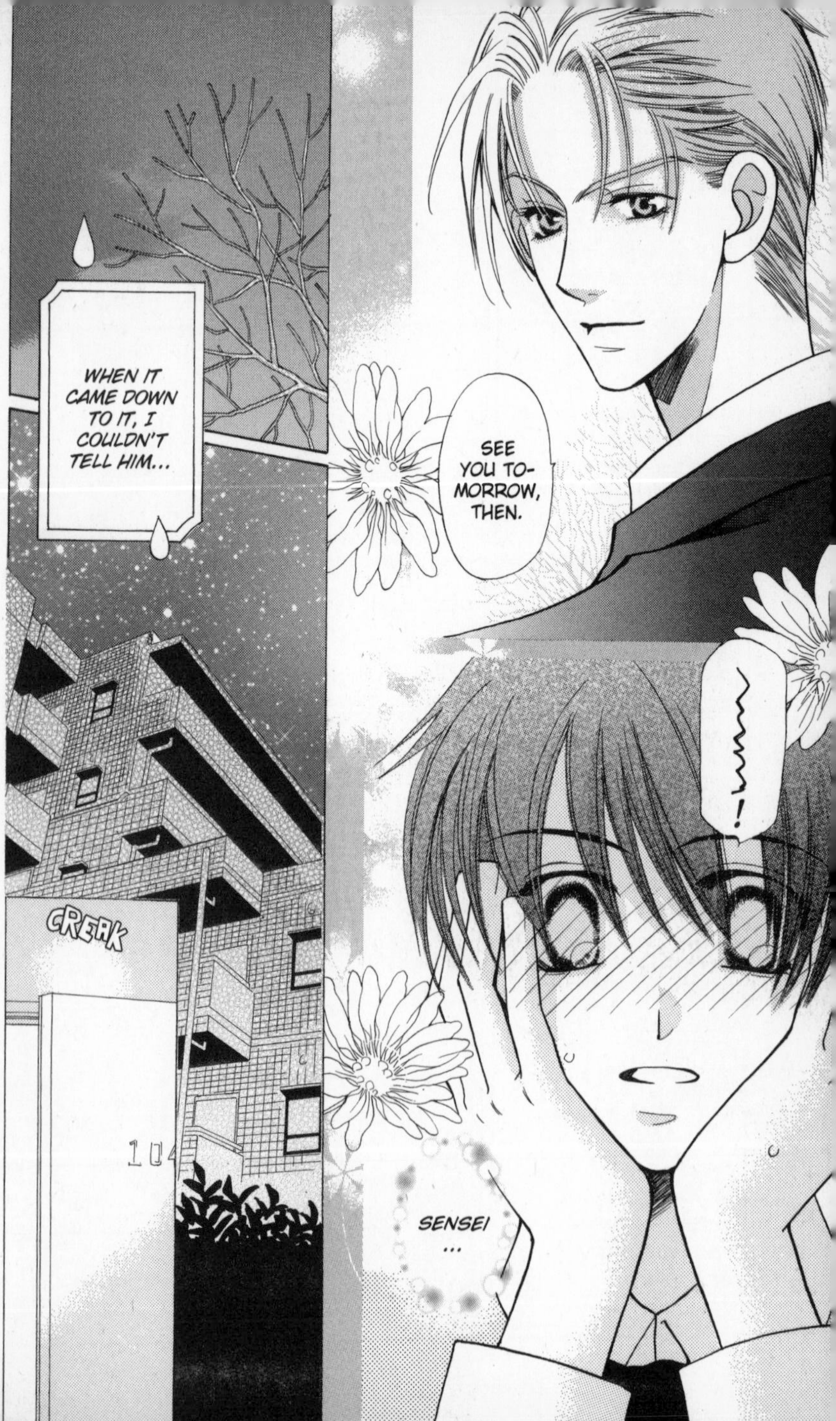
SEE YOU TO-MORROW, THEN.
!
SENSEI ...
WHEN IT CAME DOWN TO IT, I COULDN'T TELL HIM...
CREAK
104

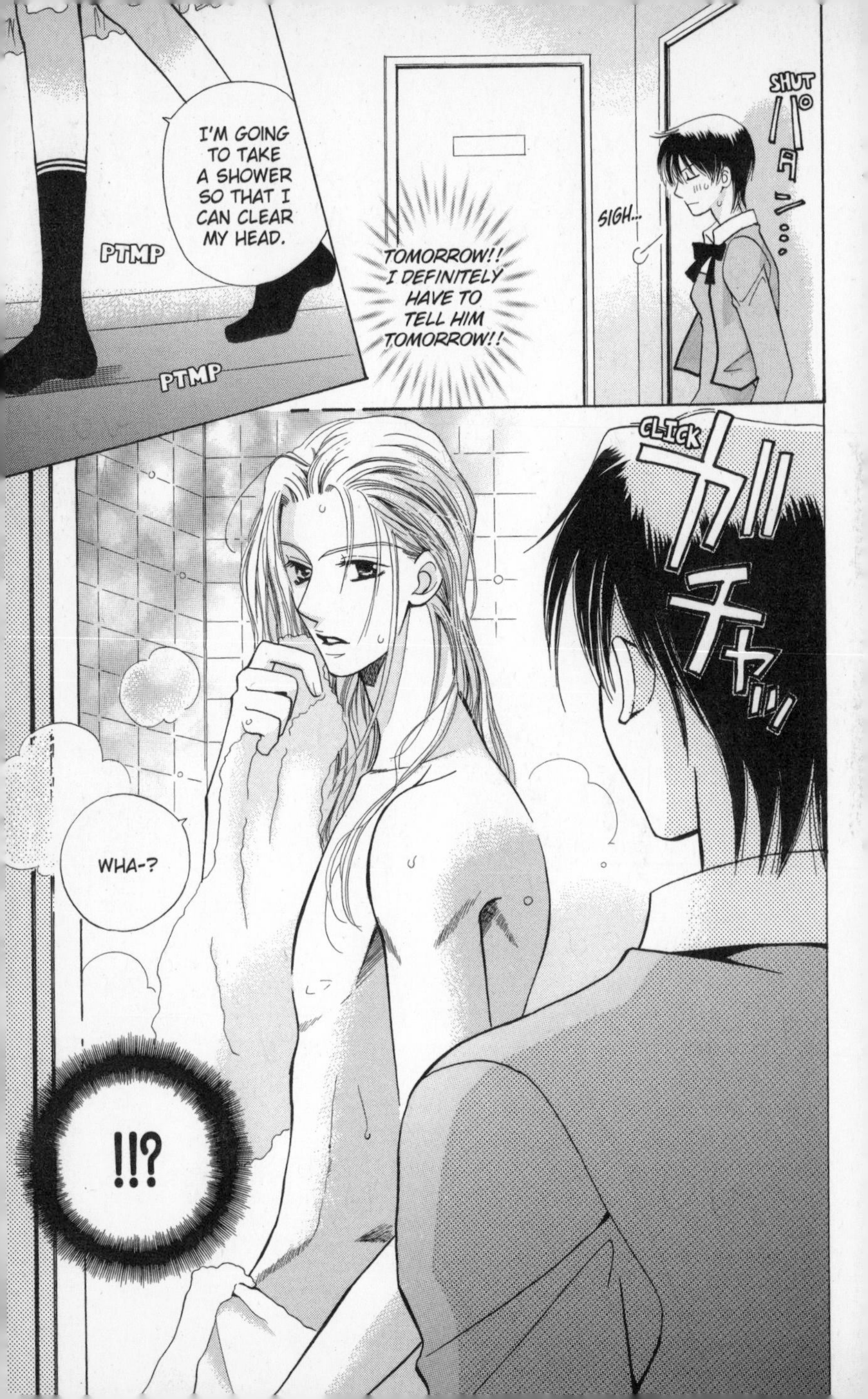
SHUT
SIGH...
TOMORROW!! I DEFINITELY HAVE TO TELL HIM TOMORROW!!
I'M GOING TO TAKE A SHOWER SO THAT I CAN CLEAR MY HEAD.
PTMP
PTMP
CLICK
WHA-?
!!?

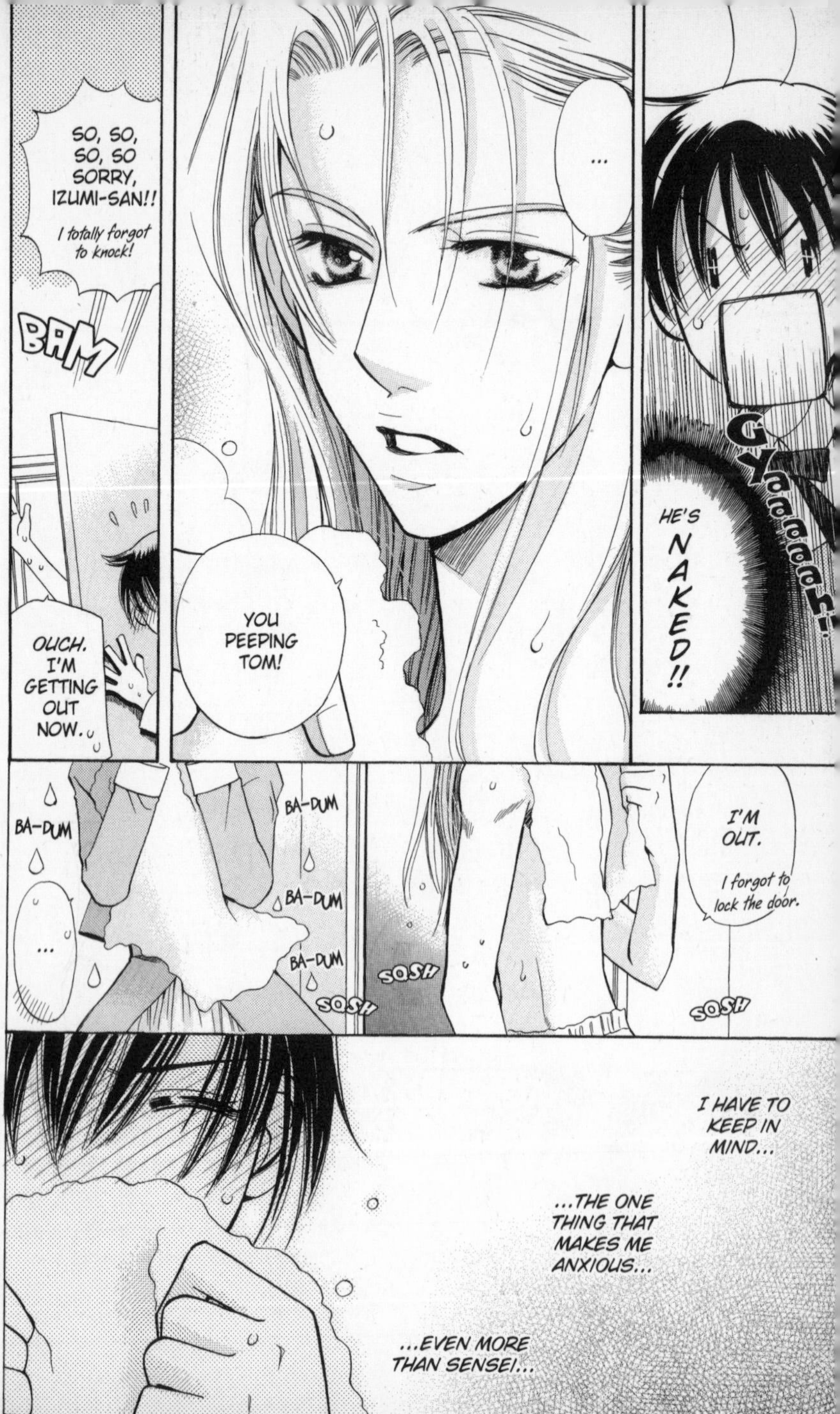
GYaaaaaah!
HE'S NAKED!!
...
YOU PEEPING TOM!
SO, SO, SO, SO SORRY, IZUMI-SAN!!
I totally forgot to knock!
BAM
OUCH. I'M GETTING OUT NOW.
I'M OUT.
I forgot to lock the door.
SOSH
SOSH
BA-DUM
BA-DUM
BA-DUM
SOSH
BA-DUM
...
I HAVE TO KEEP IN MIND...
...THE ONE THING THAT MAKES ME ANXIOUS...
...EVEN MORE THAN SENSEI...

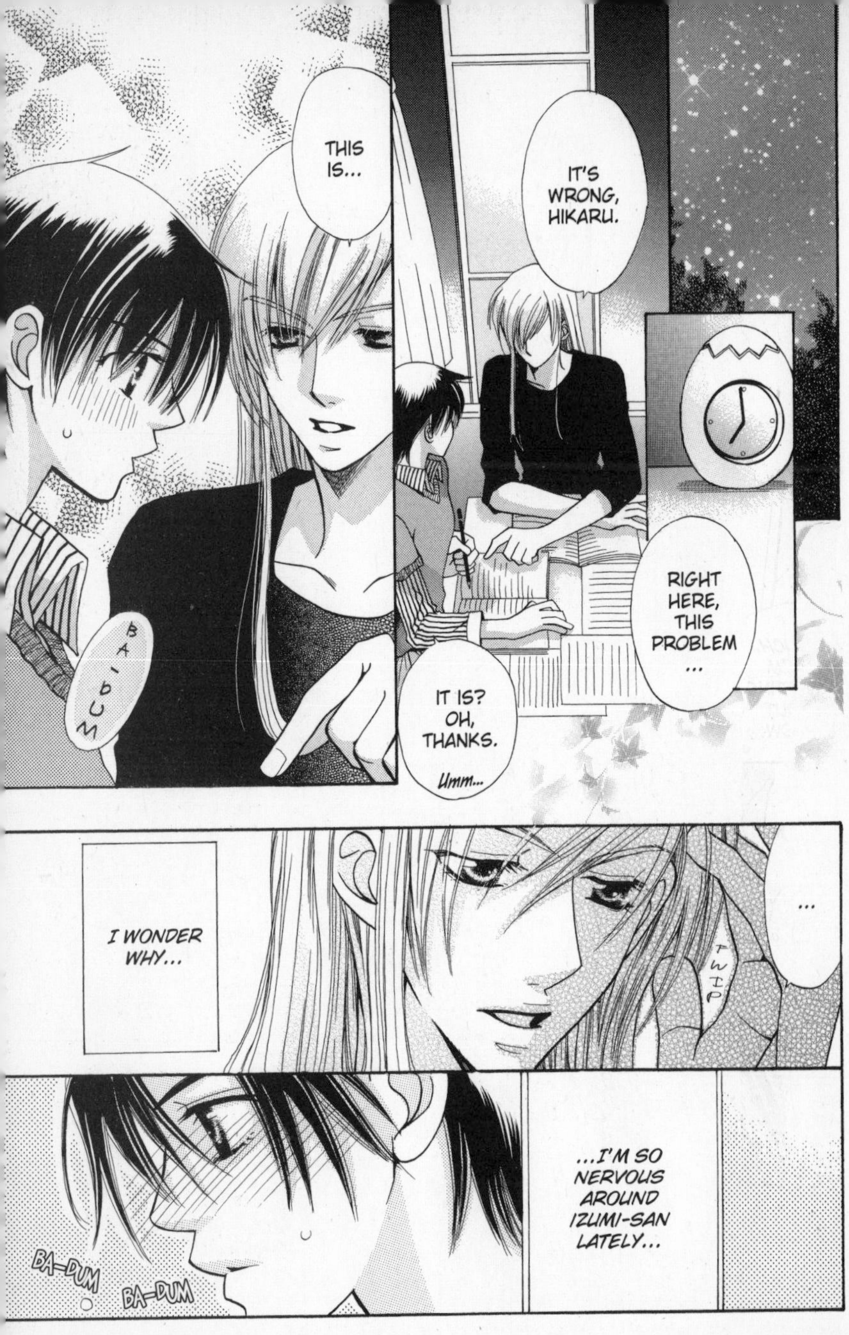
IT'S WRONG, HIKARU.
RIGHT HERE, THIS PROBLEM ...
IT IS? OH, THANKS.
Umm...
THIS IS...
BA-DUM
...
FWIP
I WONDER WHY...
...I'M SO NERVOUS AROUND IZUMI-SAN LATELY...
BA-DUM
BA-DUM

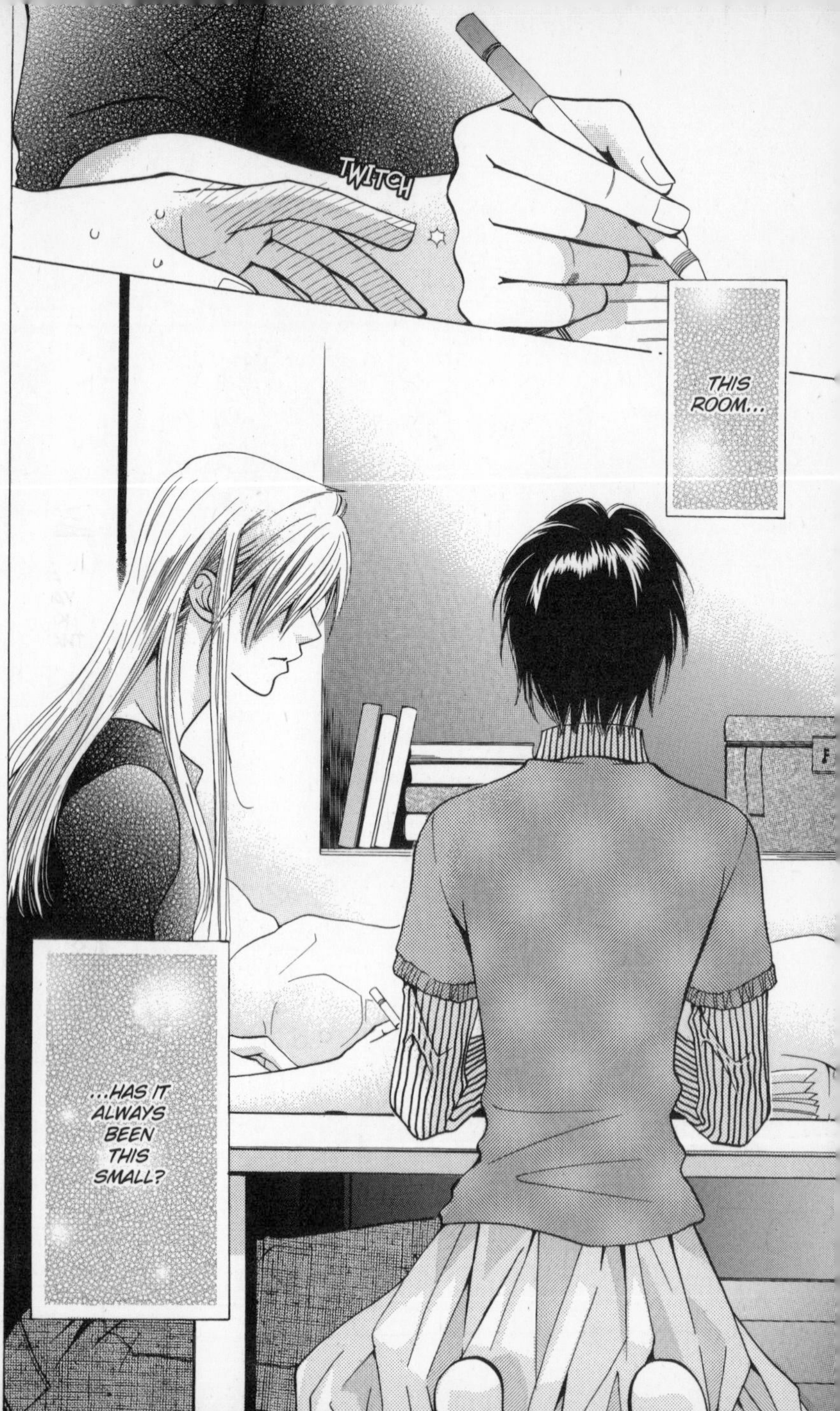
TWITCH
THIS ROOM...
...HAS IT ALWAYS BEEN THIS SMALL?

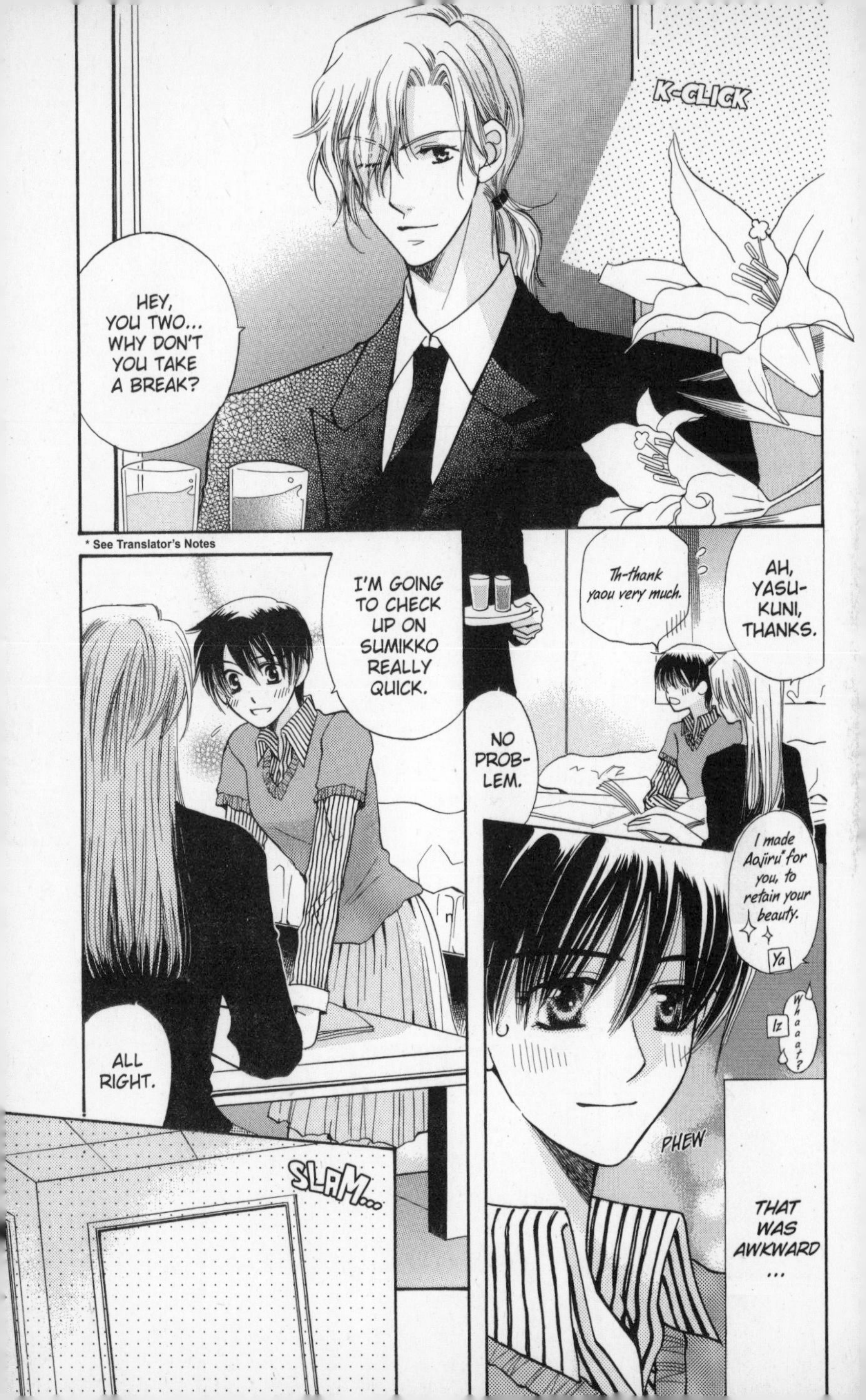
K-CLICK
HEY, YOU TWO... WHY DON'T YOU TAKE A BREAK?
AH, YASU-KUNI, THANKS.
Th-thank yaou very much.
NO PROBLEM.
I made Aajiru* for you, to retain your beauty.
Ya
Whaaat?
Iz
I'M GOING TO CHECK UP ON SUMIKKO REALLY QUICK.
ALL RIGHT.
SLAM...
PHEW
THAT WAS AWKWARD ...

* See Translator's Notes

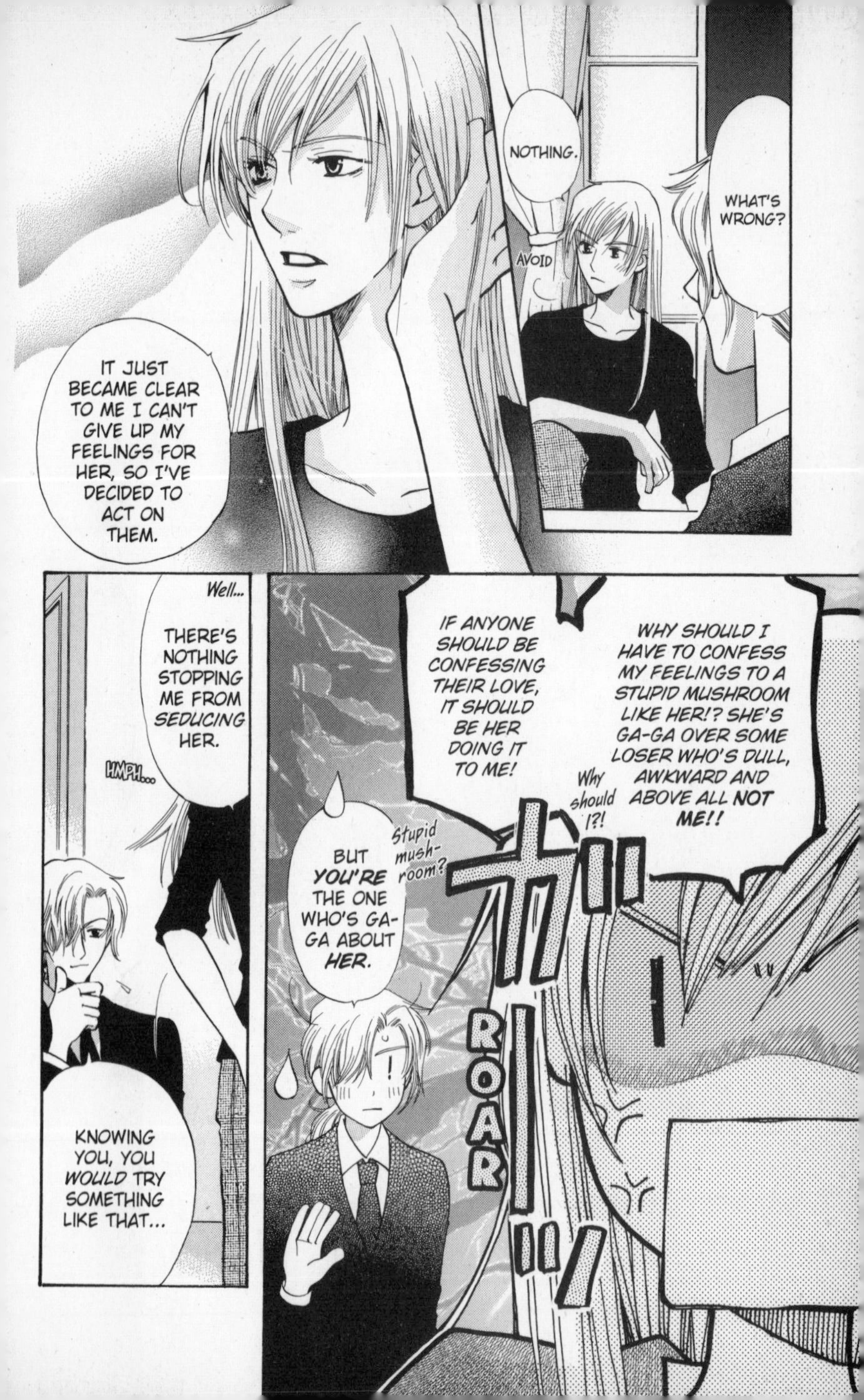
WHAT'S WRONG?
NOTHING.
AVOID
IT JUST BECAME CLEAR TO ME I CAN'T GIVE UP MY FEELINGS FOR HER, SO I'VE DECIDED TO ACT ON THEM.
WHY SHOULD I HAVE TO CONFESS MY FEELINGS TO A STUPID MUSHROOM LIKE HER!? SHE'S GA-GA OVER SOME LOSER WHO'S DULL, AWKWARD AND ABOVE ALL NOT ME!!
IF ANYONE SHOULD BE CONFESSING THEIR LOVE, IT SHOULD BE HER DOING IT TO ME!
Why should I?!
ROAR
BUT YOU'RE THE ONE WHO'S GA-GA ABOUT HER.
Stupid mush-room?
Well...
THERE'S NOTHING STOPPING ME FROM SEDUCING HER.
HMPH...
KNOWING YOU, YOU WOULD TRY SOMETHING LIKE THAT...

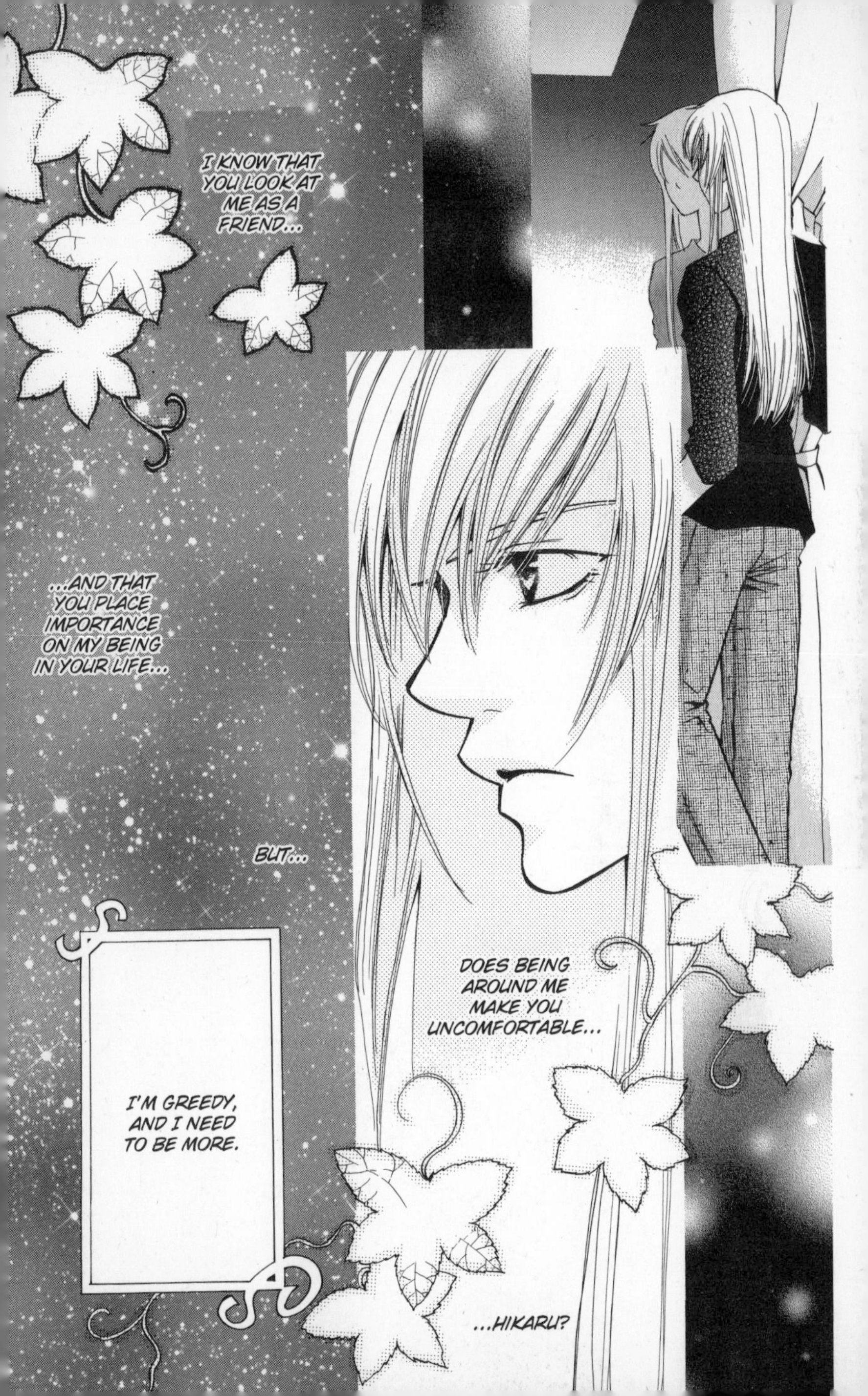
DOES BEING AROUND ME MAKE YOU UNCOMFORTABLE...
...HIKARU?
I KNOW THAT YOU LOOK AT ME AS A FRIEND...
...AND THAT YOU PLACE IMPORTANCE ON MY BEING IN YOUR LIFE...
BUT...
I'M GREEDY, AND I NEED TO BE MORE.

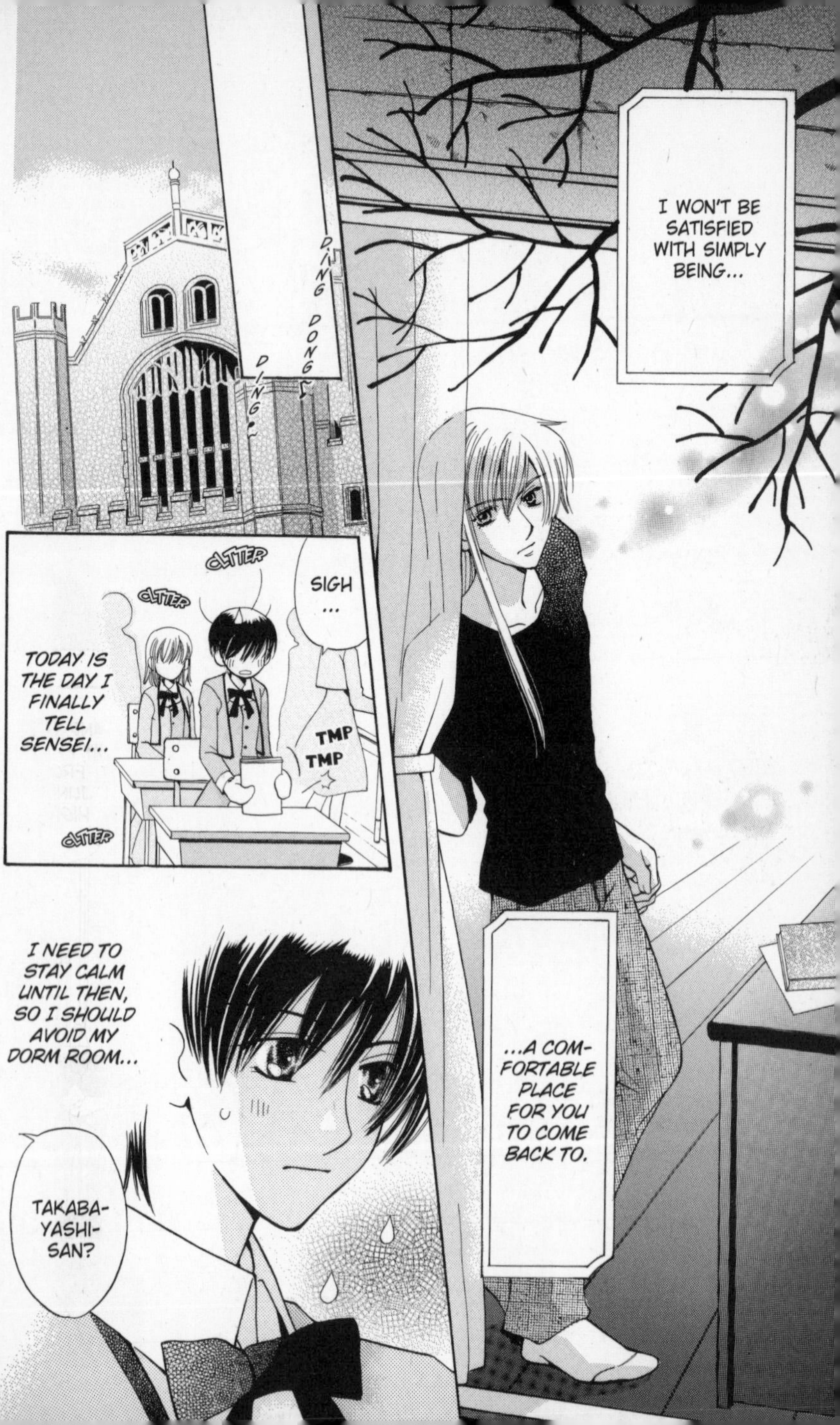
I WON'T BE SATISFIED WITH SIMPLY BEING...
...A COM-FORTABLE PLACE FOR YOU TO COME BACK TO.
DING DONG~
DING~
SIGH...
CLATTER
CLATTER
TODAY IS THE DAY I FINALLY TELL SENSEI...
TMP TMP
CLATTER
I NEED TO STAY CALM UNTIL THEN, SO I SHOULD AVOID MY DORM ROOM...
TAKABA-YASHI-SAN?

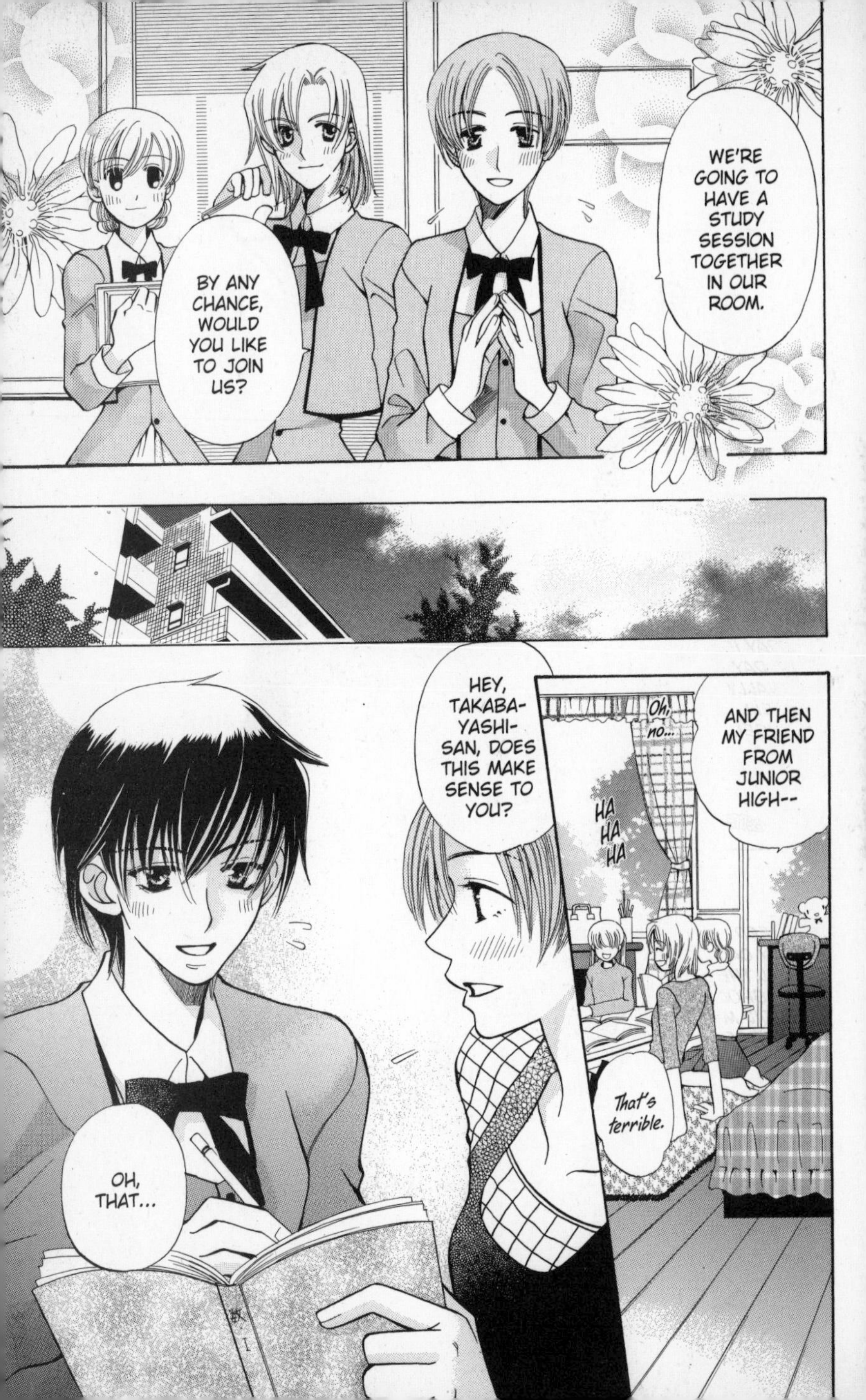

WE'RE GOING TO HAVE A STUDY SESSION TOGETHER IN OUR ROOM.
BY ANY CHANCE, WOULD YOU LIKE TO JOIN US?
AND THEN MY FRIEND FROM JUNIOR HIGH--
Oh, no...
HA HA HA
That's terrible.
HEY, TAKABA-YASHI-SAN, DOES THIS MAKE SENSE TO YOU?
OH, THAT...

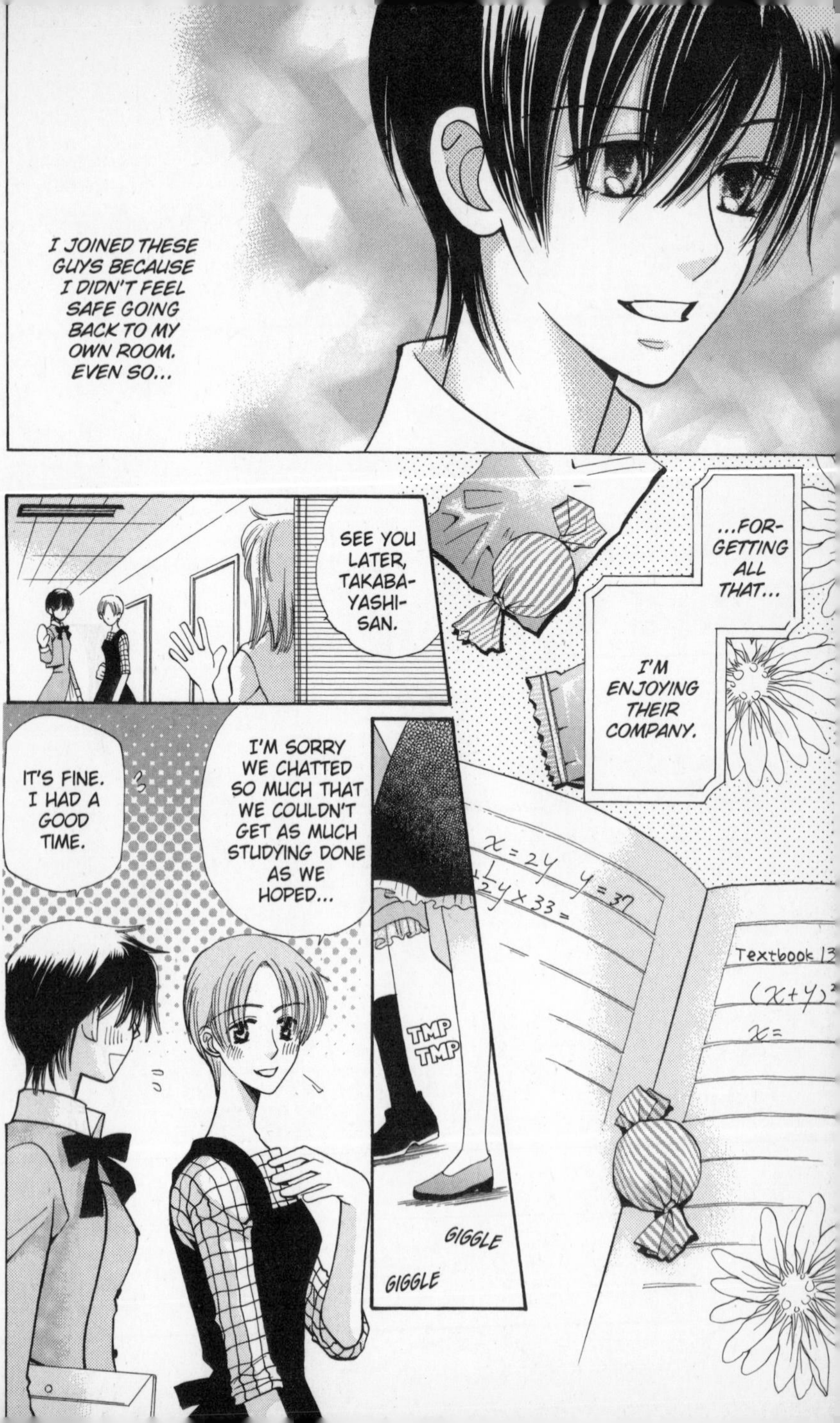
I JOINED THESE GUYS BECAUSE I DIDN'T FEEL SAFE GOING BACK TO MY OWN ROOM. EVEN SO...
...FOR-GETTING ALL THAT...
I'M ENJOYING THEIR COMPANY.
Textbook 13
SEE YOU LATER, TAKABAYASHI-SAN.
TMP TMP
GIGGLE
GIGGLE
I'M SORRY WE CHATTED SO MUCH THAT WE COULDN'T GET AS MUCH STUDYING DONE AS WE HOPED...
IT'S FINE. I HAD A GOOD TIME.

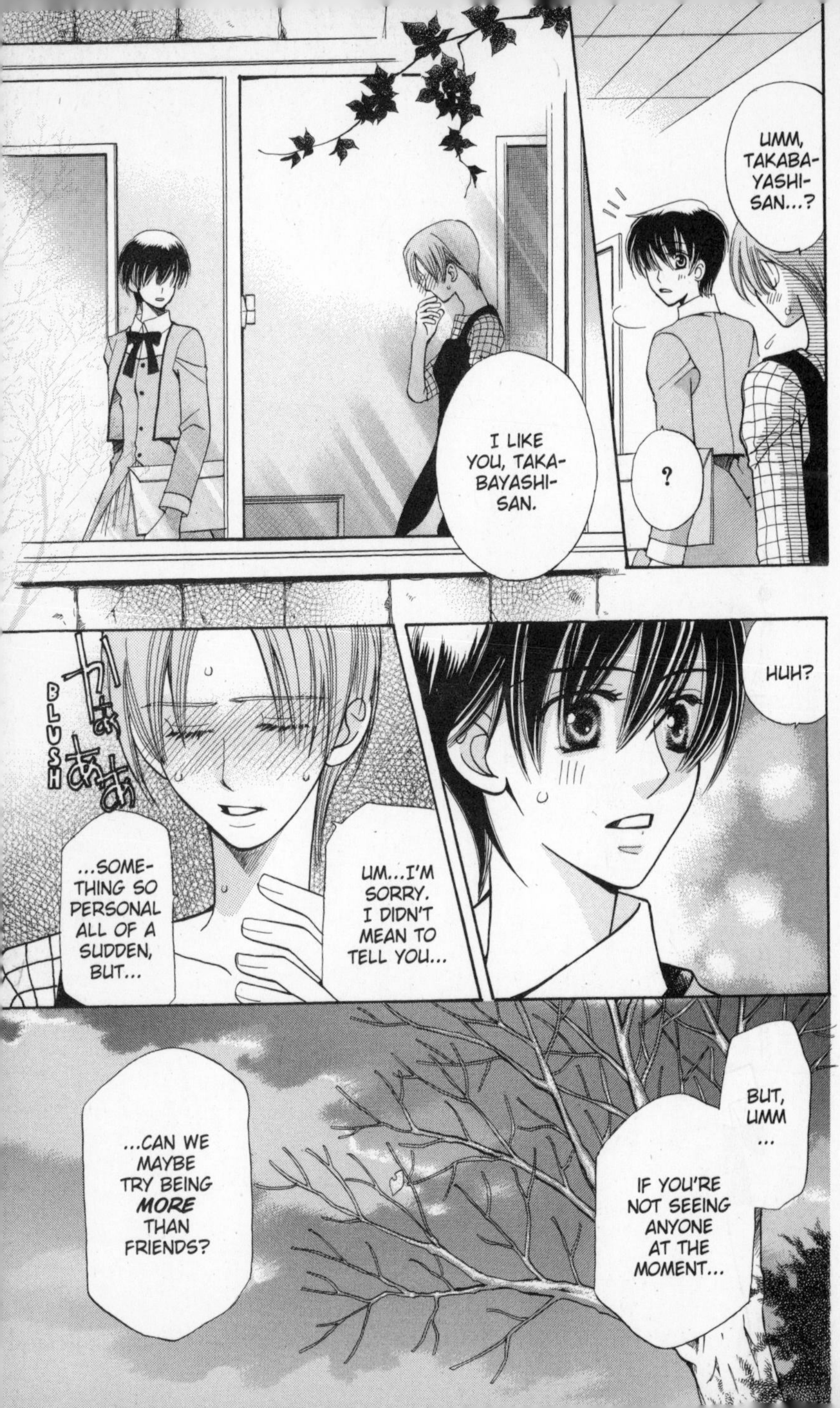
UMM, TAKABAYASHI-SAN...?
?
I LIKE YOU, TAKABAYASHI-SAN.
HUH?
BLUSH
UM...I'M SORRY. I DIDN'T MEAN TO TELL YOU...
...SOMETHING SO PERSONAL ALL OF A SUDDEN, BUT...
BUT, UMM ...
IF YOU'RE NOT SEEING ANYONE AT THE MOMENT...
...CAN WE MAYBE TRY BEING MORE THAN FRIENDS?

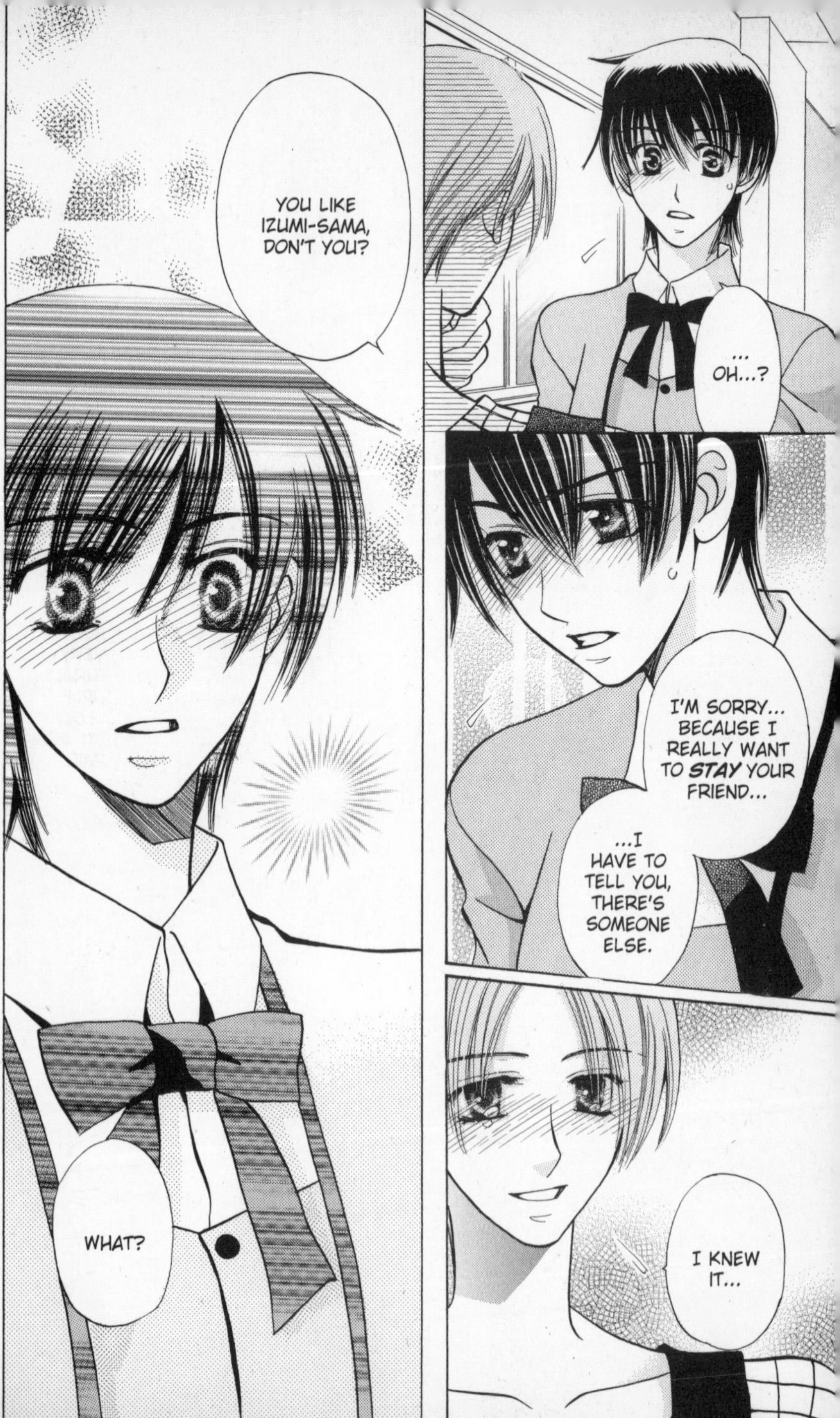
... OH...?
I'M SORRY... BECAUSE I REALLY WANT TO **STAY** YOUR FRIEND...
...I HAVE TO TELL YOU, THERE'S SOMEONE ELSE.
I KNEW IT...
YOU LIKE IZUMI-SAMA, DON'T YOU?
WHAT?

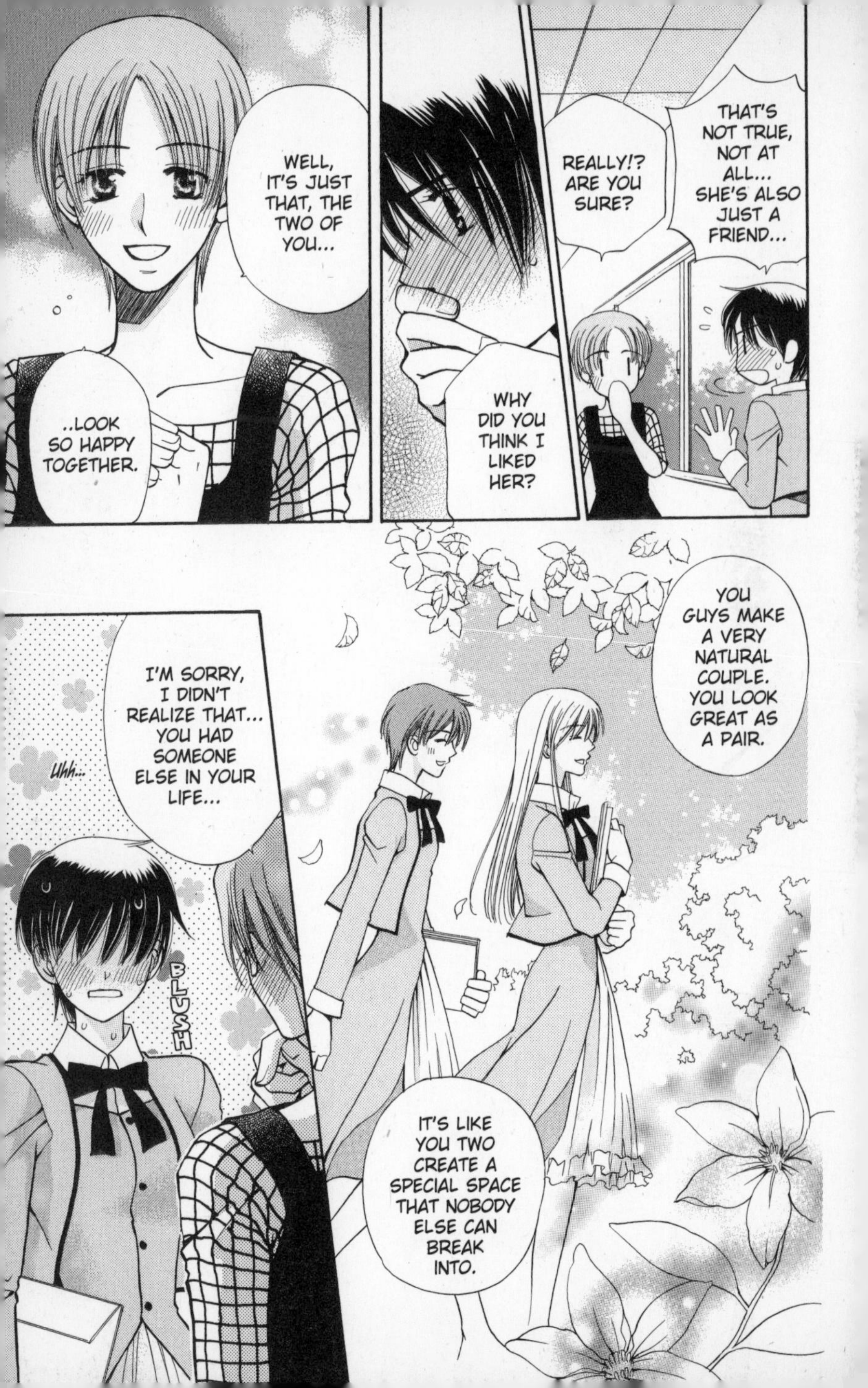
THAT'S NOT TRUE, NOT AT ALL... SHE'S ALSO JUST A FRIEND...
REALLY!? ARE YOU SURE?
WHY DID YOU THINK I LIKED HER?
WELL, IT'S JUST THAT, THE TWO OF YOU...
..LOOK SO HAPPY TOGETHER.
YOU GUYS MAKE A VERY NATURAL COUPLE. YOU LOOK GREAT AS A PAIR.
IT'S LIKE YOU TWO CREATE A SPECIAL SPACE THAT NOBODY ELSE CAN BREAK INTO.
I'M SORRY, I DIDN'T REALIZE THAT... YOU HAD SOMEONE ELSE IN YOUR LIFE...
Uhh...
BLUSH

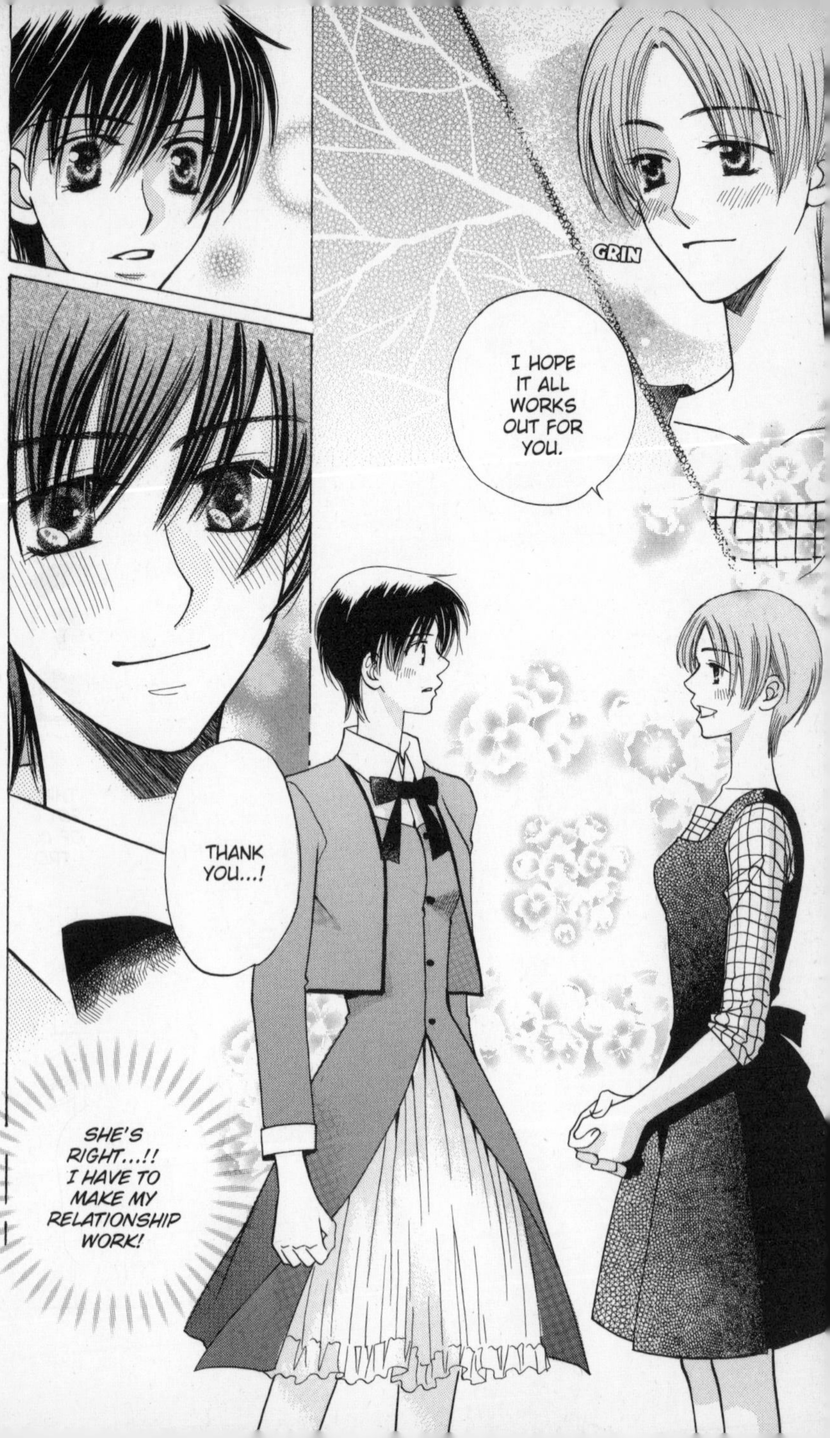
GRIN
I HOPE IT ALL WORKS OUT FOR YOU.
THANK YOU...!
SHE'S RIGHT...!! I HAVE TO MAKE MY RELATIONSHIP WORK!

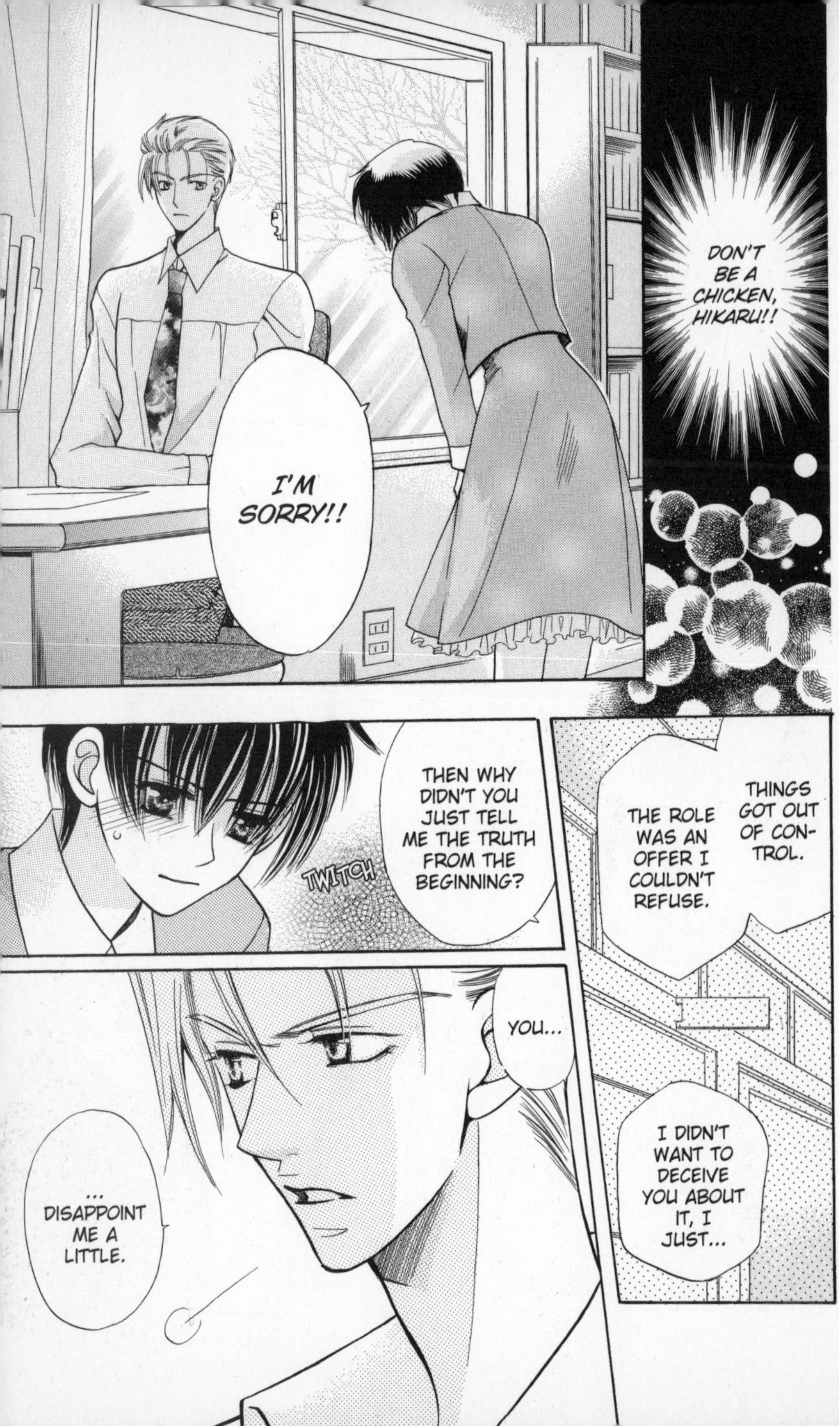
DON'T BE A CHICKEN, HIKARU!!
I'M SORRY!!
THINGS GOT OUT OF CON-TROL.
THE ROLE WAS AN OFFER I COULDN'T REFUSE.
I DIDN'T WANT TO DECEIVE YOU ABOUT IT, I JUST...
THEN WHY DIDN'T YOU JUST TELL ME THE TRUTH FROM THE BEGINNING?
TWITCH
YOU...
... DISAPPOINT ME A LITTLE.

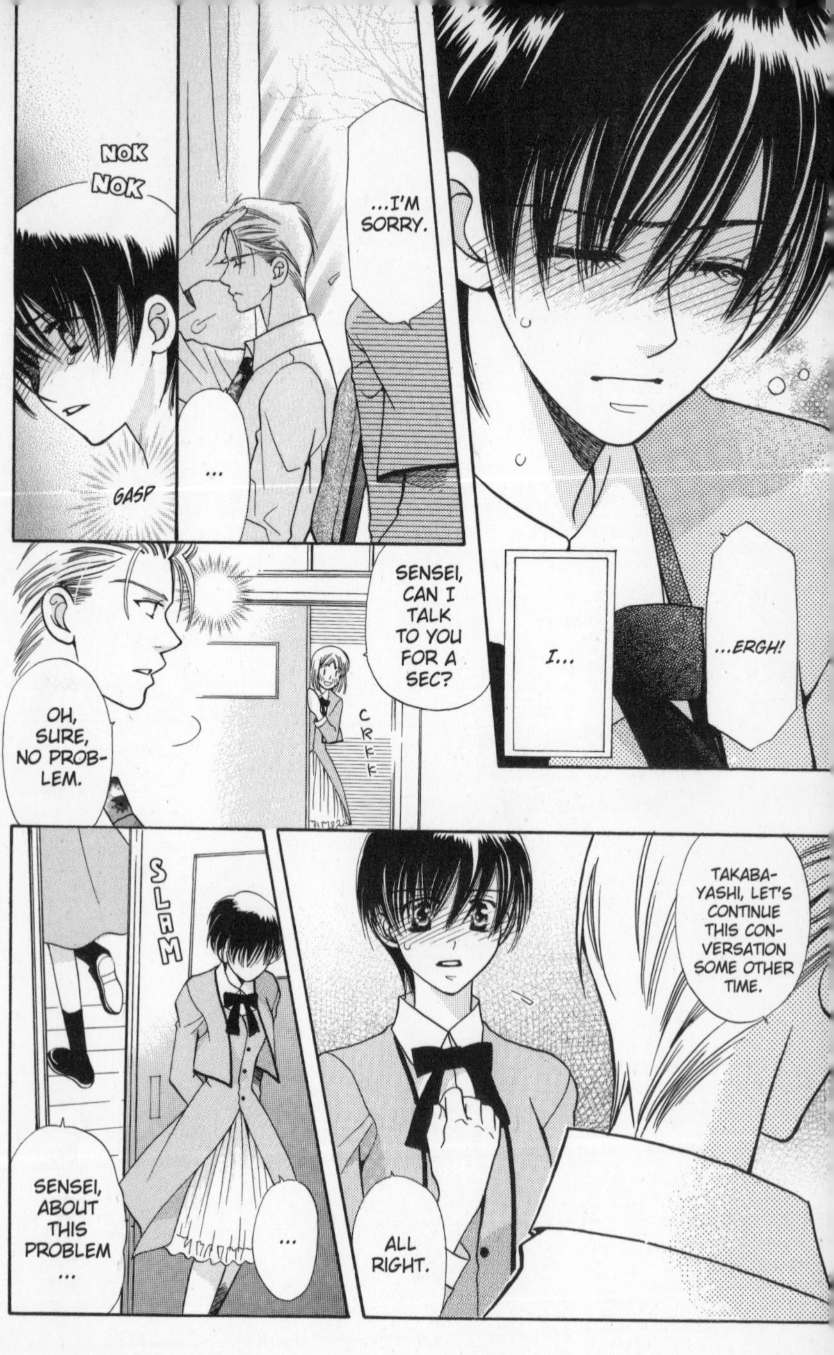
...ERGH!
I...
...I'M SORRY.
...
NOK
NOK
GASP
SENSEI, CAN I TALK TO YOU FOR A SEC?
CRKK
OH, SURE, NO PROB-LEM.
TAKABA-YASHI, LET'S CONTINUE THIS CON-VERSATION SOME OTHER TIME.
ALL RIGHT.
SLAM
...
SENSEI, ABOUT THIS PROBLEM ...

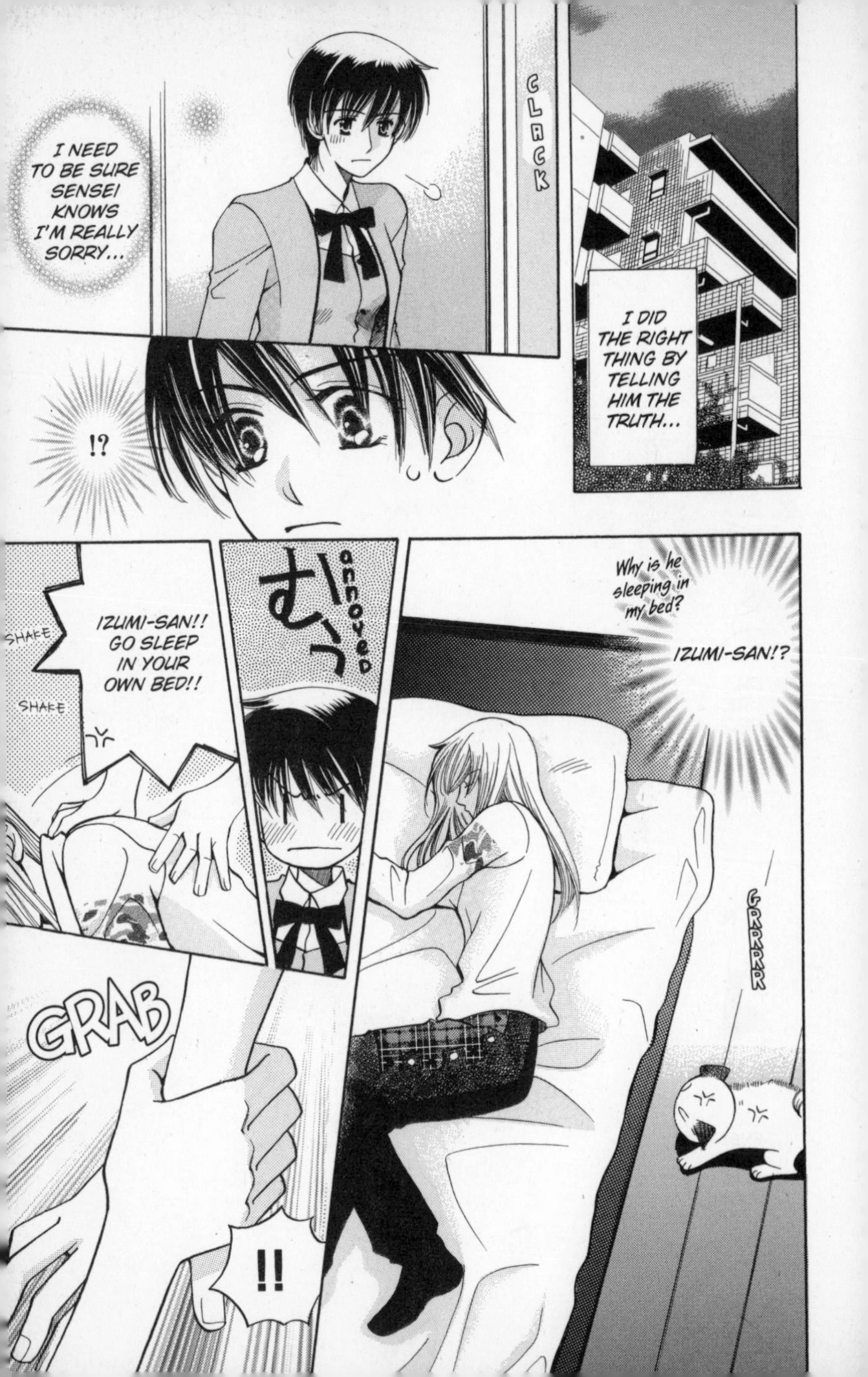
I DID THE RIGHT THING BY TELLING HIM THE TRUTH...
CLACK
I NEED TO BE SURE SENSEI KNOWS I'M REALLY SORRY...
!?
Why is he sleeping in my bed?
IZUMI-SAN!?
GRRRRR
むっ
annoyed
SHAKE
SHAKE
IZUMI-SAN!! GO SLEEP IN YOUR OWN BED!!
GRAB
!!

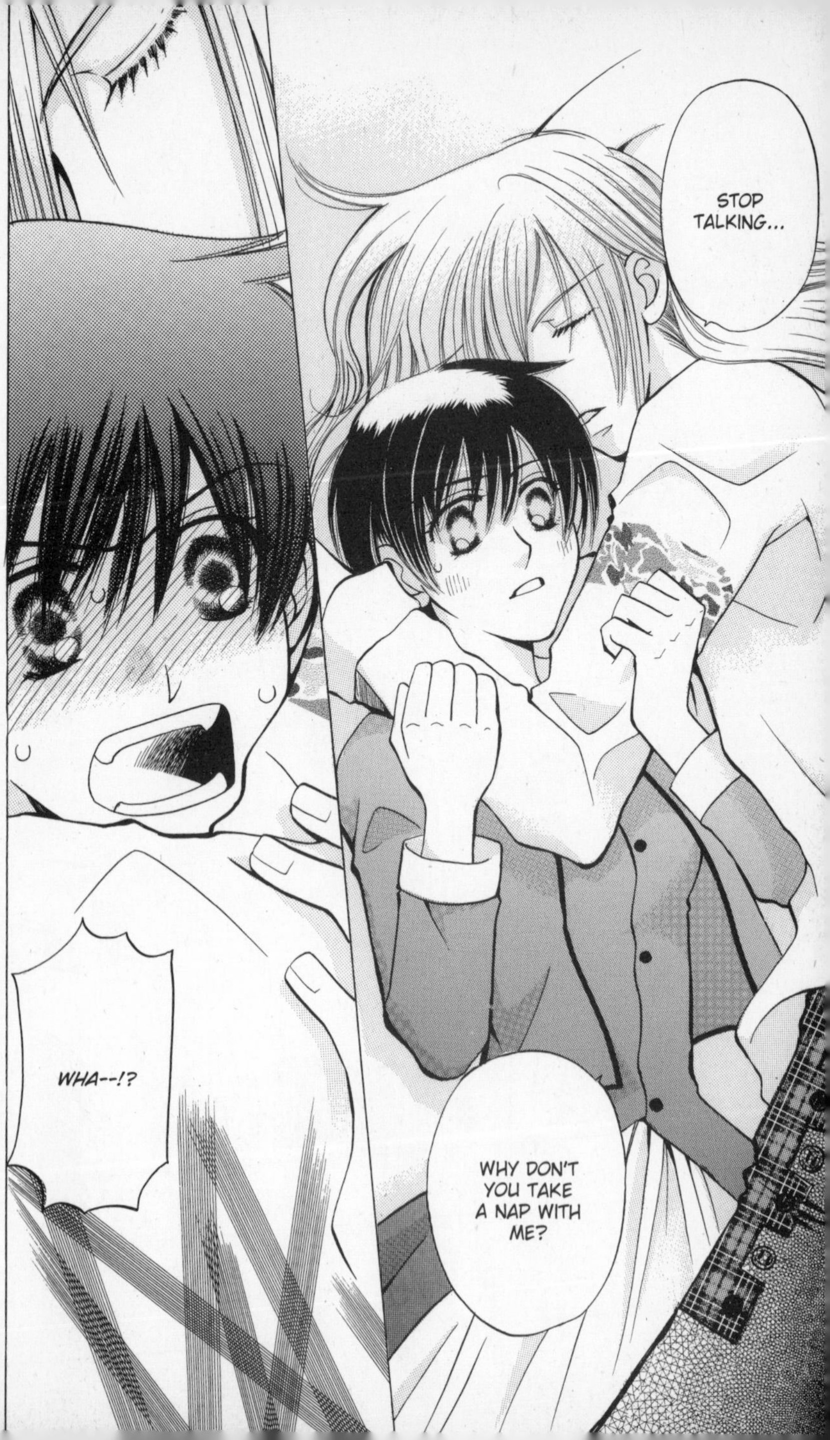
STOP TALKING...
WHY DON'T YOU TAKE A NAP WITH ME?
WHA--!?

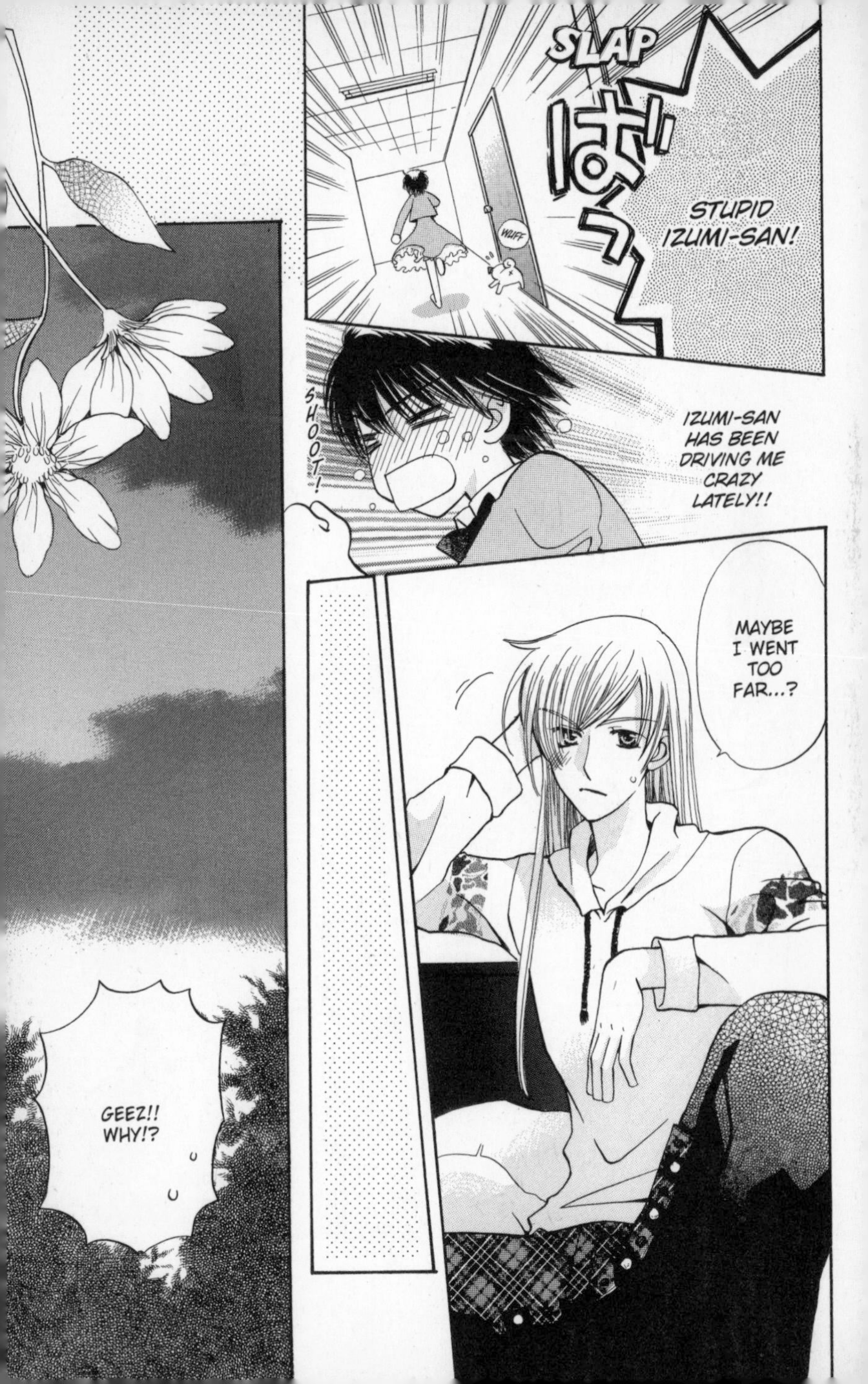
SLAP
ばっ
STUPID IZUMI-SAN!
WUFF
IZUMI-SAN HAS BEEN DRIVING ME CRAZY LATELY!!
SHOOT!
MAYBE I WENT TOO FAR...?
GEEZ!! WHY!?

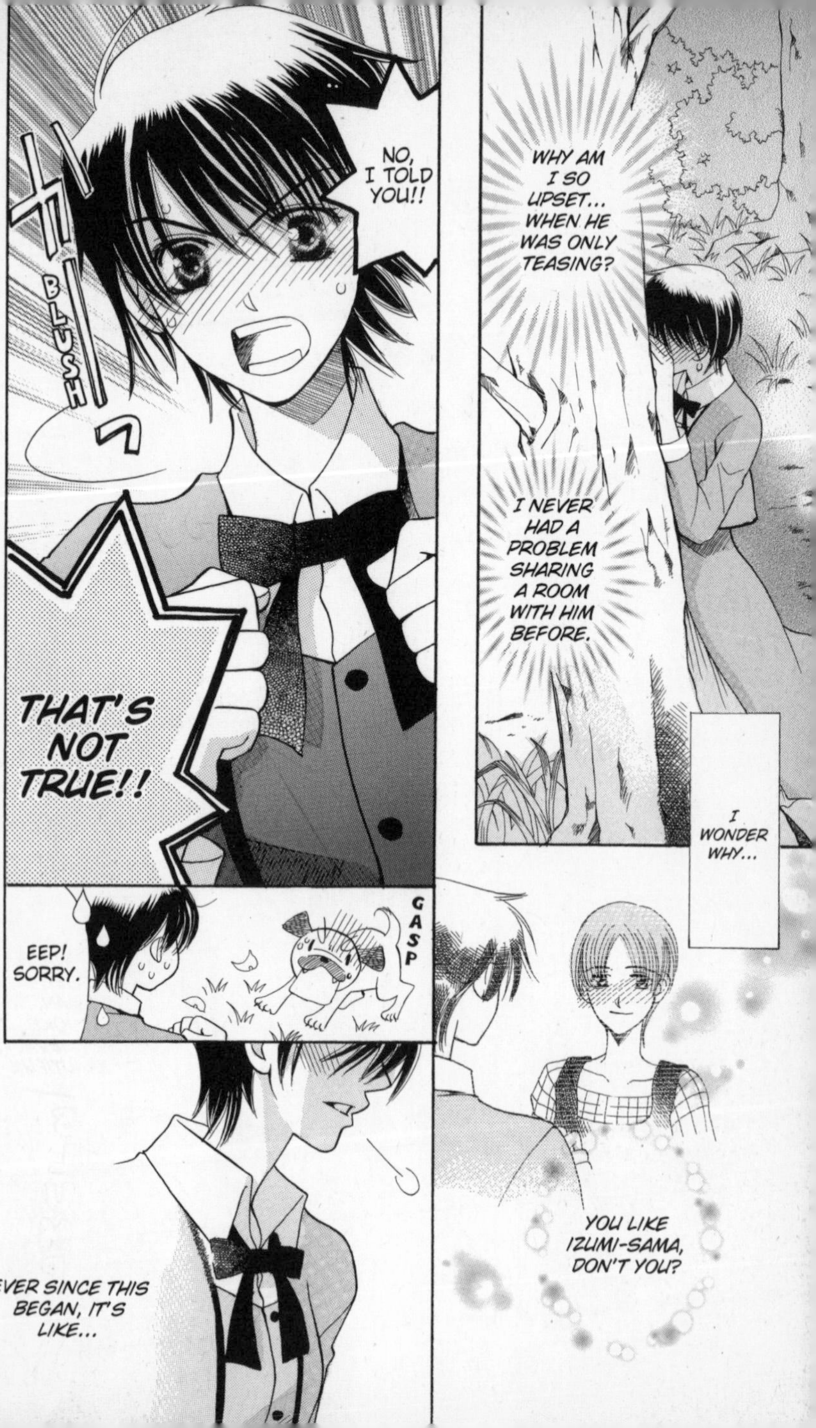
WHY AM I SO UPSET... WHEN HE WAS ONLY TEASING?
I NEVER HAD A PROBLEM SHARING A ROOM WITH HIM BEFORE.
NO, I TOLD YOU!!
BLUSH
THAT'S NOT TRUE!!
I WONDER WHY...
YOU LIKE IZUMI-SAMA, DON'T YOU?
GASP
EEP! SORRY.
EVER SINCE THIS BEGAN, IT'S LIKE...

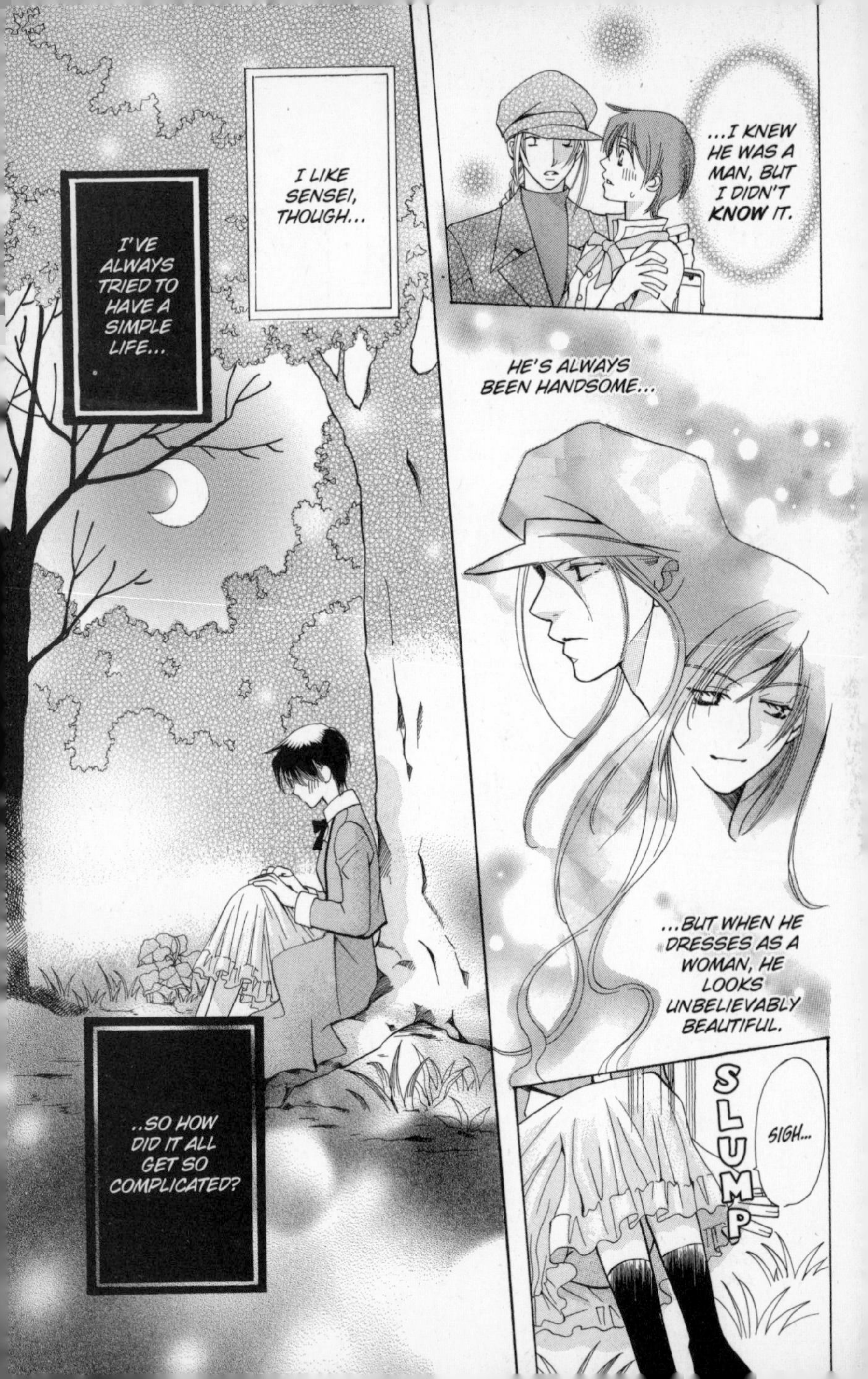
...I KNEW HE WAS A MAN, BUT I DIDN'T **KNOW** IT.
HE'S ALWAYS BEEN HANDSOME...
...BUT WHEN HE DRESSES AS A WOMAN, HE LOOKS UNBELIEVABLY BEAUTIFUL.
SIGH...
SLUMP
I LIKE SENSEI, THOUGH...
I'VE ALWAYS TRIED TO HAVE A SIMPLE LIFE...
..SO HOW DID IT ALL GET SO COMPLICATED?

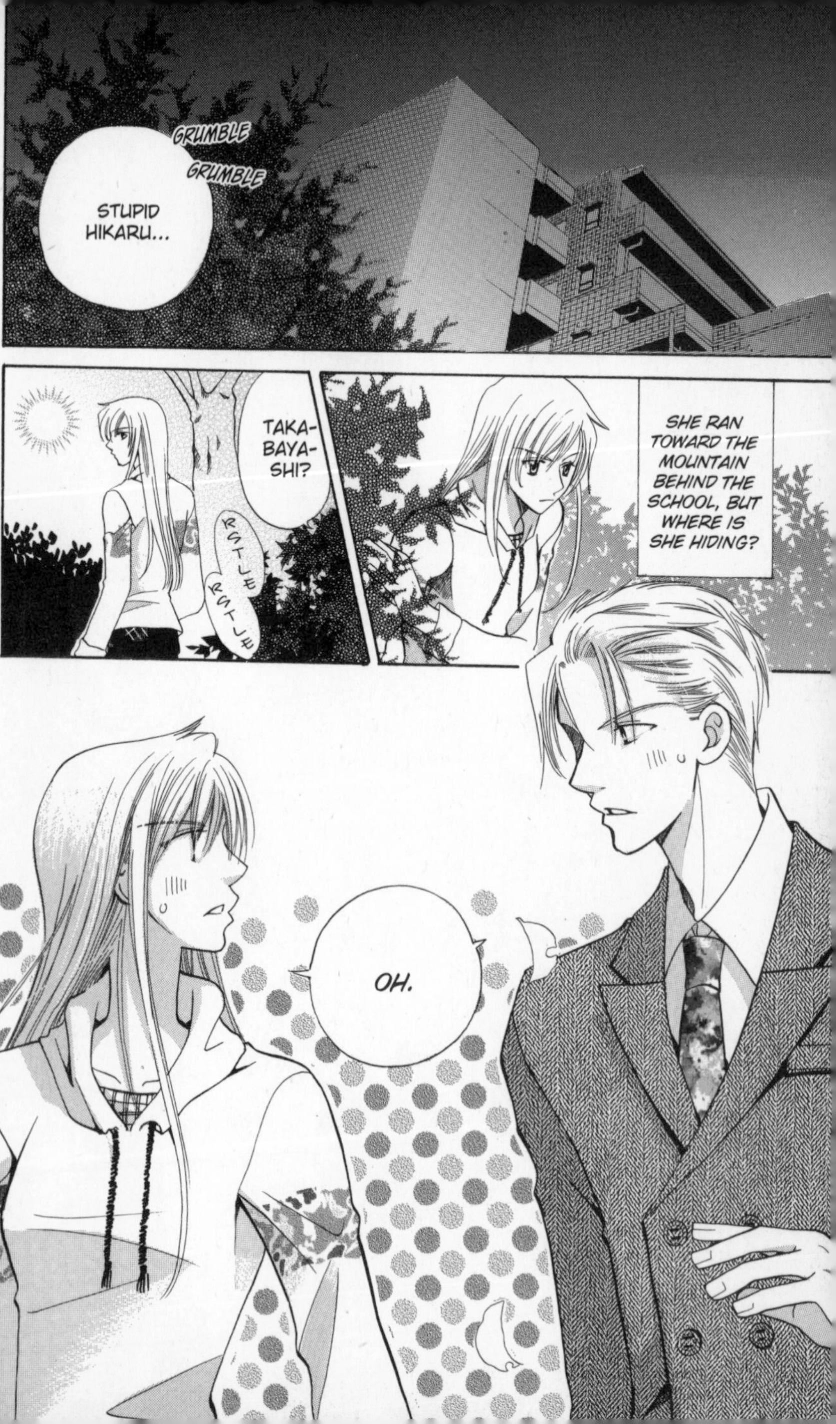
GRUMBLE
GRUMBLE
STUPID HIKARU...
SHE RAN TOWARD THE MOUNTAIN BEHIND THE SCHOOL, BUT WHERE IS SHE HIDING?
TAKA-BAYA-SHI?
RSTLE
RSTLE
OH.

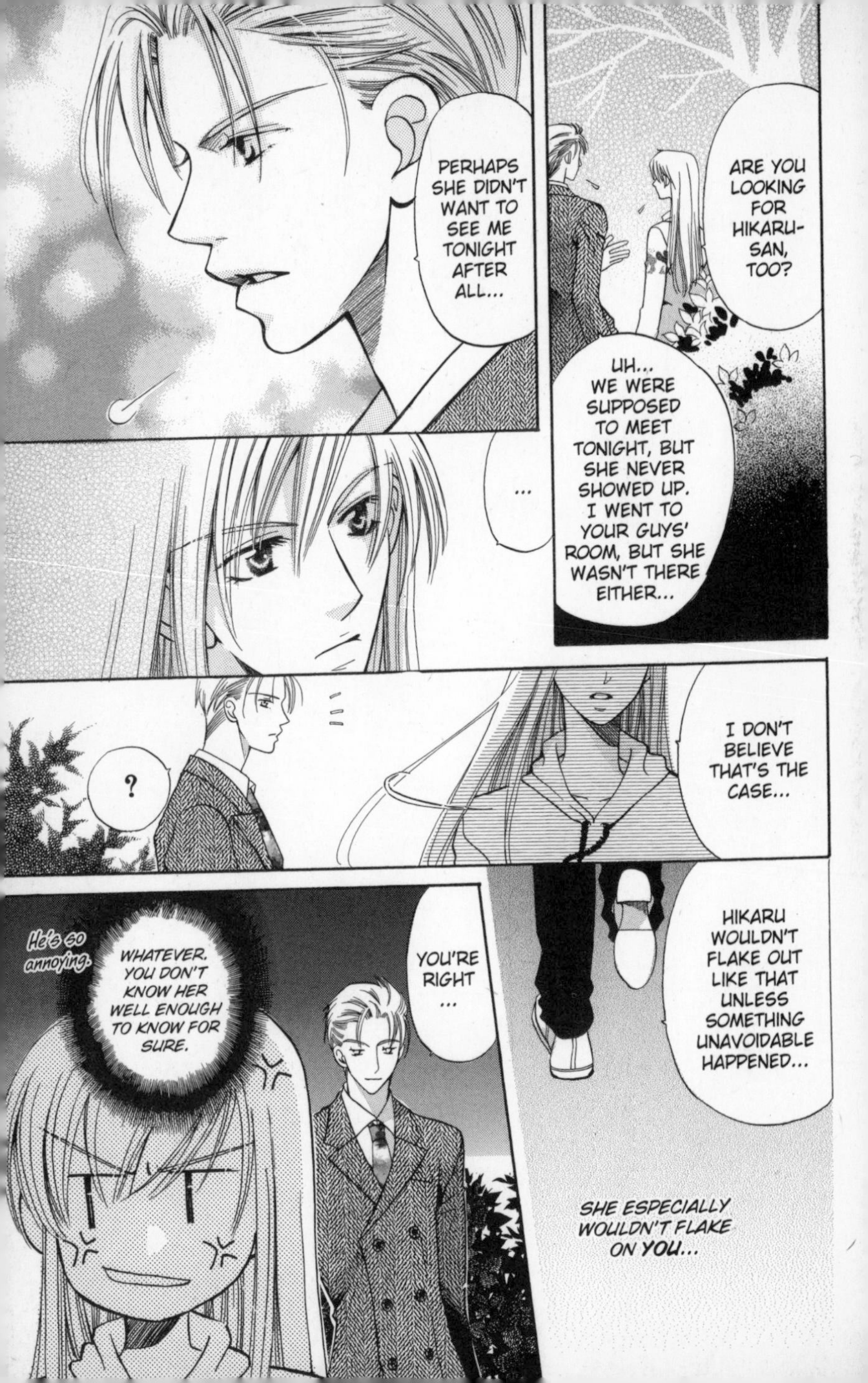
ARE YOU LOOKING FOR HIKARU-SAN, TOO?
UH... WE WERE SUPPOSED TO MEET TONIGHT, BUT SHE NEVER SHOWED UP. I WENT TO YOUR GUYS' ROOM, BUT SHE WASN'T THERE EITHER...
PERHAPS SHE DIDN'T WANT TO SEE ME TONIGHT AFTER ALL...
...
I DON'T BELIEVE THAT'S THE CASE...
?
HIKARU WOULDN'T FLAKE OUT LIKE THAT UNLESS SOMETHING UNAVOIDABLE HAPPENED...
SHE ESPECIALLY WOULDN'T FLAKE ON YOU...
YOU'RE RIGHT ...
WHATEVER. YOU DON'T KNOW HER WELL ENOUGH TO KNOW FOR SURE.
He's so annoying.

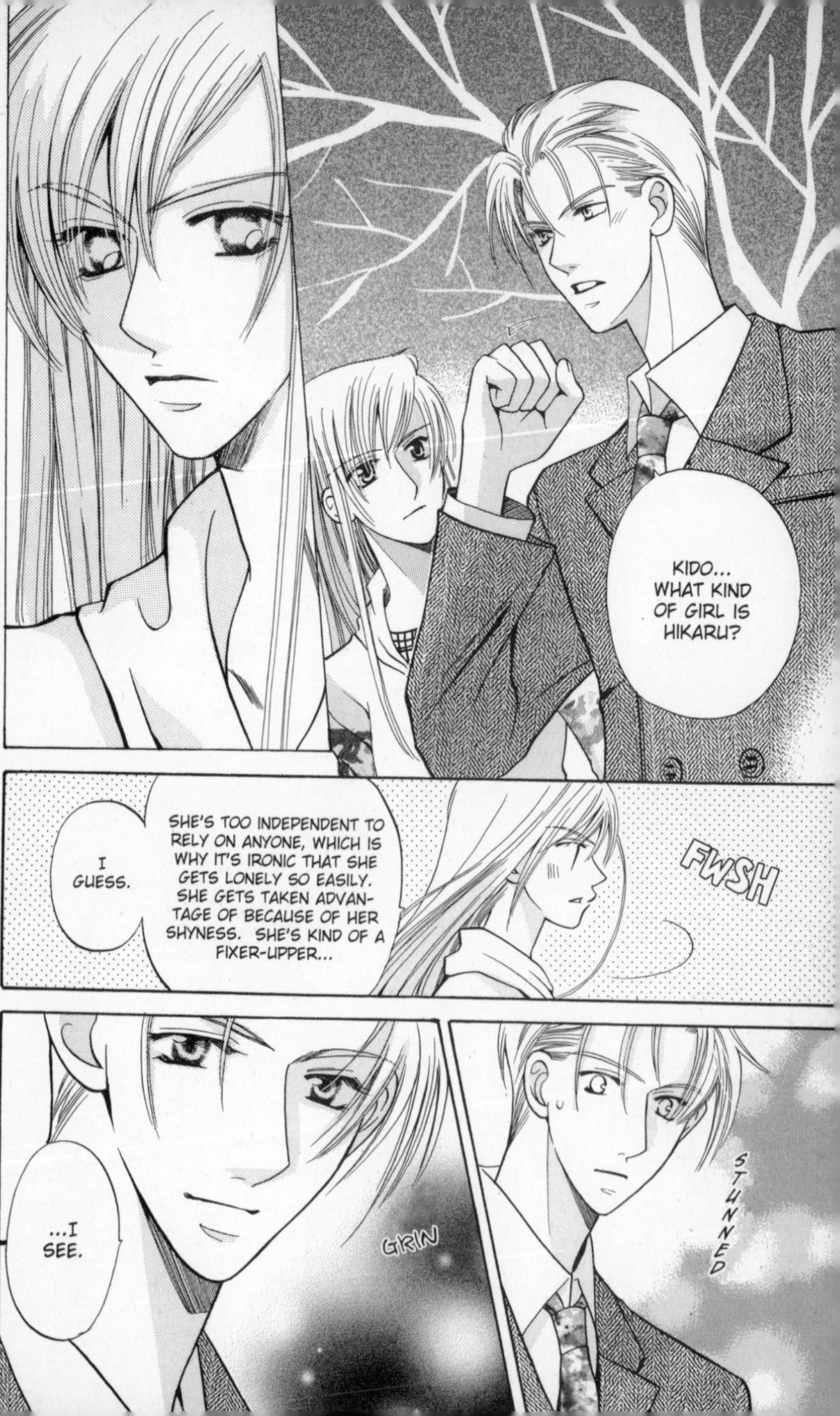
KIDO... WHAT KIND OF GIRL IS HIKARU?
FWSH
SHE'S TOO INDEPENDENT TO RELY ON ANYONE, WHICH IS WHY IT'S IRONIC THAT SHE GETS LONELY SO EASILY. SHE GETS TAKEN ADVANTAGE OF BECAUSE OF HER SHYNESS. SHE'S KIND OF A FIXER-UPPER...
I GUESS.
STUNNED
GRIN
...I SEE.

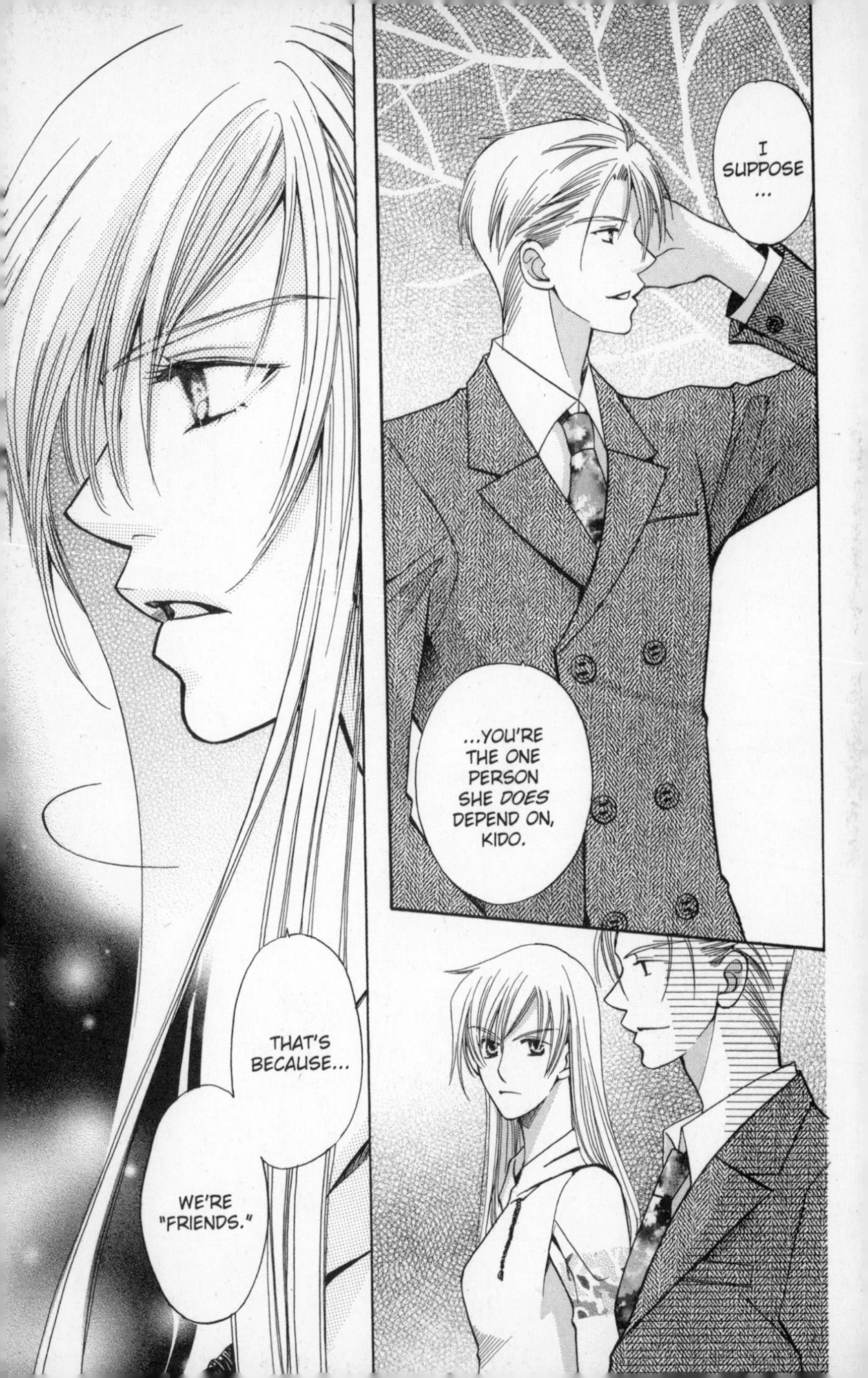
I SUPPOSE ...
...YOU'RE THE ONE PERSON SHE *DOES* DEPEND ON, KIDO.
THAT'S BECAUSE...
WE'RE "FRIENDS."

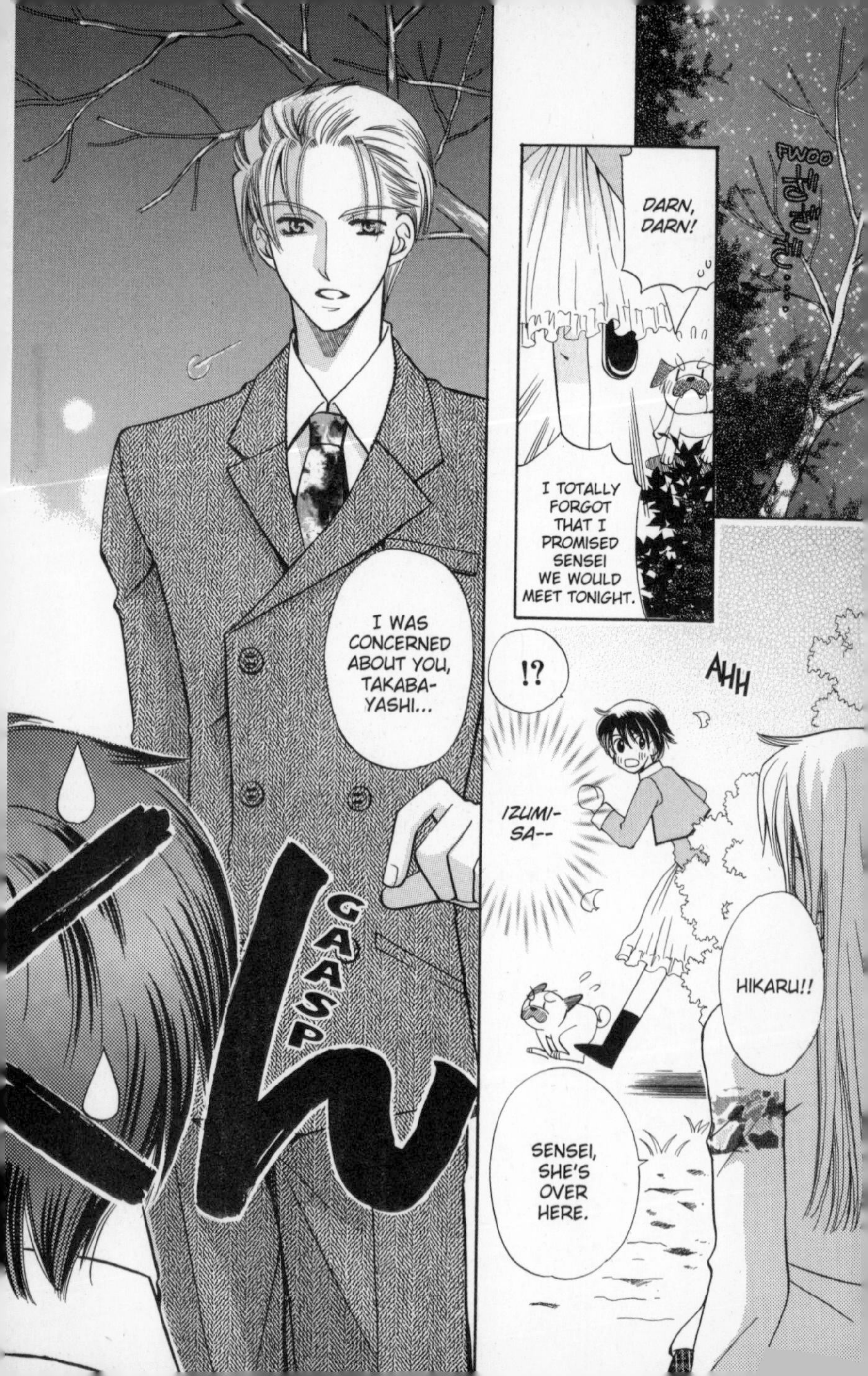
FWOO
DARN, DARN!
I TOTALLY FORGOT THAT I PROMISED SENSEI WE WOULD MEET TONIGHT.
AHH
!?
IZUMI-SA--
HIKARU!!
SENSEI, SHE'S OVER HERE.
I WAS CONCERNED ABOUT YOU, TAKABAYASHI...
GAASP

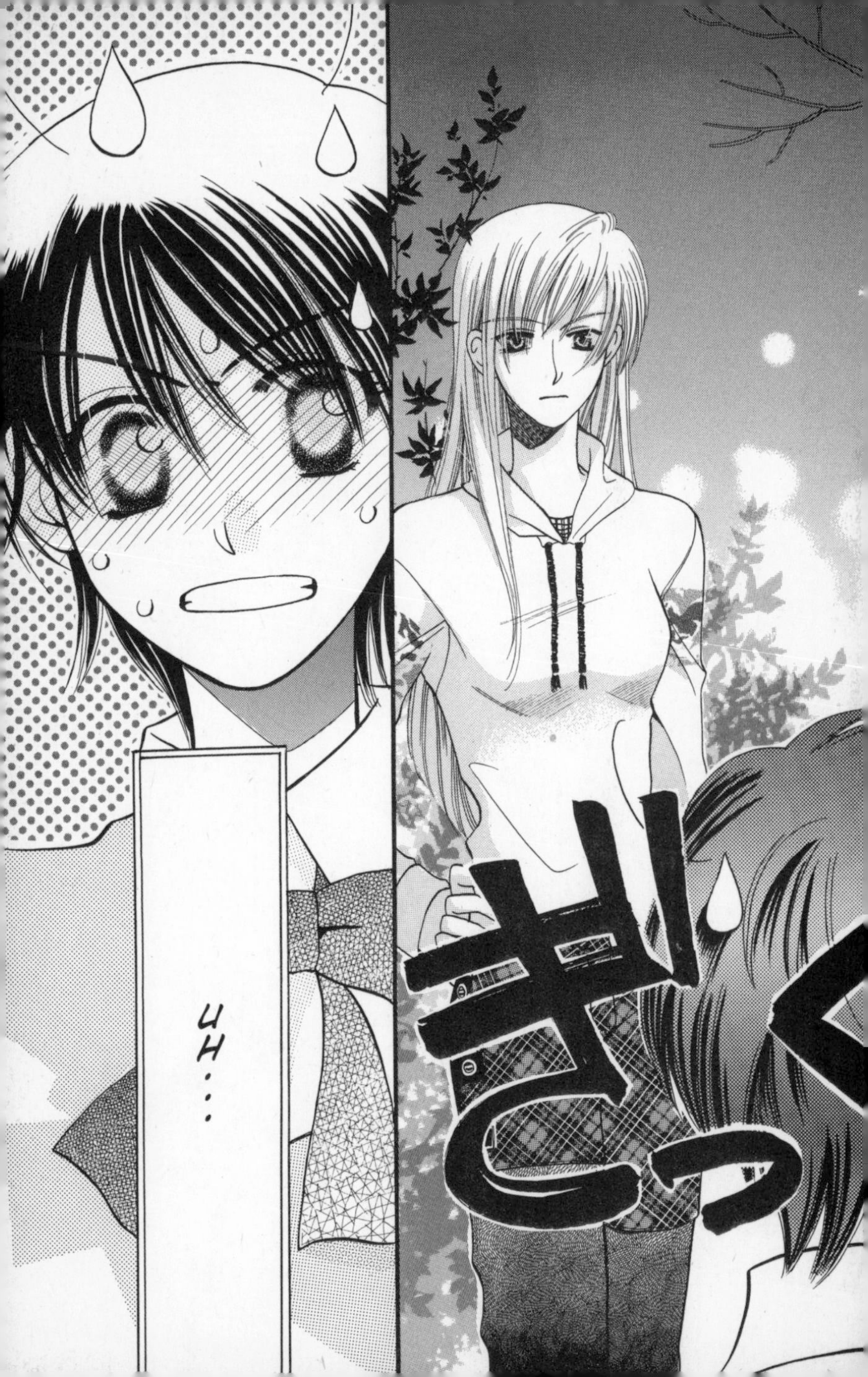
ぎくっ
UH...

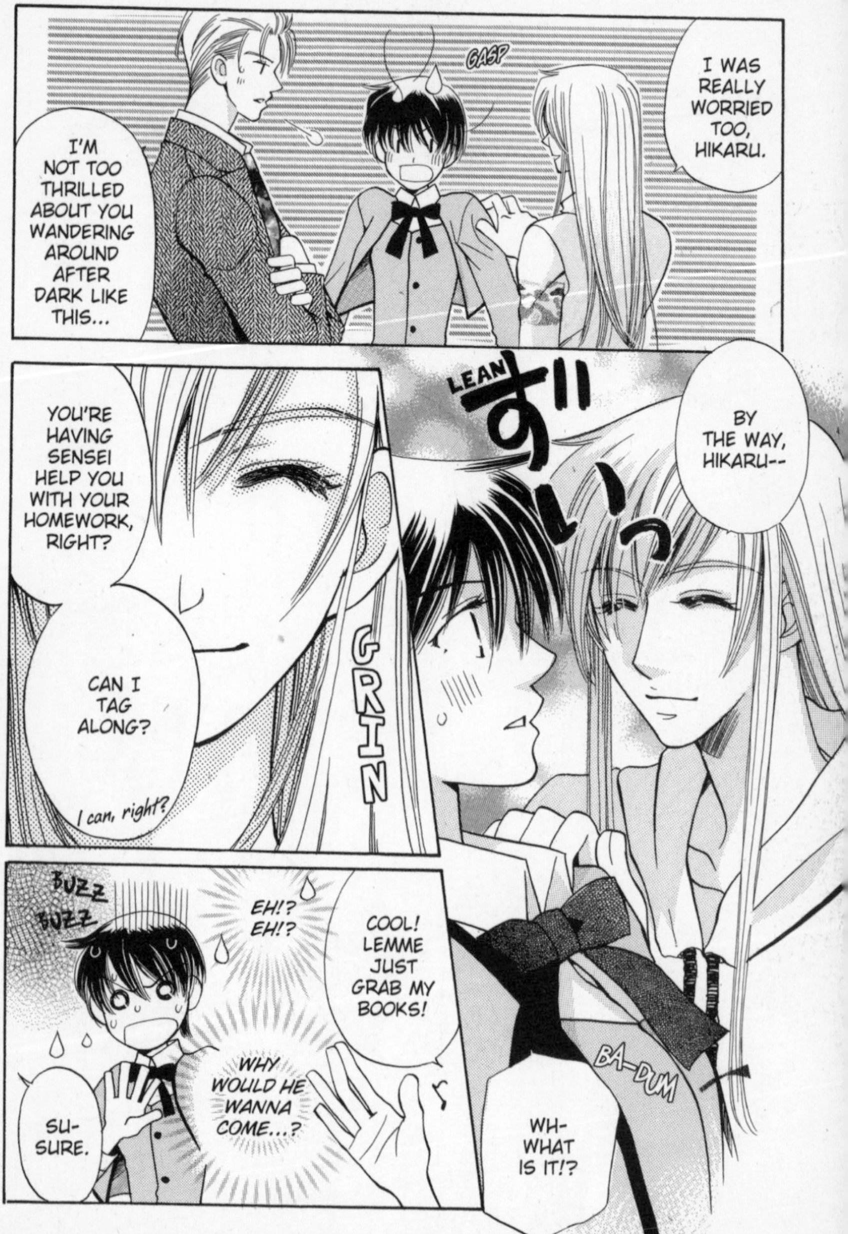
I WAS REALLY WORRIED TOO, HIKARU.
GASP
I'M NOT TOO THRILLED ABOUT YOU WANDERING AROUND AFTER DARK LIKE THIS...
LEAN
すいっ
BY THE WAY, HIKARU--
BA-DUM
WH- WHAT IS IT!?
YOU'RE HAVING SENSEI HELP YOU WITH YOUR HOMEWORK, RIGHT?
GRIN
CAN I TAG ALONG?
I can, right?
COOL! LEMME JUST GRAB MY BOOKS!
EH!? EH!?
WHY WOULD HE WANNA COME...?
BUZZ BUZZ
SU- SURE.

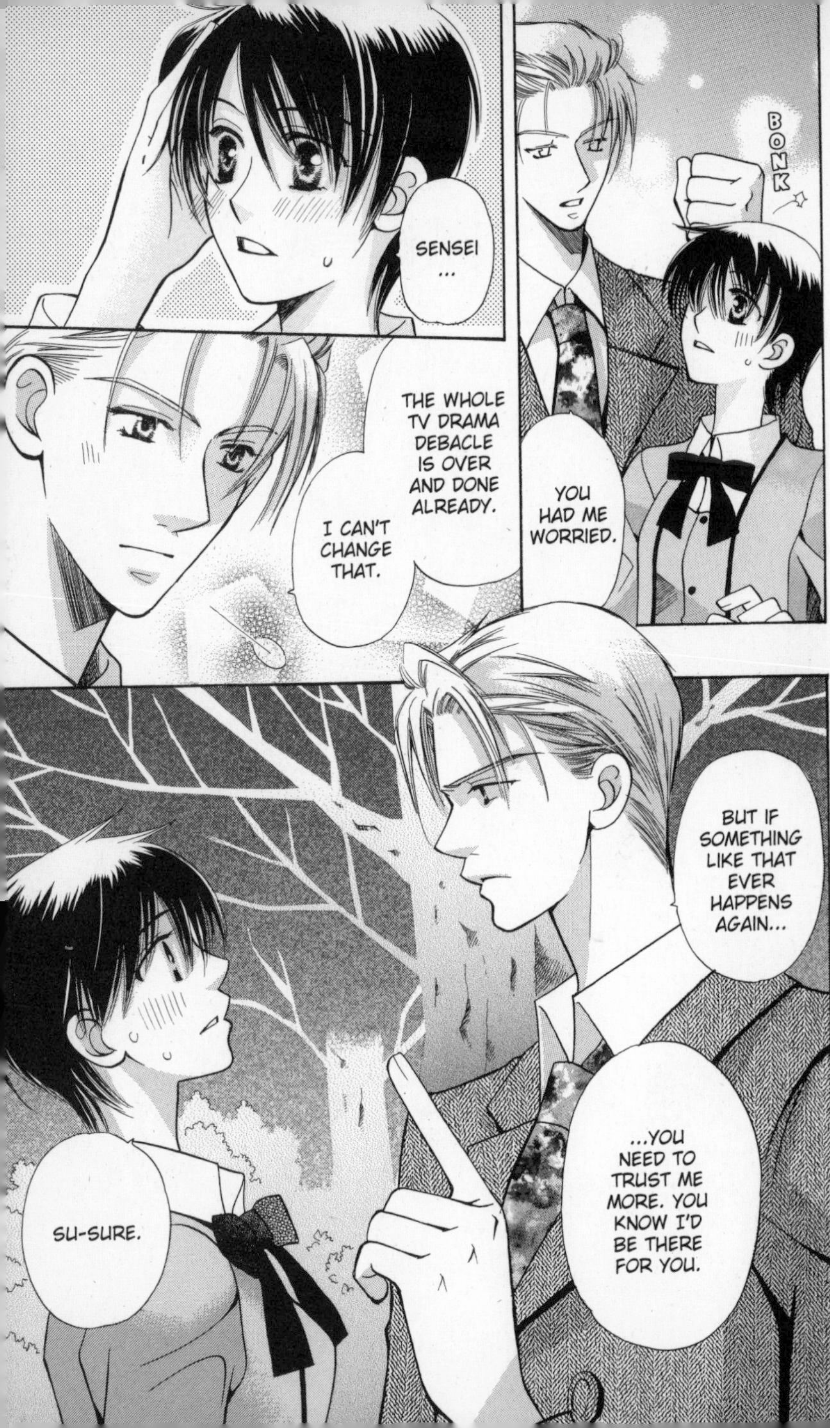
BONK
YOU HAD ME WORRIED.
SENSEI ...
THE WHOLE TV DRAMA DEBACLE IS OVER AND DONE ALREADY.
I CAN'T CHANGE THAT.
BUT IF SOMETHING LIKE THAT EVER HAPPENS AGAIN...
...YOU NEED TO TRUST ME MORE. YOU KNOW I'D BE THERE FOR YOU.
SU-SURE.

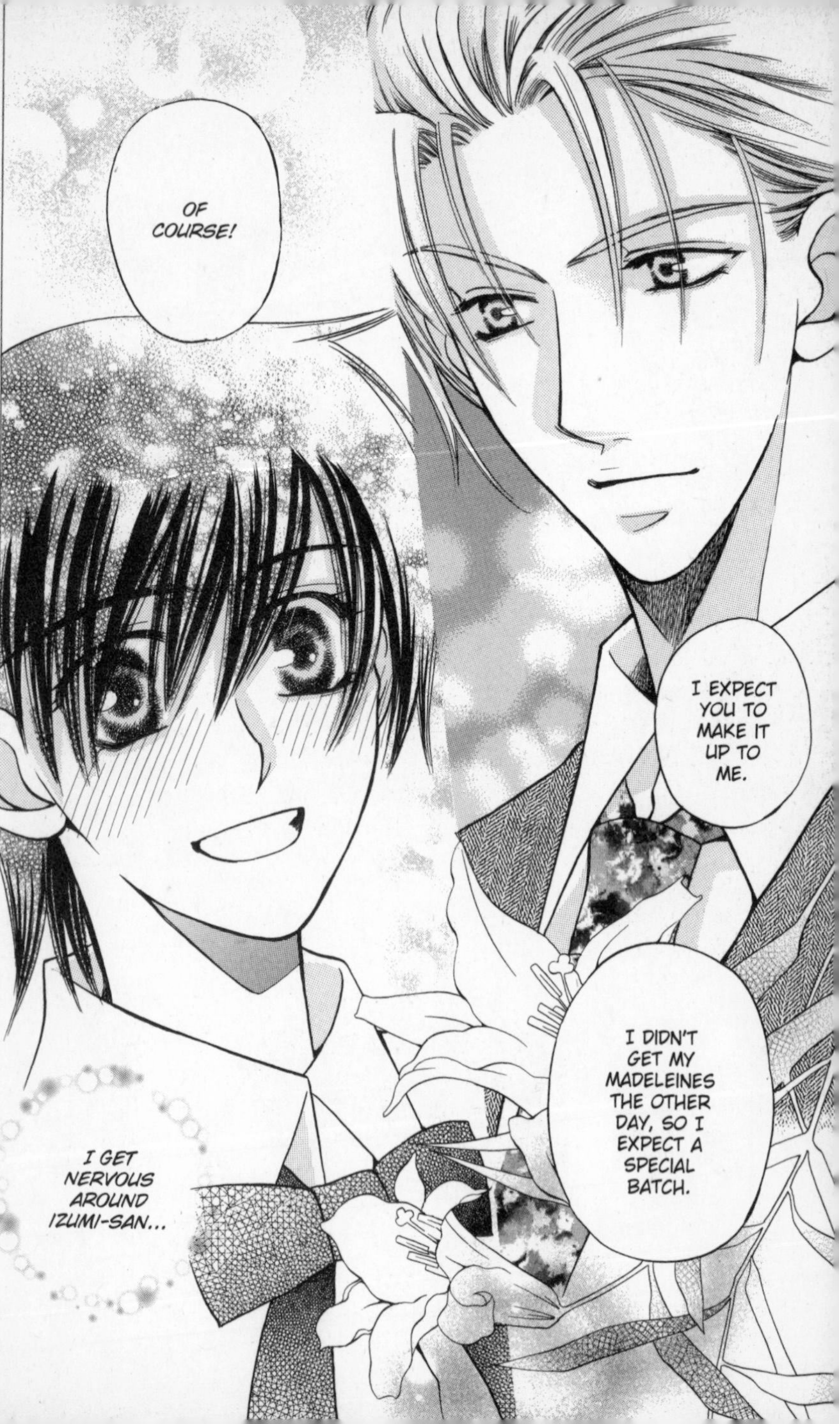
I EXPECT YOU TO MAKE IT UP TO ME.
I DIDN'T GET MY MADELEINES THE OTHER DAY, SO I EXPECT A SPECIAL BATCH.
OF COURSE!
I GET NERVOUS AROUND IZUMI-SAN...

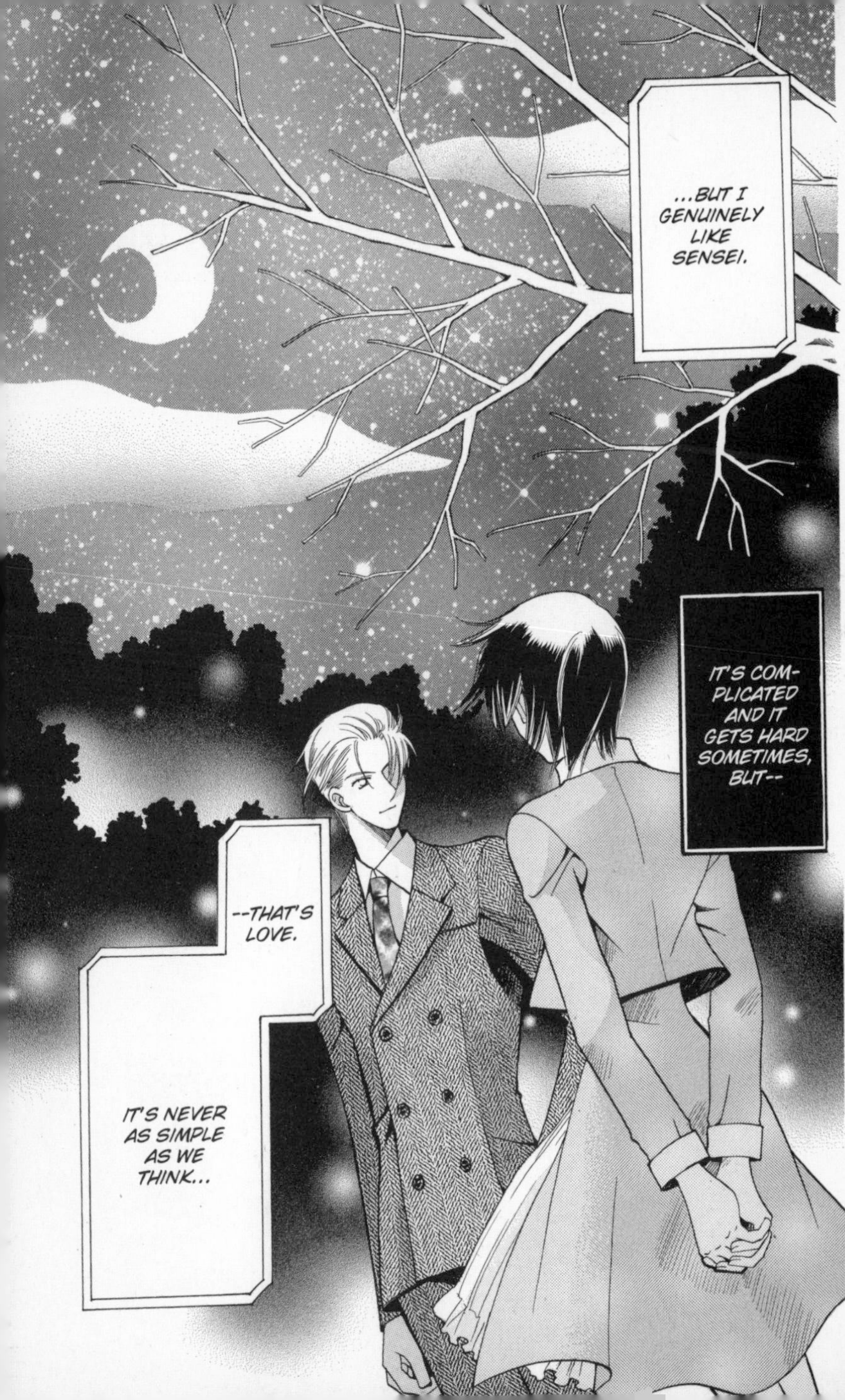
...BUT I GENUINELY LIKE SENSEI.
IT'S COM-PLICATED AND IT GETS HARD SOMETIMES, BUT--
--THAT'S LOVE.
IT'S NEVER AS SIMPLE AS WE THINK...

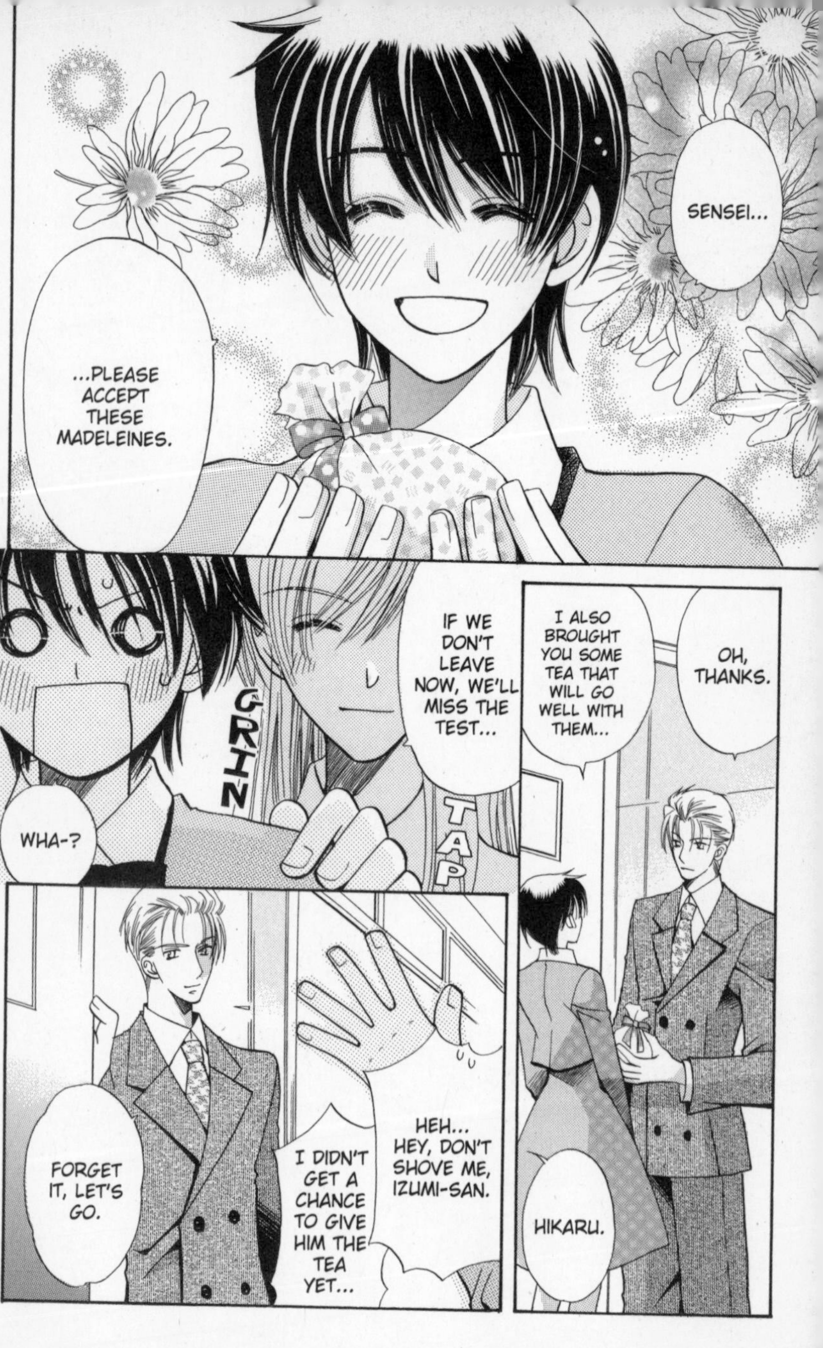
SENSEI...
...PLEASE ACCEPT THESE MADELEINES.
OH, THANKS.
I ALSO BROUGHT YOU SOME TEA THAT WILL GO WELL WITH THEM...
HIKARU.
IF WE DON'T LEAVE NOW, WE'LL MISS THE TEST...
GRIN
TAP
WHA-?
HEH... HEY, DON'T SHOVE ME, IZUMI-SAN.
I DIDN'T GET A CHANCE TO GIVE HIM THE TEA YET...
FORGET IT, LET'S GO.

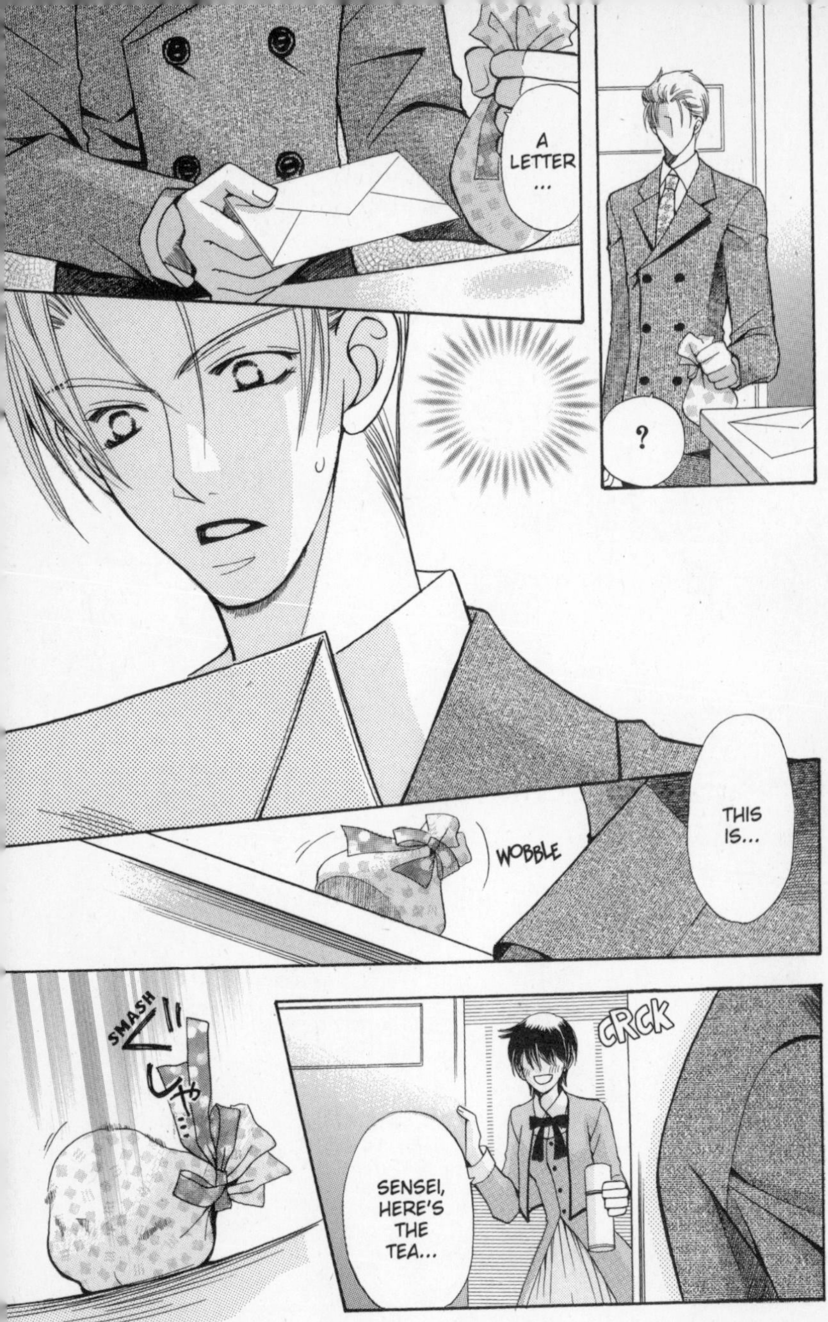
?
A LETTER...
THIS IS...
WOBBLE
CRCK
SENSEI, HERE'S THE TEA...
SMASH
しゃ

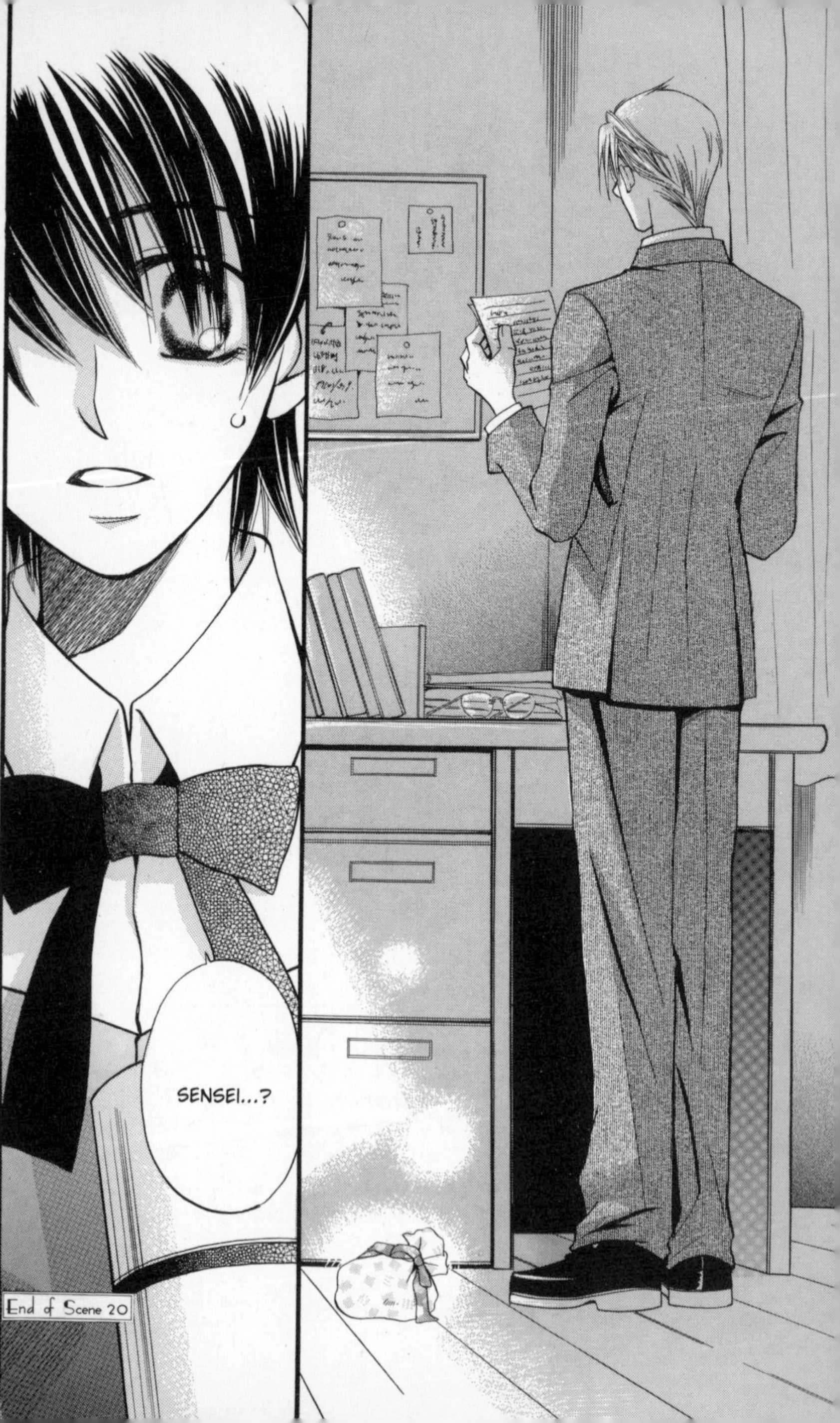
SENSEI...?
End of Scene 20

Afterword and Special Thanks!

I'd like to thank everyone who read Tenshi Ja Nai!! Vol 4! And I'd like to tell those of you who sent me letters, and those who visited my webpage, that you've been a great encouragement to me. ♡

And, as always, Hariguchi-san & Kashiwabara-san, who assist me with my art, and my editor Sugawara-san: I'd like to thank you all very much.

Also, I'd like to thank my family and friends who let me relax from time to time. [laugh]

October 13, 2004

Takako Shigematsu

I look forward to hearing from you.
http://www5b.biglobe.ne.jp/~taka_s/index.html

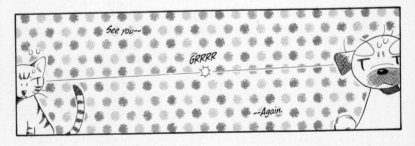

See you--

GRRRR

--Again.

- The end of Tenshi Ja Nai!! volume 4 -

Translator's Notes

Pg. 30 -- *Norritsukkomi*

A style of duo comedy popular in the Kansai region. One comedian will set up the gag, to which the other will play right into...or in this case walk right into...only to pull-out in a frantic display shortly after. Though Kurobe-san's not doing this intentionally here, it sure would make for a good set-up nonetheless.

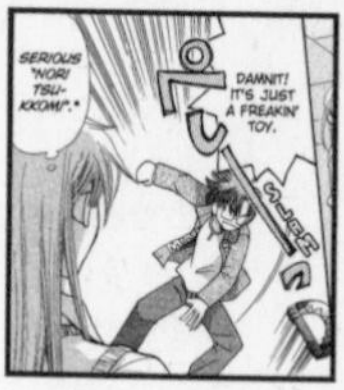
DAMNIT! IT'S JUST A FREAKIN' TOY.
SERIOUS "NORI TSU-KKOMI".*

Pg. 31 -- Game-show prop

What kind of game-show involves giant bowling balls, you might ask! On some Japanese game shows, failure to answer the questions correctly can result in outrageous punishments for the entertainment of audience and competing contestants alike. From being put in a ring with a sumo wrestler to being chased by a giant bowling ball, anything can happen on Japanese game shows.

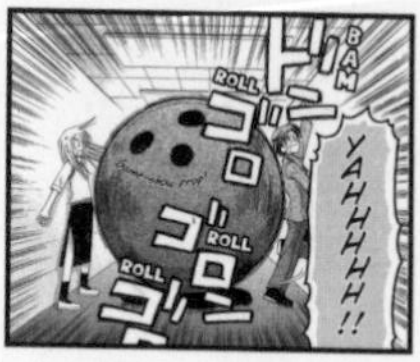
BAM
YAHHHHH!!
ROLL
ROLL
ROLL

Pg. 31 -- *Dokkiri*

The Japanese version of "candid camera" in which innocent civilians get set-up in outrageous situations only to have their frazzled, confused responses caught on tape. Getting run over by a giant bowling ball is a perfect example.

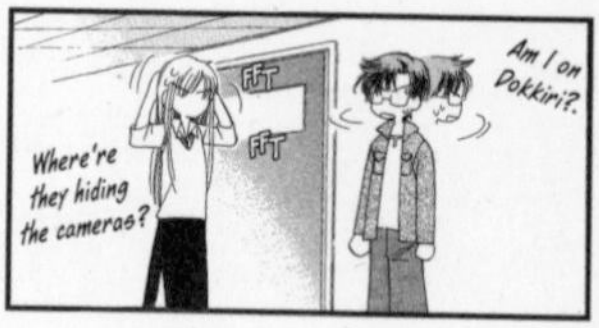
Am I on Dokkiri?
FFT
FFT
Where're they hiding the cameras?

Pg. 91 -- Kansai accent

The dialect spoken in the Kansai region of Japan is generally characterized as being both more melodic and more "harsh" by speakers of the standard language. It is also closely associated with comedy hence its presence in manga and other forms of entertainment.

Pg. 124 -- *Ossu*

An everyday greeting between male friends but originally a salutation between samurai. Keeping that history in mind, Hikaru's use of it demonstrates her fighting spirit.

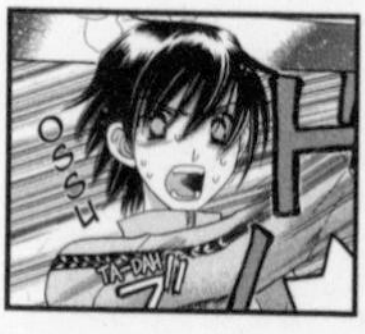
OSSU
TA-DAH

Pg. 161-- *Aojiru*

A juice made completely from tree kale leaves. With its 40 vitamins and minerals per serving, it is an all around nutritious drink with new benefits being discovered daily.

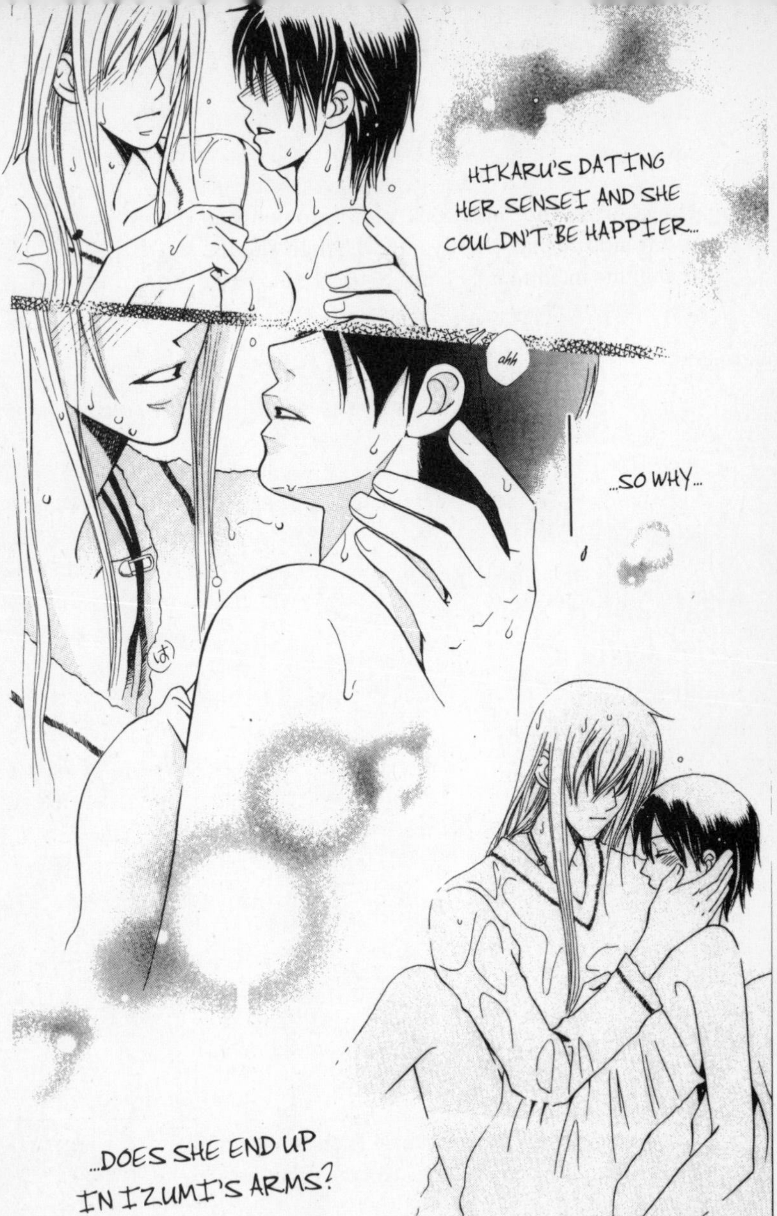
HIKARU'S DATING HER SENSEI AND SHE COULDN'T BE HAPPIER...
ahh
...SO WHY...
(は)
...DOES SHE END UP IN IZUMI'S ARMS?

Tenshi Ja Nai Volume 5
Available November 2006

NIGHT OF THE BEASTS

SPECIAL PREVIEW

Aria's got a reputation as the toughest girl in school because she can't resist protecting those who get picked on by bullies. She's especially touchy about aggressive guys, which is why she's taken by surprise when her first kiss is stolen by a complete stranger. Not only does he keep making moves on her, but it seems like every time they meet, it's at the latest crime scene of a murder spree that's plaguing Aria's neighborhood. How is it that he seems to know all about the supernatural murderer of these innocent girls? And how will Aria react to his claim only SHE can save him from a destiny so bloody that even the violent deeds of the black demon slaughtering victims all over town will pale in comparison?

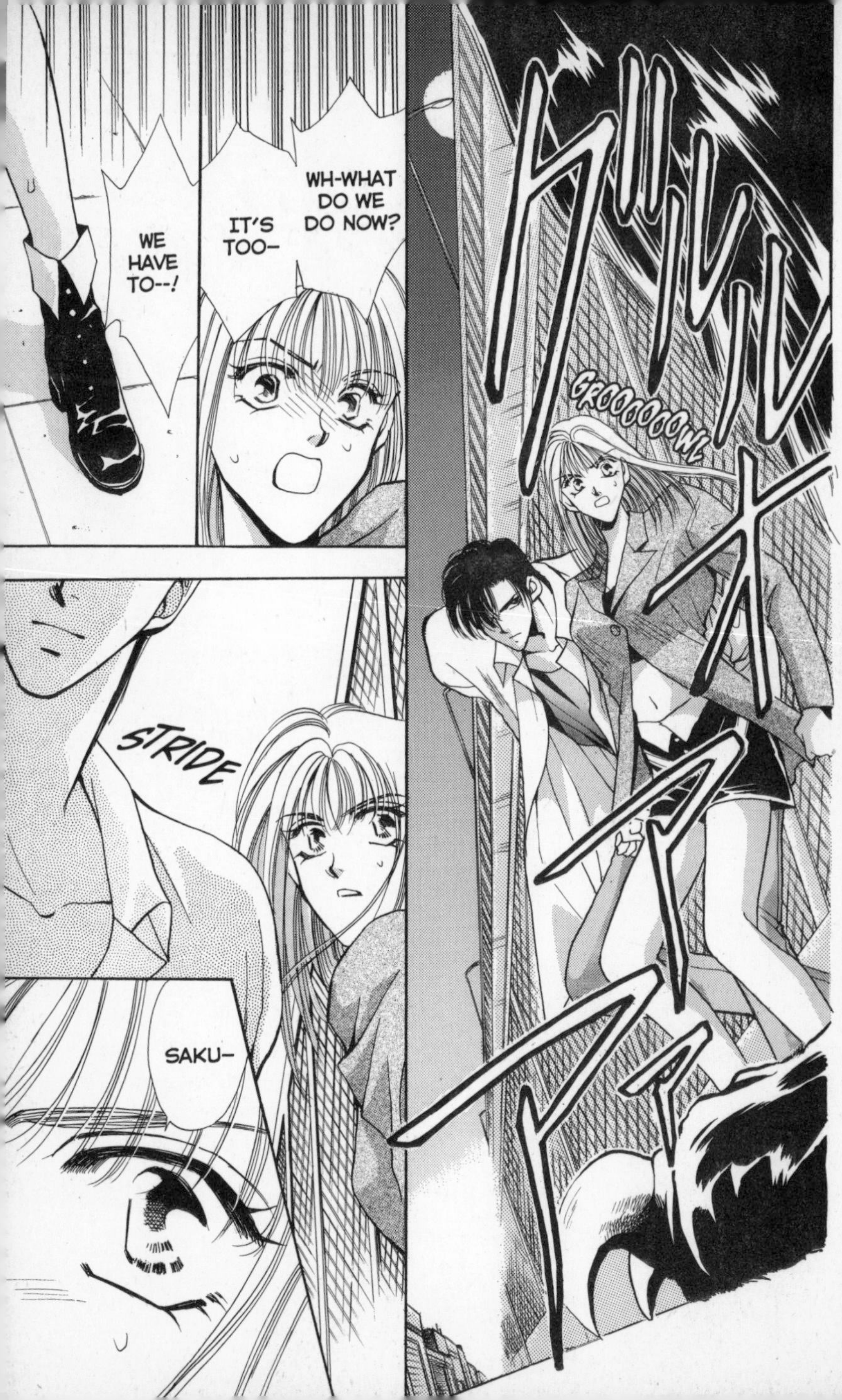
GROOOOOOWL
WH-WHAT DO WE DO NOW?
IT'S TOO-
WE HAVE TO--!
STRIDE
SAKU-

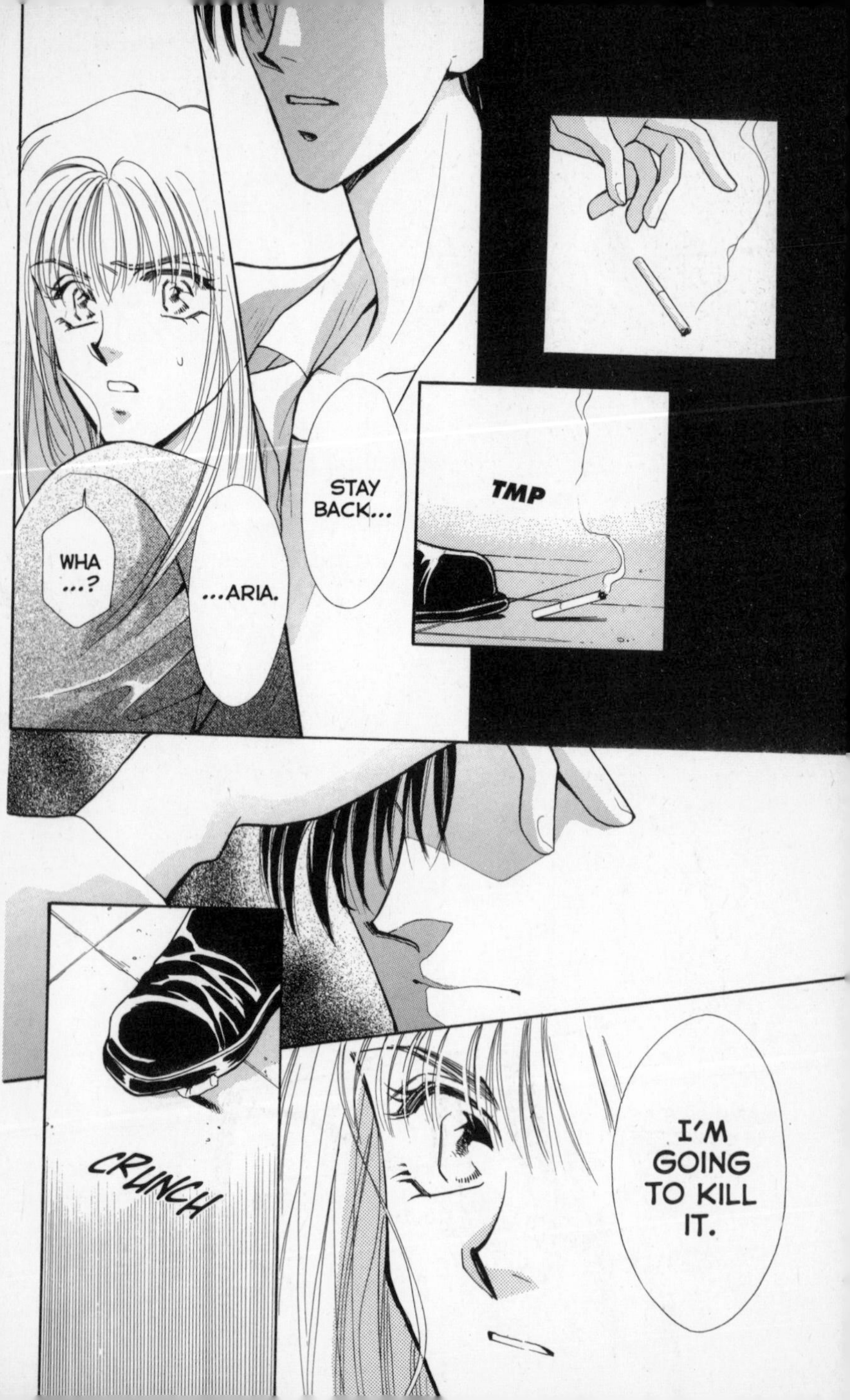
TMP
STAY BACK...
...ARIA.
WHA ...?
I'M GOING TO KILL IT.
CRUNCH

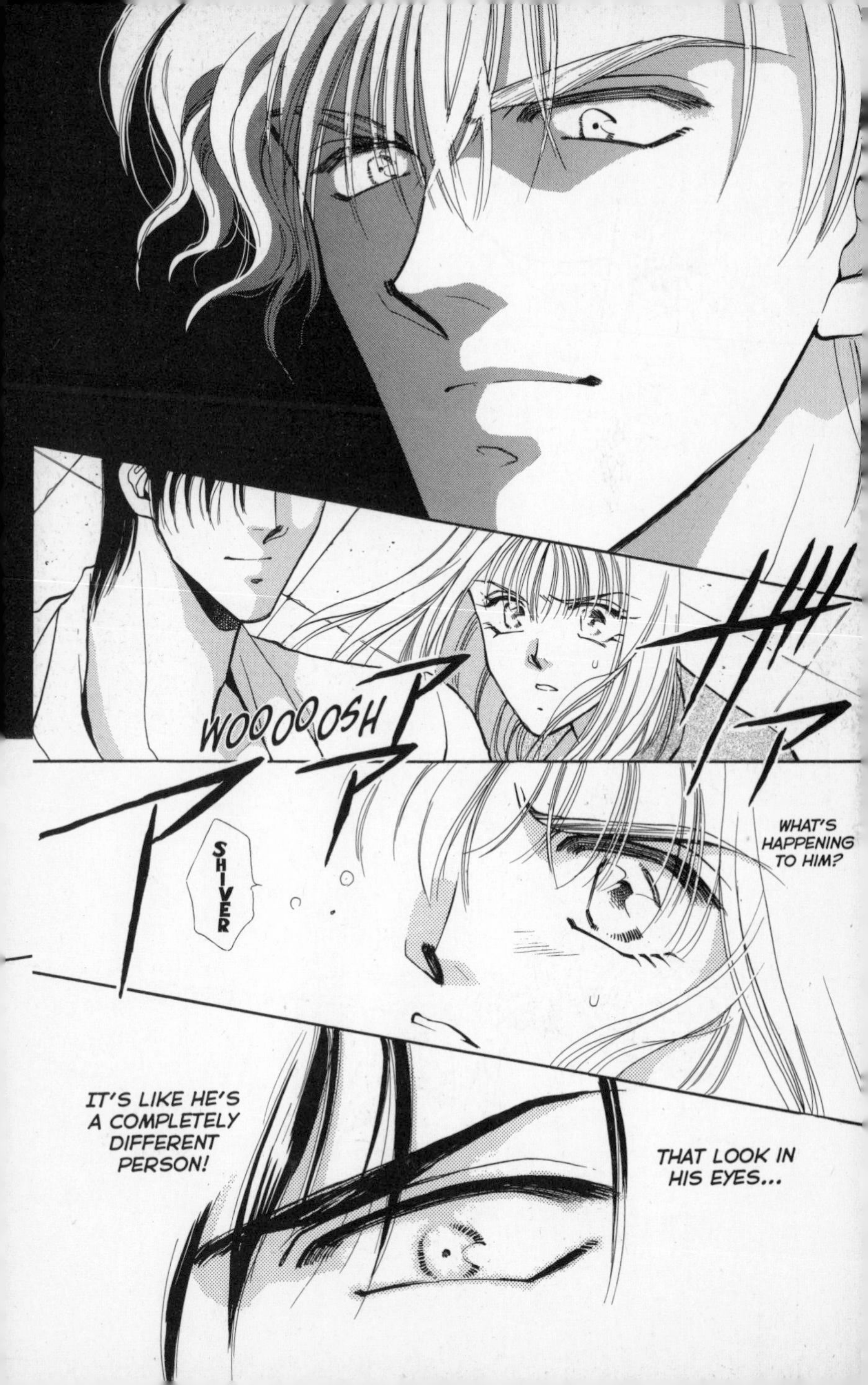
WOOOOOSH
WHAT'S HAPPENING TO HIM?
SHIVER
THAT LOOK IN HIS EYES...
IT'S LIKE HE'S A COMPLETELY DIFFERENT PERSON!

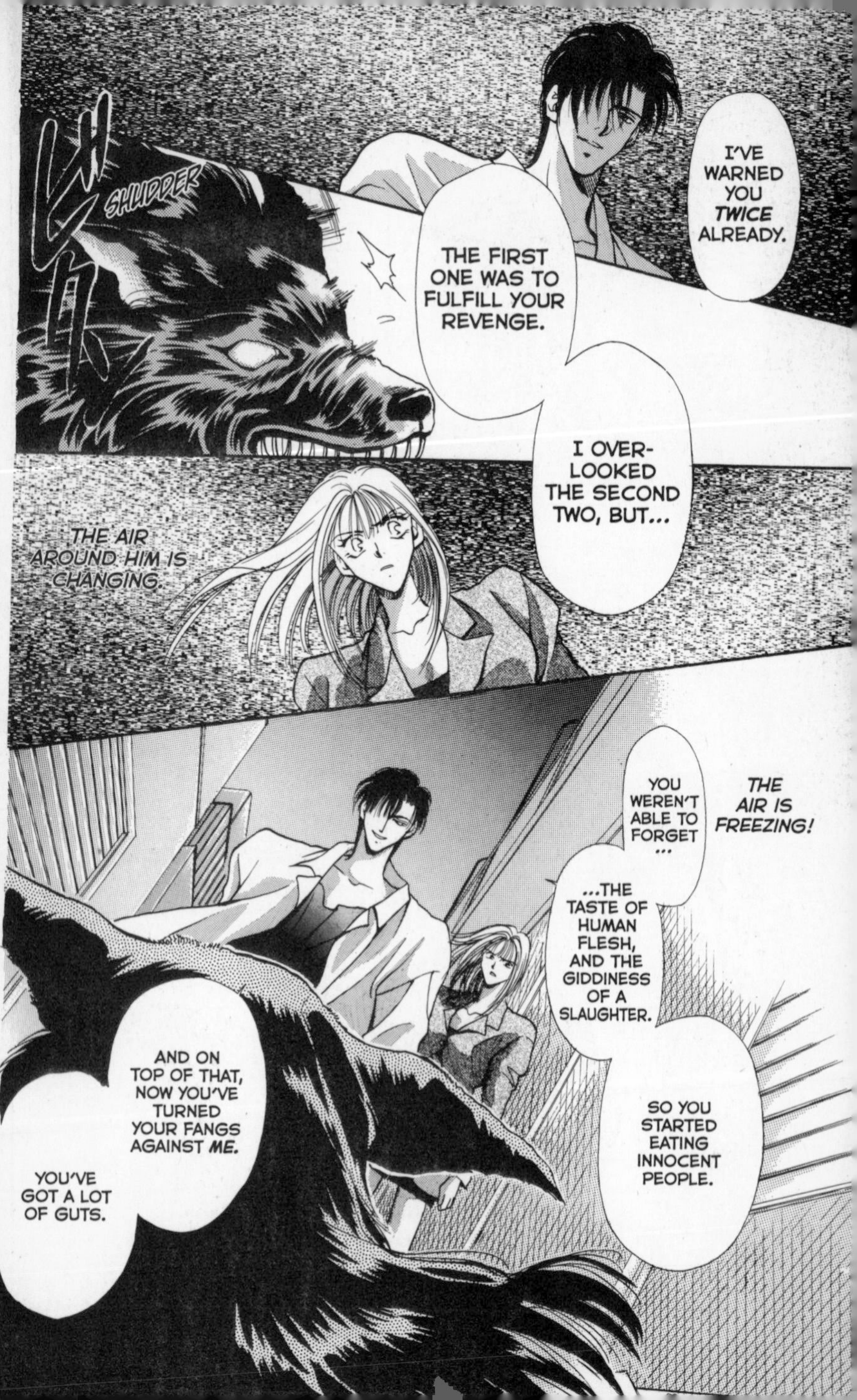
I'VE WARNED YOU *TWICE* ALREADY.
THE FIRST ONE WAS TO FULFILL YOUR REVENGE.
SHUDDER
I OVER-LOOKED THE SECOND TWO, BUT...
THE AIR AROUND HIM IS CHANGING.
THE AIR IS FREEZING!
YOU WEREN'T ABLE TO FORGET ...
...THE TASTE OF HUMAN FLESH, AND THE GIDDINESS OF A SLAUGHTER.
SO YOU STARTED EATING INNOCENT PEOPLE.
AND ON TOP OF THAT, NOW YOU'VE TURNED YOUR FANGS AGAINST *ME*.
YOU'VE GOT A LOT OF GUTS.

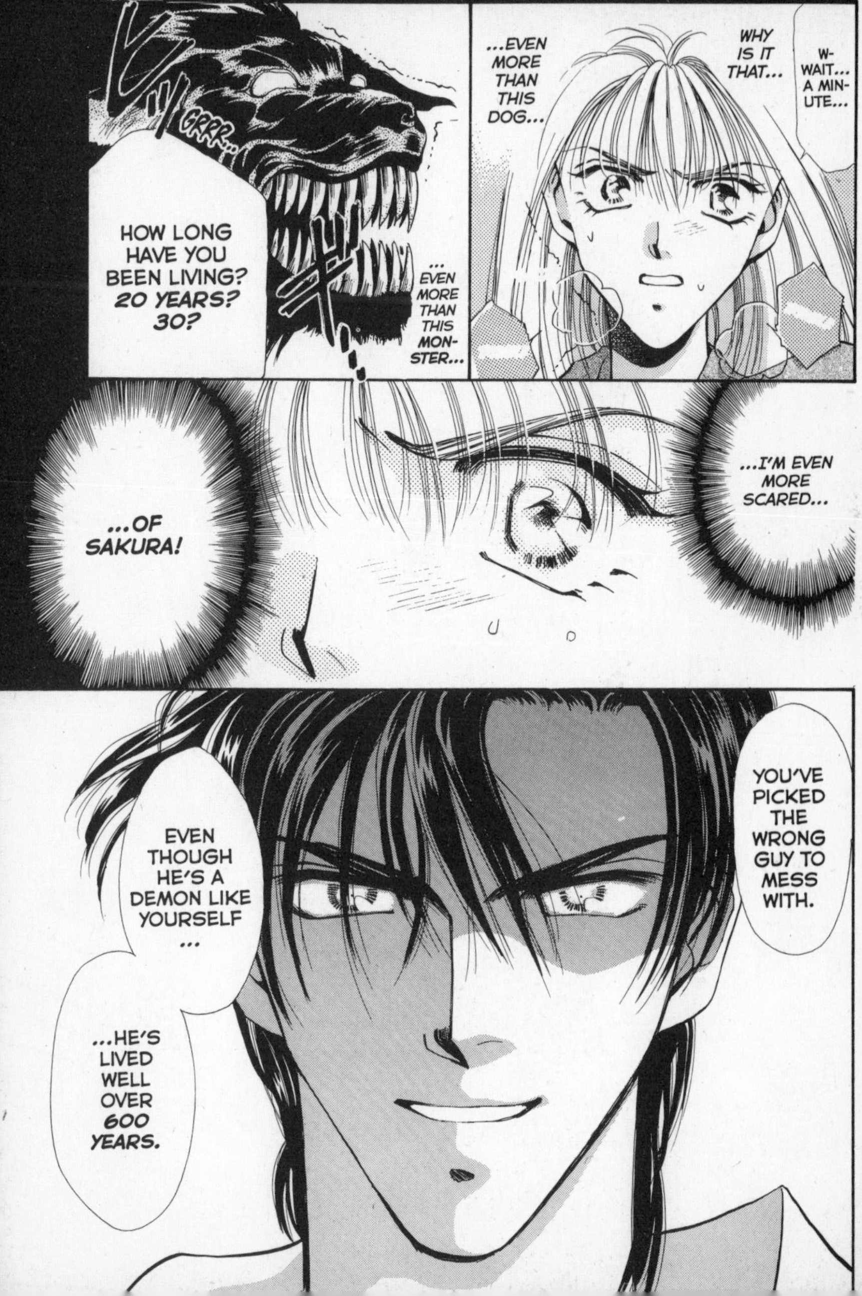
W-WAIT... A MIN-UTE...
WHY IS IT THAT...
...EVEN MORE THAN THIS DOG...
GRRR...
...EVEN MORE THAN THIS MON-STER...
HOW LONG HAVE YOU BEEN LIVING? 20 YEARS? 30?
...I'M EVEN MORE SCARED...
...OF SAKURA!
YOU'VE PICKED THE WRONG GUY TO MESS WITH.
EVEN THOUGH HE'S A DEMON LIKE YOURSELF...
...HE'S LIVED WELL OVER 600 YEARS.

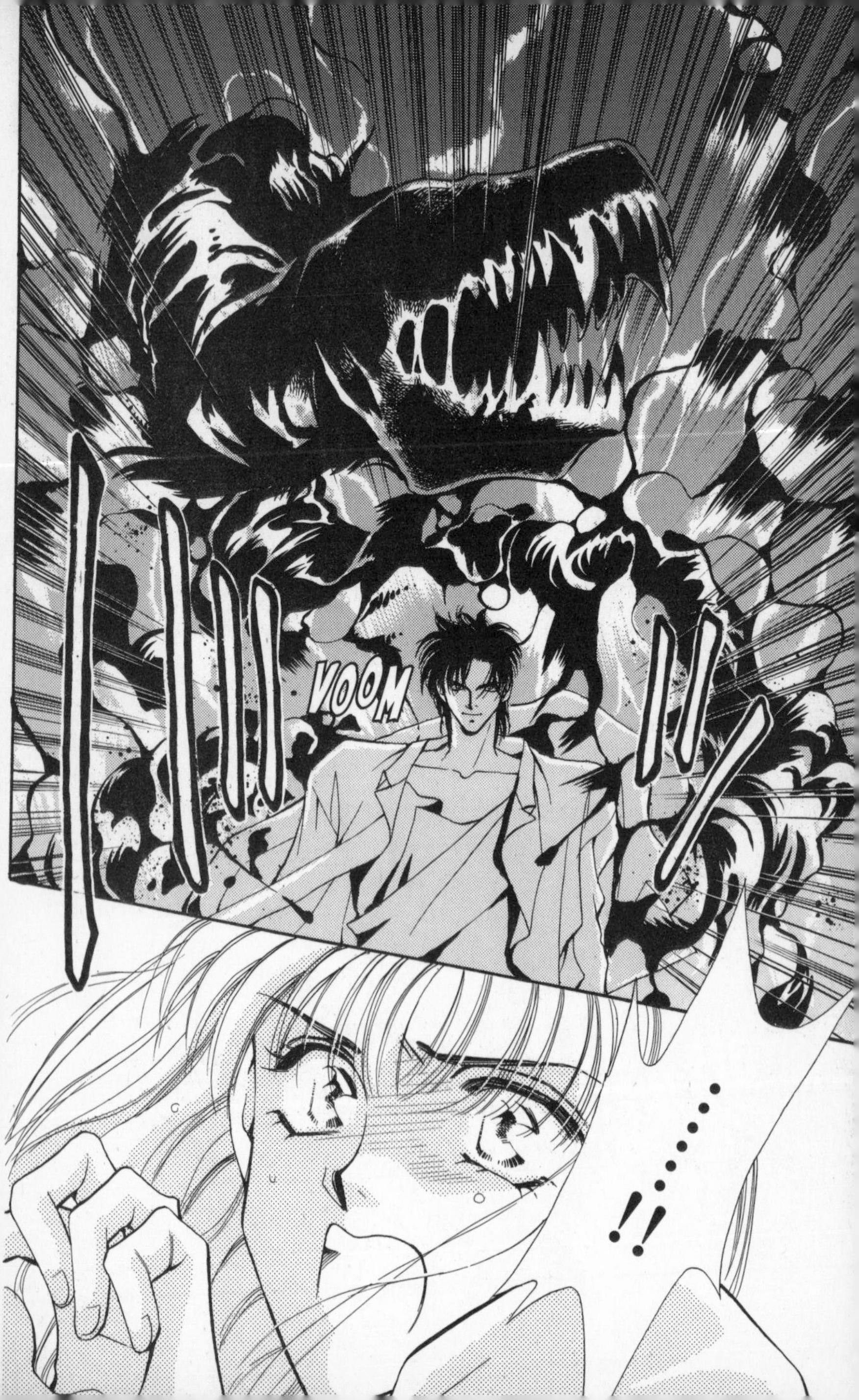
VOOM
......!!

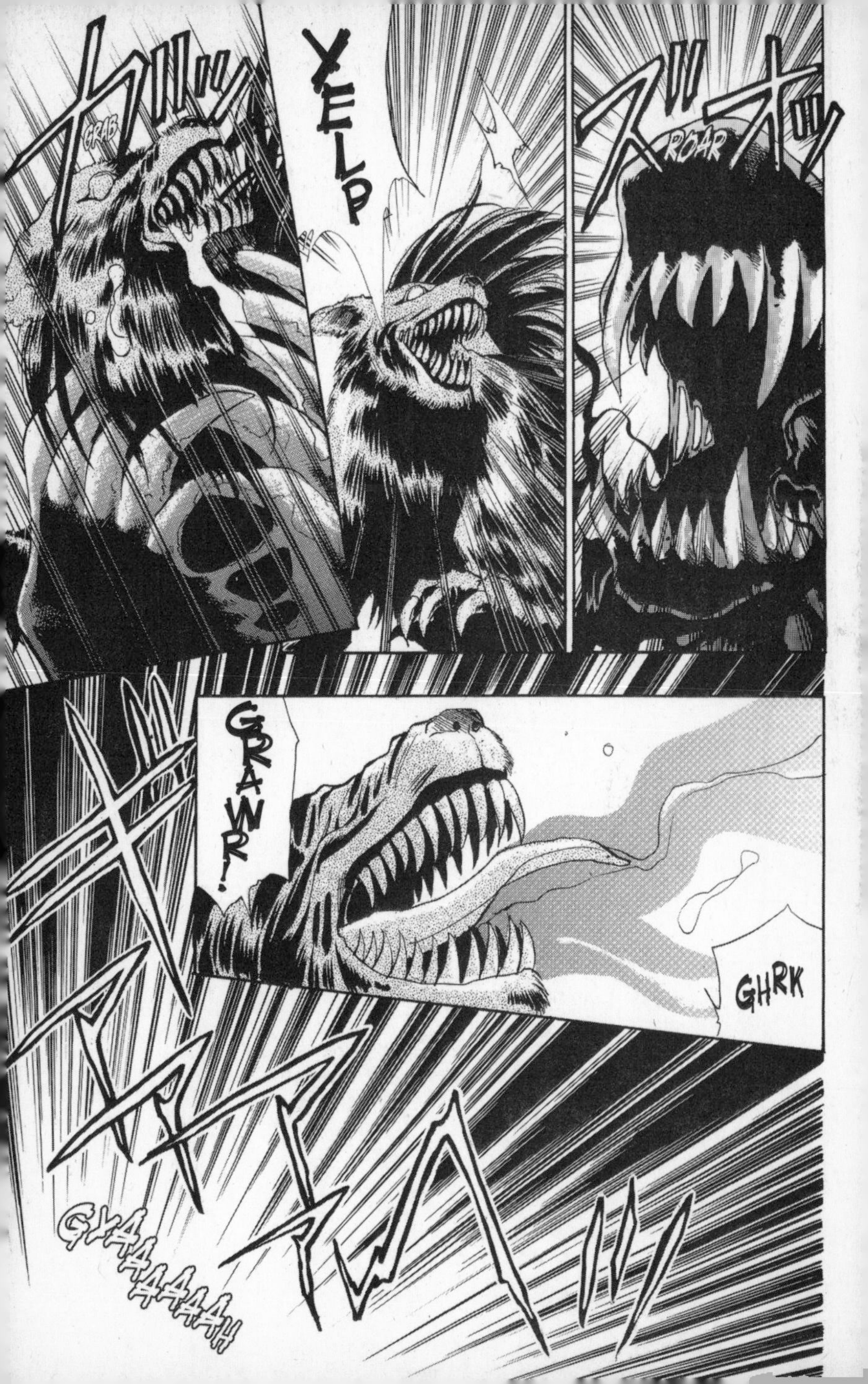
ROAR
YELP
GRAB
GHRK
GRAWR!
GYAAAAAAH

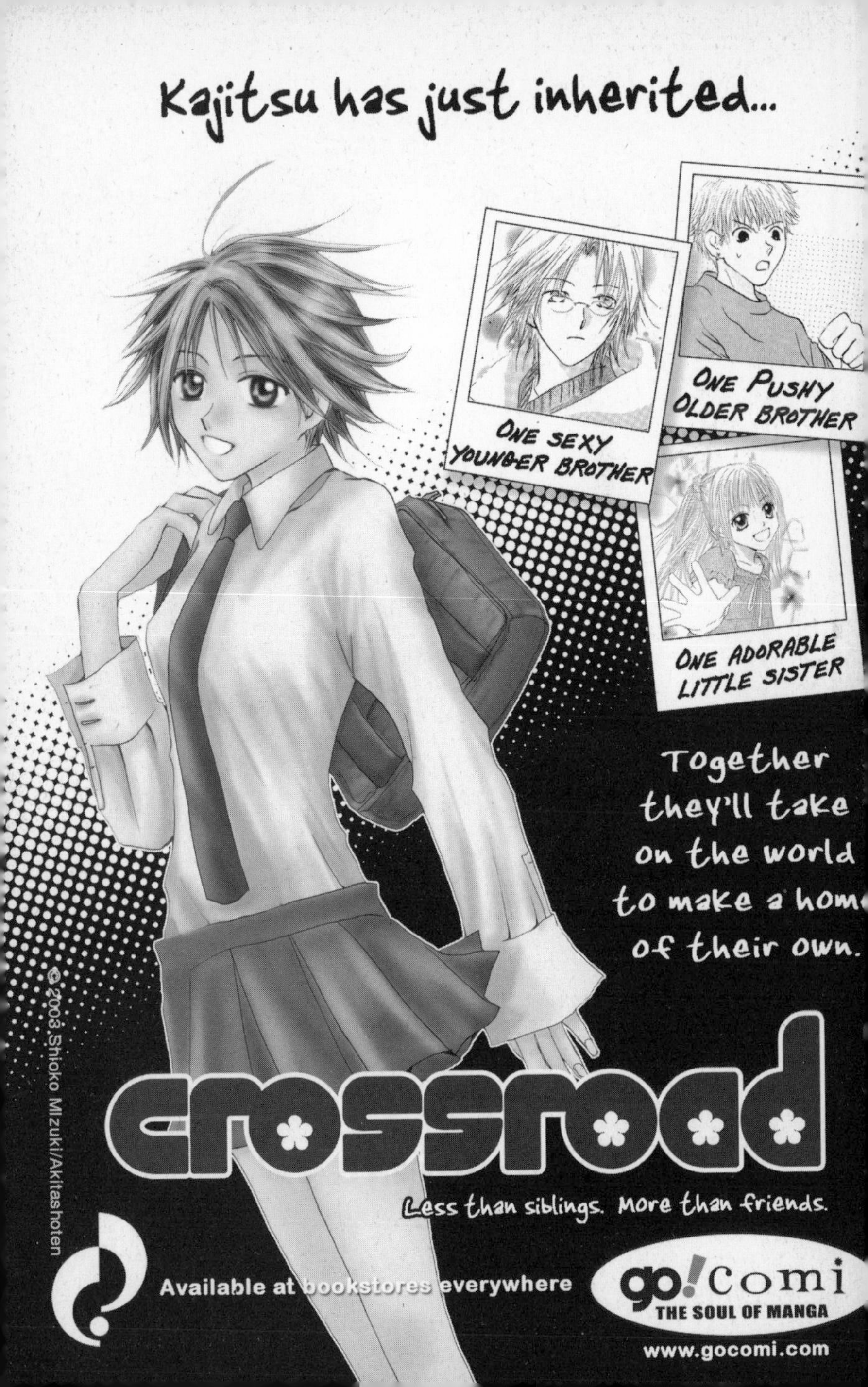
Kajitsu has just inherited...
ONE SEXY YOUNGER BROTHER
ONE PUSHY OLDER BROTHER
ONE ADORABLE LITTLE SISTER
Together they'll take on the world to make a hom of their own.
crossroad
Less than siblings. More than friends.
© 2003 Shioko Mizuki/Akitashoten
Available at bookstores everywhere
go!comi
THE SOUL OF MANGA
www.gocomi.com

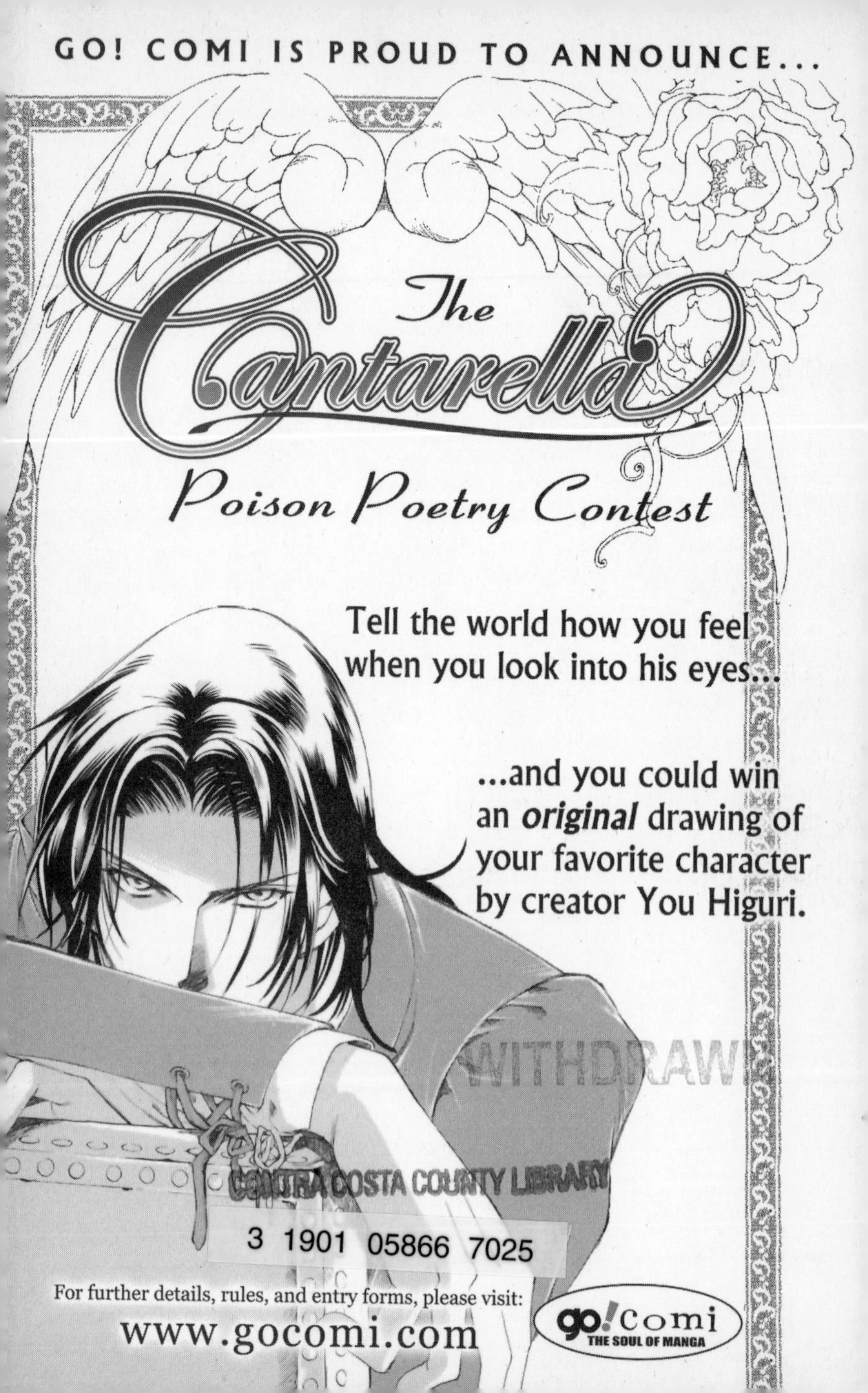
GO! COMI IS PROUD TO ANNOUNCE...
The Cantarella
Poison Poetry Contest
Tell the world how you feel when you look into his eyes...
...and you could win an *original* drawing of your favorite character by creator You Higuri.
For further details, rules, and entry forms, please visit:
www.gocomi.com
go! Comi
THE SOUL OF MANGA